Becoming a Salesforce Certified Technical Architect

Prepare for the review board by practicing example-led architectural strategies and best practices

Tameem Bahri

BIRMINGHAM—MUMBAI

Becoming a Salesforce Certified Technical Architect

Publishing Product Manager: Alok Dhuri
Senior Editor: Nitee Shetty
Content Development Editor: Ruvika Rao
Technical Editor: Pradeep Sahu
Copy Editor: Safis Editing
Project Coordinator: Francy Puthiry
Proofreader: Safis Editing
Indexer: Tejal Daruwale Soni
Production Designer: Roshan Kawale

First published: February 2021

Production reference: 2120822

Published by Packt Publishing Ltd.
Livery Place
35 Livery Street
Birmingham
B3 2PB, UK.

ISBN 978-1-80056-875-4

www.packt.com

To my mother, Raefa Arwani, my first teacher, and the most brilliant person I have ever known. To my wife, Lana, and my son, Ameer, for their love, support, and inspiration.

Contributors

About the author

Tameem Bahri is the European Salesforce CTO at Capgemini and a Salesforce CTA with a demonstrated work history in the information technology and business consultation industry, with over 17 years of experience across business transformation, digital services, innovation, process design and redesign, enterprise system security, **identity and access management (IAM)**, and enterprise solution architecture. He has worked across several industries, such as manufacturing, **Clinical Practice Research Datalink (CPRD)**, travel and transportation, energy and utilities, property management, and software development. He has led dozens of Salesforce implementations worldwide and currently heads Capgemini's program to develop the next generation of CTAs.

I'd like to thank the following people at Packt who made this book possible: Alok Dhuri, who was the first to express faith in me, and Nitee Shetty, Ruvika Rao, Francy Puthiry, and Prajakta Naik, who worked tirelessly with me to improve my drafts. I'd also like to thank the reviewer, Ali Najefi, an admirable CTA himself, for his helpful advice and support.

About the reviewer

Ali Najefi is an enterprise architect with 18 years' experience of which 13 years has been in Salesforce. He is a Salesforce CTA with a track record of delivering complex digital transformation projects on the Salesforce platform.

He has led the Salesforce architecture and design authority team, responsible for ensuring all Salesforce delivery teams adhere to Salesforce's best architecture and design principles. He has a significant interest in cybersecurity, IAM, digital data management, MDM, analytics, and AI. He has worked on several enterprise clients directing both architectural domain and delivering solutions that have proven to be secure and scalable for millions of end customers and thousands of enterprise users.

Table of Contents

Preface

Section 1: Your Journey to Becoming a CTA

1

Starting Your Journey as a CTA

Understanding the profile of a Salesforce Certified Technical Architect	4	to generate and why	11
		The actors and licenses diagram	13
		The data model diagram	15
The CTA review board's structure and format	6	The system landscape diagram	16
		The role hierarchy diagram	20
From exam to real life – how to train to become a CTA	7	The business process flow diagram	21
		The environment diagram	22
The nature of the exam – a point collection exercise	9	The contextual SSO flow diagram	23
What kind of artifacts you need		Summary	24

2

Core Architectural Concepts – Data

Differences between classic RDBMS and Salesforce	26	Data regulatory compliance	35
Understanding data governance	30	Exploring data categories	38
Understanding data security	32	Transactional data	38
Data encryption	32	Master data and master data management	38
Data restoration	33	Reference data	41
Data masking	33	Reporting data	41
Data erasure	34	Metadata	41

Big data   42
Unstructured data   42

The nature of data warehouses and data lakes   43

Choosing the right document management system   44

Understanding data architecture concepts   45

Conceptual-level data architecture

design   46
Logical-level data architecture design   46
Physical-level data architecture design   47

Designing and documenting your data model   48

Normalization versus denormalization   49
Normal forms   52
Using database relationships   55

Summary   58

3

Core Architectural Concepts – Integration and Cryptography

Integration in the enterprise – understanding the landscape   60

Integration architecture design
principles   62

Introducing the common integration styles   64

File transfer   65
Unified datastore   65
Remote procedure invocation   66
Messaging   67

Discussing the different integration tools   67

Point-to-point integration   67
Extract, transform, and load (ETL)   72
Enterprise Service Bus   74
Reverse proxies   75
API gateways   76

Stream-processing platforms   76

Exploring the modern integration approaches   77

Service-oriented architecture   77
Microservices   78
API-led architecture   80
Event-driven architecture   81

Cryptography – understanding the general concepts   82

Cryptographic algorithm types and use cases   86

Symmetric cryptography algorithms   86
Asymmetric cryptography algorithms   89
Cryptography use cases   90
Putting both integration and
cryptography together   94

Summary   94

4

Core Architectural Concepts – Identity and Access Management

Understanding the general concepts of IAM 96

Becoming familiar with the IAM terms and definitions 98

Becoming familiar with the common IAM standards 110

Understanding the common IAM standards 111

Getting to know the different types of tokens 115

Understanding the key authentication flows 120

Becoming familiar with the SAML 2.0 flows 121

Becoming familiar with the OAuth 2.0/ OpenID Connect flows 126

Summary 145

Section 2: Knowledge Domains Deep Dive

5

Developing a Scalable System Architecture

Understanding what you should know and be able to do as a Salesforce system architect 150

Determining the appropriate mix of systems 150

Design considerations for reporting and analytics 151

Org strategy 152

Mobile solutions and strategy 154

Required license types 155

Determining the right document management solution 156

Introducing the system architecture domain mini hypothetical scenario – Packt United Builder 156

The scenario 157

Internal stakeholders 157

External stakeholders 158

Requirements 158

Determining the appropriate mix of systems, and building your solution and presentation 160

Understanding the current situation 160

Diving into the shared requirements 162

Summary 177

6

Formulating a Secure Architecture in Salesforce

Understanding what you should be able to do as a security architect 180

Utilizing the appropriate platform security mechanisms 180

Designing a secure portal architecture 183

Controlling record-level security using declarative and/or programmatic features 184

Using the platform security features to control object and field access permissions 186

Designing an end-to-end identity management solution 187

Introducing the security architecture domain – Packt Innovative Retailers 190

The scenario 191

Utilizing the appropriate security mechanisms and building your solution and presentation 194

Understanding the current situation 194

Diving into the shared requirements 201

Summary 210

7

Designing a Scalable Salesforce Data Architecture

Understanding what you should be able to do as a Salesforce data architect 214

Describing platform considerations, their impact, and optimization methods while working with LDV objects 214

Explaining data modeling concepts and their impact on the database's design 222

Determining the data migration approach, tools, and strategy 224

Introducing the data architecture domain mini hypothetical scenario – Packt Online Wizz 225

The scenario 225

Building your solution and presentation 227

Understanding the current situation 228

Diving into the shared requirements 232

Summary 250

8
Creating a Lean Solution Architecture

Understanding what you should be able to do as a Salesforce solution architect 253
Selecting the right combination of declarative and programmatic functionalities 253
Augmenting your solution with the right external applications 255

Introducing the solution architecture domain mini hypothetical scenario – Packt visiting angels 256
The scenario 257

Selecting the appropriate functionalities to build your solution and presentation 259
Understanding the current situation 259
Diving into the shared requirements 261

Summary 277

9
Forging an Integrated Solution

Understanding what you should be able to do as a Salesforce integration architect 280
Recommending the right integration landscape 280
Determining the right enterprise integration architecture technology 281
Designing your integration interface using the right integration pattern 283
Selecting and justifying the right platform-specific integration capabilities 288
The scenario 291

Designing the enterprise integration interfaces to build your connected solution 293
Understanding the current situation 293
Diving into the shared requirements 294

Summary 311

10
Development Life Cycle and Deployment Planning

What you should do as a Salesforce development life cycle and deployment architect 314
Identifying project risks and developing mitigation strategies 315
Identifying the impact development methodologies have on workstreams 317
Recommend test strategies to mitigate project risks 319
Recommending the right project governance to support technical decision-making 321
Crafting the right environment

management strategy while
considering the platform's capabilities
and limitations   325
Describing the value of continuous
integration (CI) tools and source
control in release management   327

Introducing the mini-hypothetical scenario – Packt Modern Furniture   329

The scenario   330

Designing the project environment and release strategy   **331**
Understanding the current situation   332
Diving into the shared requirements   334

Summary   **340**

11
Communicating and Socializing Your Solution

Understanding what you should be able to do while communicating your solution   342
Communicating design decisions and
considerations   342
Demonstrating your visualization skills
to articulate the solution   344
Handling objection and unexpected
roadblocks   348

Practicing communicating a mini-hypothetical scenario – Packt Digital   348
The scenario   349

Articulating your solution and managing objections   351
Understanding the current situation   351
Diving into the shared requirements   352

Summary   **364**

Section 3: Putting It All Together

12
Practice the Review Board – First Mock

Introducing the full mock scenario – Packt Pioneer Auto   368
Project overview   368
Current landscape   369
Business process requirements   370
Data migration requirements   373
Accessibility and security requirements 374

Reporting requirements   375
Project development requirements   375
Other requirements   376

Analyze the requirements and creating a draft end-to-end solution   376
Understanding the current situation   377

Analyzing the business process requirements 381

Summary 412

13
Present and Defend – First Mock

Continuing to analyze requirements and creating an end-to-end solution 414
Analyzing the data migration requirements 414
Reviewing identified LDVs and developing a mitigation strategy 418
Analyzing the accessibility and security requirements 420
Analyzing the reporting requirements 430
Analyzing the project development requirements 433
Analyzing the other requirements 438

Presenting and justifying your

solution 446
Understanding the presentation structure 446
Introducing the overall solution and artifacts 447
Presenting the business processes' end-to-end solution 450
Presenting the LDV mitigation strategy 453
Presenting the data migration strategy 454
Going through the scenario and catching all remaining requirements 455
Justifying and defending your solution 457

Summary 460

14
Practice the Review Board – Second Mock

Introducing the full mock scenario – Packt Lightning Utilities 462
Project overview 462
Current landscape 464
Business process requirements 464
Data migration requirements 468
Accessibility and security requirements 469
Reporting requirements 469
Project development requirements 470

Other requirements 471

Analyzing the requirements and creating a draft end-to-end solution 471
Understanding the current situation 471
Analyzing the business process requirements 480

Summary 513

15

Present and Defend – Second Mock

Continuing with analyzing the requirements and creating an end-to-end solution 516

Analyzing the data migration requirements 516

Reviewing identified LDVs and developing a mitigation strategy 522

Analyzing the accessibility and security requirements 527

Analyzing the reporting requirements 530

Analyzing the project development requirements 533

Analyzing the other requirements 539

Presenting and justifying your solution 548

Introducing the overall solution and artifacts 549

Presenting the business processes' end-to-end solution 552

Going through the scenario and catching all the remaining requirements 558

Justifying and defending your solution 558

Summary 562

Appendix

Tips and Tricks, and the Way Forward

The anatomy of a review board scenario 564

General solving tips 566

Go through the scenario and annotate first 566

Provide a solution, not a set of options 567

You have a limited set of tools to solve a problem 567

Act like an architect, use the common architects' language 567

Managing the board 568

Help them to keep up with you 568

Tie your solution back to the requirement 568

Watch and observe their reaction if possible 568

Seed some questions 569

Show your professional attitude 569

Time management 570

Plan ahead and stick to your plan 570

Rehearse and perfect your timing 572

Practice the 2-minute pitch 572

Balance where you spend your time 573

Your presentation – make or break 573

Show confidence 573

Control the tempo 574

Own the stage 574

Use your artifacts 574

Enjoy it 575

Your exam, your way 575

Next steps 576

Practice and practice more 576

Plan some time off before the exam 576

Get in touch with the community and

study groups   577

Stay connected and share your
experience   577

**The community and available
training**   577

Salesforce training and study groups   577

Stories and lessons learned   579

Blogs and training providers   579

**Journey Towards Becoming a
Salesforce CTA – Book Club**   581

Why subscribe?   583

Other Books You May Enjoy

Index

Preface

As the Salesforce economy continues to grow rapidly, there's never been a better time to build a Salesforce-based career. Architects and architect-related skills are in higher demand than ever.

The Salesforce Certified Technical Architect (CTA) credential is ranked as one of the top enterprise architect certifications in the industry. Just run a quick search on the web for job postings, and you'll have no doubt about the value of this prestigious certificate. The very limited number of CTAs around the world gives an even more satisfying feeling of joining the club of newly certified CTAs.

This book will start by explaining a set of core concepts that every architect should master, including the data life cycle, integration, and cryptography, and build your aptitude for creating high-level technical solutions. Understanding these concepts is vital to understanding the rationale behind some of the best practices suggested in Salesforce solutions. Moreover, having that in-depth knowledge will help you significantly when it comes to explaining how your end-to-end solution works.

You will then explore specific knowledge domains that are tested in the review board. With the help of real-world examples, this book provides insights into essential topics, such as selecting systems or components for your solutions, designing scalable and secure Salesforce architecture, and planning the development life cycle and deployments. Finally, you'll work on two full mock scenarios that simulate the review board exam, helping you learn how to identify requirements, create a draft solution, and combine all elements to create an engaging story to present to the board or a client in real life.

By the end of this book, you'll have gained the knowledge and skills required to pass the review board exam and implement architectural best practices and strategies in your day-to-day work.

Who this book is for?

This book is intended for Salesforce professionals who have a solid understanding of the Salesforce platform and who have racked up several years of experience as architects. These architects would ideally like to boost their careers further by targeting the Salesforce CTA credential. The book is also intended for architects who want to add more skills to their arsenal by learning how to design secure, high-performance technical solutions on the Salesforce Platform, along with how to communicate technical solutions and design trade-offs effectively to business stakeholders and how to adopt a delivery framework that ensures quality and success.

With the current rapid growth of the Salesforce ecosystem, the borders between traditional roles in some workplaces are blurring. And with that, the value of having people with exceptional talent to link the different teams becomes vital. Future CTAs are not afraid to dig deep into business challenges and ask tough questions to reveal the real business value behind a particular requirement. They like to get to the bottom of things and roll up their sleeves when necessary to try things out in order to select the right solution approach that serves current and future potential requirements. And they do not hesitate to jump into conversations with the development teams to give guidance and best practices and then
work with the project management team to prepare that cutting-edge presentation for the stakeholders.

What this book covers?

Chapter 1, Starting Your Journey as a CTA, provides general information about the book and the certificate. We will cover what the profile of a typical CTA is, how that is related to the day-to-day activities of a Salesforce architect, and why understanding the way CTAs think is essential even for senior architects who are not necessarily targeting the CTA certificate. This chapter also provides details about the review board exam setup, whether physical or virtual.

Chapter 2, Core Architectural Concepts – Data, explores the core architectural skills related to data that an architect needs to master. Part of that knowledge is platform-agnostic, although other parts are particularly important for Salesforce architects. These skills will be used intensively in later parts of this book and, of course, during the review board itself.

Chapter 3, Core Architectural Concepts – Integration and Cryptography, explores the core architectural skills related to both integration and cryptography that an architect needs to master. Part of that knowledge is platform-agnostic, although other parts are particularly important for Salesforce architects. These skills will be used intensively in later parts of this book and, of course, during the review board itself.

Chapter 4, Core Architectural Concepts – Identity and Access Management, explores the core architectural skills related to **Identity and Access Management (IAM)** that an architect needs to master. Part of that knowledge is platform-agnostic, although other parts are particularly important for Salesforce architects. These skills will be used intensively in later parts of this book and, of course, during the review board itself.

Chapter 5, Developing a Scalable System Architecture, provides an in-depth review of some of the most tricky system architecture areas, such as determining the right selection of systems that forms the overall solution, including both on- and off-platform components, taking into consideration the platform's capabilities, constraints, and limits. This knowledge will be enhanced further using a mini hypothetical scenario.

Chapter 6, Formulating a Secure Architecture in Salesforce, provides an in-depth review of some of the most tricky areas in security, such as understanding the declarative platform security features and how they can be used to meet record-level visibility and security requirements. This knowledge will be enhanced further using a mini hypothetical scenario.

Chapter 7, Designing a Scalable Salesforce Data Architecture, provides an in-depth review of some of the most tricky areas in data, such as designing the right data migration strategy and tools, along with the different considerations the architect needs to keep in mind. This knowledge will be enhanced further using a mini hypothetical scenario.

Chapter 8, Creating a Lean Solution Architecture, provides an in-depth review of some of the most tricky areas in solution architecture, such as selecting the appropriate combination of declarative and programmatic functionality to fulfill a particular requirement. This knowledge will be enhanced further using a mini hypothetical scenario.

Chapter 9, Forging an Integrated Solution, provides an in-depth review of some of the most tricky areas in integration, such as rationally selecting the appropriate technology used to integrate with external systems, considering the platform's capabilities and limitations. This knowledge will be enhanced further using a mini hypothetical scenario.

Chapter 10, Development Life Cycle and Deployment Planning, provides an in-depth review of some of the most tricky areas in development life cycle and deployment planning, such as the ability to recommend a suitable comprehensive test strategy and mitigate the different project risks. This knowledge will be enhanced further using a mini hypothetical scenario.

Chapter 11, Communicating and Socializing Your Solution, provides an in-depth review of some of the most tricky communication areas. This includes explaining a crucial set of soft skills that an architect needs to master in order to present an end-to-end solution to the review board judges or, in real life, to internal or external clients, such as the ability to articulate the benefits, limitations, considerations, and design choices behind a proposed solution architecture in a justified and rational manner and being prepared to handle objections and adjust on the fly. This knowledge will be enhanced further using a mini hypothetical scenario.

Chapter 12, Practice the Review Board – First Mock, puts all the knowledge and skills covered in the previous chapters into action. You will be introduced to your first full hypothetical scenario. We will solve it step by step, beginning with identifying the requirement, creating a draft solution, and combining all the elements to create an engaging story to tell the judges or, in real life, internal or external clients.

Chapter 13, Present and Defend – First Mock, puts all the knowledge and skills covered in the previous chapters into action. We continue with the previous chapter's hypothetical scenario and use the draft solution to create a refined end-to-end solution and presentation. You will get hands-on experience by following a step-by-step guide where the solution is reviewed, adjusted if needed, and the artifacts' final versions are created. You will then use all of that to deliver an engaging story to tell the judges or, in real life, internal or external clients.

Chapter 14, Practice the Review Board – Second Mock, puts all the knowledge and skills covered in the previous chapters into action. You will be introduced to your second full hypothetical scenario. We will solve it step by step, beginning with identifying the requirement, creating a draft solution, and combining all the elements to create an engaging story to tell the judges or, in real life, internal or external clients.

Chapter 15, Present and Defend – Second Mock, puts all the knowledge and skills covered in the previous chapters into action. We continue with the previous chapter's hypothetical scenario and use the draft solution to create a refined end-to-end solution and presentation. You will get hands-on experience by following a step-by-step guide where the solution is reviewed, adjusted if needed, and the artifacts' final versions are created. You will then use all of that to deliver an engaging story to tell the judges or, in real life, internal or external clients.

Appendix, Tips and Tricks, and the Way Forward, provides a collection of tips and tricks to help the candidate on the day of the review, starting with best practices to follow during the presentation, followed by tips regarding time management. We then highlight different strategies used by other CTAs to pass the review board exam, and provide a set of suggested activities that a candidate who is targeting the review board should consider, including how to prepare for the last mile, what resources and groups are available in terms of getting support, and how to get into the right mindset on the day of the review board exam.

To get the most out of this book

This book is designed to help you gain the required knowledge and skills to pass the CTA exam using hands-on examples. We will be covering the seven knowledge domains that a CTA needs to master in order to pass the exam. We will tackle a mini hypothetical scenario for each domain. We will be developing the solution progressively, creating and then recreating solution artifacts as we discover and weigh different design decisions. This is precisely what many architects do in their daily lives. They dig deeper into details and, at every stage, they build a clearer picture of the solution and the correct elements required to make it. They revisit previous decisions and adjust or change them if needed.

You are strongly advised to practice recreating the solution, reconsider other alternatives, and weigh the pros and cons of each. Build your familiarity with the artifacts and diagrams needed to explain your solution. You will find that you become quicker and more efficient in creating them. Moreover, the quality of your outcome will also improve.

Diagrams will be provided at every stage and will progressively evolve; you will notice that these artifacts might end up very different from what we started with. The ability to evolve your solution and flexibly change its elements while still maintaining the end-to-end solution picture is a crucial skill that a CTA must master. You will learn much of that throughout the book.

Software/hardware covered in the book	OS requirements
MS Office (or Google Slides and Sheets)	Windows, macOS X, Linux (any)
A diagramming tool, such as LucidChart, Draw.io, or Visio	Windows, macOS X, Linux (any)
Salesforce Developer Edition	Windows, macOS X, Linux (any)

The Salesforce Developer Edition org is recommended to try out certain functionalities. You can sign up for a free org using the following link: `https://developer.salesforce.com/signup`.

You can use any diagramming tool, free or paid, or even draw the diagrams on paper or a flipchart. To practice the virtual Salesforce CTA review board, you need to become familiar with tools such as Microsoft PowerPoint and Excel or Google Slides and Sheets (the latter is preferred).

Journey Towards Becoming a Salesforce CTA – Book Club

We have created an exclusive book club for you on our Packt Community page, to share knowledge and have insightful discussions around the topics covered in this book. This book club is for all the readers, existing architects, and anyone who aims to achieve the Salesforce CTA certification.

You are welcome to discuss the book, share your own experiences, views, and best practices on designing modern, practical, and robust architectures on the Salesforce platform, and help us grow the number of Salesforce CTAs globally.

Scan the code to join the book club

Download the color images

We also provide a PDF file that has color images of the screenshots/diagrams used in this book. You can download it here: `https://static.packt-cdn.com/downloads/9781800568754_ColorImages.pdf`.

Conventions used

There are a number of text conventions used throughout this book.

`Code in text`: Indicates code words in text, database table names, folder names, filenames, file extensions, pathnames, dummy URLs, user input, and Twitter handles. Here is an example: "The logged-in, existing community user creates a `Community_Invitation__c` record and sets the required values, such as an email address."

A block of code is set as follows:

```
{
    "alg": "HS256",
    "typ": "JWT",
    "kid": "228",
}
```

Bold: Indicates a new term, an important word, or words that you see on screen. For example, words in menus or dialog boxes appear in the text like this. Here is an example: "A **data warehouse** (**DW** or **DWH**) is a central repository of current and historical data integrated from one or more disparate sources."

> **Tips or important notes**
> Appear like this.

Get in touch

Feedback from our readers is always welcome.

General feedback: If you have questions about any aspect of this book, mention the book title in the subject of your message and email us at `customercare@packtpub.com`.

Errata: Although we have taken every care to ensure the accuracy of our content, mistakes do happen. If you have found a mistake in this book, we would be grateful if you would report this to us. Please visit `www.packtpub.com/support/errata`, selecting your book, clicking on the Errata Submission Form link, and entering the details.

Piracy: If you come across any illegal copies of our works in any form on the internet, we would be grateful if you would provide us with the location address or website name. Please contact us at copyright@packt.com with a link to the material.

If you are interested in becoming an author: If there is a topic that you have expertise in and you are interested in either writing or contributing to a book, please visit authors.packtpub.com.

Reviews

Please leave a review. Once you have read and used this book, why not leave a review on the site that you purchased it from? Potential readers can then see and use your unbiased opinion to make purchase decisions, we at Packt can understand what you think about our products, and our authors can see your feedback on their book. Thank you!

For more information about Packt, please visit packt.com.

Learn more on Discord

To join the Discord community for this book – where you can share feedback, ask questions to the author, and learn about new releases – follow the QR code below:

http://packt.link/sfdserver

Section 1:
Your Journey to
Becoming a CTA

This section will focus on foundational architectural skills that every Salesforce **Certified Technical Architect (CTA)** should master.

First, we'll start by introducing some general information about the Salesforce CTA credential, why it is so prestigious, and how it is related to a Salesforce architect's day-to-day activities. We'll learn why learning to think as a CTA is essential even for senior architects who do not target the CTA credential.

Then, we'll focus on the data life cycle architectural concepts. We'll start with a historical view to understand the principles behind today's modern technology and governance. Then, we'll tackle a set of data-related concepts such as data governance, security, and compliance. We'll also learn how these concepts are relevant to the enterprise. We will explore other key components of today's modern organizations, such as data warehouses and databases.

After that, we'll move on to explore two other crucial architectural domains: integration and cryptography. We'll start by understanding the nature of modern enterprises and why both domains are critical for success. We'll then explore a set of integration styles, tools, and approaches that form the heart of today's modern integration technologies. We'll then take a turn to learn more about cryptography and its importance to secure the digital world.

Finally, we'll tackle the crucial architectural domain of **Identity and Access Management (IAM)**. We'll learn vital general concepts that any modern architect should be familiar with. Then, we'll explore common IAM standards and understand why they are essential for architects, particularly in the cloud era. We'll then explore the main authentication flows in detail and understand exactly what is happening behind the scenes.

This section has the following topics:

- *Chapter 1, Starting Your Journey as a CTA*
- *Chapter 2, Core Architectural Concepts – Data*
- *Chapter 3, Core Architectural Concepts – Integration and Cryptography*
- *Chapter 4, Core Architectural Concepts – Identity and Access Management*

1

Starting Your Journey as a CTA

This chapter will get you started by providing general information about this book and the Salesforce **Certified Technical Architect (CTA)** credential. This chapter will help you get some answers to questions such as what the typical profile of a CTA looks like, how the exam is related to the day-to-day activities of a Salesforce Architect, and why understanding the way CTAs think is important even for senior architects who are not necessarily targeting the CTA credential. This chapter also provides general details about the review board exam's structure and setup (whether that is physical or virtual) and the main artifacts needed to document an end-to-end solution.

In this chapter, we're going to cover the following main topics:

- Understanding the profile of a Salesforce Certified Technical Architect
- The CTA review board's structure and format
- From exam to real life – how to train to become a CTA
- The nature of the exam – a point collection exercise
- What kind of artifacts you need to generate and why
- Let's get started!

Understanding the profile of a Salesforce Certified Technical Architect

As the Salesforce economy continues to grow rapidly, there's never been a better time to build a Salesforce-based career. Architects and architect-related skills are in higher demand than ever.

The **Salesforce Certified Technical Architect** credential is ranked as one of the *Top Enterprise Architect Certifications* in the industry. Just run a quick search on the web for job postings and you'll have no doubt about the value of this prestigious certificate. The very limited number of CTAs around the world gives an even more satisfying feeling of *joining the club* to the newly certified CTAs.

With such rapid growth of the Salesforce ecosystem, the borders between traditional roles in some workplaces are blurring. And with that, the value of having people with that special talent to link between the different teams becomes vital. Technical architects are not afraid to dig deep into business challenges, asking tough questions to reveal the real business value behind a particular requirement. They like to get to the bottom of things, and roll up their sleeves when necessary to try things out in order to select the right solution approach that serves the current and future potential requirements. They do not hesitate to jump into conversations with the development teams to give guidance and best practices, and then work with the project management team to prepare that cutting-edge presentation for the stakeholders.

As a **CTA**, you are expected to rely on your broad knowledge across multiple technologies and your deep expertise of the Salesforce Platform to design secure, high-performance systems that maximize the potential of the Salesforce Platform. You must then combine this with an excellent set of soft skills to help you socialize and defend the proposed solution.

The candidate should be able to demonstrate deep knowledge and experience in the following areas:

- 5+ years of implementation experience, including development, across the full software development life cycle. Although having hands-on development skills is not mandatory, those who had the chance to code would normally develop a sense of *what would normally work* for a software solution, which can help with logically selecting and justifying a particular solution.

- 3+ years of experience in an architect role, which includes experience across the entire spectrum of architecture activities. This includes, but is not limited to, designing data models, integration interfaces, and end-to-end solutions; communicating and socializing a solution; and having deep hands-on experience with the platform's capabilities and potential solution trade-offs.

- 2+ years of experience on the Lightning Platform, with at least one of those in a lead architect role, implementing Salesforce applications and technologies.

- Has held a technical architect role on multiple complex deployments, or has gained equivalent knowledge through participation and exposure to these types of projects.

- Experience guiding a development team on the appropriate use of platform technology.

- The ability to identify and mitigate technical risks across the architecture, which normally comes with experience.

- Exposure to globalization considerations on a project. Projects with globalization requirements come with a particular set of challenges. Having a practical understanding of the platform's capabilities is key.

- Experience with object-oriented design patterns. Although a CTA is not necessarily expected to write code, understanding object-oriented design patterns and principles creates a more rounded architect who is more capable of explaining how a particular module would work.

- Awareness of platform-specific design patterns and limits. In order to pass the CTA review board, it is strongly recommended that they have hands-on experience with the different platform functionalities.

- Experience developing code on the Force.com platform, as well as an understanding of limitations and associated challenges, even if they're not necessarily doing hands-on coding.

- Ability to identify development-related risks, considerations, and limits for the platform.

- Experience with multiple development languages (for example, .NET, Java, or Ruby) and design frameworks. This would largely help when designing an integrated solution. Understanding what is possible and what is likely not is the key.

- Experience with common integration patterns; experience with integration on the Salesforce Platform. Any hands-on experience here is a massive plus.

- An understanding of and the ability to architect a solution to address security complexities, mechanisms, and capabilities on the Lightning Platform as part of a functional security model.

- An understanding of and the ability to design an identity and access management strategy as part of an end-to-end solution.

- An understanding of data migration considerations, design trade-offs, and common ETL tools.

- Awareness of **large data volume** (**LDV**) considerations, risks, and mitigation strategies.

- Awareness of general mobile solutions and architectures and an understanding of on-platform mobile solutions and considerations.

- Experience with project and development life cycle methodologies.

Now that we know what the CTA profile is, let's get to know the review board.

The CTA review board's structure and format

This section is mainly meant for those who are targeting the CTA exam. In order to pass the exam, you would need to set a review board with three CTA judges. You will receive a hypothetical scenario and have a limited amount of time to solve it and craft an end-to-end presentation, explaining the different elements of your solution and how you would solve the identified requirements in your scenario. The judges will then ask questions about your solution and challenge it. You are expected to justify, defend, and – if needed – change your solution accordingly.

The following are some more details about the exam:

- **Exam prerequisites**: The Salesforce Certified Application Architect credential and Salesforce Certified System Architect credential.

- **Format**: The candidate will review and solve a hypothetical scenario and then present this to a panel of three CTA judges. The presentation is followed by a question and answer session with the judges.

- **Time allotted to complete the exam**:

  180 minutes for scenario review and solution preparation

  45 minutes for scenario presentation

  40 minutes for scenario Q&A session

An exam facilitator and proctor will be onsite during the exam (or will join virtually if the exam is being executed virtually).

The following materials are provided to the candidate at the review board (onsite). No other materials are allowed. If the exam is onsite, you will need the following:

- A computer with PowerPoint, Word, and Excel (or Keynote, Pages, and Numbers for Mac)
- Flipchart paper
- Blank paper – for candidate notes only
- Pens, highlighters, and markers
- A timer

If the exam is virtual, you will need the following: A computer with PowerPoint, Word, and Excel (or Keynote, Pages, and Numbers for Mac) that the candidate can access via remote desktop.

You can deliver your artifacts/diagrams using one or more of the following tools:

- PowerPoint presentations
- Flipcharts
- Whiteboard (This is not transportable. Remember that you will normally create the solution and artifact in one room and then present it in another.)
- A combination of these

There is no *right tool*. You need to build your own habits and plans and use whatever works best for you.

Now that you have learned the review board exam's structure, let's find out how it's related to the day-to-day life of a Salesforce Architect.

From exam to real life – how to train to become a CTA

In addition to the significant career boost, there are several other reasons to learn how to design secure, high-performance technical solutions on the Salesforce Platform in the same way it's expected from a CTA. During the review board exam, you are expected to perform certain activities and think in a particular way. This should not be thought of as *activities required to pass the exam* but more of *best practices that an architect is expected to follow in order to produce a solution that delivers value and has fewer implementation risks.*

Regardless of whether you are targeting the CTA credential or not, as an architect, you will find that you can apply the knowledge in this book to your day-to-day activities. Actually, the best way to get hands-on experience with all the required domain knowledge is by following these simple steps:

1. Apply the methodology explained in this book – or your own variation of it – to your day-to-day activities. Put it in action, and you will notice that it becomes second nature after some time. This makes it easier to set and pass the review board exam. Let's put it this way: if you are practicing this day in and day out, you will be actually preparing for the review board exam during your normal working hours.

2. Set up playground environments to try things out by hand. As an architect, it is crucial to have practical experience with the different elements and technologies that form your solution. This is particularly true while working with the Salesforce Platform, considering all the flexibility it has and how it lets you easily sign up for a virtually unlimited number of developer environments. Nothing beats hands-on experience. So, the next time you are investigating how a particular **Single Sign-On (SSO)** flow works, don't just read about it: set up a playground environment and closely observe how the systems are interacting with each other. Make this one of your day-to-day activities while assessing different potential solutions for a given business challenge.

3. Make yourself familiar with the activity of documenting design decisions. While working on a Salesforce implementation project, you will come across endless cases where there is more than one potential solution. Make yourself familiar with the structured way of documenting the details of each option, as well as its pros and cons. This activity has several benefits in that it helps you organize your thoughts by putting them on paper and sharing them with others. This increases the potential of selecting the right solution/approach. Moreover, it helps you clearly communicate the different options that are available to the project's architecture board and stakeholders. And on top of that, it helps you document your solution – something that your project sponsor will love you for. This is another example of a daily activity that can significantly help you prepare for the review board. Although you might not document the different solutions and tradeoffs in the same thorough way you do in real life, the principle of identifying different approaches, trade-offs, compromises, risks, and rationally justifying a particular solution is exactly what you are expected to do during the review board.

These are not skills that you should learn and master just for the sake of passing the review board; these are valuable skills and practices that you should make part of your daily routine. And when you do so, you will find out that you are getting closer and closer to becoming ready for the review board exam. The CTA certificate will simply become the cherry on top of the cake, an assertion that you possess all the required skills and that you know how to put them all into action.

The nature of the exam – a point collection exercise

Understanding the nature of the review board exam will help you prepare for it, and will prove to be particularly valuable during the presentation stage:

- You will be requested to create an end-to-end solution and communicate it back to the judges. To do so, you will need to create a set of artifacts that will help you tell the solution as an engaging story. Your presentation should be executed in a way that will catch your audience's attention. Once you start the presentation, try to forget that you are in an exam room in front of judges; imagine yourself setting in front of a group of execs and CXOs from the company mentioned in the scenario. Forget for a moment that these judges work for Salesforce; put yourself in the right mood and mindset to present your solution to these client execs, who have solid technical knowledge about the platform and want to understand how you are planning to use it in order to solve their problems.

- The exam itself is a point collection exercise. You get points for identifying any solution requirements in the scenario. Every point counts. Some requirements are easy to spot and solve. For example, you might come across a security requirement that you can simply solve using field-level security settings. Don't overlook that or drop it from the solution story that you are going to tell. You might simply lose an easy point. However, during the Q&A stage, the judges will try to question you about the requirements that you didn't cover during the presentation. This will give you a second chance to cover them. Keep in mind that you have a limited time during the Q&A, and if you have many unidentified or non-solutioned requirements, then you could run out of time before you can cover all of them. This means losing valuable points that could be the difference between passing and failing.

- I have met many CTA candidates who dreaded the Q&A stage and I've always tried to explain that this stage should be considered as their friend, their opportunity to close some gaps caused by leaving things out, and an opportunity to express their knowledge, skills, and experience to some of the finest technical architects in the world. It is a time that the candidate should be looking forward to rather than fearing. It is true that you will be challenged and your knowledge will be put to the test, but this is exactly the moment where you can show the judges that *you belong to the club* – that you have got what it takes to join the very exclusive club of CTAs. You have to stay focused and be precise with your answers, and avoid wasting unnecessary time in describing things over and over again. Remember that the Q&A stage is your friend; you should try to make the most out of the available time. It is surprisingly similar to real-life presentations; the presenter will feel relieved when the audience starts to ask questions and the conversation becomes two-way instead of one-way.

- During the presentation, the judges might decide to change one of the requirements to check your ability to adjust quickly and get to the solution on the fly. Don't get nervous because of that, or automatically assume that they are doing so because you made a mistake somewhere. It is a part of the test.

- During the presentation (or the Q&A), you may figure out that you have made a mistake and decide to adjust. This is not a disaster. Don't lose your focus; the judges will also appreciate how you handle such difficult situations professionally and how you recover and get back on track. If you make a mistake, admit it professionally, explain the reason behind your early decision, and correct it. Also, explain in short how you would have handled such a requirement in a real-life project. However, keep in mind that if you make multiple mistakes, the likelihood of you passing will reduce.

- The judges are there to ensure that you have what it takes to create secure, scalable solutions based on the Salesforce Platform. It is good to let them know what you are thinking about and how you are making your decisions. This will help them understand your logic and therefore better understand the reasons behind making a decision that creates a sub-optimal solution. If you have valid reasoning and sound logic, then this will normally be taken into consideration. Most, if not all, of the scenarios you will be presented with can be solved in multiple ways. There is no *one* solution. The key thing to keep in mind is that your solution must be based on the right considerations and logic. This is a major skill that a CTA must have: the ability to think of the holistic solution, identify potential solutions, and rationally select a suitable one.

- Your proposed solution should be the best one you can think of from a technical perspective. You should not assume there are challenges that have not been mentioned directly or indirectly in the scenario. As an example, don't select a sub-optimal solution because you are worried about budgeting challenges that the client might have - only do this if that was mentioned in the scenario itself.

- Finally, always keep in mind that your given solutions must be presented based on the given requirements. Don't simply give a dry solution as if you are answering an exam on paper. Remember that you are supposed to be presenting to the CXOs of the client company and tie your solution to a requirement. This will attract the audience and make the overall picture much clearer. We will come across several examples of this during later chapters in this book.

Now that you understand the nature of the review board exam, let's move on and explore the artifacts you need to create in order to get solutions for the hypothetical scenario.

What kind of artifacts you need to generate and why

A Salesforce Architect is always aiming to create a secure and scalable solution that meets all required functionalities, and document them in a way that allows them to communicate them effectively with the stakeholders. This is applicable during the review board and while tackling a real-life implementation project. An **architecture diagram** is a graphical representation of a set of concepts that are part of an architecture. They are heavily used in software architecture and, when used effectively, can become a common language for documenting and communicating your solution.

Based on my experience, there are normally several discrepancies with projects in the way architectural diagrams are created. I have seen a lot of inconsistencies, a lack of detail, a lack of discipline, and fragmentation. In several cases, this can be traced back to the misuse of an **architectural description language** (for example, UML), or in some cases, the lack of using any standard at all. Sometimes, this is due to misunderstanding the value of the diagrams and relying on improper or inconsistent guidelines – and in some cases, a lack of architectural education.

In order to describe your Salesforce Technical Solution Architecture, you need the following artifacts:

- Must-haves:

  Actors and licenses

  Data model diagram

System landscape architecture diagram

Role hierarchy

Development life cycle diagram

- Good to have:

Process flows (in real-life projects, this is considered a must-have)

Environment diagram (in real-life projects, this is considered a must-have)

Contextual SSO flow

- Other diagrams, such as a data flow diagram, mind maps, and so on

---

Remember

You can deliver your artifacts/diagrams using one or more of the following tools:

PowerPoint presentations

Flipcharts

Whiteboard (this is not transportable)

A combination of these

There is no *right tool*. You need to build your own habits and plans and use whatever works best for you.

There are a few things to keep in mind regarding these diagrams:

- **Quality**: During the review board exam, you have a very limited amount of time to craft your solution and create your artifacts. The quality of your diagrams is not expected to be top-notch, but they can't be scribbled scratches. Keep this golden rule in your mind while creating your artifacts and diagrams: *they have to be pretty and must be worthy of being presented to a CXO*. In the real world, these diagrams must look perfect. During the review board exam, however, they can look less perfect, but they still have to be readable, understandable, communicate the right message, and show your professional attention to detail.

- **Use the tool that best suits your skillset**: Some architects are sharper when it comes to using PowerPoint, while others are better with hand-drawn diagrams. Don't feel restricted – choose the tool that works best for you and that you feel more comfortable working with.

- **Horses for courses**: Some tools work better for specific diagrams. Some diagrams are explained in a better way if they're drawn in an interactive environment – for instance, where the audience can see the diagram being created in front of them and relate it to a story that you are telling. A good example of this is an SSO sequence diagram. However, other diagrams are better shown pre-drawn due to the amount of time needed to create them. The data model diagram is a good example of this. Here, you need to choose the right tool for the right diagram (you must also consider the way you are planning to set your review board; in-person or virtual). For an in-person review board, I find the whiteboard more suitable for interactively drawn diagrams, while flipcharts and PowerPoints and better suited for pre-drawn diagrams and artifacts.

Now, let's discover each of these artifacts in detail.

The actors and licenses diagram

The importance of this diagram is derived from the need to clearly communicate the required Salesforce, feature, and third-party licenses with your stakeholders based on concrete use cases expected from each set of users. This diagram will help you do the following:

- Identify the key use cases for each actor. These will help you determine the right license to use.

- Clearly communicate the role of each actor within your solution. In the real world, this should also help you calculate the number of required licenses, feature licenses, or third-party licenses. Moreover, documenting the scope of each role will help you answer the common *What are these users expected to be doing?* question, which tends to become more difficult to answer with time.

For this diagram, you need to consider the following:

- Include all the actors mentioned in the scenario.

- Include all the required licenses, including feature and third-party licenses. Pay extra attention to community licenses. You need to understand the capabilities and limitations of each Salesforce license.

- Go for the best justified technical solution (license-wise). Don't think of non-standard approaches to cut down the cost. Avoid any pattern that could breach Salesforce terms and conditions.

- This doesn't have to be a diagram, but the standard actors and use cases diagram is a great fit for the purpose mentioned here. I personally find it particularly useful when it's drawn on a flipchart or a paper, but a bit difficult to create using PowerPoint, given the time restrictions. In this case, a bullet point list for the actors and licenses, along with a sub-list for activities/use cases, should do the trick.

> **What if I made the wrong decision and selected a license type that is not sufficient to cover the requirement?**
>
> Don't panic – accept the fact that you picked the wrong license, rectify that on the fly, and explain your rationale behind selecting the original license to the judges. We all make mistakes; it is how we handle the situation that matters most.

Now, let's take a look at an example. The following simplified actors and licenses diagram illustrates the activities/use cases related to three different personas, and the license(s) required by each:

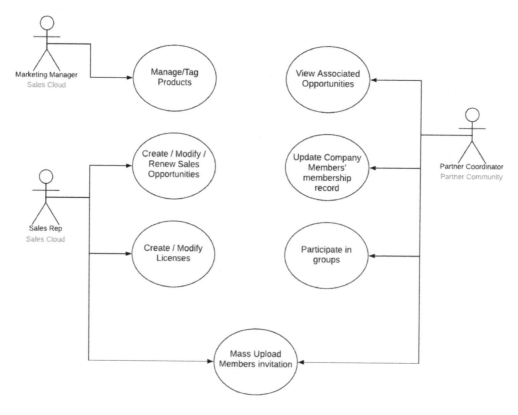

Figure 1.1 – Actors and licenses diagram example

If there was an unclear reason for picking one license over the other, add the additional rationale behind your decision to the diagram/documentation. This will help the judges – or in real life, the stakeholders – further understand your vision and the drivers behind your decision.

The data model diagram

The **data model diagram** is one of the most crucial diagrams that you need to create. Without it, you can't explain your solution properly, neither during the exam nor in real life. This diagram will help you with the following:

- Identify the custom objects versus standard objects used in your solution. Remember that standard objects come with pre-built functionalities and limitations, while custom objects have a different set of considerations (for example, some licenses have a limit on the number of custom objects that it can access). This diagram will help you identify and communicate your data model and the planned use of every object.

- Identify LDV objects. Although identifying LDVs requires more than the data model (it requires performing calculations based on the given scenario), having a well-documented data model can help you identify where things are likely to go wrong and where the data is likely going to grow more rapidly (for example, junction objects), which can help you craft a mitigation strategy.

- This diagram is also crucial for your sharing and visibility requirements. The type of relationships between objects has a direct impact on the records' visibility. This is something you cannot easily identify without a diagram that you can digest by taking a quick look at it.

- Your data model has a direct impact on your reporting strategy. By looking at this diagram, you should be able to tell where the data that's required for a particular report should be coming from.

- You can't create a solid integration strategy without understanding your underlying data model.

This diagram should include the following:

- Relation types (master-detail versus lookup).

- Cardinality (one to many, many to many, and so on).

- Object type (standard versus custom versus external objects).

- **Org-Wide Defaults (OWD)** for each object.

- Must highlight LDV objects, though you must do the math for this (it is a good practice to include these somewhere on this diagram).

- The logical data model level should be fine for the review board exam (showing the key fields for each object). In real life, you have to create a physical-level data model (showing all fields).

Now, let's take a look at an example. The following simplified data model shows the relationships between a set of standard and custom objects:

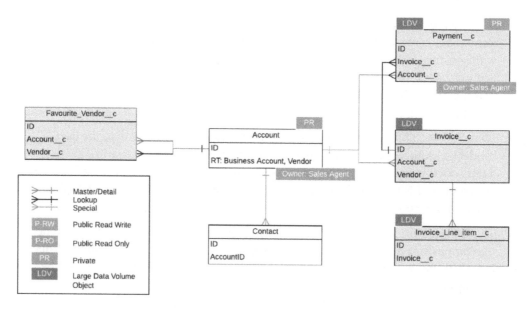

Figure 1.2 – Data model diagram example

Highlighting the owner of the records of each object type will help you illustrate part of your sharing and visibility strategy. A legend to explain your diagram would also be a nice professional touch.

The system landscape diagram

This **system landscape diagram** will help you illustrate the systems included within your solution and the relationships between them. This is extremely important because it's likely that you are going to end up creating an integrated solution that spans multiple systems. The diagram will also help you identify and document high-level information about your integration interfaces. This will be the main diagram for describing how the data will be moving across the systems (unless you decide to create a data flow diagram).

> **Remember**
>
> You are creating all these artifacts to help you explain the end-to-end solution to your audience. It is important to understand why you need each diagram and how to use it. There is no point in creating the diagram if you don't know how to use it.

For this diagram, you will need to do the following:

- Show all systems involved in the landscape architecture (including third parties, such as AppExchange products or external systems). In real life, you may also want to extend the landscape architecture so that it includes the key functionalities that are delivered by each system. During the review board, this might take more time than what you can allocate.

- Include the systems that you are planning to retire. Find a way to differentiate them from the other systems that you want to add or keep. Color coding is a good idea, but you can simply add a symbol next to the system to indicate its status. In real life, you are probably going to create multiple copies of this diagram, with each representing a snapshot in time.

- Show the proposed integration interfaces. You also need to include information such as the integration pattern, how you are planning to secure your channel, and the authentication standard used. You might find that adding all of that directly to the diagram makes it a bit too busy. Alternatively, you can use an interface reference/code on the diagram and create a supporting table with full details. Then, you can use both during the review board to explain your integration strategy.

- Remember to include **SSO** interfaces.

- Also, include any mobile devices that are part of your landscape. Add the type of the mobile app right next to that (Salesforce Mobile, Native Custom App, Hybrid App, or HTML5-based).

Now, let's take a look at an example. The following diagram shows the systems involved in a landscape where Salesforce is replacing a legacy CRM. You will also notice that it is integrated with external systems through an integration middleware (MuleSoft):

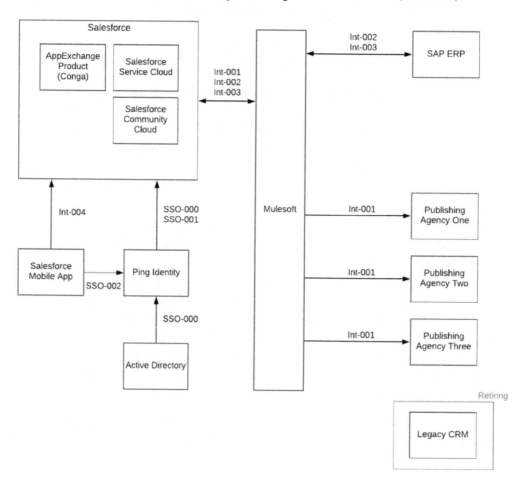

Figure 1.3 – System landscape diagram example

The following table describes the proposed integration interfaces:

Interface Code	Source/Destination	Integration Layer	Integration Pattern	Description	Security	Authentication
Int-001	Salesforce -> Mulesoft -> Publishing agency one, two, and three	Data	Data Sync - Blocking	Once the opportunity is closed, the **Send to publishers** button will become visible. When the user clicks on it, the opportunity data will be sent to the orchestration and return back the result to Salesforce	HTTPS (one way SSL/TLS)	oAuth 2.0 Web Server Flow between Salesforce and Mulesoft. Simple username/password between Mulesoft and the publishing agencies systems due to limitations.
Int-002	SAP -> Mulesoft -> Salesforce	Data	Data Sync - Batch	Batch job initiated every 30 minutes by Mulesoft to pull new/modified accounts from SAP and synch them to Salesforce	HTTPS (two way SSL/TLS)	oAuth 2.0 JWT Flow between Mulesoft and Salesforce. Simple username/password between Mulesoft and SAP.
Int-003	Salesforce -> Mulesoft -> SAP	Data	Data Sync - Batch	Batch job initiated every 30 minutes by Mulesoft to pull new orders with a status "confirmed" from Salesforce to SAP	HTTPS (two way SSL/TLS)	oAuth 2.0 JWT between Mulesoft and Salesforce. Simple username/password between Mulesoft and SAP.
Int-004	Salesforce Mobile -> Salesforce	Data	Data Sync - Blocking	Access account, contact, and order objects in Salesforce using the Salesforce mobile application	HTTPS (one way SSL/TLS)	Open ID Connect User agent flow.
SSO-000	Active Directory -> Ping -> Salesforce	Data	Data Sync - Asynch	Newly provisioned users in AD are synched via Ping to Salesforce	HTTPS (one way SSL/TLS)	Open ID Connect Web Server Flow.
SSO-001	Single Sign On for Salesforce users. Ping as IDP.	SSO	N/A	Salesforce users are authenticated via single sign-on. Here Salesforce is the **Service Provider (SP)** and Ping is the **Identity Provider (IDP)**	HTTPS (two way SSL/TLS)	Using Open ID Connect Web Server Flow.
SSO-002	Single Sign On for Salesforce Mobile App. Ping as IDP.	SSO	N/A	Similar to SSO-001. The mobile users will eventually become Salesforce users, so for this instance they would rely on Ping as and IDP	HTTPS (two way SSL/TLS)	Open ID Connect User agent flow.

Figure 1.4 – Proposed integration interfaces

Typically, you don't include data migration interfaces in a landscape architecture diagram. However, this could be beneficial, particularly during the review board, to explain what tools you are planning to use and what your proposed migration strategy is. Ensure you clearly differentiate that from the integration interfaces. Mixing data migration and data integration concepts is a common mistake.

The role hierarchy diagram

Data security and visibility is a key topic for a Salesforce architecture. The wrong data sharing and visibility architecture can significantly impact the performance of the solution and can create a major risk to compliance and security. There are several elements that form your overall data sharing and visibility architecture, including your data model, role hierarchy, territory structure, and the capabilities and limitations of some Salesforce licenses. The **role hierarchy diagram** is a common sharing mechanism, and that is why creating this diagram will help you explain your overall data sharing and visibility strategy. In real life, you might even want to include full documentation of your sharing rules.

This diagram should include the following:

- A review board, where you must create a full role hierarchy for at least one branch. You don't need to create all the branches if they are simply copied variations of the illustrated branch. For example, if you are going to create a role hierarchy that includes the head of sales for each state in USA, there is no need to create branches for all the states, as long as you can show one or two full branches for some states and indicate that a similar approach will be followed for other states. In real life, you will have enough time to create documentation for the full hierarchy.

- Roles for partner community and customer community licenses as well.

- Any license type limitations. The actors and licenses diagram will be handy at this stage.

Now, let's take a look at an example. The following diagram shows a company hierarchy based on the USA:

Figure 1.5 – Role hierarchy diagram example

Additionally, you can also include a list of sharing roles and other sharing mechanisms that you are planning to use, likely as an annexed table.

The business process flow diagram

The **business process flow** diagram will help you illustrate and communicate the targeted user experience for a given process. This is a *good to have* diagram during the review board in terms of the value it adds, but also in terms of the time it takes to create. Practice creating these types of diagrams and decide if you will include them as part of your generated artifacts or not. Again, remember that we create these diagrams to help us explain the end-to-end solution, not just for the sake of creating diagrams. In real life, diagrams that explain each business process is a must-have. It is also strongly recommended that it's in standard BPMN 2.0 format as this creates a common language between team members and avoids you losing the required details and precision.

This diagram should include the following:

- Systems included in a particular process flow. I personally prefer to use swim lanes.
- The starting action and actor.
- Activities included at each stage, and whether they are manual or automated.
- The logic that controls moving from one step to the other or from one system to the other.
- Data that's been exchanged between systems.

Now, let's take a look at an example. The following business process diagram describes a partner onboarding process. You can add as much detail as you wish for the given hypothetical scenario. In real life, this diagram is likely to be much more detailed:

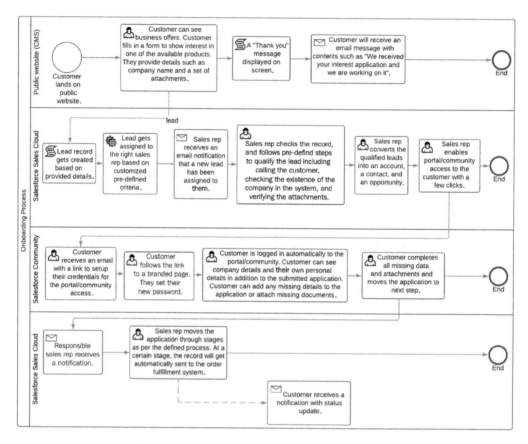

Figure 1.6 – Business process flow diagram example

Subprocesses help create reusable elements. It is recommended that you use subprocesses whenever applicable. However, this is perhaps more suitable for real-life scenarios rather than the review board.

The environment diagram

Governance is another key knowledge area that you have to cover as part of your end-to-end solution. Part of it is your environment strategy; that is, what kind of environments you are planning to use and for what. If you don't create this diagram as part of your presentation, then you are likely going to be asked to draw it during the Q&A session. This diagram is a must-have in real life and can also drive some budget-related discussions.

This diagram should include the following:

- What environment types are being planned at each stage.

- Justification for sandbox-type selection and how this is associated with the test plan. However, this probably isn't going to be something you document on the diagram itself.

- The activities you've planned for each environment and the types of tests included.

- Details about who will be deployed to each branch and at what stage.

- Make sure you fully understand the **Continuous Integration and Continuous Deployment (CI/CD)** concepts. Hands-on experience is very important here.

- Any third parties that you are planning to use (for example, automated build tools, source controls, and so on).

We'll cover examples and more details related to this diagram in the chapters to come.

I recommend that you combine this with your source code branching diagram, assuming you have enough time to do so.

The contextual SSO flow diagram

Most scenarios you get will have **SSO** requirements. This diagram (you might need more than one, depending on the used SSO standards) will help you walk your audience through the details of the target user experience without missing any points. If you didn't create this diagram as part of your presentation, then you are likely going to be asked to draw it during the Q&A session. A standard sequence diagram is highly recommended. This is one of the diagrams I personally find more suitable to be drawn in an interactive way (for instance, using a whiteboard).

For this diagram, take the following into consideration:

- You need to know how to fully draw the following flows like the back of your hand, along with all the required details:

   SAML IDP initiated

   SAML SP initiated with deep linking

   OAuth 2.0/OpenID Connect web server/Auth code

   OAuth 2.0/OpenID Connect User-Agent

   OAuth 2.0/OpenID Connect refresh token

OAuth 2.0/OpenID Connect JWT flow

OAuth 2.0 Asset token flow

- You need to understand when to use each of these standards.

- Pay extra attention to the use cases when you need to include them as part of your integration architecture (for example, an external system authenticating with Salesforce) or mobile architecture (for example, a native app authenticating with Salesforce).

- Social sign-on comes with a few caveats that you need to keep an eye on and be able to explain.

We'll cover examples and more details related to this diagram in the chapters to come.

It is recommended that you include information regarding the data that's exchanged at each step of the sequence diagram.

Summary

In this chapter, you managed to get a better understanding of the typical CTA profile. You learned how this book is structured and how you can make the most of it, as well as how to utilize your day-to-day activities in order to train for the CTA review board. You now have a better understanding of the nature of the exam and some of its key considerations to keep in mind. We also took a deep dive into some of the key tools and artifacts that can help you create a secure and scalable end-to-end solution and communicate it to your audience.

In the next chapter, we will dive deeper into some key architectural skills and knowledge areas. These skills are common for enterprise and software architects, and we are going to understand how are they applicable to the Salesforce Platform.

2
Core Architectural Concepts – Data

As you learned in the previous chapter, the expectations are really high for a Salesforce CTA. The architect is expected to have a deep understanding of the platform's features and capabilities. In addition to a very deep understanding of particular architectural concepts, the architect is also expected to have a breadth of knowledge across many architectural domains. Data is one of the key architectural domains that architects need to master. Data is all around us in our daily lives and every day, we discover a new potential for it. From sales to service, marketing, business intelligence, and artificial intelligence, data is at the heart of today's modern systems.

In this chapter, we're going to cover the following main topics:

- Differences between classic RDBMS and Salesforce
- Understanding data governance
- Understanding data security
- Data regulatory compliance
- Exploring data categories
- The nature of data warehouses and data lakes
- Choosing the right document management system

- Understanding data architecture concepts
- Designing and documenting your data model
- Using database relationships

Let's get started!

Differences between classic RDBMS and Salesforce

People have used databases in their day-to-day activities for centuries. Although they have only been given the name "databases" recently, they have been developed for years and we've invented more and more use cases for them. Most modern applications utilize a database of some sort. Theoretically, a database is simply a collection of related data. We call the software system that manages this data a **database management system** (**DBMS**). The DBMS will also be responsible for controlling access to the database.

Databases have evolved over the years from simple file-based systems to sophisticated cloud-based relational database management systems and in-memory databases.

Understanding the problems of file-based systems could help you avoid challenges that could occur in modern database systems. **File-based systems** were designed for a specific set of use cases. This was primarily driven by an attempt to digitalize the activities we – as humans – used to do. Take the manual filing system as an example. Enterprises and some libraries used to have a very organized way to store the different files and books they own. A typical arrangement would see these assets stored in labeled cabinets. The cabinets themselves might have locks to control who can open them and who cannot, and an entire set of cabinets can be kept in secured rooms or areas to ensure the right security measures are taken. The simplest way to find a document in this arrangement would be to go through all the documents one by one until you find what you are after.

Eventually, indexing systems were used to help locate what we wanted more quickly. In a simple form, we could have divisions in the filing system or a summarized index sheet that points to the location of each stored document.

This system works as long as only a small number of items are stored, or if all we want to do is simply store and retrieve items. You can probably imagine the complexity of retrieving cross-reference data or trying to get any intelligence out of the gathered data.

Relational databases became very popular at the end of the last century. They dominated the enterprise landscape and are still relevant today. The data in RDBMSes is split across multiple *related tables*, where each row of these tables has a *unique identifier* called a *primary key*. Related tables can be linked by referencing those primary keys with *foreign keys*.

Data is normally accessed using a **structured query language** (such as SQL, or SOQL in Salesforce). The speed of retrieving this data is impacted by several factors, such as the underlying infrastructure, the way data is identified and indexed, and the amount of data that can be stored and retrieved while the data's unindexed.

Relational database transactions are defined by the following four characteristics (you can remember these with the acronym **ACID**):

- **Atomic**: This means that a transaction must be treated as an *atomic unit*. All of its tasks and operations must succeed; otherwise, the entire transaction is rolled back. A database must never be in a state where a transaction is partially completed.

- **Consistent**: If the data was in a *constant state* before a particular transaction, then it should stay so once that transaction has been executed. The state of the database should stay consistent throughout the transaction. In other words, the transaction should not have a negative effect on the data in the database.

- **Isolated**: Transactions are *separate*, so there should be no dependencies between them and no shared data. This is particularly true when there is more than one transaction being executed simultaneously in parallel. No transaction will impact the existence of the other transactions.

- **Durable**: Data should be held in a *persistent fashion*, even if the system fails to restart. When a transaction updates data in a database and commits it, the database is expected to hold the modified data. In the case of a system failure before the data is written to disk, it should be updated once the system is back in action.

Relational databases are ideal for complex operations and data analysis tasks. They are designed to value *consistency over availability* and provide a *rigid structure* that the data must fit into.

In the 1990s, when the internet took off, a new challenge arose, since web applications started to produce data that wasn't necessarily structured or organized and was sometimes difficult to fit into such a rigid structure. With this came the rise of **non-relational databases**, which are now known as **not only SQL** or **NoSQL** databases.

Non-relational databases share the following three qualities (you can remember these with the acronym **BASE**):

- **Basically Available**: The system should be available, even in the event of failure (including network failure).

- **Soft state**: The state of the data in the system may change because of the eventual consistency activities.

- **Eventual consistency**: Consistency is not guaranteed, but at some point, the data will end up in a consistent state. Here, we can see the principle of delayed consistency in comparison to the immediate consistency of ACID.

Non-relational databases are highly scalable, though this comes at a cost. Data consistency is not guaranteed at every point of time, which means that different users might see different versions of the same data at the same time – despite the fact that the data would eventually end up in a consistent state. Non-relational databases – quite the opposite of relational databases – value availability over consistency.

While designing your Salesforce solution, you might find that you are presented with a challenge that requires a highly available and scalable database system. **Heroku** supports some of the most popular NoSQL databases as add-ons, such as MongoDB and CouchDB.

To understand what use cases should be considered for NoSQL, let's go through the following use cases:

- Frequently written but rarely read statistical data

- Big data (such as stats across many countries for many years)

- Binary assets (such as PDF or MP3 files), where the need would be to provide storage in a data store that can be served directly to the user's browser

- Transient/temporary data

- High-availability apps, where downtime is critical

- High-scalability apps, where there is a need to handle a very high number of transactions

The **Salesforce platform** is not designed for use cases where you need to receive and ingest tons of incoming data. Think of an *IoT* scenario as a scenario where there is normally a need for a highly available and scalable platform to receive, ingest, and aggregate the data before processing it or transferring it to another platform that would handle the processing. This is a use case where a platform such as Heroku can add a lot of value to your solution, especially since it has a built-in connector to the Salesforce platform via **Heroku Connect**. During the review board, avoid mistakes that would end up overstretching one of your solution components, such as driving IoT inbound communications into Salesforce directly.

Salesforce is slightly different from regular RDBMSes. As an experienced Salesforce architect, you are already aware that it is a *multi-tenant database* where the data of different tenants is separated using *Org IDs*. However, you need to know about some of the concepts that could be considered suboptimal in standard RDBMS design but are fine in the Salesforce world, such as the following:

- Self-relationships are absolutely fine in Salesforce. Actually, they might give you the ability to utilize some out-of-the-box capabilities that won't simply work if you model the data using two objects.

- In a regular database, it is normally not acceptable to have a table with 500 different columns. However, this is acceptable in Salesforce for some use cases, particularly if you are creating a denormalized aggregation object.

- In regular databases, you rarely notice a direct relationship from a child record to a grandparent record. While in Salesforce, this is not something out of the ordinary, such relationships could be established simply because they impact the way data is presented to the end user (for example, when establishing a lookup relation, related records will simply be displayed automatically on the page layout of the grandparent record, without the need for you to write custom code to roll these records up from the parent record to the grandparent).

- Salesforce fields are *type-aware*. In addition to their role as data containers, similar to a normal database field, they also provide built-in data type validations. You won't be able to set a number on a checkbox field, and this is not something you can turn off.

- Salesforce has its own structured data query language known as **Salesforce Object Query Language** (**SOQL**) that exchanges the flexibility of SQL for some built-in functionalities that will significantly speed up the development of most use cases.

- Data storage is an important topic that you need to keep in mind while designing your Salesforce data model. Storage space itself is one thing, as it is not very cheap compared to other platforms. But most importantly, you should keep an eye on the size of your Salesforce object to ensure the performance of certain functionalities, such as reporting, do not deteriorate with the rapid increase of object size. We will dive deeper into this topic in *Chapter 7, Designing a Scalable Salesforce Data Architecture*.

- Salesforce comes with a very solid *data access control model*. This allows us to control not only which objects and fields are accessible to a particular user, but which records too. All of this can be done by using point-and-click features rather than writing code. However, these functionalities normally create some supporting data behind the scenes in order to drive visibility requirements. You need to understand how they work and anticipate what kind of challenges you might come across while using each different sharing approach. We will also cover this in *Chapter 6, Formulating a Secure Architecture in Salesforce*.

Now that you understand the main differences between classic RDBMS and Salesforce, let's move on and explore a common topic between the two, which is also key to the success of any enterprise's data strategy – **data governance**.

Understanding data governance

Data governance, in an enterprise context, is a data management concept that aims to ensure a high level of data quality throughout the complete life cycle of the data.

The data governance concept can be extended to several focus areas. Enterprises typically focus on topics such as data usability, availability, security, and integrity. This includes any required processes that need to be followed during the different stages of the data life cycle, such as data stewardship, which ensures that the quality of the data is always up to a high standard, and other activities that ensure the data is accessible and available for all consuming applications and entities.

Data governance aims to do the following:

- Increase consistency and confidence in data-driven decisions. This, in turn, enables better decision-making capabilities across the enterprise.

- Break down data silos.

- Ensure that the right data is used for the right purposes. This is done to avoid the risk of introducing data errors into systems and to block potential misuse.

- Decrease the risk associated with regulatory requirements; avoiding fines.

- Continuously monitor and improve data security, as well as define and verify requirements for data distribution policies.

- Enable data monetization.

- Increase information quality by defining accountabilities.

- Enable modern, customer-centric user journeys based on high-quality trusted data.

- Minimize the need for rework due to a technical department being created by poorly governed activities.

Data governance bodies usually create and maintain the following artifacts:

- **Data mapping and classification**: This helps with documenting the enterprise's data assets and related data flows. Datasets can then be classified based on factors such as whether they contain personal information or sensitive data. This, in turn, influences how data governance policies are applied to each dataset.

- **Business glossary**: This contains definitions of the business terms that are used in an organization, such as what constitutes an active customer.

- **Data catalog**: These are normally created by collecting metadata from across the systems. They are then used to create an inventory of available data assets. Governance policies and information about topics such as automation mechanisms can also be built into catalog.

A well-designed data governance program normally includes a team that acts as the governing body and a group of data stewards. They work together to create the required standards and policies for governing the data, as well as implementing and executing the planned activities and procedures. This is mainly carried out by the data stewards.

A **data steward** is a role within the enterprise, and is someone who is responsible for maintaining and using the organization's data governance processes to ensure the availability and quality of both the data and metadata. The data steward also has the responsibility to utilize policies, guidelines, and processes in order to administer the organizations' data in compliance with given policy and/or regulatory obligations. The data steward and the data custodian may share some responsibilities.

A **data custodian** is a role within the enterprise, and is someone who is responsible for transporting and storing data, rather than topics such as what data is going into the system and why. Data stewards are normally responsible for what is stored in datasets, while data custodians cover the technical details, such as environment and database structure. Data custodians are sometimes referred to as database administrators or **Extract Transform Load** (ETL) developers.

Now that we understand the activities that are covered by the data governing body, as well as data stewards and custodians, let's have a look at one of the key topics they need to cover in their data strategy – data security.

Understanding data security

Data security is one of the greatest concerns for enterprises today, especially with the ever-increasing amount and value of collected data. It is all about protecting digital data from the actions of unauthorized users (such as data leaks or breaches) or from destructive forces. As part of that, there are a few concepts that you need to become familiar with, including encryption, backup and restore, data masking, and data erasure. Let's get to know each of them.

Data encryption

Data encryption can be applied at multiple levels and stages of the data life cycle. This includes when the data is stored at its final data store (encryption at rest) and while data is in motion, moving from one system to the other (encryption in transit).

Encryption in transit is typically achieved by encrypting the message before it is transmitted and decrypted at the destination. This process intends to protect data while being transferred against attackers who can intercept the transmission or carry out what is sometimes referred to as man-in-the-middle attacks. This is normally achieved by utilizing a secure channel such as HTTPS, although higher levels of security can be applied. We will do a deep dive into this topic in *Chapter 3, Core Architectural Concepts – Integration and Security*, to better understand how encryption algorithms work and how they are used to exchange data in a secure manner.

Encryption at rest is all about storing the data that's been encrypted. This makes it impossible to read and display the decrypted version of it without having access to a specific encryption key. Some applications or platforms provide this out of the box. This is a protection mechanism against attackers who can gain access to the database or to the physical disk where the data is stored.

Salesforce Shield provides an encryption solution for encrypting data at rest. This is applicable to the filesystem, the database, and the search index files. If you are planning to use Salesforce Shield as part of your solution, you need to highlight that clearly in your landscape architecture.

Data restoration

Backup and restore solutions are used to ensure data is available in a safe location/source in case there is a need to restore or recover it. In most industries, it is essential to keep a backup of any operational data. And, more importantly, you must have a clear restoration strategy. Data restoration is typically more challenging than backing it up as it comes with additional challenges, such as restoring partial data, reference data, and parent-child records and relationships.

> **Note**
> Salesforce has announced that, effective July 31, 2020, Data Recovery as a paid feature will be deprecated and no longer available as a service.

Due to this, it is important to create a comprehensive data backup and restore strategy as part of your data governance strategy. There are several tools that can be used to back up and restore data from and to the Salesforce platform, including some AppExchange products. A custom-made solution through implementing ETL tools is also possible, despite the additional build cost associated with it. As an architect, you are expected to be able to walk your stakeholders through the various options that are available, as well as the potential pros and cons.

> **Note**
> During the review board, you are expected to come up with the best possible solution technically. Cost should not be a consideration unless clearly mentioned in the scenario. Buy versus build decisions always tend to pick the *buy* option due to its quick return on investment.

Data masking

Data obfuscation (of structured data) is the process of covering the original data with modified content. This is mainly done to protect data that is classified as **personally identifiable information** (**PII**) or sensitive commercial or personal data. An example is masking national identity numbers to display only the last four digits while replacing all other digits with a static character, such as a wildcard. Data is normally obfuscated in order to protect it from users, such as internal agents, external customers, or even developers (who normally need real production-like data to test specific use cases or fix a particle bug) to be compliant with regulatory requirements.

There are two common techniques for data obfuscation: pseudonymization and anonymization. Which one you should choose depends on the degree of risk associated with the masked data and how the data will be processed. Pseudonymous data still allows some sort of reidentification (even if it's remote or indirect), while anonymous data cannot be reidentified. A common way to anonymize data is by scrambling data, a process that can sometimes be reversible; for example, London could become ndooln. This masking technique allows a part of the data to be hidden with a static or random character. On the other hand, data blurring uses an approximation of data values to make it impossible to identify a person or to make the data's meaning obsolete.

Data erasure

Data erasure (also referred to as **data clearing**, **data destruction**, or **data wiping**) is a software-based activity where specific data is overwritten with other values to completely destroy the electronic data and make it unrecoverable. This is different from data deletion, despite the fact that they sound the same. Data deletion can leave data in a recoverable format (for example, by simply removing the reference to it from an index table, while still maintaining it on the storage disk). Data erasure, on the other hand, is permanent and particularly important for highly sensitive data. It is important to understand the difference between these terms so that you can suggest the best strategy to your stakeholders, while also taking into consideration the limited control they have over how the data is ultimately being stored in Salesforce.

It is worth mentioning that encrypted data can be destroyed/erased permanently by simply destroying the encryption keys.

Another key topic the data governing body needs to cover is data regulatory compliance. With the increased amount of gathered customer and business data, it has become essential to introduce rules that govern the use of that data. As an architect, you must be aware of these regulations in order to design a *fully compliant solution*. You will likely need to work with subject matter experts to ensure your solution fulfills all regulatory requirements, but you should still be able to cover a good amount of that by yourself. You also need to be able to explain how your solution is compliant with these regulations to your stakeholders.

Data regulatory compliance

There are several data regulations in place based on industry standards and government regulations. These have been created to mitigate the risk of unauthorized access to corporate, personal, or government data. Some of the regulations that you may come across more frequently these days while designing a Salesforce solution include the following:

- **General Data Protection Regulation (GDPR)**
- **United Kingdom version of GDPR (UK-GDPR)**
- **Health Insurance Portability and Accountability Act (HIPAA)**
- **California Consumer Privacy Act (CCPA)**
- **Fair and Accurate Credit Transactions Act of 2003 (FACTA)**
- **Act on the Protection of Personal Information (APPI)**
- **Gramm-Leach-Bliley (GLB)**
- **Payment Card Industry Data Security Standard (PCI DSS)**

Failure to comply with these regulations can result in *hefty fines* and *public damage* to the enterprise's reputation, in addition to *civil and criminal liability*. We are not going to cover the details of these regulations in this book, but you are encouraged to seek additional knowledge online and from other books. We'll come across requirements that must be solved, along with considerations regarding some of the previously mentioned regulations, in the chapters to come.

The **Payment Card Industry Data Security Standard (PCI DSS**, also known as PCI compliance) is an information security standard that's applicable for all companies involved in activities related to credit card information, such as accepting, processing, storing, or transmitting credit card information from credit card providers. Salesforce Billing became PCI Level 1-compliant in 2012 and has retained its compliance every year since.

You maintain compliance with PCI by *never storing* any credit card information in Salesforce at all stages of the payment method collection stages (before, during, or after). The payment card's information should only be transmitted to the payment processors via a *token* and *never stored within Salesforce*. Each of these tokens is unique per customer, payment card, merchant, and payment processor. Once the token has been submitted, the payment processor can link it to the actual personal account number stored.

Using tokens, Salesforce can store a *representation* of the customer's payment card without storing the actual details of the card itself. If the token falls into the wrong hands, it is useless because it only works when it's being used by the original merchant and payment processor.

The information that can be stored in Salesforce while still maintaining PCI compliance includes data such as the following:

- Name on card

- Last four digits of the credit card number

- Card type

- Token

- Expiration month and year

It is important to understand how online payment mechanisms work and how to select the right one for your solution. Suggesting a non-PCI-compliant solution during the review board could open the door to many other discussions that you don't want to have. When you suggest a suboptimal solution, the judges will try to understand the rationale behind your suggestion. Failing to show enough knowledge and understanding of regulations and compliance could lead to exam failure.

For online payments, you need to know that there are generally two main ways to integrate with a payment gateway: you can either create a checkout page that's hosted on your own website (for example, Salesforce communities) or utilize a checkout page that is provided and hosted by your payment gateway.

In terms of the externally hosted checkout approach, your checkout page is hosted on a different website provided by the payment provider. When the customer clicks on the checkout button on your website, they are redirected to the payment page, which is hosted on a different domain name. The order's information and cart total amount will normally be shown on the payment page. The customer will enter their card details on this page and then hit the submit button. Notice that the card details are entered on the external payment website only; your pages and forms are never used to capture such details. Once the payment is successful, the customer is redirected to a landing page on your website. A confirmation/transaction code will also be passed back to your website.

The hosted checkout approach has the following advantages:

- **Enhanced security**: Every additional party involved in a payment transaction increases the risks associated with data breaches. You should aim to have as few data transfers as you can. Also, since the payment details are collected by the payment provider/processor, your website is not considered as part of the transaction, so the overall security level of this approach is high.

- **Less liability**: You reduce your liability as a merchant because you are not collecting any sensitive information. All of that is done by the payment provider.

- **Peace of mind for the customer**: Customers might find it more assuring to provide their payment details to a website/domain they already trust, such as PayPal. This is particularly true for smaller merchants or for newer brands.

- **Flexibility in payment methods**: Normally, hosted checkout pages provide the user with the choice to choose from multiple payment methods. This page will continue to be updated as the payment provider includes more and more payment methods. You don't need to worry about that or change anything in your code.

- **Simplified setup**: This method is the easiest to set up and maintain.

- **Limited customization**: Although the payment page is hosted on another website, many of the payment providers allow a limited level of customizations, such as setting a logo, header and footer, and a color scheme.

Regarding the onsite checkout approach, the customer provides their payment details on a page hosted on your own website (for example, Salesforce communities). You have full control over the look and feel of this page, but you are also responsible for the implementation of every required functionality, validation, and security measure.

The onsite checkout approach has the following advantages:

- **Totally seamless**: This is probably the most important advantage of this approach. The customer isn't redirected anywhere; the entire payment process feels like part of the journey and experience that you are providing to your customer.

- **One-click purchasing**: This is similar to what major merchants such as Amazon do. You are collecting the customer's payment details so that you can attach them to their account. This opens the door to introducing the one-click functionality.

- **Customization**: You can make the payment collection page in any way you like. It can be completely styled to meet your website's look and feel. This goes beyond UI styling as you can, for example, collect additional details as part of the checkout process.

If you are taking payments via a hosted page, it is much easier to fill in and submit the required forms to stay PCI-compliant. This also makes the maintenance process simpler. If there is no clear need to go with an onsite checkout approach, then it is always safer to suggest an externally hosted page approach.

Now that we have covered some of the key topics you need to know about regarding data regulations, let's understand the different data categories that are available.

Exploring data categories

Reference data and **master data** are two common data categories that an architect would typically come across in most projects. In addition to these, in this section, we will also discover the characteristics of transactional data, reporting data, metadata, big data, and unstructured data. Having a deeper understanding of these different data categories will help you craft your overall data strategy, including data governance. This will also help you speak the same language your data architects prefer to use. Let's have a look at each of them closely.

Transactional data

Transactional data is generated by regular business transactions. It describes business events. Normally, it is the most frequently changing data in the enterprise. Transactional data events could include the following:

- Sold products to customers
- Collected payments
- Created quotes
- Shipped items to customers

Transactional data is normally generated and managed by operational systems, such as CRM, ERM, and HR applications.

Master data and master data management

Enterprises normally provide key business information that supports daily transactions. Such data normally describes customers, products, locations, and so on.

Such data is called **master data**, and it is commonly referred to as *parties* (employees, customers, suppliers, and so on), places (sites, regions, and so on), and things (products, assets, vehicles, and so on).

The usual business operations normally author/create and use master data as part of the normal course of business processes. However, operational applications are usually designed for an *application-specific* use case for the master data. This could result in a misalignment with the overall enterprise requirement of high-quality, commonly used master data. This would result in the following:

- Master data being low quality

- Duplicated and scattered data

- Lack of truly managed data

Master data management (**MDM**) is a concept widely used to describe the discipline where IT and business work together to ensure the accuracy and uniformity of the enterprise master data using specific tools and technologies. Maintaining a single version of the truth is one of the highest priority topics on the agenda of most organizations.

An MDM **tool** is used to detect and remove duplicates, mass maintain data, and incorporate rules to prevent incorrect data being entered.

There are different MDM implementation styles. These styles are the foundation that MDM tools are based on. The business type, their data management strategy, and their situation will largely impact which style is selected.

The main difference between these implementation styles is in the way they deal with data, as well as the role of the MDM tool itself (is it a hub that controls the data or a tool to synchronize data with other data stores). Here are three common ones in use:

- **Registry style**: This style spots duplicates in various connected systems by running a match, cleansing algorithms, and assigning unique global identifiers to matched records. This helps identify the related records and build a comprehensive 360° view for the given data asset across the systems.

  In this approach, data is not sent back to the source systems. Changes to master data will continue to take place in source systems. The MDM tool assumes that the source systems can manage their own data quality. When a 360° view of a particular data asset is required (for example, the customer needs it), the MDM tool uses each reference system to build the 360° views in real time using the unique global identifier. There is normally a need for a continuous process to ensure the unique global identifier is still valid for a given dataset.

- **Consolidation style**: In this style, the data is normally gathered from multiple sources and consolidated in a hub to create a single version of the truth. This is sometimes referred to as the *golden record*. The golden record is stored centrally in the hub and eventually used for reporting or as a reference. Any updates that are made to the golden record are then pushed and applied to the original sources. The consolidation style normally follows these steps:

  a) Identify identical or similar records for a given object. This can use an exact match or a fuzzy match algorithm.

  b) Determine records that will be automatically consolidated.

  c) Determine records that will require review by the data steward before they can be consolidated.

  During these processes, the tool might use configured field weights. Fields with higher weights are normally considered as more important factors when it comes to determining the attributes that would eventually form the golden record.

- **Coexistence style**: This style is similar to the consolidation style, in the sense that it creates a golden record. However, the master data changes can take place either in the MDM hub or in the data source systems. This approach is normally more expensive to apply than the consolidation style due to the complexity in syncing data both ways.

It is also good to understand how the matching logic normally works. There are two main matching mechanisms:

- **Fuzzy matching**: This is the more commonly used mechanism but is slower to execute due to the effort required to identify the match. Fuzzy matching uses a probabilistic determination based on possible variations in data patterns, such as transpositions, omissions, truncation, misspellings, and phonetic variations.

- **Exact matching**: This mechanism is faster due to the fact that it compares the fields on the records with their identical matches from target records.

As a Salesforce architect, you need to understand the capabilities and limitations of the out-of-the-box tools available in the platform, in addition to the capabilities that are delivered by key MDM players in the market – particularly those that have direct integration with Salesforce via an AppExchange application.

In your review board presentation – as well as in real life – you are expected to guide your stakeholders and explain the different options they have. You should be able to suggest a name for a suitable tool. It is not enough to mention that you need to use an MDM tool – you need to be more specific and provide a suggested product name. This is applicable to all third-party products you may suggest. You may also be asked to explain *how* these MDM tools will be used to solve a particular challenge. You need to understand the MDM implementation style that's being adopted by your proposed tool.

Reference data

Think of data such as order status (Created, Approved, Delivered, and so on) or a list of country names with their ISO code. You can also think of a business account type if you wish (Silver, Gold, Platinum, and so on). Both of these are examples of reference data.

Reference data is typically static or slowly changing data that is used to categorize or classify other data. Reference datasets are sometimes referred to as **lookup data**. Some of this reference data can be universal (such as the counties with ISO codes, as mentioned earlier), while others might be domain-specific or enterprise-specific.

Reference data is different from master data. They both provide context to business processes and transactions. However, reference data is mostly concerned with categorization and classification, while master data is mainly related to business entities (for example, customers).

Reporting data

Data organized in a specific way to facilitate reporting and business intelligence is referred to as **reporting data**. Data used for operational reporting either in an aggregated or non-aggregated fashion belongs in this category.

Reporting data is created by combining master data, reference data, and transactional data.

Metadata

Metadata has a very cool definition; it is known as the data that describes other data. **eXtensible Markup Language** (**XML**) is a commonly used metadata format.

A simple example is the properties of a computer file: its size, type, author, and creation date. Salesforce utilizes metadata heavily since most of its features can be described using well-structured metadata. Custom objects, workflows, report structures, validation rules, page layouts, and many more features can all be extracted from the Salesforce platform as metadata. This enables automated merge and deployment processes, something that we will cover in the chapters to come.

Big data

Big data refers to datasets that are too massive to be handled by traditional databases or data processing applications; that is, datasets containing hundreds of millions (even billions) of rows. Big data became popular in the past decade, especially with the decreased cost of data storage and increased processing capacity.

Businesses are increasingly understanding the importance of their data and the significant benefits they can gain from it. They don't want to throw away their data and want to make use of it for many purposes, including AI-driven decisions and personalized customer-centric services and journeys. It is worth mentioning that there have been some critics of the big data approach. Some describe it as simply dumping the data somewhere in the hope that it will prove to be useful someday. However, it is also clear that when big data is used in the right way, it can prove to be a differentiator for a particular business. The future seems promising for big data, which is a key ingredient for machine learning algorithms.

As an architect, you should be able to guide the client through combining the technologies required to manage a massive quantity and variety of data (likely in a non-relational database) versus relational data (to handle complex business logic).

Unstructured data

Unstructured data became more popular due to the internet booming. This data does not have a predefined structure and therefore can't be fit into structured RDBMSes. In most cases, this type of data is presented as text data; for example, a PDF file where text mining would help with extracting structure and relevant data from this unstructured document.

The rise of big data and unstructured data takes us straight to our next topic – data warehousing and data lakes.

The nature of data warehouses and data lakes

A **data warehouse** (**DW** or **DWH**) is a central repository of current and historical data that's been integrated from one or more disparate sources. The DWH (also referred to as **enterprise data warehouse** (**EDW**)) is a system that's used for data analysis and reporting. It is usually considered the core of an enterprise business intelligence strategy.

Data stored in a DWH comes from multiple systems, including operational systems (such as CRM systems). The data may need to undergo a set of data cleansing activities before it can be uploaded into the DWH to ensure data quality.

Some DWH tools have built-in **ETL** capabilities, while others rely on external third-party tools (we will cover ETL tools and other integration middleware in *Chapter 3, Core Architectural Concepts – Integration and Security*). This ETL capability will ensure that the ingested data has a specific quality and structure. Data might be staged in a specific staging area before it is loaded into the DWH. You need to become familiar with the names of some popular data warehousing solutions, such as Amazon Redshift, which is a fully managed, cloud-based data warehouse.

A **data lake** is a system or repository of data that's stored in an *unstructured way*. Data is held in its *rawest form*; it's not processed, modified, or analyzed. Data lakes accept and store all kinds of data from all sources. Structured, semi-structured, processed, and transformed data can also be stored in data lakes (such as XML data, or data coming from databases). The data that's gathered will be used for reporting, visualization, business intelligence, machine learning, and advanced analytics. You need to become familiar with the names of some popular data lake solutions, such as AWS Lake Formation.

You also need to know which solution you should propose and for what reason. If you need to offer a platform that can provide historical trending reports, deep data analysis capabilities, and the ability to report on a massive amount of data, then a DWH is more suitable for your use case. Keep in mind that data that's been extracted from Salesforce is mostly in a structured format (files are an exception).

In many review board scenarios, you will come across the need to archive the platform data. We will discover the options that are available in *Chapter 7, Designing a Scalable Salesforce Data Architecture*, but at the moment, all you need to know is that one of these options is a DWH.

Data lakes could be the right solution if you need to store structured and unstructured data in one place in order to facilitate tasks such as machine learning or advanced analytics.

Another common requirement in today's enterprise solutions is document management systems. We will learn more about these next.

Choosing the right document management system

Electronic documents are everywhere nowadays in enterprises. An electronic document can simply be thought of as a form of electronic media content that can be used either in its electronic form or as printed output. This does not include system files or computer applications. A **document management system** (**DMS**) is a computer application that's used to store, track, and manage electronic documents throughout their life cycles. This includes activities related to these documents, such as versioning and workflows.

Document management overlaps with content management, even though they were originally different in nature. They are often seen combined today as **enterprise content management** (**ECM**) systems, mainly because many of today's electronic documents that are available for a particular enterprise are not necessarily generated by the enterprise itself.

DMSes in today's age differ in terms of complexity, features, and scope – from simple standalone applications to enterprise-scale systems that are able to serve massive audiences. Some of the key capabilities available in today's ECM systems are as follows:

- Security and access management, in a granular format
- Version control
- Comprehensive audit trails
- The ability to check in and check out the documents, with locks incorporated

As a Salesforce architect, it is important to understand the capabilities of DMSes and ECM. You must also, understand what additional tools are needed in order to incorporate a full-fledged DMS into your architecture.

Salesforce comes with built-in features that can deliver some DMS capabilities. It is important to understand the capabilities and limitations of each (including availability since some features may retire with time). These features are as follows:

- **Files**: These allow users to upload and store electronic documents. Files can be stored privately or shared with others using Chatter. Files are stored on the platform and have been considered as replacements for the old **Attachments** feature, particularly on Lightning Experience.
- **Salesforce CRM Content**: This allows users to create, duplicate, and develop enterprise documents. A good example is a presentation or a flyer. It also allows you to share this content with other internal or external users, such as customers or partners.

- **Salesforce Knowledge**: This is more like an enterprise knowledge base. It allows users to create and curate knowledge articles and publish them using a controlled workflow. It allows internal and external users (through communities) to search these knowledge articles and use them in multiple ways (for instance, attach them to a case). Knowledge articles can be organized into libraries, which makes them easier to maintain and share.

- **Documents**: These are mostly used to store static files in folders without needing them to be attached to records. This is particularly useful when you need to refer to a static resource (such as a logo) in a Visualforce page, for example.

Most enterprises will already have a DMS of some sort; for example, enterprise-wide applications such as Microsoft SharePoint, Box, Google Drive, One Drive, and others. You will most likely need to integrate with these systems in order to access and manage external documents within the Salesforce UI, rather than create things from scratch. In order to do that, you can use another out-of-the-box tool in Salesforce called **Files Connect**. It is important to get some hands-on experience with Files Connect to get a better understanding of how it works. And, since it has its own limitations, it is also important to become familiar with some of the other alternatives available on AppExchange. You are not expected to know the names and capabilities of all the tools under the sun – just make yourself familiar with some of them and understand exactly what they are capable of.

As an architect, you will come across several DMS requirements and challenges. You will also definitely come across business requirements that require your skills and experience to design a solid data architecture. Next, we will learn more about key data architecture concepts.

Understanding data architecture concepts

Previously, we covered the importance of data, as well as the importance of data architecture for the enterprise. The data architect – who you, as a Salesforce architect need to work closely with or, in smaller projects, act as one – needs to tackle the data architecture in a similar fashion to a normal building architecture. And to a good extent, similar principles should be followed in software architecture.

First, it is imperative to understand the business processes and create a conceptual and logical blueprint. Then, you need to know the underlying technology in order to build the detailed design and implementation. To understand these better, let's take a closer look at the three stages of data architecture design.

Conceptual-level data architecture design

The data architect, at the conceptual-level stage, needs to gain a deep understanding of the business knowledge, business processes, and operations. This includes knowledge related to data flows, business rules, and the way data is used or supposed to be used in the enterprise. This could be extended to areas such as financial, product, marketing, and industry-specific knowledge domains (such as manufacturing, insurance, and so on). The data architect can then build a blueprint by designing data entities that represent each of the enterprise's business domains.

The architect will also define the various taxonomies and data flows behind each business process. The data blueprint is crucial for building a robust and successful data architecture. On many occasions, this activity is done at the project level, rather than the enterprise-wide level. And, it is usually included as part of the business analysis activities. Typically, the following areas need to be covered:

- The key data entities and elements (Accounts, Products, Orders, and so on)

- Data entity relationships, including details such as data integrity requirements and business rules

- The output data expected by the end customers

- Required security policies

- The data that will be gathered, transformed, and used in order to generate the output data

- Ownership of the defined data entities and how they will be gathered and distributed

Logical-level data architecture design

This data architecture design is sometimes also referred to as **data modeling**. At this stage, the architect will start considering the type of technology being dealt with and define the data formats to use. The logical data model connects business requirements to the technology and database structure. The data architect should consider the standards, capabilities, best practices, and limitations of each of the underlying systems or databases. Data flows have to be defined clearly at this stage. Typically, the following areas need to be covered:

- **Data integrity requirements and naming conventions**: Naming conventions should be defined and consistently used for each database involved. The data integrity requirements between the operational data and the reference data should be considered and enforced – especially if the data needs to reside in multiple underlying systems (at the conceptual level, all of these data entities should, ideally, belong to the same conceptual entity).

- **Data archiving and retention policies**: Data cannot be piled up on top of each other indefinitely. Failing to address data archiving and retention policies at an early stage normally has an impact on the project's overall cost, poor system performance (particularly during data updates or data queries), and potential data inconsistencies. The data architect should work with stakeholders in order to define the data archiving and retention strategy based on business operations and legal or compliance requirements.

- **Privacy and security information**: While the conceptual design is more concerned with defining which data element is considered sensitive, the logical design dives into more details to ensure that confidential information is protected, and that data is visible only to the right audience. The data architect also needs to work on the strategy related to data replication and how to protect the replicated data both during transition and at rest.

- **Data flows and pipelines**: At this stage, details about how data flows between the different systems and databases should be clearly articulated. These flows should be consistent with the flows defined at the conceptual level and should reflect details such as the required data transformations while in the pipeline, as well as the frequency of the data ingestions.

Physical-level data architecture design

This data architecture design is also known as the **internal level**. This is the lowest level of data design. At this stage, the architect is concerned with the actual technical aspects of the underlying system or database. It can even go as far as defining how the data is stored in the storage devices (such as within the specific folder structure).

As a Salesforce architect, you are likely going to be involved in the conceptual design and are heavily expected to be involved in the logical design. Your involvement in the physical design isn't going to be as intensive and will be mostly in an advisory context.

In *Chapter 1*, *Starting Your Journey as a CTA*, we covered the importance of creating a data model diagram during the review board exam. This is likely to be based on the logical model (you will see several examples throughout this book). In real life, a logical model diagram is also required during the design phase of your project, while a physical model diagram is a must-have during the implementation phase.

You are expected to document (or lead the activity of documenting) the full Salesforce physical data model of your solution. This includes providing a full description of each standard and custom object used, how it is used (even for standard objects, it is not enough to mention that you are using the account object; for example, you must clearly explain how it is used), and the source of data in each integrated field, with a clear description of all involved data flows.

Next, we will understand more about the principles behind designing and properly documenting a data model.

Designing and documenting your data model

The importance of your data model's design cannot be emphasized enough. It is sad to see it being overlooked in many cases in Salesforce due to the fact that Salesforce comes with a pre-built data model, in addition to great flexibility for creating and changing custom fields and objects.

However, the proper data model design could be the difference between a smart, flexible, and scalable solution that delivers valuable real-time insight that justifies all efforts required to enter the data. This may also glorify the database with tons of dumped data and provide an overall feeling that data entry is an overhead.

Your data model is the foundation of your solution. You can read through the solution by understanding its data model, and your solution should be as strong as its foundation. You need to get your data model design right, and in order to do so, you need to understand key concepts in data modeling. This starts with normalization versus denormalization, going through three of the standard normal forms for database design, and finally understanding the common relationship types between database tables and how that is reflected in Salesforce.

Normalization versus denormalization

Normalization is the process of arranging data in a database efficiently based on its relationships. This approach aims to remove data redundancies as it wastes disk space, slows down queries, and costs more processing time to execute **create, read, update, and delete** (**CRUD**) operations. Moreover, redundant data might also increase data inconsistency. For example, when the same data persists in multiple places and gets updated in one of them, you need to ensure that the change gets reflected in all other occurrences; otherwise, you may risk having data inconsistencies. Normalization should aim to get rid of data redundancy, but not at the cost of losing data integrity.

Normalization is based on the concept of what is known as the **normal forms**. The dataset has to meet specific criteria in order to be considered in one of these normal forms. There are three main normal forms (1NF, 2NF, and 3NF), all of which we will cover shortly, and others such as BCNF, 4NF, 5NF, and so on, which we are not going to cover in this book for brevity.

Denormalization can be considered the opposite of the normalization process. In a denormalized dataset, we intentionally use redundant information. This is done for several purposes but mostly to improve the performance while executing queries and performing analytics. There is an associated overhead, of course, in keeping all the redundant data consistent and aligned.

The denormalization process reduces the number of tables (though it consumes more storage) and simplifies complicated table joins, which effectively enhances the performance while querying data that resides in multiple tables. The concept that's adopted by denormalization is that by placing all the data in one place, we could simplify the search process as it only needs to be executed on one table.

While designing your data model, you may come across use cases that could be better solved using a normalized set of tables. In other cases, denormalization could be the answer. Let's take a look at two user stories to understand things better.

> *As an account manager, I want to store the addresses of all my customers so that I can generate an important report showing the number of shipments we sent to each of these addresses in a given period of time.*

The focus of this user story is on analytics/reports. Considering the standard reporting capabilities in Salesforce, it makes sense to store the account and account address details in two separate tables. This will also enable us to link the shipment records to the right address straight away, as well as build the desired report with minimal efforts, despite the fact that Salesforce is doing additional processes behind the scenes to query data from multiple tables.

The following figure represents the proposed data model and an example of the data that's stored:

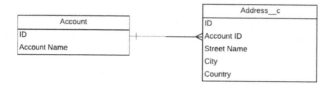

Account

ID	Name
1	Acme
2	Globex Ltd

Address

ID	Account ID	Street Name	City	State	Country
1	1	No.1 Atlantic Street	London		United Kingdom
2	1	No.5 Florence Avenue	London		United Kingdom
3	1	No.27 Argyle Street	San Francisco	CA	USA
4	2	50a Glebe Point	Los Angeles	CA	USA
5	2	44 Grosvenor Street	Los Angeles	CA	USA

Figure 2.1 – Data model in a normalized form example

Now, let's explore the second user story.

> *As an account manager, I want to store the addresses of all my customers so that I can quickly find contact addresses when looking at my customer record page and list views.*

The focus here is on the user experience while entering or viewing the data. In this case, it makes sense to use a denormalized dataset. These denormalized fields can easily be added to list views and page layouts. They can also be edited using fewer clicks. We will come across more complicated scenarios where we could utilize a denormalized dataset to reduce data storage throughout this book. Although theoretically, a denormalized dataset consumes more storage data, in Salesforce, the data storage for the records of most objects is roughly 2 KB (with a few exceptions, such as a person account and articles). This is true regardless of the number of fields in it, as well as if these fields are filled in or not (some field types are exceptions, such as rich text fields). As we mentioned earlier in this book, there are some concepts of data modeling that may look different in Salesforce.

The following figure represents the proposed data model and an example of the data that's stored:

Account	
ID	
Account Name	
Street Name1	
City1	
State1	
Country1	
Street Name2	
City2	
State2	
Country2	
Street Name3	
City3	
State3	
Country3	

Account

ID	Account Name	Street Name1	City1	State1	Country1	Street Name2	City2	State2	Country2	Street Name3	City3	State3	Country3
1	Acme	No.1 Atlantic Street	London		United Kingdom	No.5 Florence Avenue	London		United Kingdom	No.27 Argyle Street	San Francisco	CA	USA
2	Globex Ltd	50a Glebe Point	Los Angeles	CA	USA	44 Grosvenor Street	Los Angeles	CA	USA				

Figure 2.2 – Data model in a denormalized form example

We can summarize the differences between normalized versus denormalized datasets as follows:

- The normalization process relies on splitting data into multiple tables. The aim is to reduce data redundancy and increase consistency and data integrity. On the other hand, denormalization relies on combining data in order to speed up the retrieval processes. In Salesforce, it could also be used to reduce data storage and reduce the size of **LDV** objects. Despite that, this is not a common benefit in other databases.

- Normalization is usually used in **online transaction processing** (**OLTP**) systems, where the speed of insert, delete, and update operations is key. On the other hand, denormalization is used with **online analytical processing** (**OLAP**), where the query's speed and analytics are key.

- Data integrity is hard to maintain in denormalized datasets, unlike normalized datasets.

- Denormalization increases data redundancy.

- The denormalization process reduces the number of tables and potential join statements, while both of these are increased with normalization.

- Typically, denormalized datasets take more disk storage. As we mentioned earlier, this is not necessarily true in Salesforce.

The standard Salesforce data model is in normalized form by default. In order to further understand the normalization process, you need to understand the three main different types of normal forms.

Normal forms

As we explored earlier, normalization is all about arranging data in a database efficiently based on its relationships. There are three common forms of data normalization. Let's explore each of these.

First normal form

A database is considered in the first normal form if it meets the following conditions:

- **Contains atomic values only**: Atomic values are values that cannot be divided. For example, in the following figure, the value of the Phone Number column can be divided into three different phone numbers. Therefore, it is not in the first normal form (not 1NF):

Table 1

Customer ID	Phone Number
1	0794312000, 0214312000, 0914312000
2	0912239382
3	0773322000, 0214332000,

Figure 2.3 – Table 1, which does not meet the first normal form (1NF)

- **No repeating groups**: This means that the table does not contain two or more fields/columns that are representing multiple values for the same data entity. For example, in the following figure, we can see that the Phone Number 1, Phone Number 2, and Phone Number 3 fields represent multiple values for the same data entity, which is the phone number. Therefore, this table is not in 1NF:

Table 2

Customer ID	Phone Number 1	Phone Number 2	Phone Number 3
1	0794312000	0214312000	0914312000
2	0912239382		
3	0773322000	0214332000	

Figure 2.4 – Table 2, which does not meet the first normal form (1NF)

To bring the table shown in *Figure 2.3* into 1NF, we must split the table into the following two tables:

Table 1

Customer ID	Phone ID
1	1
1	2
1	3
2	4
3	5
3	6

Phone ID	Phone Number
1	0794312000
2	0214312000
3	0914312000
4	0912239382
5	0773322000
6	0214332000

Figure 2.5 – Table 1 from Figure 2.3 modified to meet the first normal form (1NF)

Second normal form

A database is considered in the second normal form if it meets the following conditions:

- It is in 1NF.

- Non-key attributes function based on the primary key. This is particularly applicable to cases where we have a composite key. (In Salesforce, the ID field is always the primary ID. There is no use for composite keys, which means that this condition is always met.) For example, the following table is not in 2NF because `Address City` is dependent on a subset of the composite key (which is `Site ID`). This can be clearly seen in the second and fourth rows. Therefore, this table is not in 2NF:

Customer ID	Site ID	Address City
1	1	San Francisco
2	3	London
3	5	Los Angeles
4	3	London

Figure 2.6 – A table that doesn't meet the second normal form (2NF)

To bring the table into 2NF, we must split the table into the following two tables:

Customer ID	Site ID
1	1
2	3
3	5
4	3

Site ID	Address City
1	San Francisco
3	London
5	Los Angeles

Figure 2.7 – The table from Figure 2.6 modified to meet the second normal form (2NF)

Third normal form

A database is considered in the third normal form if it meets the following conditions:

- It is in 2NF.

- Non-key attributes are not transitively dependent on the primary key. Take the following table as an example. The ID field is the primary key. The table is in 1NF and 2NF. The Name, Partner Number, and Bank Code fields are functionally dependent on the ID field. So far, so good. However, the Bank Name field is actually dependent on the Bank Code field. Therefore, this table is not in 3NF:

ID	Name	Partner Number	Bank Code	Bank Name
1	John Due	1234	XYZ-000242	Bank 1
2	Jane Doe	5432	ABC-004444	Bank 2
3	Richard Roe	7867	MM-00432	Bank 3

Figure 2.8 – A table that doesn't meet the third normal form (3NF)

To bring this table into 3NF, we must split the table into the following two tables:

ID	Name	Partner Number	Bank Code
1	John Due	1234	XYZ-000242
2	Jane Doe	5432	ABC-004444
3	Richard Roe	7867	MM-00432

Bank Code	Bank Name
XYZ-000242	Bank 1
ABC-004444	Bank 2
MM-00432	Bank 3

Figure 2.9 – The table from Figure 2.8 modified to meet the third normal form (3NF)

Now that we've covered the three normalization normal forms, let's explore the types of relationships that can be created between the different database tables.

Using database relationships

As we saw earlier, one of the goals of the normalization process is to remove data redundancy. To do that, we must divide tables into multiple related subject-based tables. There are three main types of relationships: one-to-one, one-to-many, and many-to-many. Let's take a look at these in more detail:

- **One-to-one relationship**: In this type of relationship, each record in the first table has one – and only one – linked record from the second table. And similarly, each record from the second table can have one – and only one – matching record from the first table. In this relationship, one of the tables is effectively considered an extension of the other. In many cases, the additional attributes will simply end up being added to one of the tables. That is why this relationship is not very common. However, it still has its valid cases, including splitting the data for security reasons. In Salesforce, this is particularly useful considering the rich sharing model available. You can implement one-to-one relationships in many ways, with the most common being to create a lookup relationship from each object to the other, with an automation script (trigger, workflow, process builder, and others) to ensure both lookup fields are always populated with the right values and each object is linked to its counterpart:

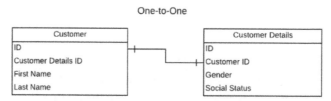

Figure 2.10 – One-to-one relationship

- **One-to-many relationship**: This common type of relationship occurs when a record in one table (sometimes referred to as a parent) is associated with multiple records of another table (sometimes referred to as a child). There are plenty of examples of this, including a customer placing multiple orders, an account with multiple addresses, and an order with multiple order line items. In order to have this relationship, you would need to use what is known as primary keys and foreign keys. In the child table, the primary ID would be the unique identifier for each record in that table, while the foreign key would be referring to the unique identifier of the parent's primary key. This type of relationship can be created in Salesforce using lookup fields or master-detail fields. This book assumes you already know the differences between the two. We will also cover some particular differences that you need to remember in later chapters:

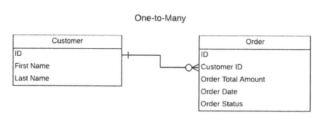

Figure 2.11 – One-to-many relationship

- **Many-to-many relationship**: This type of relationship occurs when multiple records from the first table can be associated with multiple records from the second table. This is also a common type of relationship that we come across every day. Think of the students and courses example, where each student can attend multiple courses and each course can have multiple students attending it. In order to create a many-to-many relationship between two tables, you need to create a third table, often called a bridge table or a junction table. This many-to-many relationship would effectively be broken into two one-to-many relationships. The junction table's records would hold the value of two foreign keys, each pointing to a record from the two main tables.

Junction objects can be created in Salesforce by creating a custom object with two master-detail fields, or with two lookup fields (in this case, it is more often referred to as a bridge rather than a junction). Both approaches are valid and have their most suitable use cases. You can even create a junction object using a mix of master-detail fields and a lookup field. This is assuming you put all the validation and business rules required in place to ensure they are always populated with the right values. We will come across examples of and use cases for Salesforce junction objects in later chapters:

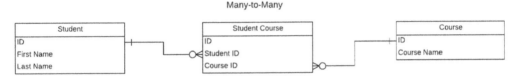

Figure 2.12 – Many-to-many relationship

Keep in mind that the cardinality of these relationships can take different forms. For example, a one-to-many relationship might actually be better represented as one-to-zero-or-many if there are occurrences where the first table will have zero related records from the second table, as illustrated in the students and courses example earlier.

The following diagram illustrates a list of other relationships' cardinalities. The one-and-only-one relationship could be a bit confusing. It is used when the relationship between two records from two different tables cannot be modified. Think of the example of a user and a login ID. Once a login ID is associated with a user, it cannot be assigned to any other user after that. And, of course, it can be associated with one user only. This differs from the ownership relationship between a user and a mobile phone, for example, where the relationship itself might get updated in the future if the phone were to be sold to another owner:

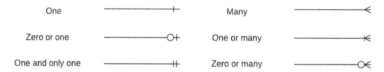

Figure 2.13 – Table relationships cardinalities

Summary

In this chapter, you learned some historical information about database design, as well as how a proper design can be crucial to the overall Salesforce solution. You also learned about some key concepts, such as reference data, reporting data, and big data, in addition to general information about document management systems.

We then covered various data modeling principles and activities, including the process of normalizing and denormalizing data. We also covered other common architectural knowledge areas, such as normal forms, database relationships, and cardinality.

All this knowledge will be required when you're designing your secure and scalable Salesforce solution. In the next chapter, we will cover another set of required common architectural skills. This time, we will focus on the ever-growing and always-interesting integration domain.

3
Core Architectural Concepts – Integration and Cryptography

In this chapter, we'll continue to discover the general architectural concepts that a Salesforce CTA should be familiar with. In today's world, we rarely come across a single implementation where Salesforce is completely isolated. In most cases, Salesforce will become the heart of the enterprise's business transformation process, which means that it has to be connected with dozens of other new and existing applications. Integration cost is sometimes overlooked or underestimated, despite the different studies that point out that around 25-35% of the total project cost would likely be spent on integration.

Coming up with the right integration architecture is crucial to the success of a Salesforce project. Moreover, securing the internal and external integration interfaces is becoming more and more important, especially with the progressive move toward API economy and data monetization. The Salesforce architect is expected to be able to design a secure and scalable integrated solution.

In this chapter, we will discover general architectural concepts about integration and cryptography. Building that breadth of knowledge will help us dive deeper into Salesforce-specific topics in the chapters to come. In this chapter, we're going to cover the following main topics:

- Integration in the enterprise – understanding the landscape
- Introducing the common integration styles
- Discussing the different integration tools
- Exploring modern integration approaches
- Cryptography – understanding the general concepts
- Cryptographic algorithm types and use cases

Let's get started!

Integration in the enterprise – understanding the landscape

The digital enterprise landscape is continuously becoming more sophisticated. Gone are the days when the enterprise used to have less than 10 systems covering most of its business processes. Today's enterprises have hundreds, if not thousands, of different applications that are either bought, built in house, or a combination of both. This is in addition to a set of legacy systems that are still surviving the axe. Nowadays, it is very common to find that an enterprise has dozens of websites, multiple instances of ERP systems, and many other departmental applications, in addition to several data warehouses or lakes.

One of the reasons why enterprises end in such situations is because of the complexity associated with building business applications. Building a single application that runs all business processes is nearly impossible. Maintaining it and adapting to day-to-day business challenges and requested changes is even more challenging. Spreading business functions into smaller chunks of applications has always made sense. It provides the business with enough flexibility and agility to move at the pace they need, rather than being bound by the technical boundaries of a bigger all-in-one solution. Moreover, it gives the business the opportunity to pick and choose the best suite of applications that best serve their needs. This would mean combining the best **customer relationship management (CRM)** system with the best **order management system (OMS)** and the best **enterprise resource planning (ERP)** solution.

In the past 20 or so years, we've seen that vendors offered focus applications for specific core functions. We also noticed the continuous addition of functionalities to existing applications, which caused some sort of *functionality spillover*. For example, we have seen many pieces of customer care software that got extensions to include a limited billing functionality due to the difficulty in drawing clear functional separations between systems. For instance, if a customer raises a dispute for a bill, will that be considered something to be handled by customer care or the billing applications?

On the other hand, users do not really care about these boundaries or the systems that are involved behind the scenes. They expect a business function to be executed, regardless of the system or systems involved in delivering it. For example, when a customer places an order online, this will likely require coordination between several systems to deliver several functionalities, such as checking the history or credit score of the customer, checking inventory, computing tax, creating the order, fulfilling the order, handling shipment, sending a bill, collecting payment, and more. These processes can span across multiple systems, but from the customer's perspective, that was a single transaction and that drives a lot of customer expectations.

In order to support such distributed functionalities, which are yet expected to work as a coherent business process, these applications need to be integrated in an efficient, secure, scalable, and reliable fashion.

The typical *enterprise integration needs* are as follows:

- **Get the right information**: Get precise knowledge of a particular piece of information created by different systems and enterprise business processes. This knowledge has to be structured in a consumable way that can support other business needs.

- **Get that information to the right place**: This requires mechanisms to handle information transactions across heterogeneous environments, which may be based on different technology stacks and reside on different servers/hardware and operating systems.

- **Get that information at the right time**: Ideally, this requires distributing the information in real time to reflect the actual state of a particular data entity.

- **Flexibility and embracement of change**: This is done to adapt to external factors, such as market demand, a shift in customer behavior, new legislation, or a shift in social philosophy.

- **Coordinate business processes**: This is a challenging operation that may require modeling the enterprise business's processes, how they are interlinked, and what kind of information they exchange. This may require having a deep understanding of the business and a certain know-how of the enterprise.

So, what makes a good integration architecture? We'll find that out in the next section.

Integration architecture design principles

Like any complex technical architectural topic, there are several considerations and consequences that you need to keep in mind while designing the target integration strategy and architecture. Actually, integration is one of the key areas where *sub-optimal* designs could have a significant impact on the overall solution.

The main decision points are usually as follows:

- **Native integration**: Simply put, if you can develop a single standalone application that can fulfil all business needs on its own, without any need to collaborate with any other application, then you can avoid a lot of complexity driven by integration requirements. However, in reality, this is not something you can normally achieve. As we discussed earlier, many of the attempts to extend an application so that it includes other functionalities can end up creating a complex system that is hard to manage and maintain, slow to react to market needs, and hard to adjust to meet new business requirements. This problem exists in the Salesforce world as well, although in a more limited way. Many Salesforce products are natively integrated, with many considered the best in the market, and with the ability to deliver different user experiences. For example, Salesforce Communities provides a native solution to exposing a customer portal that is natively integrated with your CRM. Salesforce communities offer a very good sharing model and an easy way to control the look and feel of the community itself. It makes sense to favor that over a solution where you need to build a custom-made customer portal over some technology, then figure out a way to integrate it with Salesforce in a secure and compliant way. Moreover, using the native integration keeps the doors open for using other natively-integrated features in the future.

- **Simplicity**: This goes beyond the integration architecture. Simplicity is an aim that architects and developers should always strive for. Avoid complicated solutions as much as possible and always keep the golden *80-20* rule in mind. Fulfilling 80% of use cases using a simplified architecture should be preferred over targeting a solution that covers 100% of the use cases using an over-complicated architecture. Keep your integration code simple and tidy. In some use cases, however, you may still need to introduce some complex modules to deliver highly sophisticated functionalities.

- **Application dependencies**: Integrated applications should have minimal dependencies on each other. This allows solutions to evolve independently without being tied to each other's roadmaps. It also allows us to replace an application completely without it impacting the other integrated systems. Tightly coupled applications have many dependencies on each other and rely on many assumptions regarding how each of them works. When an application is modified, the assumptions could change, which would, in turn, break the integration. In a loosely coupled integration, the integration interface is specific enough to deliver a particular functionality, but generic enough to allow for a change if needed.

- **Timing**: Ideally, the integration architecture should aim to minimize the duration between the moment an application is sending data and another application is receiving it. The integration architecture should aim to share small chunks of data as frequently as possible, rather than waiting to exchange a huge block of data that may not necessarily be related. Data sharing latency should be taken into consideration while designing the architecture. The longer a data exchange process takes, the more likely it will become more complex and prone to other challenges, such as a change in the data's state. Bulk data exchanges can still be used for the right use cases, such as archiving operational data.

- **Synchronous versus asynchronous**: In a synchronous process, a procedure waits until all of its sub-procedures finish executing. However, in an integrated environment, where the integrated applications might be on different networks or might not necessarily be available at the same time, you may find more use cases where the procedure doesn't have to wait for all of its sub-procedures to conclude. It simply invokes the sub-procedure and then lets it execute asynchronously in the background, making use of the multi-threading ability available in many of today's applications.

- **Integration technology**: Selecting the right technology is essential. Depending on the integration techniques available, there might be higher dependencies on specific skillsets, hardware, or software. This might impact the speed and agility of your project.

- **Data formats**: Data that's exchanged between different applications must follow a pre-agreed format. In the enterprise world, this is unlikely. Therefore, the integration process must have an intermediate step where the data is translated from one format into another. Another related challenge is the natural evolution of data formats. Flexibility to accommodate the changes and extensions of a data format plays a great role in defining the flexibility of the integration architecture.

- **Data versus functionality**: Integration is not necessarily about sharing data. The integrated applications could be looking to share functionality. Think of the use case where one application needs to invoke a particular functionality in another system, such as checking for a particular customer's credit score. There will likely be a set of parameters being sent to the other end in order to facilitate the logic of the remote process. Invoking remote functionalities can be difficult and could have a significant impact on how reliable the integration is. As a Salesforce architect, you need to be aware of specific integration patterns, and you need to understand the limitations of the platform. We will cover this in *Chapter 9, Forging an Integrated Solution*.

There are several considerations that an architect should take into account when designing an integration strategy or a distributed solution. Now, we need to understand what key integration styles are available and what they should be used for.

Introducing the common integration styles

When designing an integration architecture between two or more systems, the key challenge is *how* to actually achieve that. There are some common integration styles that architects should be familiar with. You need to become familiar with them and understand how and when to use each of them. In today's world, some of these integration styles have evolved and are used as part of modern enterprise integration platforms. Let's take a closer look at each of them.

File transfer

In this integration style, applications produce a file containing the data that other applications would consume. This file is normally in a format that can be read by all the target systems and shared to a repository that can be accessed by all concerned systems. These systems are responsible for transforming the file into any other format they are expecting, while the file's producer is responsible for generating the data files on regular intervals based on business needs. One of the challenges with this approach is based on the produced file types, as some applications might not be able to produce data in a standard format, such as XML. This is particularly true for legacy applications. The timing of this approach and its limited scalability has always been an issue too. Moreover, this approach is only good for exchanging a snapshot of data at a given point of time. It lacks the agility, scalability, and speed required by today's integrated applications.

In today's world, the customer is expected to receive a payment receipt immediately after completing a payment. They will receive an order confirmation email once the order has been submitted, with another email coming later, confirming the dispatch date. Failing to deliver a similar or better user experience means that your overall solution is falling short of today's *digital customer experience*, which is considered one of the most important success factors for digital businesses. However, this approach is still valid for the right use cases, particularly when there is a need to replicate reporting data from a legacy system or an external system that doesn't support APIs, and doesn't grant you access to its data via any other mechanism.

Unified datastore

Think of it this way: if a set of integrated applications are designed to rely on a common database, then they are pretty much integrated in a consistent fashion all the time. If one application updates the data, the other systems will get access to the latest updated version of the data as soon as they attempt to retrieve it. Only cached data might be out of date. Moreover, there is no need to do any data transformations as all the involved systems are *built* to work with the given underlying structure. The challenge with this approach is in terms of the high dependency between the applications themselves and between them and the database. Moreover, with today's ever-changing landscape of technologies, expecting all systems to work with a unified database is not realistic. This approach was very popular in the early days of distributed systems, particularly with the client-server architecture. Today, it has received a bit of a boost by the concept of data lakes. Many enterprises are experimenting with a concept where all their operational data is centralized in a data lake, with a rich set of APIs on top to provide a flexible interface for other applications to integrate with.

Realistically, this approach has many challenges, including the fact that today's enterprise applications are designed and built to work with their own databases. Attempts to change that are very expensive and time-consuming. Moreover, they could cause the original application to lose key functionalities or end up creating a performance bottleneck.

Remote procedure invocation

This is an integration style that is used when there is a need for more than just exchanging data. As you might have noticed, the two previous approaches replicate data from one system to another. However, that might not be enough. We normally require the applications to take specific actions once the data they rely on has changed. For example, a change of order status in application A might trigger the creation of a legal entity in application B. In order to simplify this process and reduce application dependencies, **remote procedure invocation** (**RPI**) has been introduced, where the logic of creating that legal entity in application B will be encapsulated and made available for other systems to invoke.

Historically, there were several technologies that implemented the RPI concept, such as CORBA and .NET remoting. In today's world, the most preferred technologies are web services. If you are not familiar with web services, you can think of them as a set of encapsulated functionalities built using commonly used open standards and protocols. The main functionality of a web service is to facilitate exchanging data between systems. It also inherits some of the RPI concepts since the invoked web services can, in turn, invoke another action in the target application. Web services rely mostly on two common standards, SOAP and REST, with the latter being considered more modern due to its small data footprint and its simplicity as it can be easily invoked by clients, including a browser or a mobile app.

A note to avoid confusion: in today's world, the concept of web services is sometimes confused with the concept of **application programmable interfaces** (**APIs**). An API is a software interface that's used to expose the logic and functionalities of a particular application to other applications. This allows unrelated applications to integrate and interact without knowing how each of them is actually built. The mix between the two concepts comes from the fact that many modern systems have built their own APIs in the form of web services, using standards such as SOAP and REST. Some have even gone further and exposed these web services to the public, such as AWS, Google, and others.

Messaging

Messaging is an asynchronous style of integration where two or more systems are loosely integrated via a message bus, which contains several virtual pipes that connect a sender to a receiver (called channels), and message routers, which are components that determine how to navigate the channels' topology to deliver the message to the right receiver. In this style, the integrated systems are not necessarily required to be up and running at the same time. The asynchronous nature of this style also means that it is more capable of scaling to support highly demanding applications. However, the message bus itself might end up becoming a bottleneck if it is not designed in a way that enables smooth auto scaling. This integration style provided the principles of the **enterprise service bus** (**ESB**), which is highly adopted in today's enterprises. We will cover ESBs and other integration tools later on in this chapter.

Now that we've explored the different integration styles, let's have a look at some of the modern integration approaches and tools. As a Salesforce architect, you need to have a solid understanding of the differences between these tools in order to select the right one for your project.

Discussing the different integration tools

Before we discuss some of the common types of integration tools available today, we need to explain *why* we need these tools. As a Salesforce Architect, you are expected to guide the client and the integration team when it comes to selecting the right set of tools that support the agreed integration strategy. And you should be able to challenge sub-optimal design decisions based on valid logic and rational. Picking the wrong tool or taking shortcuts without considering their potential impact could prove to be very costly, and this might impact the project/program in multiple ways and become a major risk to the success of your Salesforce implementation. During the CTA review board, you are always expected to justify why you selected your integration tools.

Historically, a common way to integrate two applications together is through a direct channel with no third-party app or mediator in-between. This can be done with what has become known as **point-to-point integration** (**P2P**). Let's take a closer look at it.

Point-to-point integration

As an architect, you need to understand the capabilities and limitations of P2P integrations and why you would likely need an integration tool (on some occasions, it is also called a piece of *middleware*) in an enterprise context. This section describes various P2P connections.

Unique channel establishment

A **unique channel** is established between each pair of applications that need to interact with each other. The number of unique channels required to connect N number of systems can be calculated using the formula $N(N-1)/2$. For example, if you need to connect three systems through a one-way-direction interface, you would need three unique channels. But in order to link 10 different applications, you would need $10*(10-1)/2 = 45$ unique channels. All of this is assuming there's a one-way-direction of course. Each of these channels has to be developed, documented, tested, and maintained on a regular basis.

Despite that, this cost should not be considered the full cost of the P2P approach. The real cost will start to show up on the macro level, as the cost to add additional systems to the landscape or to connect additional systems to it is not linear. Try to calculate how many new integration channels would be needed to add three more applications to the previously mentioned landscape. Practically, enterprises won't necessarily expect that the new applications will be linked to each and every other application. However, the cost is still unpredictable and, depending on the nature of the new applications and their business functionalities, the cost could rise dramatically.

The *hub-and-spoke* approach requires much fewer channels. In this approach, each application is a spoke, and is only connected to the hub for any given transaction. This results in a much more flexible landscape, with the ability to easily predict the number of new channels required to hook an additional system. The following diagram compares the number of channels required for both approaches:

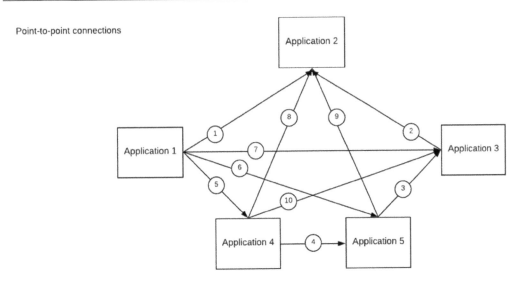

Point-to-point connections

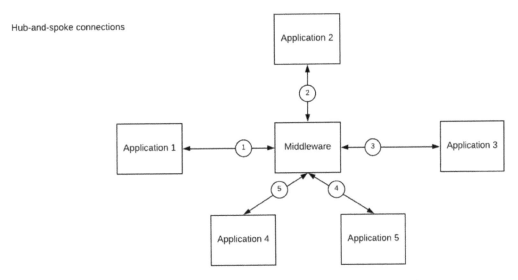

Hub-and-spoke connections

Figure 3.1 – The number of unique channels in both the P2P and hub-and-spoke connections

Each of the unique integration channels is expected to *handle any required data transformations*. This will require your developers to know both integrated applications well. Moreover, the logic for the data transformations is going to be hidden within each channel, reducing the ability to reuse or manage them centrally.

Process orchestration

Process orchestration needs to be handled on the channel level as well. This includes any exception handling and retry mechanisms. Take, for example, a scenario where we have an order intake application, A, which collects the customer and order information from an online web page. It then passes that to an order management application, B, which stores the customer data and the order data separately. Let's assume that both applications have secure APIs that can be invoked by the other applications. In this case, application A is going to invoke application B's customer creation API, and once it receives a response that the process has been completed successfully, it will invoke the order creation API to create an order related to the recently created customer. The integration channel will have to be built to handle the potential failure of customer creation for any reason, including the unavailability of application B. It will likely need to implement a retry mechanism with a comprehensive exception handling and logging capability. A notification mechanism would also be very valuable to have. A rollback capability would also be very desirable. Remember that all of this will have to be repeated for every single P2P integration channel in the landscape. This will require a massive amount of effort and would inevitably reduce the overall reliability of the integrated solution.

Overall reliability

The **overall reliability** of the integrated solution is an important topic to consider, particularly while using P2P connections. Imagine an integrated solution of three different applications: A, B, and C. For a particular business process, application A needs to communicate with application B, which, in turn, is going to communicate with application C. When utilizing P2P connections, this can be thought of as three systems sequentially connected. This means that the overall integrated solution's reliability can be calculated using this formula: $R = A1\text{-}R * A2\text{-}R * A3\text{-}R* \ldots * AN\text{-}R$.

Here, $AN\text{-}R$ is the reliability of the application, A.

For this example, let's assume that the applications had the following reliabilities:

- $A1\text{-}R = 0.9$
- $A2\text{-}R = 0.8$
- $A3\text{-}R = 0.5$

Here, the overall solution would have a reliability of $0.9 \times 0.8 \times 0.5 = 0.36$.

So far, we have assumed that the reliability of each of the given applications does not change with time and does not get impacted by any external factor (for example, a reduced server capacity or network lag). We also haven't considered historical failure rates for each of these applications. Using a hub-and-spoke approach instead of P2P would significantly increase the overall reliability of your solution as it simplifies the connections. The hub itself can turn into a bottleneck, but you have less things that could go wrong.

Limited capabilities

Due to the fact that all data transformations and process orchestrations are taking place on each individual channel, many of these channels end up as simple and straightforward integrations. And, while simplicity is an architectural goal that should be aimed for, the limited technical capabilities imposed by P2P would effectively limit the business's ability to introduce complex business differentiator services.

Turns IT into a blocker

Over time, P2P integrations would inevitably become difficult to maintain and support. Teams will worry before attempting to change anything in them, and the process of deploying any new feature or even a hot fix will become increasingly slow and costly. This would effectively turn the IT department into a blocker rather than an enabler for the enterprise.

High dependencies

Typically, tightly coupled integrated applications have high dependencies on each other. We discussed this earlier, in the context of reliability and cost of ownership. However, it can also be extended to other dimensions. Consider a use case where 3 out of the 10 integrated applications mentioned earlier have reached their end of life and need to be replaced. Due to the high dependencies in a P2P-based landscape, this will likely have a direct impact on all the other applications in the landscape.

Scalability

Due to all of the previous reasons, it is easy to understand why P2P is not the right option to design a scalable enterprise solution.

You need to keep all of the considerations we discussed in this section in your mind while proposing your integration architecture. In the CTA review board exam, you are expected to come up with the best technical solution. And in real life, you need to be able to articulate the pros and cons to your stakeholders and walk them through the different options they have, as this will help them select the most suitable one for them. We will discuss more Salesforce-specific integration topics in the chapters to come.

Now that we understand the challenges with P2P connections, let's discover the different available integration tools. Some of them support the hub-and-spoke integration architecture by nature.

Extract, transform, and load (ETL)

In this method of data integration, the data is *copied* from one or more data sources into a destination data store that does not necessarily share the same structure as the data source(s). This integration method follows some principles from the *file transfer integration* style and in the more modern ETL tools, they also use some of the principle inherited from the *messaging* style:

- **Data extraction** involves accessing one or more data sources and extracting data from them.

- **Data transformation** includes all activities that take place on the data before it's delivered to its final destination, including data cleansing, data formatting, data enrichment, data validation, and data augmentation.

- **Data loading** includes the processes required to access and load the data into the final target data store.

ETL tools may *stage* the data into a *staging area* or *staging data store* in order to run complex transformations on it, such as de-duplication, custom logic, or data enrichment by looking up external reference data. Normally, the staging data store would co-exist with the ETL tool on the same server to provide the quickest possible response time. The three ETL processes take time, so it is common to have them scheduled or running in an asynchronous fashion. Most of the modern ETL tools can be scheduled to run a particular job every few minutes. Some ETL tools can also expose a triggerable end point, which is simply an *HTTP listener* that can receive a message from specific authorized senders in order to trigger one or more ETL jobs. For example, a listener can be exposed to receive a specific type of outbound messages from a particular Salesforce instance. Once that outbound message is received, the listener triggers one or more ETL jobs to retrieve or update data in Salesforce, as well as other systems.

Most of today's ETL tools come with *built-in connectors* for different types of application databases, such as Salesforce, Microsoft Azure, Amazon Redshift, Amazon S3, SAP, and many others. In addition, they also come with adapters to generic database APIs, such as **Open Database Connectivity (ODBC)** and **Java Database Connectivity (JDBC)**. Some even provide connectors for the **File Transfer Protocol (FTP)** and the **SSH File Transfer Protocol (SFTP)**. These connectors allow us to access a particular application database in an optimized fashion. For example, the Salesforce connector could be built to automatically switch between using the Salesforce's standard REST API, the Salesforce SOAP API, or the Salesforce BULK API, depending on the operation that's been executed and the amount of data being dealt with.

Today, several ETL products are provided in a SaaS fashion. In this case, you need to understand how the ETL tools can connect to a database behind a firewall. The enterprise's hosted applications and database would normally reside behind the enterprise firewall. Most enterprises have strict regulations that prevent such resources from being exposed. These are known as **demilitarized zones (DMZs)**. A DMZ is a physical or logical subnetwork that is used by the enterprise to expose external-facing materials and contents – mainly to the public, who are untrusted users. Resources in these DMZs can be accessed by cloud-based applications. However, this is not how cloud-based ETL tools get access to the enterprise's locally hosted applications. One of the most popular ways to achieve this is by installing a *client application* on the enterprise's local network. This is a trusted application provided by the ETL tool product provider, and its main duty is to facilitate communication between the enterprise's local applications and databases and the cloud-based ETL tool. The security team will still need to configure the firewall to allow the client to communicate back and forth with the cloud-based ETL tool.

ETL tools are very suitable for *data replication* operations. They are designed and built to provide a robust and scalable service, since they can deal with millions – even billions – of records. ETL tools are also ideal for data replications that require a lot of time, such as replicating media files. They are very flexible and easy to work with.

As a Salesforce architect, you need to know about some of the popular ETLs that are used today. You also need to understand the limitations of the out of the box tools such as Salesforce Data Loader, which is too simple to be categorized as an ETL tool. Some of the most popular ETL tools that are used with Salesforce today are Informatica PowerCenter, Informatica Cloud, Talend, Jitterbit, and MuleSoft (although MuleSoft is normally considered more of an ESB tool, it actually supports both integration methods).

Enterprise Service Bus

Enterprise Service Bus (ESB) is a name given to a particular method of data integration where the different applications are integrated via a communication bus. Each different application would communicate with the bus only. This decouples the applications and reduces dependencies. This allows systems to communicate without knowing the details of how other systems operate. This integration method follows principles from the *messaging* integration style, as well as the *remote procedure invocation* style. ESB tools have developed this concept even further and currently support different architectural concepts such as microservices, API-led connectivity, and event-driven architectures. We will cover all these concepts later on in this chapter.

ESBs supports both synchronous and asynchronous type of communications, which makes it ideal for integrations operating on the business logic layer, where RPI is a key capability to look for. ESBs also utilize *built-in connectors* to connect to different types of applications and data stores, similar to ETL tools. The connector here would also transform the data from the source system format into the bus format. Considering that ESBs are usually stateless, the state of each message in the bus is included as part of the message itself. While the data is travelling through the bus, it is considered to be in a **canonical data format**. A canonical data format is simply a model of the data that supersets all the other models of the same data in the landscape. This canonical data is normally *translated* into target data models. The **Cloud Information Model (CIM)** is a good example of a canonical data model. Describing CIM is beyond the scope of this book, but becoming familiar with it is strongly recommended.

ESBs can handle complex orchestrations. For example, an application, A, might be sending customer details to the ESB, which, in turn, would communicate with multiple external applications to do a real-time credit check, followed by an invocation to the CRM system, to start a customer onboarding journey. The customer onboarding journey then generates a unique customer ID that is returned to application A with a success message. ESBs can handle complex orchestrations and can use a supporting database as a temporary storage or as a cache for some data. The database would normally co-exist with the ESB tool on the same server to provide the quickest possible response time.

The ESB also handles any kind of required data cleansing, data formatting, data enrichment, data validation, and data augmentation, as well as translations from/to different data formats. For example, you can imagine an application, A, sending data in the **Intermediate Document (IDoc)** format to the ESB, which receives it, augments it with other data coming from a lookup/reference data source, and then translates that into the formats expected by the recipients, such as XML, CSV, JSON, and others.

ESBs can also provide multiple interfaces for the same component, which is particularly useful for providing backward compatibility, especially for web services. ESBs are normally designed to be very scalable and capable of handling a very high load of traffic, and several modern ESBs are offered today in a SaaS fashion with an option to host them locally. Due to their stateless nature, ESBs are not considered ideal for long-running operations such as replicating a massive amount of data between systems or moving large media files.

As a Salesforce Architect, you need to know some of the popular ESBs that are in use today. You also need to understand when and why to propose utilizing an ESB as part of your landscape. Make sure you fully understand the differences between ESBs and ETLs, as well as which is good for what. Also, make sure you understand why, in most cases, that enterprises should utilize a piece of middleware of some sort instead of P2P connections. And, make sure you understand the *ideal* use cases for ESBs in order to recognize if they are utilized in the most optimal way in a given implementation or not. ESBs and ETLs are very common in Salesforce solutions, and we will come across several examples of where we propose using them in the chapters to come. Some of the popular ESB tools that are used with Salesforce today are MuleSoft webMethods Integration Server, IBM Integration Bus, TIBCO ActiveMatrix Service Bus, and WSO2 Enterprise Integrator.

Reverse proxies

A **reverse proxy** is the opposite of a forward proxy: while the forward proxy is used as an intermediary the client uses to connect to a server, the reverse proxy is something the server (or servers) would put between itself and potential clients. For the end client, any retrieved resources in this case would appear as if they were *originated by the proxy server itself*, rather than the server or servers that sit behind it. A reverse proxy is often used to provide a more secure interface to deal with untrusted clients (such as unauthorized internet users), as well as shield the other applications behind it that might lack the ability to handle excessive load or be unable to provide the right security measure required (such as the inability to support HTTPS). A reverse proxy can provide capabilities such as transforming HTTPS requests into HTTP, handling cookies and session data, transforming one request into multiple requests behind the scenes and then combining the responses, and buffering incoming requests to protect the shielded servers from excessive load. Some of the providers of reverse proxy products are VMware, Citrix Systems, and F5 Networks.

API gateways

API gateways are historically used to protect your internal web services (or APIs – remember that we are using the two terms interchangeably in the web context as most modern APIs are offered as web services). The enterprise's internal APIs might not be designed to handle topics such as authentication and scalability, so an API gateway would provide a layer on top to protect the APIs, as well as to enable a set of other functionalities, such as monetizing the APIs, providing real-time analytics, and protection against **denial of service (DoS)** attacks.

API gateways are very similar in concept to reverse process. You can actually think of an API gateway as a special type of reverse proxy. On some occasions, you might have both of them in your landscape, where the API gateway sits behind the reverse proxy, which handles load balancing. API gateways can normally be configured via an API or a UI. On the other hand, reverse proxies are normally configured via a config file and require a restart so that they can use a new set of configurations. API gateways also provide advanced API functionalities such as rate limiting and quotas and service discovery.

As a Salesforce architect, you need to know about some of the popular API gateways that are in use today. Some of the most popular ones that are used with Salesforce today are MuleSoft, Microsoft's Azure API Management, Google (Apigee), and IBM API Management.

Stream-processing platforms

Stream-processing platforms are systems designed to make the most out of parallel processing. This allows them to fully utilize the computational capabilities of their server. Ideally, they are utilized in event-driven integrations. This process inherits some principles from the *messaging* integration style. Actually, stream-processing platforms are often referred to as *message queue platforms*. We will cover the event-driven integration approach shortly.

Stream-processing platforms can handle huge amounts of incoming data since they are designed to make use of elastic scaling. They are also normally easy to encapsulate in containers, which makes them easy to deploy on different platforms, including the cloud, on-premises, or hybrid environments. Due to their capabilities and nature, stream-processing platforms are considered ideal in use cases where there is a need for a massively scalable messaging platform, such as an IoT server. Some of the most popular stream-processing tools in use today are Apache Kafka, Amazon Kinesis, Redis, and RabbitQ. Salesforce Heroku supports some of these technologies, such as Kafka.

With that, we have covered the challenges that may arise from P2P connections, as well as the need for middleware. We have also discovered different types of middleware with different values driven out of each. We will now discover some modern integration approaches, such as service-oriented architecture, microservices, API-led connectivity, and event-driven architecture.

Exploring the modern integration approaches

The technological landscape is ever changing, and as a Salesforce architect, you are dealing with modern tools and technologies every day. It is very important to align the knowledge we covered earlier with today's modern integration approaches. Some of these approaches are becoming less popular nowadays, but their concepts are still the basis of other more modern approaches. In order to fully understand the modern integration approaches and be able to lead discussions with your client, enterprise architects, and integration architects about the most appropriate integration strategy to use, you need to have a wide knowledge of today's modern integration approaches, in addition to a deep and solid understanding of their basis. In my experience, technology enthusiasts might get carried away with new concepts and terminologies. And, while staying up to date with the latest and greatest market trends is very important, it is your duty, as a senior architect, to understand which of these approaches are most suitable for your client and project.

Service-oriented architecture

Service-oriented architecture (**SOA**) is an approach of software development that aims to encapsulate business logic into a *service* that makes the most out of reusable code. Each service contains the code and data integrations required to fulfill a particular business use case; for example, placing a shopping order or onboarding a new customer.

These services are loosely coupled and utilize an *enterprise service bus* to communicate with each other. This means that developers can save time by reusing existing SOA services across the enterprise.

SOA services are logical representations of particular business activities with clear specific outcomes. They are provided more or less as a *black box* for consumers who don't need to worry about how these services are working. Services can consist of multiple other underlying services.

SOA emerged in the late 1990s, and was the base for other modern integration approaches such as microservices and the event-driven architecture. Some critics of SOA mention challenges regarding its performance, maintainability, and the difficulties associated with designing it to the right level of granularity.

A simplified SOA-based architecture would look as follows:

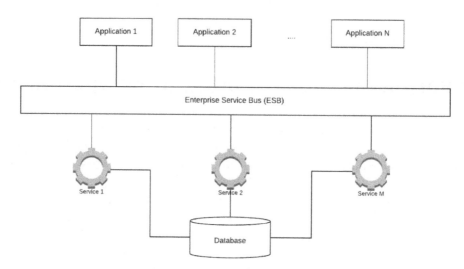

Figure 3.2 – An example of a SOA-based architecture

Microservices

Microservices are a modern interpretation of SOA. They are also made up of loosely coupled and reusable components with a clear functionality and outcome. Rather than communicating through an ESB, microservices communicate with each other directly. The services can use different technologies and protocols.

The microservices architecture is very much geared toward the cloud. It utilizes the **Development and Operations** (**DevOps**) concepts to allow decentralized small teams to take complete ownership of a particular service, deliver its functionality using their preferred technology, and rapidly release it to the enterprise using lightweight containers.

Microservices are typically used as building blocks for other enterprise applications. They are finely grained services, and they have access to their own data stores in order to access all the data that they need access to. Microservices are never supposed to access the same data store/database as this would create a dependency between them and every other data store. The microservices principles favor encapsulation and independency over reusability; redundant code is considered an acceptable side effect.

Microservices became popular since their introduction in 2014 due to their relationship with DevOps concepts. Due to the similarity between SOA and microservices, it is good to understand some of the key differences between these particular integration approaches:

- **Synchronous calls**: Reusable SOA services should be available throughout the enterprise via the use of synchronous protocols such as SOAP or REST APIs. Synchronous calls are less preferred in the microservices architecture as it may create real-time dependencies, which may cause latency. An asynchronous approach is preferred, such as publish/subscribe, which would enhance the resilience and availability of the services.

- **Communication**: SOA services utilize the ESB to communicate, which could make ESB a performance bottleneck. Microservices are developed independently, and they communicate directly using different protocols and standards.

- **Reuse**: SOA is all about increasing reuse, whereas in the microservices architecture, this is less important – especially considering that achieving some reusability at runtime could create dependencies between the microservices, which reduces agility and resilience. With microservices, duplicating code by copying and pasting it is considered an accepted side effect in order to avoid dependencies.

- **Data duplication**: In SOA, the services can directly access and change data in a particular data source or application. This means that multiple SOA services would likely be accessing the same data store. Microservices always aim to reduce dependencies. A microservice should ideally have local access to all the data it needs in order to deliver its expected functionality. This means that there might be a need to duplicate some data. This also means that the data could be out of sync between the different services. Data duplication adds a considerable amount of complexity to the design and potential usage of microservices, so it has to be balanced against the expected gains from the microservice's independence.

- **Granularity**: Microservices are designed to do one specific task; they are very specialized and therefore finely grained. On the other hand, SOA services reflect business services, so they can range from small to bigger enterprise-wide services.

- **Speed**: As we mentioned earlier, speed was one of the weaker sides of SOA due to several factors. Microservices are lightweight, more specialized, and usually utilize lightweight communication protocols such as REST. They generally run faster than SOA services.

A simplified microservices-based architecture would look as follows:

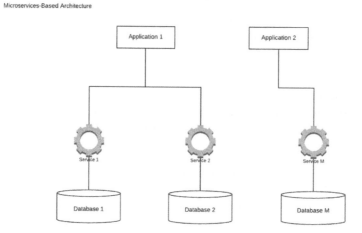

Figure 3.3 – An example of a microservices-based architecture

API-led architecture

The **API-led architecture** is an API strategy where all external and internal services are exposed as managed APIs, regardless of how they were implemented (microservices, SOA services, web services driven out of a monolithic application, or based on other architectures). **Managed APIs** in today's modern terms do more than just provide governance capabilities such as security policies, throttling, versioning, and automatic service discovery. The principle has extended beyond that to include developer portals where they can experiment with APIs before using them, productivity tools, and a mechanism to register and pay for API usage. In this approach, APIs are usually organized on three different layers:

- **System APIs**: They are meant to access core systems and services. They provide a simplified insulating layer between the service consumer and the underlying system or service.

- **Process APIs**: They are meant to interact, transform, and shape the data coming from the underlying system APIs or from other process APIs, effectively breaking down data silos. They have no dependency on the source systems where the data came from, nor on the target systems where the data will be delivered. Both system APIs and process APIs can be used to connect to existing microservices, as well as other enterprise services, depending on the use case.

- **Experience APIs**: They are meant to allow easy access and data consumption for the end user or application. They typically communicate with one or more process APIs to deliver a specific functionality.

Microservices are known to create many endpoints, which are normally difficult to control and monetize. The API-led architecture aims to create an API strategy that governs the way the different enterprise services interact between each other, as well as with external consumers, by utilizing the capabilities of lightweight standards such as REST and combining them with modern API gateway capabilities.

Previously, we mentioned that microservices are typically *consumed by applications*. The API-led architecture aims to turn these applications into a smaller and lighter set of APIs. This can help enterprises take steps toward the *API economy*. For example, an enterprise could create a set of APIs on top of their rich set of services, which are built with different technologies and based on different architectures, and then utilize an API manager to expose these services externally and internally with different applicable policies and subscription mechanisms. Moreover, this approach is also seen as an enabler for rapid application development since you can reuse APIs that are built on top of different business processes. MuleSoft Anypoint Platform is a tool that enables enterprises to deliver API-led integration architecture.

Event-driven architecture

Event-driven architecture is an approach of software development that utilizes *events* to communicate and trigger actions in integrated and decoupled applications. An *event* is simply a change in status of a particular object. For example, a change in the customer status value could fire a *customer status change* event that would, in turn, trigger a set of actions in integrated systems, such as starting a particular marketing journey.

The event-driven architecture inherits some principles from the *messaging* integration style, as we mentioned earlier. The event-driven architecture has three main components: event producers, event routers, and event consumers. The producers publish events to the router, the routers handle filtering and pushing the events to the subscribed consumers, and the consumers receive the event, parse it and transform it into a format suitable for their needs, and then use it, typically to update their own version of the data or to fire subsequent logic. Stream-processing platforms, modern ESBs, or event routing buses such as CometD are usually used as routers.

Now that we've covered the important topic of modern integration approaches, we can move on to another key set of architectural concepts. Cryptography is one of the foundations that the modern digital communications are built on. They have been used for centuries but flourished with the digital era. Cryptography concepts are closely related and intensively used in integration. In the next section, we will go through some general cryptography concepts, understand the key cryptography algorithm types, and discuss some of their use cases in detail.

Cryptography – understanding the general concepts

Cryptography has a tight relationship with several other architectural domains, such as integration and **identity and access management** (**IAM**). It also has tight relationships with data, as we discovered earlier when we discussed both encryption at rest and on transit. As a Salesforce Architect, you need to have a general understanding of the value of cryptography, the different types of cryptography algorithms, and a high-level understanding on the way they work. This will help you understand the details of some of the day-to-day activities that take place in Salesforce implementation projects, such as securing an integration channel using **TLS** or **two-way TLS** (also known as **mutual authentication**), or how authentication tokens are *digitally signed*.

Encryption is the process of converting original readable data (also known as **plaintext**) into a form that can't be read by unauthorized parties (also known as **ciphertext**). Encryption is not a method of preventing others from interfering with data; rather, it is a mechanism that denies access to the readable form of that data to unauthorized parties. In other words, the attacker would end up with a version of the data that is not useful and cannot be converted back into a useful format in a reasonable timeframe.

Let's take ancient encryption algorithms as an example. The transposition cipher was one of the classic and very basic ways to encrypt messages sent with messengers across unsafe territories. In a transposition cipher, the order of a word's letters is rearranged based on specific logic. A statement such *hello world* could end up as *ehlol owrdl*. If the message falls into the wrong hands, they can still destroy it or tamper with it, but ideally, they shouldn't be able to read it.

Another example of ancient encryption is substitution ciphers, which rely on replacing letters or symbols with other letters or symbols based on a rule known only to the message generator and the authorized parties. For example, *London* becomes *Mpoepo* by replacing each letter with the next letter in the English alphabet. Typically, the message can be easily decrypted once you know two things: the *algorithm* and the *key*. In this example, the algorithm is the *substitution cipher* and the key is the *letter order in English alphabet + 1*.

These algorithms are obviously very simple to crack today, especially using computers. Today's cryptography algorithms are much more sophisticated and harder to break.

Until modern times, cryptography and encryption mainly referred to the same thing. However, during World War I, there was a leap in the techniques that were used for cryptography. First, rotor cipher machines were used, and then more computational capabilities were developed during World War II.

Modern cryptography relies on *computer science practices* and *mathematical theory*. They are designed to provide a mechanism that protects the contents of the encrypted data by rendering the attempts to break them infeasible. Theoretically, all encryption algorithms can be broken, given enough time and considering the available computational power (the most basic form of attack is brute force, which, tries every possible key in turn until the right one is found). However, considering that this process could be infeasible makes these algorithms *computationally secure*. For example, in order to break AES-256 using brute-force, an attacker would need to try an average of 2^{255} keys. It is estimated that this would take 27 trillion trillion trillion trillion trillion years on a high-end PC from 2016. Obviously, this time is becoming shorter with the advances we see every day in computer technology, but it should still hold for a while. Until then, breaking this encryption is simply infeasible and therefore it is considered to be *computationally secure*.

We have come across some terms already, but let's list some of the terms that you need to be familiar with:

- **Key/encryption key**: An encryption key is an input parameter that controls the output of a cryptographic algorithm. As we saw earlier, the key is an essential element in the cipher process. The key is also required to decipher the ciphertext. Without it, the ciphertext can be considered useless. Actually, in *Chapter 2, Core Architectural Concepts – Data*, we came across a data destruction mechanism that relies simply on destroying the encryption keys. By doing so, the encrypted data is rendered useless and unrecoverable.

  The key is considered the top-most important element of a cryptography process. The attacker can figure out the algorithm that was used to encrypt a piece of information (it could be something publicly available, such as the algorithms used by TLS, which we will cover later on), but that shouldn't be a problem as long as the *key* is still kept secret. The process of generating long encryption keys is extremely complex. **Symmetric cryptography algorithms** typically use keys that are 128 and 256 bits long. On the other hand, **asymmetric cryptography algorithms** typically use 1,024 and 4,096 bits-long keys. We will cover symmetric and a symmetric cryptography algorithms toward the end of this chapter.

- **Key management**: This is the process of managing cryptographic keys. This includes generating, exchanging, storing, using, replacing, and destroying keys. Secure key management is critical to the enterprise. It involves crafting enterprise policies, training users, and defining organizational and departmental interactions. Keys and certificates are typically managed in a *repository*. Key management is a wide domain to cover, and it is beyond the scope of this book.

Recently, cloud providers started to support a mechanism called **bring your own encryption (BYOE)** or **bring your own key (BYOK)**, which aims to give clients more confidence in storing data in the cloud by giving them full control over their encryption keys, rather than relying on key repositories provided or hosted by the cloud provider. Salesforce Shield supports the BYOK concept.

- **Initialization vector**: This can be generally thought of as an *initial value* used during the cipher process, likely at the beginning of an iteration. This pseudorandom value is used to ensure that each message is encrypted differently. Even if the same message is encrypted twice, the result will look different each time. This helps in further securing the cipher text as the attacker won't be able to realize that two blocks of ciphertext are actually based on the same plaintext, which significantly reduces the attacker's ability to analyze the patterns.

  The IV is not supposed to be kept secret, unlike the key. Actually, many algorithms would set the IV as the first 128 bits of the ciphertext. If the message falls into the wrong hands, the attacker can easily extract the IV, but it is useless without the key. For the recipient (who has the key), decrypting the message using the key and the unique IV is straightforward.

  If you are familiar with the Salesforce `Crypto` class, you will notice that it has the `encryptWithManagedIV` and `decryptWithManagedIV` methods, which don't expect any IV as an input parameter, unlike the standard encrypt and decrypt methods. Both `encryptWithManagedIV` and `decryptWithManagedIV` would extract the IV from the encrypted message itself, and would expect it to be at the beginning of the ciphertext. If you are not familiar with the Salesforce `Crypto` class, have a look at the online documentation. We will come across this class in the chapters to come, but it is still a good idea to have a look at the online documentation and understand the different functionalities provided by that class.

- **Salt**: The salt is a piece of pseudorandom data that is added to the input. A salt is mainly used with one-way hashing algorithms. For example, the system capturing the user password can add a salt value to it before hashing the combined text. This makes it more difficult for the attacker to guess the length of the original password. Moreover, considering that the salt value will be random each time, for two similar inputs, the output would be totally different.

  Coming back to the password example, even if the attacker managed to crack one of the passwords, they will have no way of guessing if there are other users who used the same password and therefore compromise their accounts as well. In more technical terms, salting would increase the entropy for low-entropy inputs.

Similar to the IV, the salt value is not supposed to be kept secret. Typically, it will be stored in the database next to other user details.

- **Certificate**: The certificate is an electronic document that contains an encryption key called the *public key*, in addition to other information, such as the *issuer*, the purpose of the certificate, and some other data.

  The certificate is used to prove the *authenticity* of a particular entity (such as a web server) who owns the *private key* of the certificate's *public key*. Public keys and private keys are terms that are used in asymmetric cipher algorithms, as we will discover shortly. The certificates themselves can be *digitally signed* by the issuer. For public websites, the issuer here would be a third independent entity called the **certificate authority** (**CA**). Some examples of CAs are Comodo, GeoTrust, and Symantec.

  Let's take a look at a simple example to understand the use of certificates. When you visit a secure HTTPS website, the website presents its certificate to your browser. The certificate contains the server's public key. This is issued by a CA, so the certificate itself will contain the digital signature of the CA that confirms the authenticity of the certificate. Using the public key and the CA signature, the browser can make sure that the server it is communicating with is indeed the right one, as well as that the communication with that server will be protected against a man-in-the-middle attack. The certificate that's issued or signed by CA authorities is normally referred to as a **CA-signed certificate**.

  Later, we will discover how the TLS protocol works, which will help you further understand the value and use of digital certificates. We will also discover how digital signatures work in more detail.

- **Block cipher**: This is the name given to cryptography algorithms that operate on *fixed-length* groups of bits (called *blocks*). For example, the **Advanced Encryption System** (**AES**) algorithm encrypts 128-bit blocks using different lengths of keys, such as 128, 192, or 256 bits.

Now that we've covered some high-level general information about cryptography and explored some of the common terms that are used today, let's move on and understand the different types of cryptography algorithms. We came across some of them earlier, and you have definitely come across some of them in your projects.

Cryptographic algorithm types and use cases

The two types of cryptography algorithms that we will dive into are symmetric cryptography algorithms and asymmetric encryption algorithms. We will also dig into the details of hashing algorithms, digital signatures, and **message authentication codes (MACs)**.

Symmetric cryptography algorithms

This is the family of algorithms that relies on a *symmetric key* for both encrypting the plaintext and decrypting ciphertext. As we discussed earlier, storing the key in a secure and safe way is absolutely crucial for this type of algorithm. The need for sharing the key between both parties (sender and recipient) is one of the main drawbacks of these types of algorithms as the attacker could intercept the used channel and get access to the key. There have been several workarounds during history (remember, some of these algorithms have been around for many years). More streamlined approaches have been adopted in the digital world, and we will find out more about that when we dive deeper into how TLS works.

There are several symmetric cryptography algorithms that are also considered **reciprocal ciphers** or **self-reciprocal ciphers**. This is simply a type of cipher algorithm that can take plaintext and pass it through the specific algorithm logic to turn it into cipher text using the encryption key. Then, it takes the ciphertext and passes it through the exact same logic using the same key to generate the plaintext again. Examples of this include the XOR cipher and the Beaufort cipher, in addition to the famous World War II Enigma machine.

There are two main types of symmetric cryptography algorithms: *stream ciphers* and the *block ciphers*. We covered the latter earlier, while the former is out of scope for this book. Some examples of popular, modern symmetric cryptography algorithms include the **data encryption standard (DES)**, Blowfish, and AES and its different versions; that is, AES128, AES192, and AES256. These three versions of AES are supported by the Salesforce Crypto class.

There are also some derived symmetric cryptography algorithms that operate slightly differently than the algorithms we just saw. While the likes of AES aim to encrypt plaintext in order to generate ciphertext, hashing algorithms are designed to ensure the integrity of a particular message. MAC algorithms are used to provide this hashing functionality, plus some sort of authentication. Let's look at both in more detail.

Hashing algorithms

Hashing algorithms are algorithms that are created to solve the following simple problem: *How can a recipient ensure that a received message hasn't been changed or tampered with?* Hashing algorithms create a *digest* out of plaintext. The digest (also known as a *hash value*) cannot be reversed back into plaintext. Hashing algorithms are one-way functions, which are simply functions where their output can't be inverted. Hashing algorithms have the following properties:

- Deterministic, in that for the same message, you always get the same result (unless you use a salt value, as we discovered earlier).

- Due to their nature, it is infeasible for the attacker to try to generate a message that yields a particular given hash.

- Even a small change to the original plaintext should significantly change the hash value so that the new hash value appears completely unrelated to the old value. This is sometimes referred to as the *avalanche* effect.

- Typically, hashing algorithms *do not need or use a key*. Again, remember that the purpose of hashing algorithms is to ensure the integrity of the original plaintext. Hashing algorithms have a wide usage in computer systems. They are used in digital signatures (which is something we will discover in detail shortly) and MAC algorithms, as well as for generating encryption keys, creating index data, detecting duplicate data, and creating message checksums.

- Examples of popular, modern hashing algorithms include the **Message-Digest Algorithm** (**MD5**), Whirlpool, and **Secure Hash Algorithm** (**SHA**) and its different versions; that is, SHA-1, SHA-256, and SHA-512. These three versions of SHA are supported by the Salesforce Crypto class.

The following diagram explains the general mechanism of a hashing algorithm:

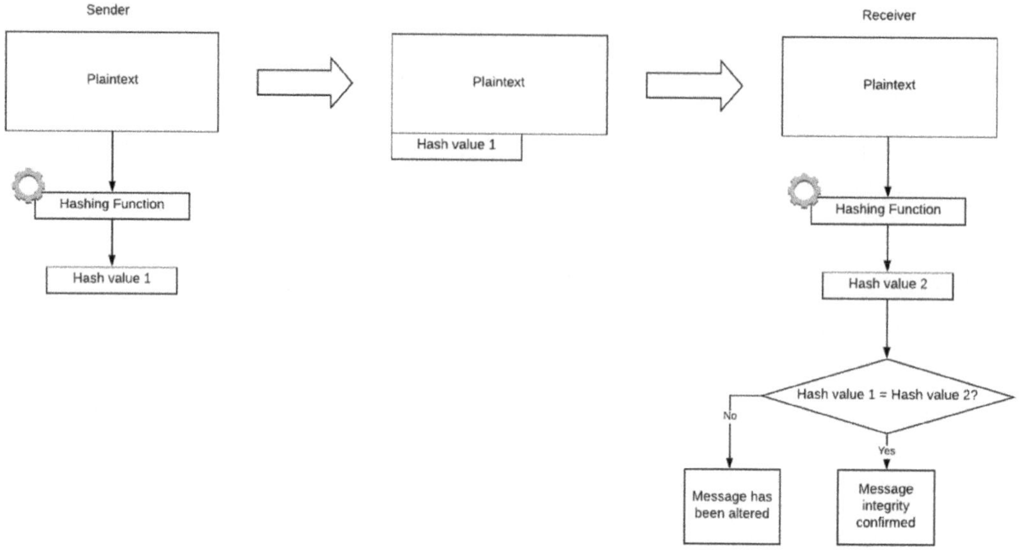

Figure 3.4 – An illustration of the way hashing algorithms work

MAC algorithms

MAC algorithms are similar to hashing algorithms in the sense that both generate a one-way digest/hash of the plaintext. However, MAC algorithms are mainly created to *verify the authenticity of the message sender*, in addition to verifying that the message itself hasn't been tampered with. In order to do that, MAC algorithms use a *key* in their process. Typically, this is used to encrypt the hashed value itself. The key should be known to both the sender and the receiver. It can be used to verify that that the entity that generated the hash owns a copy of the same key, which is proof of the authenticity of the message itself.

Examples of popular modern MAC algorithms include the **keyed-hash message authentication code (HMAC)** and its different versions; that is, hmacMD5, hmacSHA1, hmacSHA256, and hmacSHA512. All these versions are supported by the Salesforce Crypto class.

The following diagram explains the general mechanism of a MAC algorithm:

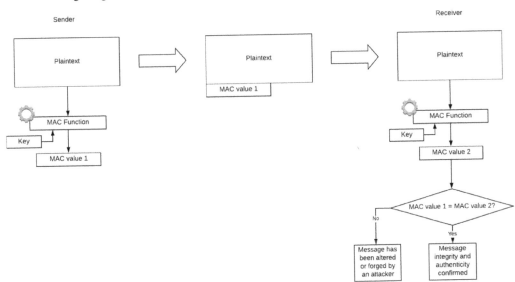

Figure 3.5 – An illustration of the way MAC algorithms work

Asymmetric cryptography algorithms

Also known as **public-key cryptography algorithms**, these are designed to create an encryption mechanism where two communicating entities can use a pair of different keys. The first is called a *private key*, which should be kept secret, while the second is called a *public key*, which is safe to be distributed.

In such algorithms, an application can encrypt a message using the public key, and this message can only be decrypted using the paired private key. It is just like having a bag with a lock that can be locked with one key but opened using another key. The process of generating the key pair for asymmetric cryptography algorithms is much more complex than the process used to generate symmetric keys. Moreover, asymmetric algorithms are typically more complex and time consuming to run.

Asymmetric cryptography algorithms have many applications but they are mainly used for the following two use cases:

- **Message confidentiality**: As we mentioned earlier, it is completely safe to distribute the public key. The private key has to be kept secret alongside the entity who should receive and decrypt the cipher messages. In this case, asymmetric algorithms solve one of the main challenges that's experienced with symmetric algorithms, which is distributing the key. Using an asymmetric algorithm, the message is encrypted with the public key, and can only be decrypted using the private key by the entity that originally issued both key pairs. In this mechanism, the owner of the private key can ensure the confidentiality of the received messages. Examples of well-known asymmetric cryptography algorithms include ElGamal, RSA, and the Diffie-Hellman key exchange.

- **Digital signature**: In this case, the *private key* is used to *sign* a particular message effectively by generating a *digest/hash* value of that message. The signature can be verified by anyone who has access to the *public key*. The verification process proves that the entity who signed the message has access to the private key, and that proves the authenticity of the sender. Moreover, we have already learned that hash values are used to ensure that a particular message has not been tampered with. This might sound similar to what we mentioned previously about MAC algorithms, but you need to remember that we are using the *public key* here to verify the digital signature. Distributing public keys is never a problem. Examples of some popular asymmetric cryptography algorithms that are used for digital signatures include RSA-SHA1, RSA-SHA256, RSA-SHA384, and RSA-SHA512, all of which are supported by Salesforce's `Crypto` class.

Now that we've covered both types of cryptography algorithms and their variations and key use cases, let's go through a real-life example that we come across every day while browsing secure websites.

Cryptography use cases

Let's try to understand the high-level details of how **TLS** works. Then, we'll move on and look at a special case of it known as **two-way TLS** (also known as **two-way-SSL** or **mutual authentication**). As a Salesforce Architect, you are likely going to come across both topics in your projects. It is very important to understand how both of them work as you might be asked to explain that during the review board or in real life.

Understanding how TLS works

Transport Layer Security (**TLS**) is a cryptographic protocol that has superseded the **Secure Sockets Layer** (**SSL**). It is designed to secure any communication between two computer applications over a network (such as the internet). There have been four versions of TLS so far (1.0, 1.1, 1.2, and 1.3). Salesforce keeps updating its platform to support the latest and most secure versions of TLS. You should aim to use the latest available version of TLS whenever possible and avoid any versions earlier than 1.2.

When a communication channel is secured by TLS, the communication between two parties (normally referred to as the *client*, such as a *browser*, and the *server*, such as *packtpub.com*) has one or more of the following properties:

- **Private connection**: A symmetric encryption algorithm is used to encrypt the data transmitted. The key that's used for this encryption is unique per session and will be generated as part of a *handshake* process. The handshake process itself is also secure, even against a man-in-the-middle attack.

- **Authentic identity**: The identity of the two communicating parties can be verified using an asymmetric cryptography process that utilizes *CA-signed certificates*. Verifying the identity of the communicating parties can be made optional, but it is normally required at least for the server. For example, when the client attempts to open an HTTPS website – If both parties' identities are verified, then this becomes a two-way TLS secured channel. We will explain how that works shortly.

- **Reliable**: Each exchanged message will also include a MAC value to ensure that the message itself hasn't been modified or tampered with.

Now, let's look at the high-level details of what happens when a user attempts to navigate to a secure website such as `https://www.salesforce.com`:

1. The client (the browser, in this case) starts the handshake process. The client provides a list of the cipher suites (and their versions) that it is willing to support.

2. The server (`https://www.salesforce.com`, in this case) checks if it is willing to support and use any of the cipher suites provided by the client. For example, Salesforce stopped supporting TLS 1.1 for its production orgs on October 25, 2019. If the browser is configured to use a version no later than TLS 1.1, then the connection will be denied. If the server agrees to use one of the cipher suites supported by the client, it will send back a response containing its CA-signed certificate. (Remember, the certificate will also contain the public key.)

3. The client will validate the given certificate with the mentioned CA authority (verifying digital signature). This step is required to assure the client that the website it is communicating with is authentic and indeed what it is claiming to be. If the certificate is verified successfully, the client extracts the public key from the certificate.

4. The client generates a random pre-master key and encrypts it with the public key. This means that this pre-master key can only be decrypted by the holder of the private key. The client now sends this encrypted pre-master key to the server.

5. The server uses its private key to decrypt the pre-master key.

6. Both the client and the server use the pre-master key to compute a new shared key called a **shared secret** or **session key**. *Step 4*, *Step 5*, and *Step 6* can also be achieved using the Diffie-Hellman key exchange, but this is outside the scope of this book.

7. The client sends a new test message that's been encrypted using the session key. This is now a simple symmetric encryption.

8. The server decrypts the message using the session key and confirms that the process was successful. This means that both parties have successfully exchanged a unique asymmetric cryptographic key that is secure and known only to them, even if there was a third-party attacker listening to the entire conversation. The session key will be secure and known only to the client and the server.

9. From now on, any communication between the two parties will take place using the session key for the rest of the session. All exchanged messages are also protected with a MAC that utilizes the session key.

With that, you've seen how this example contained most of the terms we covered earlier, including certificates, digital signatures, symmetric and asymmetric cryptography, and MAC values. Now, let's move on to two-way TLS.

Understanding how two-way TLS works

Two-way TLS, or what is still referred to sometimes as two-way-SSL, is pretty much similar to standard one-way TLS with one main difference. In one-way TLS, the client validates the server's certificate to confirm the server's identity. The client will be confident of the identity of the server after successful identity verification, but the server will have no way to confirm the identity of the client. This is probably less important in our previous examples since public severs are accessed by thousands or millions of users every minute; they serve them all without the need to confirm their identity. But what if the server is providing services that should only be available to a limited set of clients? This is exactly where two-way TLS is used, and this is why it is sometimes referred to as mutual authentication or two-way authentication.

The flow of two-way TLS looks as follows:

1. The client (typically an application rather than a browser, in this case) starts the handshake process. The client provides a list of the cipher suites (and their versions) that it is willing to support.

2. Similar to *Step 2* from the one-way TLS description.

3. Similar to *Step 3* from the one-way TLS description.

4. The client generates a random pre-master key and encrypts it with the public key. This means that this pre-master key can only be decrypted by the holder of the private key. The client sends its own certificate, along with this encrypted pre-master key, to the server.

5. The server validates the client's certificate with the mentioned CA authority (verifying digital signature). In addition, the server could be configured to restrict access to specific clients only. In this case, the server will compare the given certificate to a repository of *permitted client certificates* that it holds. If the given certificate is among them, it will proceed to the next step.

6. The rest of the steps are similar to the one-way TLS description.

Two-way TLS is a very popular mechanism particularly in the SaaS world due to the fact that many production environments (in the Salesforce world, these are known as *production instances*) will share the same infrastructure, domain name, and IP range. Two-way TLS provides a convenient way to ensure that the right instance can be accessed by the right set of client applications. Let's look at a quick example to explain this further.

Putting both integration and cryptography together

Let's assume you have a Salesforce instance that has been integrated with a set of cloud-based and on-premises hosted applications through an ESB middleware such as *MuleSoft CloudHub*, which is a cloud based, multi-tenant, and fully managed platform. You need to ensure that only your enterprise's Salesforce instance can communicate with your enterprise's MuleSoft CloudHub instance and vice versa. Using two-way TLS here would provide that functionality and would ensure your data is secure and always encrypted on transit. However, in the next chapter, we are going to learn that you might need to add another authentication layer to that architecture for some use cases.

Summary

We have covered a lot of ground in this chapter. We started by looking at the general concepts surrounding integration before moving on and looking at some of the older and more modern integration approaches. We achieved this by looking at different types of tools and mechanisms. We also learned about some of the ideal use cases for each of these tools.

We then moved on to a closely-related architectural topic: security and cryptography. We learned some key concepts in the wide and complex world of cryptography and tied them back to some real-world examples that we come across every day.

Finally, we tied all this together and learned how integration and cryptography can work side by side in the enterprise landscape.

In the next chapter, we will cover another key architectural concept. **Identity and access management (IAM)** architectural concepts are now extensively used in modern distributed solutions. These IAM concepts are closely related to both the integration and encryption domains, and they are very common in cloud-based solutions such as Salesforce. While looking at such IAM concepts, we will look at their definitions, standards, and flows.

4
Core Architectural Concepts – Identity and Access Management

In this chapter, we will continue our efforts to understand the general architectural concepts that a Salesforce CTA should be familiar with. **Identity and access management (IAM)** is one of the most challenging topics that an architect needs to deal with. During a normal project, you might find yourself working with multiple IAM experts from different technological backgrounds. You need to be able to speak the same language as they do, understand their vision, and challenge their architectural design (if needed). As a Salesforce CTA, you are expected to step away from the standard platform knowledge to provide expert guidance in other related matters. Integration was a good example, IAM is another.

In this chapter, we're going to cover the following main topics:

- Understanding the general concepts of IAM
- Becoming familiar with the common IAM standards
- Understanding the key authentication flows

Understanding the general concepts of IAM

The **IAM** architecture is the activity of defining the processes, tools, monitoring mechanisms, and governance required in order to grant the enterprise's internal and external users access to the right digital assets in a well-governed and secure manner. The IAM architecture needs to ensure that users are granted the right level of access privileges based on internal and external requirements, such as enterprise policies or regulatory compliance.

The users included in an IAM architecture could be external (and in this case, we usually use the term **customer identity and access management** (**CIAM**)) or internal (where we simply use the term **IAM**).

The IAM strategy aims at creating a *unified digital identity* for the enterprise's customers and employees, along with a set of tools and processes to manage this identity and the access rights associated with it.

The IAM architecture is critical in today's connected enterprise applications. We discussed on several occasions prior to the rapid growth in the value of data and how enterprises are coming up with different approaches to make the most out of it, including *API monetization*, which requires exposing the company's internal resources to the public. Obviously, doing that without the right security planning and strategy is a recipe for disaster, especially considering the sharp rise in ransomware, phishing, whaling, and social engineering attacks. Besides, it is common nowadays to expect a particular transaction to span across multiple systems.

Integrated distributed systems are everywhere. In some use cases, there is a need to hook some systems together via scalable and secure integration interfaces. In other use cases, there is a need to facilitate a mechanism to *swirl the user's chair* between these multiple systems in the easiest possible way, particularly without requiring the user to *log in* again to other applications. Moreover, social networks are a part of the daily lives of most, if not all, of today's internet users. Hence, having a mechanism to integrate with them is becoming a standard expectation in today's **customer experience** (**CX**) world.

We also came across some of the common regulatory compliances, such as **GDPR**, where the responsibility of safeguarding the user's personal data is considered a part of the enterprise's responsibilities. Other regulations, such as **NYDFS**, require a comprehensive mechanism to ensure capturing and monitoring of the activities of logged-in users in an audit log. A solid IAM architecture is a key element in ensuring compliance with such regulations.

The four key components of an IAM solution are as follows:

- **An identity repository**: A place or a system that keeps the personal details of each user. This can take different shapes and forms.

- **A management toolbox**: To manage, edit, add, and delete the aforementioned data.

- **A monitoring platform**: Providing continuous monitoring of user activities and storing this in a secure audit log.

- **A policy enforcer**: To regulate and enforce the user's access privilege.

Some of the modern IAM tools offer all these capabilities in a single platform. However, you are likely to need some additional configurations in the other connected systems to facilitate the expected functionalities.

We see a wide set of tools used to authenticate users today (which is a mandatory step in regulating and enforcing access privileges and policies), such as user credentials, tokens, digital certificates, fingerprint readers, iris readers, face recognition, smart cards, and hardware tokens. In the past few years, there has been an increase in utilizing multi-factor authentication, which relies on a combination of information you know (such as user credentials) with something you should exclusively have access to (such as your email inbox or your mobile phone).

In the coming sections, we will go through a set of IAM concepts and principles that you need to become familiar with. This will help you speak the same language as your IAM team members as well as other IAM architects.

Becoming familiar with the IAM terms and definitions

The following list of terms and definitions are commonly used to define and describe the various elements of an IAM architecture. Some of them are more straightforward than others, but we still wanted to list them here to ensure that you have a comprehensive list that you can come back to later and use as a reference:

Identity

This is what we use to recognize a particular individual or thing. As humans, we normally use names to identify ourselves. However, you might come across more than one person with the same name, especially when we deal with a huge number of individuals. In systems, we usually utilize a unique alphanumerical identifier to recognize someone, such as a national ID, social security number, or even an employee ID. Other systems utilize a unique identifier in a specific format, such as the email address format. Salesforce is a good example of such a system. Once the identity of a particular user is recognized, all operations would run under its context. Therefore we can apply the various security policies and run the appropriate monitoring activities based on the given identity. In order to recognize a particular identity and start using it, you need to ensure that the person claiming it is authentic. And this is where authentication comes into the picture.

Authentication

This is a term given to the process or series of processes used to uniquely, securely, and confidently identify a particular individual or thing. This step is becoming obvious in today's applications, where the user is expected to prove their identity using one or more techniques, and once that is done, the application would operate based on the recognized identity (sometimes referred to as the *logged-in user* or *authenticated user*). Authentication normally takes place by requesting one or more of the following inputs from the individual/thing: Something that is known only to that individual (such as a password or unique key); something that the individual/thing has (such as a physical ID card, dongle, or an embedded chip); or something related to the physical structure of the identified object (such as a fingerprint or iris scan). Once the individual/thing is authenticated, there will be a need to determine *what* they are allowed to see within the current system. This is where authorization comes into the picture.

Authorization

This process takes place after authenticating a particular user in order to grant the right privileges to see, do, and have things within a particular system. In software applications, it is common to have a **super user** (also known as an **administrator**) who defines the allowed policies and permissions within a particular system. The administrator would likely also be responsible for defining/creating other users.

Enterprises should aim to apply the *principle of least privilege* while designing their authorization strategy. This requires that users, applications, and devices are granted the minimal sufficient privileges required to operate normally and deliver their desired functionality. You should keep that in mind while designing your overall security architecture and particularly avoid granting *service users* (also known as *integration users*) more privileges than necessary.

Identity store

This is a common name given to databases or systems with directory structures that are used to hold information about the users (or, in general, *identities*, which are also known as *principals*) that a particular system is using. Information held in identity stores may include personal details, such as names, phone numbers, and email addresses, in addition to any other information required to authenticate a user, such as the unique user identifier or passwords (remember, passwords should never be stored in plain text or even in an encrypted form that can be decrypted; passwords are normally stored as hash values that are impossible to reverse/decrypt as we discussed previously), and any other data that uniquely describes the user. The identity store can also contain the user's *group memberships*, which defines the privileges granted to a particular user. The identity store can simply be a database or something more advanced, such as **Microsoft Active Directory** (**AD**).

Identity provider (IDP)

The IDP (or IdP) is a trusted system that manages identities for known users/principals. It normally includes capabilities such as creating, updating, and generally maintaining the different identity information. Moreover, it provides authentication services that can be used by other applications. The main difference between modern IDPs and identity stores is that the former could provide identity maintenance and authentication services either by using their own capabilities or relying on connected identity stores. In other words, the IDPs do not necessarily need to maintain the values used for authentication (such as passwords) as it can connect to the identity store that does, and rely on the identity store itself to provide the authentication services while providing a layer on top of that to facilitate and standardize the entire process and associated user experience.

Similarly, the IDP doesn't need to maintain the personal information of identities as these could be maintained in an identity store, with the IDP providing a set of services on top in order to display, change, and synchronize the data between the applications utilizing the IDP services and the related identity stores. That doesn't mean that the IDPs don't have the capability to hold such information natively. Modern IDPs provide the option of either hosting such information or using the services of a connected identity store. Ping Identity, Okta, and other providers are examples of IDPs. Salesforce itself offers limited IDP capabilities.

Service provider

The applications that provide specific services for internal or external users are generally referred to as *service providers (SPs)*. However, in the context of IAM, we can add that service providers are typically applications that rely on other identity providers to provide IAM capabilities (including user management and authentication). Service providers typically have their own user repositories (such as databases) and user access control management consoles (where particular permissions are assigned to specific users). In the use case where an SP is relying on an IDP to handle authentication, identity management, and potentially authorization (commonly known as **Single Sign On (SSO)**), there is a need for a special setup where the identity privileges maintained in the IDP would be translated into specific local SP user privileges. In simpler cases, this setup will be limited to authentication and a small set of identity management activities. There are many examples of SPs. Salesforce itself can be considered an SP. Depending on its role in a particular SSO setup, Salesforce can play the role of IDP, SP, or both. Other SP examples include applications such as Workday, SAP, and many others.

Single Sign On

The term *SSO* is used to describe the process where a user is allowed to authenticate *once* in order to access *multiple* applications. The common form of SSO is where a user authenticates to one application using any of the previously mentioned authentication mechanisms (such as credentials), and then attempts to access resources that belong to another application, which is linked with the same SSO mechanism. The user won't need to authenticate again in this case. This can occur either on the **user interface (UI)** level or the *business logic* level (typically via APIs). SSO eliminates the need to *re-authenticate*, which could be a tedious process. Therefore, it is considered a technique to improve user productivity. Moreover, it provides a *centralized mechanism* to monitor user authentication activities and therefore increases security and compliance.

The SSO setup utilizes an IDP to provide centralized user authentication and policy enforcement capability. For example, it is very common nowadays to see enterprises implement SSO to ensure that all their systems are following the same login policies (such as password complexity requirement, login restrictions, and additional verification mechanisms). These policies and regulations would be enforced by an IDP, which acts as the central unit for the SSO setup. All applications that utilize this IDP would be considered SPs.

As a Salesforce architect, you need to understand that most, if not all, of the enterprise applications that you might deal with would normally have their own user repositories/databases and have built most of their functionalities based on the assumption that there is a logged-in user (also known as **context user**) identified from that local repository. For example, think of applications such as Workday, SAP, Oracle NetSuite, MS Dynamics, and Salesforce. They all expect the user to *log in* and be identified as a *context user* or *application user* against their local data stores.

Therefore, in an SSO setup, users will typically be replicated multiple times across the systems. The IDP will control the full list of users, including their authentication mechanisms (such as their hashed passwords), while each of the SPs would maintain a list of users allowed to work with that particular application and would rely on the IDP to authenticate those users, so they might not hold any authentication data locally. There will be a need for a unique identifier for each user to map the local users to the IDP's users. This is what is referred to usually as a **federated identifier**. The federated identifier can take multiple shapes and forms, such as an email address, social security number, or simply a unique enterprise ID.

The following diagram is an example illustrating the global and local data stores in an SSO setup:

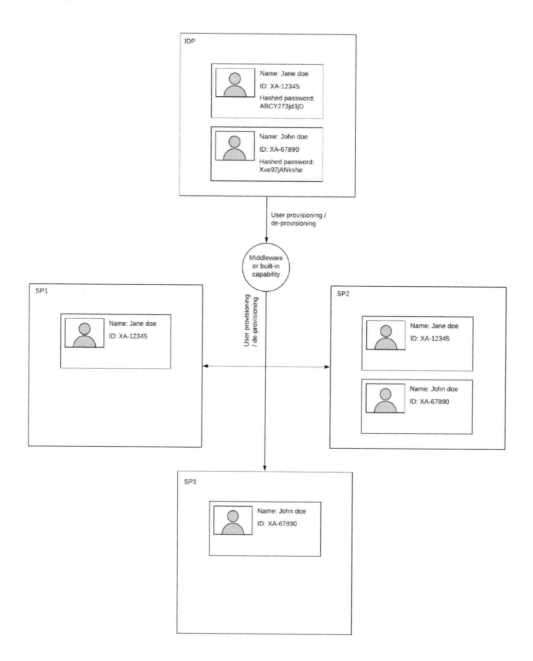

Figure 4.1 – Example of global and local data stores in an SSO setup

Multi-Factor Authentication (MFA)

This term is used to describe the security mechanism where a successful authentication process would require the user to pass more than one identity validation process using different methods. For example, the user might be requested to provide something they know (such as a password), and something they have (such as a one-time token received on a mobile phone), and something they physically possess (such as a fingerprint). In MFA, the user is normally requested to pass three (or more) different security layers. A more relaxed security mechanism is normally referred to as **Two-Factor Authentication (2FA)**, which requires passing just two identity validation processes. A common example (that Salesforce professionals are familiar with) is requesting the user's credentials as the first step. Upon successfully passing the validation, the user is then redirected to another page with a single input field, and a one-time token is sent to the specified user's email address. The user would be requested to enter that **one-time-password token (OTP)** into the input field.

Again, this relies on something the user knows (the password) and something they have (access to their own email inbox). MFA and 2FA ensure that the attacker can't gain access to the desired resource(s) by simply guessing or stealing a user's password (or any other single authentication mechanism, such as an ID card). Many enterprises are making this approach mandatory nowadays.

Having an SSO setup makes this process easy and streamlined. The tasks of defining the 2FA/MFA policies, executing them, and providing a comprehensive log on their use is something the IDP would be handling in full. This means that the SPs don't need to worry about implementing any of this; they can simply rely on the IDP to handle all of that and then authenticate the user who passes the IDP checks based on the trust relationship they have.

This means that the enterprise can be more agile and flexible in changing and developing their security policies. For example, an enterprise might decide to add a new layer of authentication on top of what it has today. With the right setup, they would need to introduce this only once to the IDP that manages the entire SSO process for the enterprise.

User provisioning and de-provisioning

Provisioning is the process of creating a user in an identity repository. That includes global and local identity repositories. Normally, there will also be a set of roles assigned to the user in each repository. De-provisioning is exactly the opposite process and involves deactivating or deleting an identity from global and local identity stores, including any roles associated with it.

Streamlining the provisioning and de-provisioning processes is important for enterprises as new employees would be joining every day while others would be leaving. It is also key to ensuring that you can turn off all user access to all relevant systems from a single location. This adds a multitude of benefits in terms of optimization, efficiency, security, and compliance.

Role-Based Access (RBA)

Most enterprise-size applications come with a tool or a module to manage the user's privileges to access specific functionalities, database objects, records, or fields. The same principle can be applied to the entire resources available on a network. The tool would normally be called **role-based access control (RBAC)** in this case and is used to assign specific roles to users, which controls what these users can see and do across the entire network. Depending on the RBAC tool itself, roles might also be referred to as **group memberships**.

Upon identifying the user via authentication, the authorization server determines the roles applicable for the logged-in user. Sometimes, both activities can be done by the same system. Enterprises would ideally aspire to have a centralized tool where they can manage all available roles and their assignments. In an SSO setup, this normally takes place in two steps:

- **Define and manage a set of global roles**: The global roles would be defined and assigned to the appropriate users in the centralized RBAC system. These roles could be based on users' responsibilities, job description, or functionality done on a particular system, such as *System admin – North America*, or *Salesforce system admin – North America*. More than one role can be associated with the same user; for example, when the same user needs to access more than one system with a different privilege level on each.

- **Define and manage local application roles**: For each SP application, there will be a need to define a set of roles/profiles/permissions that can be assigned to the application users. These local roles are mapped to global roles. Although not necessarily a one-to-one mapping, for example, the *Salesforce system admin – North America* global role could be translated into a Salesforce profile called *Salesforce system admin* for the North America instance, plus a set of permission sets, feature licenses, and third-party licenses that ensure that the specified user can carry out all the functionalities expected of them.

The *role translation* process is something that can take place in multiple ways. A common way is to assign that task to a user provisioning tool. Some of the modern IDPs have this built-in capability. For example, some IDPs, such as Ping Identity, can *provision* and *de-provision* users in Salesforce using standard Salesforce APIs or using the **System for Cross-domain Identity Management (SCIM)** standard. Another common approach is utilizing an integration middleware to handle this task.

The following diagram is an example illustrating the global and translated local roles in an SSO setup:

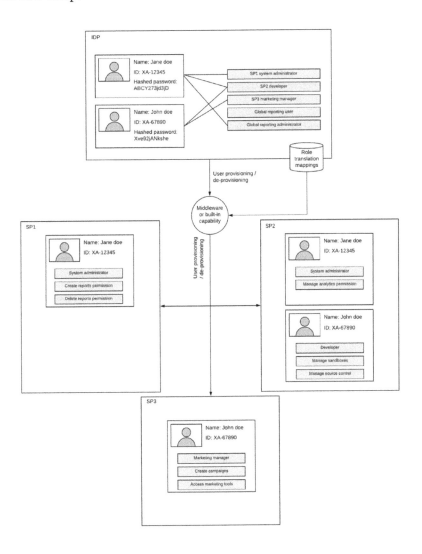

Figure 4.2 – Example of global and translated local roles in an SSO setup

Biometric authentication: This is a term given to the process of uniquely identifying a person using *biological attributes*, such as a fingerprint, retina scan, voice and facial recognition, and more. There are even studies for uniquely identifying people by the way they walk. Biometric authentication gained a lot of traction in the market recently due to the quick technological advances in this field. At the beginning of the millennium, topics such as face recognition were nothing more than science fiction. Today, it is there by default in many modern smartphones. And similar to what happened many times before, throughout history, the innovative use cases that depend on such technologies have followed. Today, you can do your online shopping using your smartphone and then pay online using details of a credit card stored safely in your phone's *e-wallet*, which is secured using your fingerprint or your facial features. The success of such technologies and the level of convenience they bring suggests many more use cases coming in the near future.

Many enterprises have adopted some sort of biometric authentication as a 2FA or MFA mechanism, where the user logs in to a portal using one authentication mechanism (for example, a password). Once that is done, a *push message* will be sent to a mobile application that the user should have on their mobile. The user would then open the application, which utilizes the mobile device's biometric authentication capability to authenticate the user again. Once the authentication is done successfully, a message will be sent back to the server, which then proceeds with the next steps defined in its authentication process (such as completing the authentication process, creating a session cookie in the user's browser, running some pre-defined validations, and then redirecting the user to a landing page).

The following diagram illustrates the use of biometric authentication as a second-factor authentication mechanism:

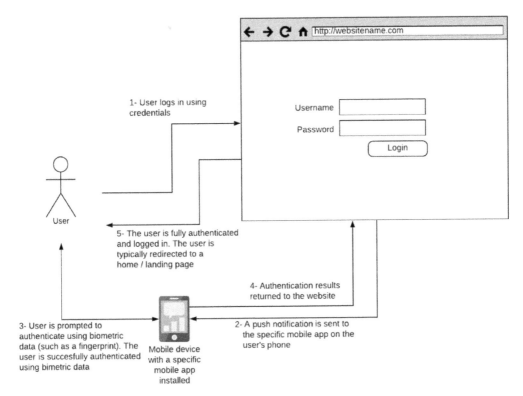

Figure 4.3 – Using biometric authentication as a second-factor authentication mechanism

- **Identity as a service (IDaaS)**: This is a solution that provides identity services in an SaaS fashion. It normally offers an online portal with some tools and control panels to configure it and style it in the desired way. Some of these solutions offer different levels of IAM capabilities, such as user provisioning and de-provisioning. Some providers also provide their solution in a form that can be hosted on-premises. Examples of these providers include Okta, Microsoft Azure identity management, Ping identity, and, to some extent, Salesforce. Like all the other products that we mention throughout this book, you need to memorize some of these names to suggest the right solution during the CTA review board.

- **Risk-based authentication (RBA)**: This technique uses different tools and algorithms to calculate a risk score for the user trying to access a secure resource or attempting to authenticate. Based on the calculated risk score, the user might be asked to provide a second-factor authentication or more. The algorithms to calculate the risk score of a particular user could depend on many factors, such as an IP address range, the specific time of the day, the existence of cookies from a particular domain in the user's browser, the last time that a particular user has logged in successfully, and many other more advanced algorithms besides that could rely on anything from complex logic to machine learning and artificial intelligence. RBA provides a convincing way to ensure a high level of security without unnecessarily cluttering the user experience. Several IDPs provide various levels of RBAs as part of their solution.

- **Lightweight Directory Access Protocol (LDAP)**: This is a protocol that was designed to provide a standardized mechanism to interact with data stored in a *hierarchical directory structure*. LDAP can store and retrieve data from these structures efficiently, which was one of the reasons it became so popular. **Microsoft Active Directory (AD)** is an example of a tool that stores the enterprise data (usually, policies, roles, and permissions) in a *hierarchical structure*. These types of tools are normally referred to as *directory service databases*.

  LDAP is a protocol that can communicate and interact efficiently with directory service databases such as Microsoft AD. In the CTA review board scenarios as well as in real life, you might come across use cases where LDAP is used to communicate with other directory service databases, such as Apache Directory, OpenLDAP, JXplorer, or others. You need to understand which tools and IDPs are built to work with AD specifically, such as **Microsoft Active Directory Federation Services (ADFS)**, or LDAP in general (such as the IDaaS products mentioned earlier).

- **Service user versus context user authentication**: In some use cases (particularly when accessing APIs), authentication can typically take one of two flavors. You either authenticate using a named principal (also known as a **service user**) where you only need to authenticate a single integration user, or you follow a per-user policy, which means that you authenticate at least once per every user in the connected system.

Operations executed in the target systems would operate under the context of the integration user in the first case, which means you have less opportunity to provide a finely grained access privilege for each connected user. In contrast, in the second case, operations in the target system would operate under the context of the logged-in user (also known as the context user), which allows you to define different permissions, roles, and profiles for each connected user. The following diagram illustrates the two different approaches:

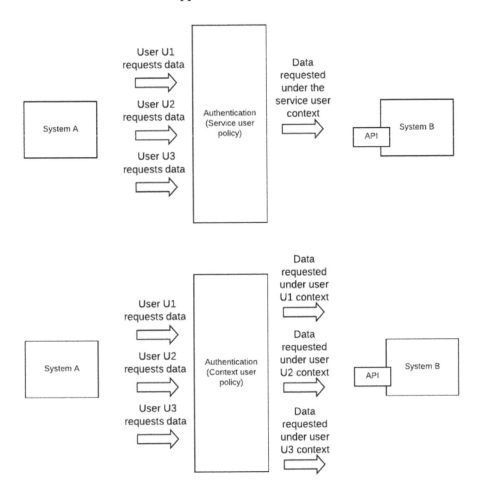

Figure 4.4 – Difference between service user and context user authentication

Now that we have covered the common IAM terms and concepts and learned how they work together, let's move on and find out more about three of the most common IAM standards.

Becoming familiar with the common IAM standards

IAM is a complex domain, and in order to ensure that its desired functionalities are delivered in a secure, consistent, and compliant way, several standards and protocols have been developed throughout time. As an architect, you need to become very familiar with these standards, understand how they operate and how they differ from one another, and exactly when to propose using any of them. Moreover, some of these standards have known and well-defined processes that describe precisely how to use the given standard to authenticate a user for a given use case. These processes are referred to as the *authentication flows*.

To understand the *authentication and authorization* concept and how standards are used therein, let's take a simple example. Assume you are traveling from the UK to the USA. When you attempt to cross the US border control, they would want to verify your identity. And let's assume that there is also a need to check some other information related to what you are *allowed to do*, such as driving a car in the US while using a UK driving license. In this case, the US border control would need to communicate with the UK and make a request to *verify* your identity. Once that is verified, they will ask *what you are authorized to do*. The identification/authentication process can take many forms. For example, you could be identified using your passport, and the passport *authenticity* itself could be *verified* using the special security measurements/electronic chip embedded within it. Your passport can be scanned, and a real-time call could be made to a specific online endpoint to retrieve a list of things that you are allowed to do, such as driving a normal-sized car in the US for a given period of time.

In this example, the UK is acting as the *identity provider*, while the US border control is the *service provider*. Your passport is representing some sort of *authentication token*, which is protected with a security measure. In the digital world, this could be a digital signature. The *way* the data is exchanged and the *formats* used represents a *standard/protocol* used for the given task, and the *exact sequence* of the authentication and authorization process steps represent the authentication/authorization *flow*.

When designing an IAM strategy for a client, it makes all the sense to rely on one of the industry standards rather than attempting to re-invent the wheel. In addition to saving time and effort, this will ensure that your authentication mechanisms are secure, scalable, and compliant. Deviating from the standards could lead to huge security gaps and would almost certainly result in a failure in the IAM domain during the CTA review board.

Understanding the common IAM standards

In this section, we will get to know some of the most common IAM standards, and then move on to further understand the type of tokens involved in these standards, and finally go through a set of authentication flows that you should become very familiar with. Let's start with the list of common IAM standards.

Security Assertion Markup Language (SAML)

The SAML standard was created in 2001. It is currently in version 2.0, which was released in 2005. SAML is considered a standard for both authentication and authorization, and it is based on XML. In SAML, the SP can ask an IDP to authenticate and authorize a user/principal using a *SAML assertion request*. The IDP would respond with a *SAML assertion response*. In other flows, the principal can start from a particular web page that contains links to various systems (SPs). Each link contains an IDP-generated SAML assertion. Once that link is clicked, the assertion is sent to the target SP, and the SP verifies the SAML assertion based on a *trust* relationship established between the SP and the IDP. The principal is then granted access to the SP. SAML assertions are signed using **XML Signature Wrapping**, which is an advanced form of digital signature. Verifying a digital signature (as we discussed previously in *Chapter 3, Core Architectural Concepts – Integration and Cryptography*) requires access to the *public key*, which is normally presented as a *digital certificate*. The *trust* is established between the IDP and SP using the *digital certificate*. In the setup phase, the architect/developer/configurator would normally upload a certificate shared by the IDP to the SP. The SP will then use this certificate to verify SAML assertions received in the future from the IDP. There are other steps involved in setting up the connection between the SP and the IDP using SAML, which could slightly differ depending on the technology used. Salesforce supports both **SAML V1.1** and **V2.0**. In your solution, you should aim at using the latest supported version. Later on in this chapter, we will get to know two SAML-related flows: the **SAML IDP-initiated flow** and the **SAML SP-initiated flow**. SAML is best suited for SSO, is not very suitable for mobile phones or JavaScript, and is not very popular with APIs.

Open authorization (OAuth)

OAuth is an open standard that was created to solve a particular problem, normally referred to as *access delegation* or *secure delegated access*, which is simply allowing an application (normally referred to as *client*) to access resources or perform activities on a server (normally referred to as *resource server*) on behalf of a *user*. The standard facilitates this process *without* the need for the *user* to share their *credentials* with the *client*. This is done by utilizing *tokens* issued by an *IDP*, upon the *user's* approval, which contains a description of what the client is *authorized* to access and do on the *resource server*. Its current version is 2.0, and that is the minimal version you should aim to use. OAuth is normally considered an *authorization* standard, although there have been some debates around considering it an authentication standard based on the assumption that the authorization process can be considered a *pseudo-authentication*. In order to understand this topic and to understand what we precisely mean by *access delegation*, let's take a simple example.

Assume you are leaving for a short trip, and you want your friend Suzanne to take care of your house while you are away. You want Suzanne to be able to access your house, garage, and two out of the four rooms in your house. Before you leave, you hand over to Suzanne a keychain that contains keys for the main house door, the two rooms, and the garage. Suzanne can now access the house and specified rooms using the keys without you being around. In this example, Suzanne is the *client*, you are the *user*, the house and rooms are the *resource server*, and the keychain is the *token* that authorizes Suzanne to access specific resources only. The keychain and the keys have been created by a locksmith who, in this case, resembles an *IDP*. This locksmith has created the keys based on your own *permission/approval*. For someone watching Suzanne accessing the house, it may seem that she is the house owner. This is an assumption based on the fact that she has the keys. In this case, the authorization that the key chain holder has can be used to *pseudo-authenticate* the person and assume they are the house owner. Now let's take another example from the digital world, which many of us have experienced.

You are on a nice website to review books. You have just finished reading a nice book and created a great review.

After submitting the review, the website shows you a **Share on Facebook** button with a message asking you whether you are interested in posting your review on Facebook. You like the idea, so you hit the button. This is your first-ever time doing this. The website here will attempt to get permission/authorization to post on Facebook on your behalf. So, it redirects you to Facebook; if you are not already logged in, Facebook will show you the standard login page. After you authenticate, Facebook will show you a page with a message informing you that the website is requesting permission to post on your behalf. The page will also contain *approve* and *reject* buttons. Once you hit the *approve* button, a token will be issued by Facebook to the website, granting the website the limited privilege to post on your behalf. The website will use this token to authenticate to Facebook and post your review on your Facebook wall, and for your Facebook friends, this will look like an activity done directly by you. Note that you shared your credentials with Facebook only; you have never shared them with the website or any other entity.

Typically, there will be another token issued to the website that allows it to get a fresh new token next time without the need for this whole set of activities. The next time you post a review on the website and hit the same button, the website will use the tokens granted to it in the previous step to authenticate again to Facebook and post on your behalf. Depending on the settings of these tokens, this can continue to happen until you *revoke* these tokens. In the previous example, this is equivalent to claiming back the keychain from Suzanne or completely changing all the locks. Later on, in this chapter, we will get to know some OAuth2.0 and OpenID Connect (which is based on OAuth2.0) flows, such as **web server**, **user-agent**, **refresh token**, **JWT bearer**, **device**, **asset token**, and **username-password**.

OpenID Connect

OpenID is based on OAuth2.0, but it is designed for a different purpose. It is designed to provide a federated authentication mechanism that is similar to SAML. It adds a set of different functionalities on top of OAuth2.0, but the one you should be particularly aware of is an additional token generated called the **ID token**. The ID token contains information about the authenticated user, such as first name, email, federated identified, and the requesting *client*, in addition to custom attributes that could be added by the IDP. This token can help confirm the identity of the individual for whom this token has been issued.

The ID token itself is *digitally signed*, and therefore it is easy to validate it and confirm whether its contents have been tampered with. Because the IDP's digital signature secures the ID token, and because it contains key information about the user it is generated for, including the federated identifier, it can be used to authenticate this user by other systems (service providers) who trust the IDP (trust is established using a digital certificate). OpenID Connect is widely used today; most social networks, such as Facebook, Twitter, Google, and others, support it. Using social networks as IDPs to log in to other websites is called *social sign-on*, and in most cases, it will be utilizing OpenID Connect. However, that doesn't mean that OpenID usage is limited to that alone. Many enterprises are using it as their SSO standard.

Kerberos

This authentication protocol is used over networks (such as a local enterprise network) to provide SSO capabilities. It uses *tickets*, which is similar in principle to tokens. Kerberos is named after the Greek mythological three-headed dog, Cerberus, who guards the entrance to the underworld. Kerberos is used in most systems apart from, most remarkably, Microsoft Windows. **Integrated Windows Authentication (IWA)** is a Microsoft product that utilizes Kerberos (it can also work with other protocols such as **NT Lan Manager (NTLM)**) to allow Windows users to use AD for SSO.

Imagine this scenario; you are an employee of a company that utilizes AD to manage all its employees' identities. You arrive at the office in the morning, open your Windows-based laptop, and authenticate to join the domain using your AD credentials (which, behind the scenes, creates a Kerberos ticket). And now you want to access your company's instance of Salesforce (which has a unique MyDomain URL). But you want to do that without the need to authenticate again.

Kerberos, IWA, and a tool such as Salesforce Identity Connect, Microsoft ADFS, or Ping Identity (which would facilitate the authentication flow between Salesforce and AD) would all combine to deliver this functionality. The details of setting up Kerberos or IWA are beyond the scope of this book, for the sake of brevity. We are not going to describe the Kerberos protocol itself, but we will discover how it is utilized during a SSO flow in *Chapter 13, Present and Defend – First Mock*.

The standards mentioned utilize and generate tokens as part of their design. Tokens have a crucial role in IAM. They are involved in many different operations and come in different formats and for different purposes. We will now go through the most common types of tokens that you might come across as a Salesforce architect.

Getting to know the different types of tokens

As a Salesforce architect, you are expected to lead the activities of designing and implementing IAM strategies for your Salesforce implementation. Tokens are an essential element of the IAM standards, and you need to know more than just their names.

The following tokens are by no means a complete list of all possible tokens; the list is too long and probably requires a dedicated book. The following sections cover a selected set that Salesforce architects designing solutions for B2B and B2C are likely to come across.

Access token

This is a term used by OAuth2.0 and OpenID Connect. The *access token* is the ultimate token that your applications are after. This is the token that will allow an application (remember, we referred to that as a *client*) to authenticate to a *resource server* and request resources (such as retrieving specific data) on behalf of the *user*. The access token can be used to authenticate against web services as well, typically bypassing the token itself in the header. The access token can be formatted in multiple forms depending on the system issuing it. For example, Salesforce-issued access tokens take the shape of a normal session ID, which will look similar to the following example:

```
00DR00000008oBT!AQwAQCPqzc_
HBE59c80QmEJD4rQKRRc1GRLvYZEqc80QmEJD4
```

The value of this token cannot be decoded. It is a unique hash and is not supposed to be decrypted or decoded. By itself, it doesn't contain any information. However, it can be used to access resources on a resource server because a copy of the same token will be cached by the server, usually in a key/value pair dictionary along with its expiry date. Access tokens have relatively short longevity (such as 30 minutes, 60 minutes, and 120 minutes). It is determined by the system administrator who would decide the time for *session timeout*.

Another example is Azure-issued access tokens, which are formatted as **JSON Web Tokens (JWTs)**. JWT tokens contain some standard and custom attributes/payload (also known as **claims**). You can use an online tool such as www.jwt.io to see a live example of a JWT and its decoded value.

Refresh token

This is another term used by OAuth2.0 and OpenID Connect. *Refresh tokens* are issued for clients in specific use cases (depending on the client type and the authentication flow used). The refresh token normally has a longer longevity than the access token. Sometimes, they can be set so that they *never expire* (until they get revoked). The refresh token should be stored in a *secure location* by the *client application* and used to get a new access token periodically or whenever needed. You can see refresh tokens in action right now using one of the applications on your smart mobile phone.

Perhaps you have noticed that some apps require you to sign in once, the first time you start the application. You never need to enter your credentials again the next time you open the app, even if you open it after a few days or weeks. This is because the application has been configured to utilize a *refresh token*. When you authenticated for the first time, the application received both an *access token* and a *refresh token*. The access token has a short TTL; let's assume a few hours. The application will continue to use it as long as it is still valid.

Let's assume you opened the application after 2 weeks. The application will use the cached access token to communicate with the resource server, but will immediately get a response back, indicating that the token has expired. The application will respond by utilizing the refresh token to get a new access token. Once that is done (and we will see that flow later on in this chapter), the application will use the *newly retrieved access token* to communicate with the resource server. All of this is done in a completely transparent way for the user.

ID token

This is a token that is exclusive to OpenID Connect. As we mentioned before, it provides a mechanism for the client application to verify the identity of the user for whom this token has been issued. The ID token contains information such as the time of issue and the time of expiry. In addition to data regarding the authenticated user, such as the user's unique identifier (also known as the federated identifier), depending on the IDP setup, the federated identifier could be a value such as the employee ID, email address, or a different sort of unique identifier. The ID token also contains information about the client application that the token has been issued for. Most importantly, the token will also contain the IDP's digital signature, which can be used to verify the token's contents. The ID token format is based on *JWT,* which is a data structure based on JSON. Applications can request an ID token using the same OAuth2.0 flows if the right parameters are passed. For example, in the web server flow, the client application can get an ID token if it included the *openid* scope as part of the passed scope arguments. We will see further details about this later in this chapter.

JWT token

JWT is a standard to format data that can be used to assert the identity of a party to other parties as well as asserting a set of information (referred to as *claims*) that is included in the token itself. The ID token is one of the tokens that use the JWT format, as mentioned earlier. JWT tokens can either be signed (similar to the example we gave before while describing the ID token), and in this case, it will be called the **JWS (JSON Web Signature)** token, or encrypted, and in this case, it will be called the **JWE (JSON Web Encryption)** token.

Commonly, when a JWT token is referred to, it is implicitly assumed that it is a signed JWT (effectively, a JWS). If a JWT token is neither signed nor encrypted, this is explicitly clarified by calling it an **Unsecured JWT**. The body of a JWT is encoded. It normally looks like the following example (the three dots represent text that we have trimmed off for the sake of simplicity):

```
eyJhbGciOiJIUzI1NiIsInR5cCI6IkpXVCJ9.eyJzdWIiOiIxMjM0NTY3
ODkwIiwibmFtZSI6IkpvaG4gRG9lIiwiaWF0IjoxNTE2MjM5MDIyfQ.SflKxw
RJSMeKKF2QT4fwpMeJf36PO...
```

Once you decode a JWT token using a tool such as www.jwt.io, you will notice that the JWT token consists of three main parts – a header, a payload, and a signature (remember, when we use the term JWT by itself, we are normally implicitly indicating that this JWT is actually a JWS). The header and the payload sections could look like the following example:

```
{
    "alg": "HS256",
    "typ": "JWT",
    "kid": "228",
}
{
    "iss": "www.packtpub.com",
    "sub": "11050225117732",
    "email": "testemail@packtpub.com",
    "email_verified": true,
    "aud": "825249835659",
    "iat": 1401908271,
    "exp": 1401912171
}
```

The attributes such as `iss`, `aud`, `iat`, and `exp` are what we referred to earlier as claims. These are standard claims; they are part of the standard JWT tokens. An IDP might add custom claims and include additional information in them. Here is an explanation of the meanings of some of these claims:

- `iss` (issuer): This claim is used to hold an identifier about the principal that issued the token.

- `aud` (audience): This claim is used to hold an identifier for the recipients the token is issued for, such as the client application.

- `iat` (issued at): This is the time the token was issued at.

- `exp` (expiration time): This is the time after which the token should not be accepted.

- `alg` (algorithm): This is the algorithm used for encryption or digital signatures.

- `kid` (key ID): This is an optional header claim. It is not necessarily included by all OpenID providers. When Salesforce is configured as an OpenID provider, its ID tokens (remember, they are in JWT format) will contain this optional header claim. This claim contains an identifier to the key that was used to sign the token. Salesforce (and some other OpenID token providers) use multiple private keys to sign JWT tokens, and therefore they need to provide a `key id` (`kid`) to help the recipients identify which public key can be used to verify the signature. If you look at this public URL, `https://login.salesforce.com/id/keys`, you will see multiple keys listed by Salesforce. Each is identified using a unique key ID (kid).

  The applications that receive a signed JWT from Salesforce would extract the value of the *kid* header claim and then use it to look up the correct public key from the list published regularly by Salesforce to verify the token's signature. This all happens transparently, and the user won't be bothered with it unless the signature is invalid, of course, where an exception will be thrown.

One thing to keep in mind is that Salesforce, similar to other OpenID providers, can regularly change the keys used to sign their tokens. The client application should never attempt to hardcode a *kid*, but instead should attempt to *resolve it dynamically,* as we mentioned earlier.

Session token

Also known as the session ID, this is a common term used with web applications. The session token is a unique string (normally, a hash value) that identifies a particular session for the currently logged-in user. Session IDs are heavily used on websites, and they are normally stored within a cookie. The session ID can normally be mapped to a key-value dictionary in the application server, which contains information about the logged-in user and what they are authorized to do. If an attacker manages to get hold of a session ID/session token, they would normally be able to impersonate the victim at the target application server.

This is why users are always advised to *log out* after they finish working with a particular secure website in order to destroy their sessions. This is also the reason why session IDs are normally configured to have a short lifetime, particularly with financial services applications (such as online banking) where the session can expire after a very short period (such as 5 minutes) of idle time. The token's **time-to-live** (**TTL**) can be *fixed* (which means the token will expire after the given time, regardless of whether the user is active) or can be extended based on user activity. This means the token will expire only after a specific given period of idle time (where the user is simply not doing any interaction with the server); in this case, it is normally called a *sliding token*.

Authorization code

This is a special type of token. It is used in one of the OAuth2.0/OpenID flows (the *web server* flow). It has a very short TTL, and it is created by the authorization server and returned back (via browser) to the client application. The client application would then send the authorization code back to the authorization server in order to exchange it for an access token (and optionally, a refresh token).

Due to the fact that the authorization code is returned via the browser, and although this step happens very quickly, the authorization code is visible to the end user and can be observed using some tools. This is particularly why its TTL is so short, as this reduces the risk of being stolen by an attacker (who can use it to get an access token).

SAML assertion

Similar to JWT tokens, SAML assertions can be used to authenticate a user to a particular resource server/service provider. They contain information such as the user identity, issue time, and expiry time. They can also be secured using multiple mechanisms, including **XML Signature Wrapping**. Applications can utilize SAML assertions to authenticate to APIs as well.

Salesforce security token

When you attempt to access Salesforce APIs and authenticate using a basic authentication mechanism (username/password), you need to append the security token to the password provided. The token itself is a case-sensitive alphanumeric key. You should try to avoid basic authentication as much as possible and utilize one of the standards mentioned before, such as OpenID Connect.

Now that you are familiar with all types of tokens, let's look at the different authentication flows and observe the generation of each type of these tokens throughout the process.

Understanding the key authentication flows

For each of the following flows, we will go through the flow's sequence diagram, cover the high-level details of each step, and provide potential use cases and key considerations. In order to draw and read a sequence diagram properly, you need to make yourself familiar with the standard symbols used. The following diagram lists the most common UML sequence diagram symbols:

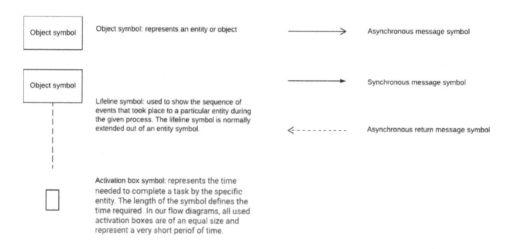

Figure 4.5 – Common sequence diagram symbols

These flows are not specific to Salesforce; they are open standards and used across different technologies. You need to become very familiar with all of them. During the CTA review board, you will likely need to explain one of these flows. The best way to explain a flow is to draw its sequence diagram and walk the audience through it. It is strongly recommended that you practice drawing these diagrams over and over until you fully memorize them. Also, practice explaining them to an audience.

This will all help during the review board presentation and in your daily activities in general.

Ready? Buckle up, here we go.

Becoming familiar with the SAML 2.0 flows

SAML 2.0 has three main flows, the **IDP-initiated**, the **SP-initiated**, and the **SAML bearer assertion** flow. We will cover the first two; the SAML bearer assertion flow is very similar to the OAuth 2.0 JWT flow, which we will cover later in this chapter.

SAML IDP-initiated flow

The following diagram represents a SAML IDP-initiated flow. This flow is usually used by enterprises that provides a central location/page for their employees to access all applications (service providers) linked to the same enterprise identity provider:

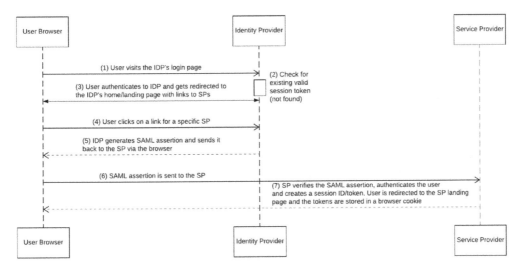

Figure 4.6 – SAML IDP-initiated flow

1. The user visits the IDP login page or the IDP home page.

2. The home or login pages will check whether the user is authenticated by checking whether there is a stored cookie for the IDP domain with a valid session token. Let's assume that this is the first login by the user for the given day and that there is no valid session token found. The user should see the login page at this stage.

3. The user enters their username and password (or authenticates in whatever way defined by the IDP). If the IDP is configured to use 2FA or MFA, then the other factors will be requested before the user is authenticated. Once the user is authenticated, they are redirected to the IDP's home page.

4. The user lands on the IDP's home page/landing page. The page contains links for all available applications (service providers) that are using the IDP for SSO. The user clicks on one of those links.

5. The IDP generates a SAML assertion, signed with the IDP's private key/certificate. The assertion is sent via the browser to the SP.

6. The assertion is sent to the SP.

7. The SP receives the assertion, validates it using the IDP's public key/certificate. The user is authenticated, and a session token for the specific SP domain is created and saved in a browser cookie. The user is redirected to the SP home page. The next time the user attempts to access the SP, the SP will detect the cookie with the session token. And if it is still valid, the user will be allowed to access the desired page. Otherwise, a new authentication flow will start over. The only difference is that this time it will start from the SP rather than the IDP. This is what is referred to as SP-initiated flow.

SAML SP-initiated flow

The following diagram represents a SAML SP-initiated flow. This flow is used when a user attempts to access a *deep link* of a particular SP. That could be a URL saved in bookmarks, a link in an email, a URL from the browser history, a URL that the user knows by heart, or even the URL of the SP's home page. The idea here is that the user is trying to access one of the SP's resources. The SP needs to authenticate the user before it allows access to that resource. This is a very common flow:

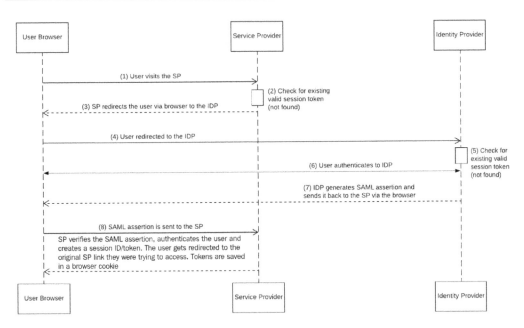

Figure 4.7 – SAML SP-initiated flow

8. The user visits the SP using a deep link or simply by trying to access the SP's home page.

9. The SP checks for an existing and valid session token stored in a cookie associated with the SP's domain. Let's assume that this token hasn't been found because this is the first time the user has attempted to access this application/SP today.

10. The user is redirected to the IDP via the browser with a SAML assertion request. The idea here is to get the IDP authenticating the user and then return the user back to the SP's page/URL that the user was attempting to access (for example, the URL in the deep link such as `http://www.packtpub.com/books/SF_TAHandBook.html`). The target URL is passed in a parameter called `RelayState`. In the previous example, the value of this parameter would be `/books/SF_TAHandBook.html`. This parameter will eventually be passed back to the SP following user authentication, which will help redirect the user to the right URL.

11. The user is redirected to the IDP login page (with the `RelayState` value).

12. The IDP checks for an existing and valid session token stored in a cookie associated with the IDP's domain. Let's assume that this token hasn't been found because this is the first time the user has logged in to the IDP today.

13. The user enters the username and password (or authenticates in whatever way defined by the IDP). If the IDP is configured to use 2FA or MFA, then the other factors will be requested before the user is authenticated.

14. Once the user is authenticated, a SAML assertion will be created, signed with the IDP private key/certificate, and returned to the SP via the browser, along with the `RelayState` value.

15. A SAML assertion is sent to the SP via the browser, along with the `RelayState` value.

16. The SP receives the assertion, and validates it using the IDP's public key/certificate. The user is authenticated, and a session token for the specific SP domain is created and saved in a browser cookie. The user is then redirected to the SP page specified in the `RelayState` value. The user lands on the URL they were trying to access in *step 1*.

Let's look now at the next time the user attempts to access another page from the same SP, assuming the SP session cookie is still valid:

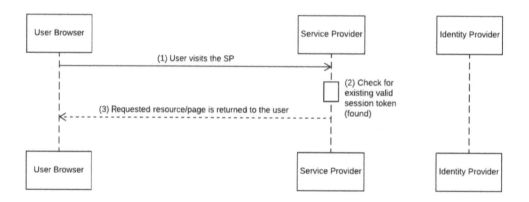

Figure 4.8 – Continuing the SAML SP-initiated flow following user authentication with a valid SP session

1. The user visits the SP using a deep link or simply by trying to access the SP's home page.

2. The SP checks for an existing and valid session token stored in a cookie associated with the SP's domain. Let's assume that the token from the previous authentication is still valid.

3. The user is granted access to the desired resource.

Now let's have another look at the scenario where the user attempts to access a page from the SP following expiry of the SP's session token, but prior to expiry of the IDP's session token. This could happen if the expiry time of the IDP token is set to a higher duration than the session token of the SP:

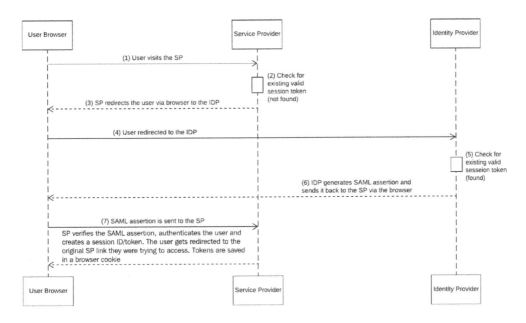

Figure 4.9 – Continuing the SAML SP-initiated flow with an expired SP session and a valid IDP session

1. The user visits the SP using a deep link or simply by trying to access the SP's home page.

2. The SP checks for an existing and valid session token stored in a cookie associated with the SP's domain. Let's assume that the token from the previous authentication has expired.

3. The user is redirected to the IDP via the browser with a SAML assertion request. The value of `RelayState` is also populated and passed.

4. The user is redirected to the IDP login page (with the `RelayState` value).

5. The IDP checks for an existing and valid session token stored in a cookie associated with the IDP's domain. Let's assume that the IDP found an active/valid session token.

6. A SAML assertion is created, signed with the IDP private key/certificate, and returned to the SP via the browser, along with the `RelayState` value.

7. A SAML assertion is sent to the SP via the browser, along with the `RelayState` value.

8. The SP receives the assertion and validates it using the IDP's public key/certificate. The user is authenticated, and a session token for the specific SP domain is created and saved in a browser cookie. The user is then redirected to the SP page specified in the `RelayState` value.

These are the most common SAML2.0 flows. Let's now explore the OAuth2.0/OpenID Connect flows.

Becoming familiar with the OAuth 2.0/OpenID Connect flows

Remember that OpenID Connect is based on OAuth2.0, so most of the following flows are applicable for both.

Let's get familiar with some of the terms used in these flows:

- **Client app**: An application that is trying to access resources on a resource server on behalf of the user. For example, a website such as www.mywebsite.com could be trying to access resources from a Salesforce instance such as `MySFinstance.my.salesforce.com`.

- **Authorization server**: This is the server that will grant the right authorization to the logged-in user. For the sake of simplicity, we will assume that it is also handling the process of identifying the user attempting to log in (effectively authenticating the user and acting like an IDP) and that it has access to the identity store where the identification mechanisms for the users are kept (such as user credentials). `Login.salesforce.com` is an example of such a server.

- **Resource server**: This is the server with the resource that the client application is trying to access on behalf of the user. For example, this could be a Salesforce instance such as `MySFinstance.my.salesforce.com`, from where the user is simply trying to access a particular page or a web service.

- **Client ID/consumer ID**: A unique alphanumeric ID for a given client app. The authorization server generates this value for a specific client app upon registering the app with the authorization server. The app registration is typically done as part of the setup process, but it can happen dynamically in some cases.

- **Client secret/consumer secret**: A unique alphanumeric value representing a highly confidential value that the client app should never expose to the user or external entities apart from the trusted authorization server. Similar to the *client ID*, the authorization server also generates this value for a specific client app upon registering the app with the authorization server.

There are other terms that we will come across, but we will explain each in time. All set? Let's proceed to the flows.

Web server flow

This flow is also known as the **authorization code flow** or **auth-code flow**. This scenario is typically used when a website/web application is trying to access resources from a resource server on behalf of the user. Websites/web apps are hosted on servers, and to use this flow, the website/web app should be able to safely store the highly confidential *client secret* value. That value should never be exposed to end users, never returned to the browser, never exchanged over non-secure channels, and never exposed to any entity but the authorization server. If the website/web app (which is the *client app* in this case) is unable to meet this requirement, you need to consider a different flow.

This flow facilitates server-to-server communications but requires user interaction, at least during the first authentication. The flow can grant the client app an access token, and optionally an ID token (if the openid scope is specified during the process), and a refresh token (if the refresh_token or offline_access scopes are specified during the process). Having a refresh token allows the client app to communicate with the authorization server to request a new access token when the current access token expired.

As mentioned earlier, refresh tokens can be configured to *never expire*. This means that a web server flow can be used to establish a never-expiring (until revoked) authenticated connection between the client app and the resource server. This flow can also be used to authenticate middleware to a target application (for example, authenticating MuleSoft to Salesforce, or vice versa). Remember that there will still be a need for human interaction at the setup phase where the first authentication occurs.

Let's have a look at the sequence diagram:

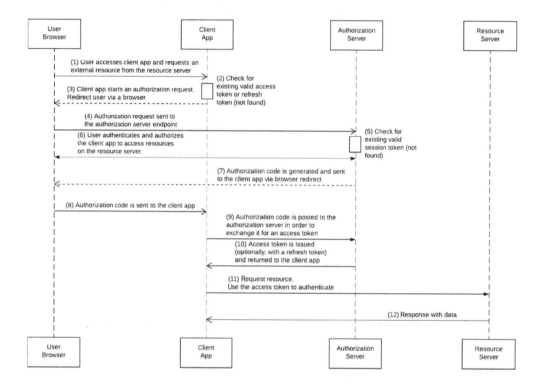

Figure 4.10 – OAuth2.0/OpenID Connect web server flow

1. The user visits the client application (website/web app). For the sake of simplicity, assume that the website itself has already identified and authenticated the user locally (using its own authentication mechanism). However, the website is also trying to access some of the user's data stored on the *resource server* on behalf of the user. For example, the website could be trying to retrieve the user's full profile.

2. The website checks for an existing and valid access token or refresh token for the current user and the target resource server. These tokens would typically be stored on the server hosting the website, either in memory, or in a more persistent data store such as a database, or both, identified by the user who owns them and the target system they are meant to be used with. The tokens should be stored safely on the server where an attacker and other users (even a system administrator) don't have access (for example, they could be encrypted while stored in the database and protected while in memory).

Let's assume that the application didn't find any tokens for the current user, which are meant for the target resource server, most likely because this is the first time that this user tries to retrieve data from the resource server.

3. The client app starts the authorization process by sending an authorization request. This process is sometimes called *the* OAuth *dance*. The client app does an HTTP redirect via the browser to the target *authorization endpoint*, such as `https://login.salesforce.com/services/oauth2/authorize`, and passes a set of parameters. The key parameters passed are `client_id`, which is the unique alphanumeric ID for the client app, and `redirect_uri`, which is the URI that the user will be redirected to following successful authentication. This URI must also be registered with the authorization server (this is also done during the setup process). `response_type` defines the OAuth2.0 grant type; this is pretty much defining the type of authentication flow used. For the *web server* flow, the value of this parameter must be `code`. There are several optional parameters that you can use to configure the behavior of the flow. One of them is particularly important, which is `scope`. This parameter contains a list of the permissions the application requests to be authorized to use upon successful authentication. The authorization server normally defines the possible values of this parameter. However, there are some common scopes, such as `full` (allows access to all data accessible by the logged-in user), `openid` (requesting this scope while using either the user agent flow or the web server flow enables the app to receive a signed ID token), and `refresh_token` (enables the app to receive a refresh token under specific conditions). For example, the full URI of the redirect could look like `https://login.salesforce.com/services/oauth2/authorize?client_id=3M20PaInvUgL9bbWFTS&redirect_uri=https://www.packtpub.com/oauth2/callback& response_type=code`.

4. The authorization request is sent to the authorization server.

5. The authorization server checks for an existing and valid session token stored in a cookie associated with the server's domain. Let's assume that this token hasn't been found because this is the first time the user has logged in to the authorization server today.

6. The user is presented with a login screen served by the authorization server. The user enters their username and password (or authenticates in whatever way defined by the authorization server). If the server is configured to use 2FA or MFA, the other factors will be requested before the user is authenticated. Once that is complete, the user will be presented with a screen asking for approval to allow the *client app* to access *specific scopes* on the *resource server*. The screen will look like the following screenshot:

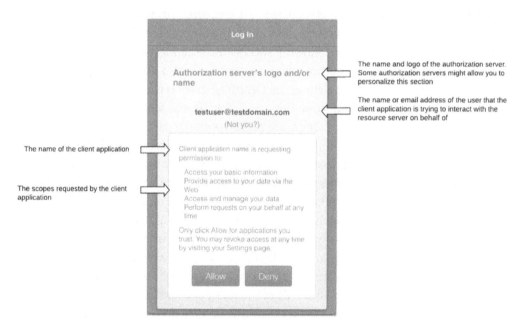

Figure 4.11 – Example of an OAuth2.0/OpenID Connect authorization approval screen

7. The user is authenticated, and an authorization code generated and returned to the client app via the user browser (redirect). The authorization code will be returned to the given `redirect_uri`. For our previous example, the returned *auth code* could look like this: `https://www.packtpub.com/oauth2/callback& code=aPYmiDiLmlLnM2NhXEBgX01tpd1zWeFSjzk4CUTZg0Hu3kC==`.

8. The authorization code is sent to the client app via the browser. Please note that due to the redirect via the browser, the authorization code might be exposed to attackers. However, it has a very short TTL, and there are other protection mechanisms that prevent attackers from making use of it, such as the need for a *client secret* value (which is supposed to be known only to the client app).

9. The client app receives the authorization code. It uses it to get an *access token* from the authorization server. This is achieved by posting the authorization code and other values to a specific server endpoint. The other parameters passed include `grant_type` (this value must be `authorization_code` for the given flow), `redirect_uri` (the value of this parameter is used for validation only at this stage and should match the value used in *step 3*), `code` (this parameter contains the value of the authorization code), `client_id` (this contains the ID of the client app, and `client_secret` (this is a crucial parameter, and it should contain the highly sensitive client secret value known only to the client app). Suppose the attacker has access to the client secret. In that case, they can use the authorization code to get the access token (some other protection mechanisms are usually included, but the attacker will find them easier to dodge). This is why the client secret must be stored in a safe location of the server hosting the client app.

10. The authorization server receives the post request and issues an access token. Optionally, depending on the values passed in the `scope` parameter, the server can also generate a *refresh token* and an *ID token* (OpenID Connect). These tokens are returned to the caller (typically, in JSON format).

11. The client app receives the tokens. Optionally, if the client app receives an *ID token*, the app should validate that token (by validating its signature using the public key of the authorization server). The client app uses the *access token* to request the desired resource from the resource server.

12. The resource server responds by sending the requested resource.

Now let's assume that the user refreshed the page. The client app would attempt to retrieve the user's profile details again from the resource server. However, this time, we already have the tokens. The flow would look like this:

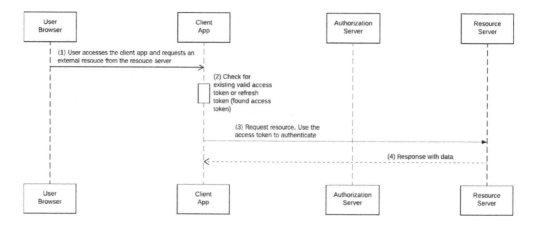

Figure 4.12 – OAuth2.0/OpenID Connect web server flow, following initial authorization

Please note that the previous diagram assumes that the *access token* is still valid. If not, the client app will use the *refresh token* to get a new token in a process known as the *refresh token flow*.

Refresh token flow

This approach is used to get a new access token using a refresh token. Let's have a look at the sequence diagram:

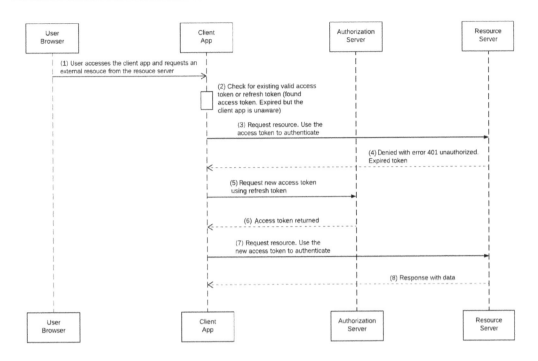

Figure 4.13 – OAuth2.0/OpenID Connect refresh token flow

1. The user visits the client application (website/web app). The website tries to access some of the user's data stored on the *resource server* on behalf of the user, such as the user's full profile.

2. The website checks for an existing and valid access token or refresh token for the current user and for the target resource server. Let's assume that the application found both. However, the application is unaware that the access token has expired. Some access tokens contain information within them, which indicates their expiry date, while some don't. Assuming that the application has no way to find out that the access token has expired, it will try to use it to get the desired resource.

3. The client app uses the *access token* to request the desired resource from the resource server.

4. The resource server returns a response indicating that the token has expired. The resource server would typically have a storage (in memory or in a database) to keep all active access tokens and refresh tokens. Expired or revoked tokens will get purged from that storage. In this case, the resource server looked for the expired access token in its storage and didn't find it (or found it, but with a flag indicating that it expired, depending on the setup of the resource server itself).

5. The client app uses the refresh token to get a new access token by posting the following parameters to the authorization server endpoint: `grant_type`: the value for this flow must be `refresh_token`; `client_id`: the client app's unique ID; `client_secret`: contains the client app's secret value; `refresh_token`: this parameter will contain the refresh token itself.

6. The authorization server receives the post request, issues an access token, and returns it to the client app.

7. The client app receives the *access token* and uses it to request the desired resource from the resource server.

8. The resource server responds by sending the requested resource.

User agent flow

Also known as the **implicit** flow, this flow is considered less secure than the web server flow and is mainly used for client apps that are unable to provide secure storage for the *client secret* value. JavaScript **SPAs** (**single page applications**) are a good example. Mobile applications are another. Let's have a look at the sequence diagram:

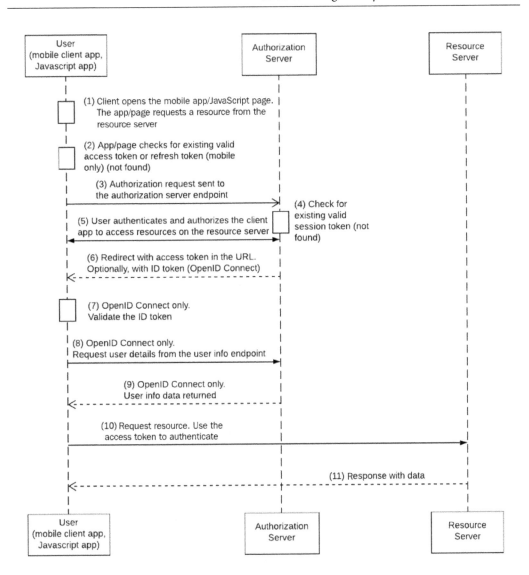

Figure 4.14 – OAuth2.0/OpenID Connect user agent flow

1. The user starts the mobile application (or visits the JavaScript-based SPA). Let's assume that this is the first time the user opens this application, and let's also assume that the mobile application is designed to work with data coming from one source, which is the resource server.

2. The application checks for a valid access token or a refresh token. Considering that this is the first time the user launches the app, no tokens will be found. The mobile app starts the OAuth2.0/OpenID Connect *user agent* flow. The passed parameters are very similar to those passed in the *web server* flow, except that the `response_type` parameter's value should be `token` this time. By way of example, the full URI of the redirect could look like this: `https://login.salesforce.com/services/oauth2/authorize?client_id=3M20PaInvUgL9bbWFTS&redirect_uri=myapp://callback&response_type=token&state=mystate`. One other thing to notice here, besides the `response_type` value, is the fact that native mobile applications can register and use custom protocols such as `myapp://` and then define a callback such as `myapp://callback`. Due to the nature of the user agent flow, and the fact that it is less secure than the web server flow, it normally doesn't return a refresh token. An exceptional case is when the client app uses a custom protocol in the `redirect_uri` value. In the preceding example, the flow can return an access token, a refresh token, and an ID token assuming the right scopes are used, as explained earlier.

3. The authorization request is sent to the authorization server.

4. The authorization server checks for an existing and valid session token stored in a cookie associated with the server's domain. Let's assume that this token hasn't been found because this is the first time the user has logged in to the authorization server today.

5. The user is presented with a login screen served by the authorization server. The user enters their username and password (or authenticates in whatever way defined by the authorization server). If the server is configured to use 2FA or MFA, the other factors will be requested before the user is authenticated. Once that is complete, the user will be presented with a screen asking for approval to allow the *client app* to access *specific scopes* on the *resource server*. This will be a screen similar to *Figure 4.9*.

6. The user is authenticated and an access token generated. A refresh token and an ID token will also be generated if the right scopes are used (let's assume so, which is a likely case for mobile applications, mainly because they normally want to provide a better user experience by not requiring the user to authenticate again the next time the application is opened). The endpoint would parse the response and extract the three tokens from it.

7. This is an optional (but strongly recommended) step for if an ID token is received. The client app validates the ID token by verifying its digital signature.

8. This is an optional step. The client app can use the information in the ID token to request the full profile details of the logged-in user.

9. This is an optional step related to *step 8*. Full profile details are returned.

10. The client app uses the access token to request the desired resource from the resource server.

11. The resource server responds by sending the requested resource.

You should be able to explain and justify the flow you are planning to use in your solution. The *web server* flow is preferred over the *user agent* due to its better security measures. However, when the client app cannot store the *consumer secret* value safely and securely (such as in mobile applications or JavaScript-based applications), the *user agent* flow provides an acceptable level of security for most enterprises.

JWT bearer flow

We came across JWT tokens before in this chapter, and we discussed their structure and the fact that they have a signature section that contains the author's digital signature. The signature can be validated by any entity with access to the public key of the JWT's author. This flow is typically used when you authorize a *client app* to access data on a *resource server* without user interaction (to log in). The digital signature in the JWT itself will be used to authenticate the *client app*. Considering that there is no user interaction expected in this flow, the client app must either be approved/authorized by a user at an earlier stage (likely, using some other flow such as the web server; the user should authorize the client application using a screen similar to *Figure 4.9*), or be authorized by an admin (the setup for that depends on the authorization server). For example, if Salesforce is the authorization server, there is a setting called *Admin approved users are pre-authorized* that can be enabled on the *connected app* functionality.

Let's now have a look at this flow's sequence diagram:

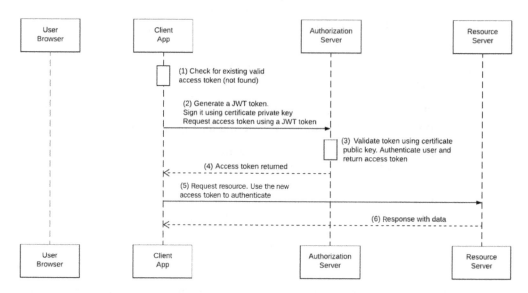

Figure 4.15 – JWT bearer flow

1. The *client app* checks for a valid access token. This could be because the client app is configured to retrieve some data from the resource server periodically (for example, every day), and it needs to have a valid access token in order to do that. Let's assume that it didn't find any. It is also fair to assume that there is no refresh token available. If a refresh token is available, it makes sense to use it in order to get a new access token (the *refresh token flow*) rather than going through the JWT bearer flow.

2. The *client app* generates a JWT and signs it using its private key/certificate. Generating a JWT is relatively easy and quick, and there are many ready-made libraries that can be used for almost all programming languages.

3. The authorization server receives the JWT and validates its signature using the public key/certificate of the *client app*. There might be a need to share the public key with the authorization server during the setup stage. Once the signature is validated, the authorization server can extract the *user identifier* from the JWT (this is typically stored in a variable called *sub*). The authorization server uses the user identifier to locate the user in its identity store. If a match is found, and if the client app has been authorized for the scopes already, the authorization server generates an *access token* for the given *client app* to access the *resource server* on behalf of the identified user.

4. The access token is returned to the client app.

5. The client app uses the access token to request the desired resource from the resource server.

6. The resource server responds by sending the requested resource.

The device flow

In order to understand this flow, we need to clarify what we mean by *device* here. This is mainly referring to electronic devices that can connect to the internet, but that have limited input or display capability. Smart TVs and appliances are great examples. Many smart TVs come today with built-in operating systems, such as Google Android, and require the user to be authenticated before they can work properly. In addition, they also need to be authorized to access specific resource servers in order to perform specific operations. For example, a smart TV might need to access your Google profile in order to display the recommended shows for you based on your profile permissions and known behavior. This flow has to been designed to be as simple as possible to use, considering the limitations in the *devices*. Let's have a look at the sequence diagram:

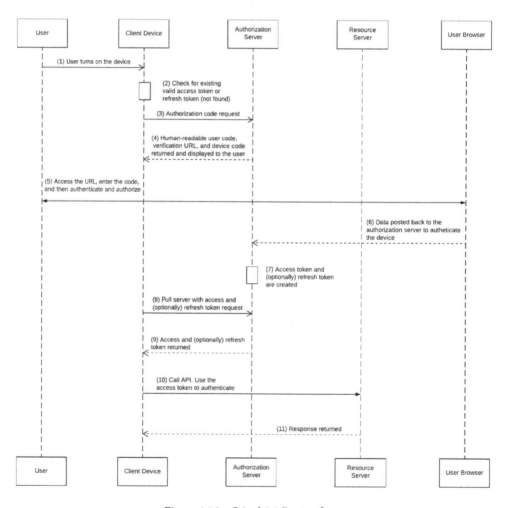

Figure 4.16 – OAuth2.0 Device flow

1. The *user* turns on the *device* (for example, turns on the smart TV).

2. The *device* checks for a valid access token or a refresh token. Let's assume that both are not available because this is the first time the user uses this device.

3. The device posts an authorization code request to the authorization server endpoint.

4. The authorization server verifies the request and issues a human-readable user code/authorization code, normally with a verification URL and a device code.

5. These values are normally displayed on the *device's* screen. You would normally see a message on your smart TV screen with the user code, device code, and the URL that the user should use in order to verify the device. The user is then expected to use a different device (such as a laptop or mobile phone) to open the URL. The URL would lead the user to a page where they can input the device code and the user code. Once this step is done, the device will be recognized by the authorization server. On some occasions, the user will also be requested to log in using one of the social network providers (such as Google) and authorize the application. This will look very similar to the web server flow; the user will have to *authorize* the *device* to access specific *scopes* on the *resource server*.

6. The collected data will be used to authenticate and authorize the device. The browser then posts this information to the authorization server.

7. The access token and, optionally, the refresh token will be generated.

8. During this period, the device will periodically pull the authorization server for the tokens. Once they are available, they are sent to the device.

9. Access and refresh tokens are sent to the device and stored securely.

10. The device uses the access token to request the desired resource from the resource server.

11. The resource server responds by sending the requested resource.

The asset token flow

This flow is mainly created for IoT devices. This could be a bit confusing as smart TVs and appliances could also be considered IoT devices. However, this flow serves a different purpose. It is an open standard meant to verify and secure communication with connected devices, particularly those who do not have any sort of screens to use. In other words, the device won't be able to display a human-readable code to use. This is common nowadays for many IoT devices such as smart sensors and smart house devices. The user for such devices normally needs to *register* them before they can be used. Once a device is registered with an IoT management platform, it can be managed and controlled remotely. In addition, its data will start flowing securely to the IoT aggregation platform. The asset token (based on JWT) will be used to uniquely identify and authenticate the specific device (also known as an *IoT asset*). Let's have a look at the sequence diagram:

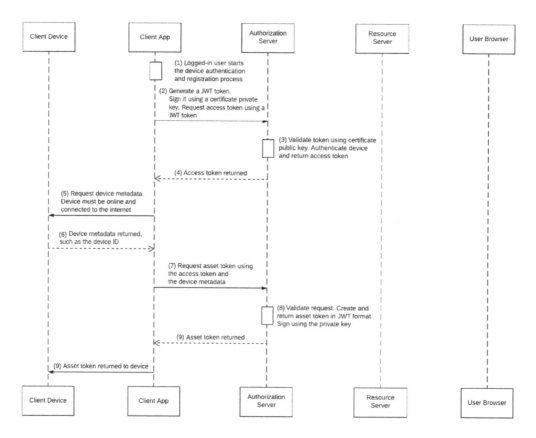

Figure 4.17 – OAuth2.0 Asset token flow

1. The logged-in user attempts to register a new device. Using a specific portal (that we are going to refer to as the *client app*), the user enters the device ID and clicks a link to start the authentication and registration process.

2. The client app generates a JWT, signs it using its private key/certificate, and uses it to request an *access token* from the authorization server.

3. The authorization server receives the token, validates it, and issues an access token (*steps 2* and *3* are meant to request an access token from the authorization server and can be accomplished using either the *JWT* or the *web server* flows).

4. The access token is returned to the client app.

5. The client app invokes a specific API from the device to request *device information*. The device is assumed to be online and connected to the internet.

6. The device responds by sending device information, such as the device ID, serial number, and others.

7. The client app receives the full device information. It can now request an *asset token* using the *access token* and, optionally, an *actor token*. The actor token can be used to pass information (metadata) about the asset/device itself to the authorization server, which could include custom attributes known by the client app (for example, the account ID that this particular asset should be linked with). The actor token itself is in JWT format and can be signed to allow the authorization server to validate it when received. Both the access token and the actor token are posted to the authorization server to exchange them for an asset token.

8. The authorization server receives the tokens, validates them, and issues an *asset token* (in JWT format) signed using its private key/certificate. The asset token can include the standard and custom attributes that describe the asset itself, originally passed in the actor token.

9. The asset token is returned to the device. The device can use it from there onward to authenticate to the resource server (the IoT aggregation platform) and send its data.

The username-password flow

This flow utilizes the user credentials (username/password) to retrieve an access token. This flow does not return a refresh token and is meant to be used for specific use cases, mainly when the client app has been developed by the same authority as the authorization server. A high trust level can be assumed in this regard. For example, we can imagine a website called `mywebsite.com` trying to access resources from its own subdomain, `api.mywebsite.com`. However, you are encouraged to consider an alternative flow if possible. Let's have a look at its sequence diagram:

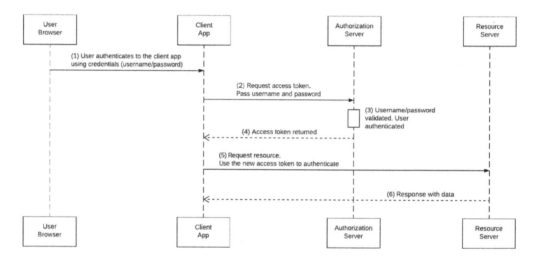

Figure 4.18 – Username-password flow

1. The user authenticates to the *client app* using credentials, assuming this is the first time the user has attempted to access the client app today and no session token is available.

2. The client app uses the received credentials to request an *access token* from the authorization server. The app will pass the following parameters: `grant_type` (the value for this flow should be `password`); `client_id` (the client app's unique ID); `client_secret` (the client secret of the app), `username` (the username captured from the user); and `password` (the password captured from the user). It is worth mentioning that when using this flow to authenticate to a Salesforce API, you need to concatenate the *Salesforce security token* to the password.

3. The authorization server validates the credentials and issues an access token.

4. The access token is returned to the client app.

5. The client app uses the access token to request the desired resource from the resource server.

6. The resource server responds by sending the requested resource.

   That concludes the key authentication flows we wanted to cover. This is by no means a complete list. However, I hope that this will get you up to speed with the most common standards and flows you may encounter in your day-to-day work.

Summary

This was a long chapter, full of in-depth technical knowledge. We started by covering some general concepts regarding IAM. We learned the importance of crafting a well-designed IAM strategy and how that could significantly impact the end user experience as well as overall system security and compliance. We then became familiar with some key IAM terms and definitions, including *identity*, *authentication*, *authorization*, *identity store*, and others. We then moved on to discover some of the most common IAM standards, including SAML, OAuth2.0, OpenID Connect, and Kerberos, along with the different types of tokens they generate or use, such as the access token, refresh token, session token, and ID token.

That all set the scene to dive deeper into some of the common and standard authentication flows. We had an in-depth review of nine different flows, including SAML IDP-initiated, SAML SP-initiated, OAuth web server, OAuth JWT flows, and others.

That concludes this part of the book, where we discussed several common architectural concepts, including data, integration, security and cryptography, and IAM. In the next part, we will dive into more Salesforce-specific knowledge areas and go through some hands-on exercises that will help you to prepare for the CTA review board.

Section 2:
Knowledge Domains Deep Dive

This section will focus on the seven knowledge domains that a CTA is expected to master. We will explore what is expected from a CTA to know and cover during the review board exam for each domain. We will get a clear understanding of Salesforce capabilities that can be used to meet certain functionalities. You will also get practical experience of how design decisions are made and justified during the CTA review board exam. We will utilize a mini hypothetical scenario for each chapter and learn how to solve and present such scenarios. We will create a set of artifacts and diagrams together that can help us deliver an engaging end-to-end solution presentation.

This section has the following topics:

- *Chapter 5, Developing a Scalable System Architecture*
- *Chapter 6, Formulating a Secure Architecture in Salesforce*
- *Chapter 7, Designing a Scalable Salesforce Data Architecture*
- *Chapter 8, Creating a Lean Solution Architecture*
- *Chapter 9, Forging an Integrated Solution*
- *Chapter 10, Development Life Cycle and Deployment Planning*
- *Chapter 11, Communicating and Socializing Your Solution*

5
Developing a Scalable System Architecture

Designing scalable solutions is a challenging task. Scalable solutions include solutions that perform well under huge customer demands or during a particular demand spike, as well as those solutions that can continuously add value to the business and enable it to embrace futuristic market trends without compromising the quality of the service.

As a Salesforce system architect, you are expected to lead the design of such solutions, utilizing the rich set of Salesforce products as well as third-party products and applications from the ecosystem. You must do all this while keeping the desired user experience, the imposed governance limits, and the nature of the client's business model in mind.

In this chapter, we'll start to dive deeper into the different Salesforce-specific knowledge areas required to pass the CTA review board. We will then put that knowledge into action by utilizing a mini hypothetical scenario that has a particular focus on system architecture. We will solve that scenario step by step, creating a justified, crisp recommendation at each stage.

We're going to cover the following main topics in this chapter:

- Understanding what you should know and be able to do as a Salesforce system architect

- Introducing the system architecture domain mini hypothetical scenario – Packt United Builder

- Determining the appropriate mix of systems, and building your solution and presentation

Let's get started!

Understanding what you should know and be able to do as a Salesforce system architect

According to Salesforce's online documentation, a CTA candidate should meet a specific set of objectives, all of which can be found at the following link: `https://trailhead.salesforce.com/en/help?article=Salesforce-Certified-Technical-Architect-Exam-Guide&search=release+exam+schedule`.

Let's have a closer look at each of these objectives.

Determining the appropriate mix of systems

The Salesforce platform is a fantastic tool that can deliver value to customers. However, it is not a solution for every challenge that you can come across. The Force.com platform provides a SaaS solution in a multitenant environment. As someone with good experience with the platform, you should understand that there are several governor limits that you need to keep in mind.

In addition, you should always aim for the best solution technically, which can deliver high value to the customer in the shortest possible time. Specialized solutions that can be *configured* to fulfill the customer's needs typically provide a shorter time to market and a higher return on investment. Make yourself familiar with some of the common **AppExchange** solutions and some other third parties. Understand their *capabilities*, as well as *when*, *where*, and *how* to use them.

These scenarios will normally be created so that they still have a very decent number of requirements that can be fulfilled using native platform capabilities. Every time you suggest a third-party solution (whether this is via AppExchange or a completely different platform), you need to provide a valid and logical justification. Cost shouldn't be the driver for your decision, as the client should normally benefit more from a better designed technical solution.

Design considerations for reporting and analytics

You need to know about the standard Salesforce reporting capabilities. The four standard report formats are as follows:

- Tabular
- Summary
- Matrix
- Joined reports

You need to get some hands-on experience with them to understand their capabilities and limitations.

Standard Salesforce reports are an excellent tool for reporting on data hosted on the platform with a limited number of records. However, they are not suitable for reporting on multi-million records objects. Trending reports and reports that span over multiple years tend to include a large number of records. Ensure you make your calculations based on the numbers shared in the scenario and – if required – based on reasonable assumptions. Then, determine your reporting strategy based on that.

When it comes to reporting requirements on a multi-million records dataset, you can consider options such as **Tableau CRM (formerly Einstein Analytics)**, **Tableau**, and other third-party BI tools such as **Power BI**. You don't have to recommend a Salesforce product. Recommend what you believe would be a better solution. Salesforce products are normally easier to integrate with the Salesforce platform. They get updated regularly with more features that continuously keep making them easier to use and integrate with other Salesforce products.

Org strategy

This is one of the key decisions you need to help guide your customer to make in real life and during the review board. You need to help your client decide whether the solution can be better delivered using a single Salesforce org or multiple orgs. Every time you come across this decision, you need to remember a number of key pros and cons for both approaches. Let's take a look.

Single org

Your solution is delivered using a single Salesforce production org. This approach has the following pros:

- Users from multiple departments and business units can work together and collaborate on the same set of records.

- It is typically easier to introduce unified processes using this approach. Think of a unified sales process using the opportunity object across multiple countries.

- All the platform data is on a single instance; therefore, it is easier to build reports that use this data.

- Security configurations, policies, profiles, and permissions are all managed in a single place.

- You already know that data visibility can be controlled using several platform features. However, having the data on the same instance can make it easier to share between different users, business units, and departments if needed.

- Each user would typically consume one Salesforce license and use one set of login credentials.

- Integration interfaces are easier to maintain, considering that we are only dealing with one Salesforce org.

- Easier to build a 360° view of the customer as we have all the platform data in one place.

However, this approach has the following cons:

- You need to keep any regulations that could prevent you from selecting this approach in mind.

- Due to the fact that you might be accommodating several business units with different processes and requirements, the single org could grow quickly in terms of complexity. This means it might end up becoming very difficult to maintain.

- You have a higher chance of hitting the governor limits.

- Due to the org's complexity and the fact that changes could impact many users and business units, innovations and changes could become slow and limited.

- The advantage you get in terms of maintaining all policies, profiles, and permissions in a single place could also be a disadvantage when these configurations grow too complex to maintain.

- Different teams could be working on conflicting features, which might end up breaking each other. A thorough regression test strategy is key in such an environment.

- Difficult to administrate locally.

Now, let's look at multi-org environments.

Multi-org

Your solution is delivered using multiple Salesforce production orgs. They can be completely autonomous or designed to be in a master-child architectural style where a master org pushes or pulls data to/from multiple child orgs or is designed without a central org, where some of the orgs are connected directly to each other in order to exchange data. This approach has the following pros:

- Fewer chances to hit the governor limits.

- Innovation and time to market are better than the single org approach since changes that are made to each org do not impact the other orgs.

- Fewer chances of conflicts between different business units as they can work on their own orgs.

- Less complexity in general in each org.

- Easy to administrate locally.

- Better ability to handle different regulatory requirements.

- Higher flexibility with release cycles since each org could have its own.

However, they also have the following cons:

- More difficult to get a unified process across the orgs. Even though you can partially facilitate this using deployment features such as the unlocked packages, the separate orgs are more difficult to govern and, therefore, are more likely to end up using different processes.

- Limited capability to collaborate with users from multiple orgs. Although some third-party products can partially bridge the gap, the single org will always provide much better capabilities in terms of collaboration.

- More difficult (and time-resource-consuming) to maintain the integration interfaces.

- Users who need to access multiple Salesforce instances will consume a Salesforce user license per instance. You may also need to introduce a single sign-on capability to provide a better user experience.

- The cost of third parties could increase, depending on their licensing structure.

- Less capability to report on data across multiple Salesforce instances. However, you can use tools such as Tableau CRM or Tableau to bridge the gap.

- There might be a need for multiple release strategies, toolsets, and teams maintaining them.

- You need to consider all of these points and more while deciding on the most suitable org structure. Sometimes, you may come across a clear requirement that pushes you directly to one option. I normally start by assuming a single org strategy and update my assumption while going through the multiple scenario requirements.

Now, let's look at mobile solutions.

Mobile solutions and strategy

There are four main types of mobile applications that you can consider in your solution:

- Salesforce mobile app (which is built and continuously updated by Salesforce)

- Native apps (which are apps built for specific platforms, such as *iOS*, using specific programming languages)

- Hybrid apps (which are apps built using cross-platform frameworks such as PhoneGap, JavaScript, HTML5, and other technologies)

- HTML5 apps (which are HTML5-based apps, developed using web technologies such as JavaScript and CSS)

Each of these applications is most suitable for specific use cases. The following table can help you determine the right mobile strategy for your solution:

Capability	Salesforce mobile app	Native app	Hybrid app	HTML5 app
Performance	Optimal	Optimal	Sub-optimal	Sub-optimal
Distribution	Via stores (such as App store). Mobile publisher can be used to facilitate branded listing	Via stores (such as App store)	Via stores (such as App store)	Web
Access to camera	Require customization	Yes	Yes	No
Access to geolocation	Yes	Yes	Yes	Yes
Access to contacts and calendar	Yes	Yes	Yes	No
Offline	Limited	Optimal	Limited	Very limited
UI capabilities (such as pinch, swipe, spread)	Good	Optimal	Limited	Limited
Customized UI	Limited	Optimal	Limited	Limited
Cross-platform	Yes	No	Yes	Yes
Branding capabilities	No (except when using mobile publisher)	Yes	Yes	Yes
Required development skills	None. Lightning components and visualforce if there is a need for custom functionalities	Native development languages such as Objective-C and Java	Specific frameworks. HTML5, Javascript, CSS	HTML5, Javascript, CSS
Speed of development	Fast	Slow	Medium	Medium

Figure 5.1 – Capability comparison between the different types of mobile apps

You are expected to explain your mobile strategy as part of your solution while considering the scenario's context and shared requirements. As a CTA, you are not only expected to simply list the different options, but you are also expected to walk the audience to the right option based on their requirements, logical assumptions, and valid justifications.

Required license types

You need to specify the required licenses for your solution, including any third-party licenses. For example, if your user uses a third-party service such as Conga Composer to generate PDF documents, you need to include that license in your solution. You don't need to go into a granular level of detail during the review board. This will be required in your real-life solutions as you will have much more time to go through the full list of license types provided by that specific vendor. These lists keep changing, and you are not expected to memorize every single one of them.

For Salesforce licenses, it is normally enough to identify and use one of the main licenses, such as Sales Cloud, Service Cloud, Salesforce Platform, Salesforce customer community, Salesforce customer community plus, Salesforce partner community, Tableau CRM, Marketing Cloud, and Pardot. You can make yourself familiar with the up-to-date list of licenses and their capabilities (particularly the objects and functionalities they are allowed to work with) by going to the following link: `https://www.salesforce.com/editions-pricing`.

Determining the right document management solution

We've already covered the different types of **document management solutions** (**DMSes**) offered by the Salesforce platform. We also briefly mentioned some of the most common solutions in the market and how to connect them to Salesforce in *Chapter 2, Core Architectural Concepts – Data*. Make sure you get some hands-on experience with Files Connect. You can check out the full official guide using this link: `https://help.salesforce.com/articleView?id=collab_admin_files_connect.htm`.

Now, let's put all this knowledge into action. In the next section, you will be introduced to a mini hypothetical scenario that focuses on the system architecture domain.

Introducing the system architecture domain mini hypothetical scenario – Packt United Builder

The following mini scenario describes a challenge with a particular client. We will go through the scenario and then create a solution step by step. To get the most out of this scenario, it is recommended that you read each paragraph, try to solve the problems yourself, and then come back to this book, go through the suggested solution, and compare it to yours and take notes.

> **Note**
> Remember that the solutions listed here are not necessarily the *only* possible solutions. Alternate solutions are acceptable as long as they are technically correct and logically justified.

Without further ado, let's proceed to the scenario.

The scenario

Packt United Builder (**PUB**) is a global property developer. It has 200 offices across 20 regions, including 15 US states, France, Germany, Italy, UAE, and Singapore. PUB provides services that include property design, build management, and maintenance. It runs its own property development projects, as well as special bespoke projects for B2B and VIP B2C customers.

PUB has over 5 million B2C customers and around 100k B2B customers, in addition to a wide network of suppliers and contractors in around roughly 50k companies.

PUB manages around 100k properties worldwide. Each property has an average of 10 smart fire monitoring devices and security devices and sensors. All of them are connected to the internet and send status messages at least every 30 seconds. PUB expects its portfolio of managed properties to grow by 10% every year for the coming 5 years.

PUB has been struggling with its disconnected systems, leading to poor data quality and additional work for its employees. They have piloted a solution based on Salesforce in Italy and want to roll that out to the other regions. Each region has its own set of property development and management regulations that the businesses must adhere to. PUB has also struggled in rolling out a universal mechanism to provision and monitor sensors in their managed properties. Currently, the data flowing from these sensors is gathered in multiple disconnected systems with low capabilities and value to the business.

Internal stakeholders

The following PUB employees will be using the new system:

- 300 designers and property development specialists, who meet with customers, design bespoke properties, and supervise the development process.

- 10,000 project managers and engineers, who supervise the building teams and report on project progress.

- 5,000 specialists, who look after the minor properties and their scheduled maintenance.

- 10,000 sales agents, who are responsible for managing the sales cycle of properties, maintenance contracts, and bespoke properties.

- 100 regional directors, who need regular reports on the property development progress, as well as the sales and property management operations.

- 50 property supervisors, who deal with cases reported across the managed properties and ensure the customers are served based on their agreed support levels.

Next, let's look at the external stakeholders.

External stakeholders

PUB has also identified external users who will be using the system:

- **5 million B2C customers**: These are individuals who purchased or leased one or more PUB properties at a given point in time.

- **100k B2B customers**: These are companies that purchased or leased one or more PUB properties at a given point in time. PUB believes that most of these records are up to date.

- **50k suppliers and contractors**: These are companies who provide different services for PUB, depending on different types of agreement.

Now, let's look at the requirements.

Requirements

PUB has shared the following requirements, which describe the current and desired solution. PUB uses several systems to run their business:

- A single custom multi-lingual public website that provides company information, office addresses, phone numbers, and inquiry forms to prospective customers. PUB plans to retain the website and update it as needed to accommodate the new system.

- Seven different monitoring systems, disconnected and with no logic built in them. These systems are hosted on-premises with publicly accessible web services that receive signals directly from the different sensors installed in the managed properties. PUB finds little value in these systems and would like to replace them with the new system, which will act as a unified platform to receive, interpret, and react to the different signals received from the different types and models of used sensors around the world.

- Four different ERP systems – one in the USA, one in Europe, one in UAE and the Middle East region, and one in Singapore and the eastern Asia region. Due to regulatory requirements for fire and safety systems, these ERP implementations have very different data requirements. For this reason, they have remained separate.

- A custom design application, designed specifically to be used by the designers on their corporate tablets. The application is used to display and adjust the different design elements while being with the client. The application creates a PDF file as an output, which should ideally be kept with the set of documents that describe the property, such as the document that explains the location of the installed sensors. Currently, all these files are stored on different systems in each region. PUB would like to use the new system as a centralized tool to store such documents in a structured and regionally compliant way. PUB has a preference to utilize their newly purchased Microsoft SharePoint Online software for this, as long as it can be fully integrated with the new system.

- PUB has a set of CRMs (not Salesforce, except Italy) that are used to track the project development and sales activities, which are different by nature in each region. PUB would like all of these disconnected applications to be replaced with the new system. Some of these CRMs are integrated with PUB's regional ERP systems. PUB would like to have the new system fully integrated with the ERP systems so that customer and order data can be replicated to the right ERP system based on the region.

- PUB has a central system that's used for scheduled maintenance operations. The system had several challenges during the past years and is now considered inefficient. PUB would like it to be replaced with the new system.

- All existing systems are connected with the corporate Azure **Active Directory (AD)** for internal user single sign-on. PUB would like to still have the new system utilizing Azure AD for single sign-on between the new system and the retained ERPs.

- Germany has rolled out a mobile application that allows employees to access the German CRM from anywhere in the world, as long as they are connected to the internet. PUB would like to have something similar for the new system to be rolled out globally.

In addition to these points, PUB realizes that in order to deliver the best customer experience, it also needs the following capabilities delivered as part of the new system:

- Customers should be able to download a PUB-branded mobile application to view their online account, raise tickets against their properties, and update their profile. The application should provide a very modern and bespoke user experience and UI.

- PUB does little communication with its customers currently. PUB would like to be able to send regular marketing materials to its customers based on their preferences.

- PUB realizes that the data that's gathered from the sensors in the managed properties could reveal valuable business trends that can help PUB deliver a better and more efficient service. The same is also applicable to the maintenance data. PUB would like to be able to analyze data from the past 5 years in order to come up with valuable market trends.

PUB would like to get your assistance in designing a scalable and future-embracing solution based on their shared requirements and vision.

Determining the appropriate mix of systems, and building your solution and presentation

You would typically start by quickly skimming through the scenario to understand the big picture and build some initial thoughts about the solution. Then, you should go through the scenario again, section by section, and incrementally build your solution.

Understanding the current situation

Starting with the first part of the scenario, the sections starting with the statements *The following PUB employees will be using the new system* and *PUB has identified external users who will also be using the system* can help us identify the different roles and personas involved and determine the licenses needed for each.

However, that paragraph on its own can give us a good idea of the type of licenses we will need, though we will need to cover the entire scenario before we can finalize it. We can start by drawing the actors diagram. We will add the licenses to it once we have formalized a better idea for the solution. At this stage, the actors diagram looks as follows:

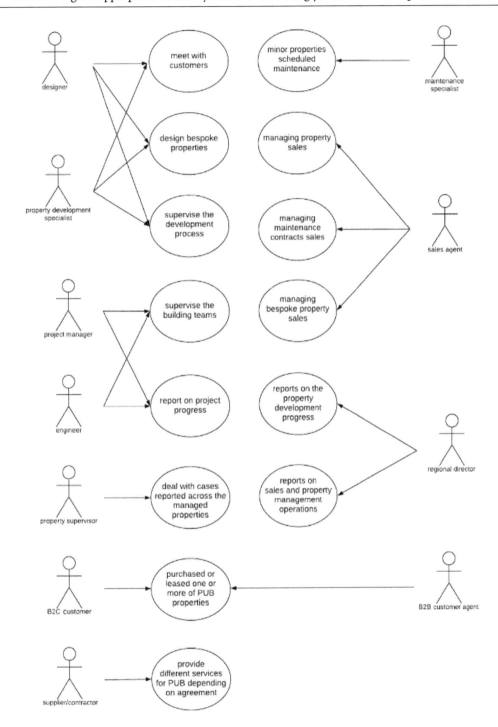

Figure 5.2 – Actors diagram – first draft

The *Requirements* section describes the current PUB system landscape and how they see the to-be landscape. This section also contains several hints that can help us determine the right org strategy and mobile strategy, in addition to some other requirements.

The structure of the CTA review board scenario could be a bit different, especially considering that full scenarios are much longer than this mini scenario. However, in most cases, there will be a section describing the current landscape, as well as several other sections providing multiple requirements that can help you determine the to-be landscape and other design decisions related to system architecture.

Diving into the shared requirements

Let's go through the requirements one by one and identify the different requirements in them so that we can add more elements to our solution. The first requirement starts with the following statement:

A single custom multi-lingual public website that provides company information, office addresses, phone numbers, and inquiry forms to prospective customers

Based on this statement, we can start by adding the custom website to the to-be landscape. We know that we are going to propose Salesforce as part of the solution, and we can utilize web-to-lead forms to provide an integrated mechanism for the inquiry forms. We can have all of this on our landscape diagram and integration interfaces. These artifacts will now look as follows:

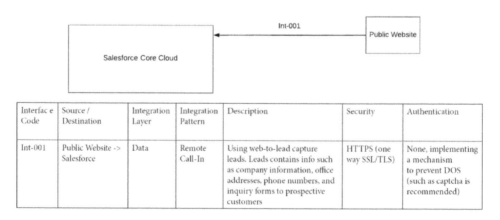

Interface Code	Source / Destination	Integration Layer	Integration Pattern	Description	Security	Authentication
Int-001	Public Website -> Salesforce	Data	Remote Call-In	Using web-to-lead capture leads. Leads contains info such as company information, office addresses, phone numbers, and inquiry forms to prospective customers	HTTPS (one way SSL/TLS)	None, implementing a mechanism to prevent DOS (such as captcha is recommended)

Figure 5.3 – Landscape architecture and integration interfaces

Now, let's move on to the next requirement, which starts with the following statement:

Seven different monitoring systems, disconnected and with no logic built in them

This is where we learn about seven IoT platform systems that PUB is not particularly a fan of. We can add these systems to the landscape diagram and highlight that they are going to be retired. Including the retiring systems in your diagram will help you tell the full story during the presentation. Reading through the scenario, we understand that PUB is looking for a unified platform that can integrate with all kinds of sensors and provide some sort of intelligence. This is communicated via the statement *react to the different signals received.* The question here is, can we utilize the Salesforce core cloud as a platform to receive these messages? We know that we can develop a really good decision engine on Salesforce, but we also know that there are several platform limitations we should keep in mind.

The scenario mentioned that there are 100k properties worldwide, each with an average of 10 sensors, and each sensor sends two messages every minute. This means that every day, there are *100,000 * 10 * 2 * 60 * 24 = 2,880,000.000* messages being received. Even without considering the data storage required to store that number of messages, you can clearly see that this number would hit the governance limit of the number of inbound API calls.

Buying more allowance is not the right decision here, either. This is a very high-cost solution that is not justified, mainly because you are using the platform for something it is not designed for. Alternatively, you should consider an off-platform solution.

You could propose a solution that you are familiar with and know that it fulfills the requirements, or you could simply suggest a custom-built application hosted on top of a PaaS platform such as **AWS** or **Heroku**. *PaaS* platforms are designed to deal with such massive amounts of traffic; some even provide built-in modules to deal with IoT devices.

Selecting Heroku has its advantages as you can utilize **Heroku Connect** to sync data with Salesforce core if needed. In real life, several other factors impact this decision. During the review board, you can simply play it safe and pick Heroku, just in case you need to utilize Heroku Connect to fulfill other requirements that you haven't identified yet.

Do you need an *ESB* or an *API manager* to receive these messages before passing them to Heroku? Currently, there is no requirement that drives this decision. You can easily develop secure custom web services and expose them via Heroku. These web services are publicly accessible because Heroku itself is cloud-based. We haven't come across a requirement that justifies including an ESB in the landscape. The landscape architecture diagram and the integration interfaces table will now look as follows:

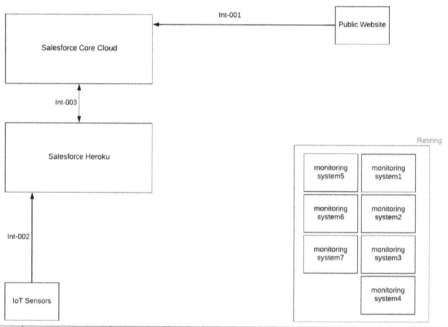

Interface Code	Source / Destination	Integration Layer	Integration Pattern	Description	Security	Authentication
Int-001	Public Website -> Salesforce	Data	Remote Call-In	Using web-to-lead capture leads. Leads contains info such as company information, office addresses, phone numbers, and inquiry forms to prospective customers	HTTPS (one way SSL/TLS)	None, implementing a mechanism to prevent DOS (such as captcha is recommended)
Int-002	IoT sensors -> Heroku	Data	Remote Call-In	Sensors send regular status update toHeroku roughly every 30 seconds	HTTPS (one way SSL/TLS)	oAuth 2.0 asset token flow
Int-003	Salesforce <-> Heroku	Data	Batch Data sync - Asynch	Bi-directional data synch between Salesforce core cloud (force.com) and Heroku using Heroku connect. Assumed objects: Account and cases	HTTPS (one way SSL/TLS)	oAuth 2.0 web-server flow

Figure 5.4 – Landscape architecture and Integration interfaces – second draft

Let's look at the next requirement, which starts with the following statement:

Four different ERP systems. One in the USA, one in Europe, one in UAE and the Middle East region, and one in Singapore and the eastern Asia region

Based on this statement, we know that these ERPs will continue to be part of the landscape, and we also learn new and important information. There are strict regulatory requirements regarding the way data is stored for fire and safety systems in each region. This could help us determine the right org strategy approach.

Remember that you are expected to determine the org strategy as part of your solution. You will find requirements that can help guide you; we can find one of these requirements here. I personally always start by assuming that the solution will be delivered using a single org, then go through the requirements one by one and, at each stage, reevaluate and determine whether that assumption is still valid.

In this case, the question that should come to your mind is, *Can I meet these regulatory requirements using a single Salesforce org?* Clearly, this wasn't possible with the ERP systems, so it is fair to assume that you won't be able to meet that using a single Salesforce instance. Salesforce Shield can't help you in this situation, and neither would the sharing and visibility settings.

Based on that, you should think of selecting a multi-org strategy. You need to justify your decision during the presentation without exhausting the topic or spending more time on it than you should. For example, you could summarize your decision in the following way:

I am proposing a multi-org strategy due to the regulatory requirement for fire and safety systems data. These regulations cannot be met using a single org. Therefore, I am proposing an org strategy where each region will have its own Salesforce org. Each org will be hosted locally within the region. I am also assuming that the Italian org can be repurposed to become the European org. The scenario didn't specify the regulatory requirements exactly, so I am assuming that hosting this data within the same region would be sufficient to stay compliant. The scenario didn't mention a need for a unified global process across regions either, so I am assuming that the four regional orgs are completely autonomous.

This statement justifies your rationale and also explains the assumptions you used to come up with this decision. In most cases, the scenarios will be designed to allow you some room for assumptions. Be reasonable and logical with your assumptions, and communicate them clearly. Reading and presenting the preceding paragraph shouldn't take more than 60-90 seconds. Your presentation time is very precious, and you should make the most of it.

Let's move on to the next paragraph/bullet point, which starts with the following line:

A custom design application, designed specifically to be used by the designers on their corporate tablets

There are two requirements in this paragraph. The custom-built tablet application has to use the new system to store the generated PDFs. Moreover, these PDFs have to be stored in an enterprise-level DMS. With a clear preference from PUB to utilize Microsoft SharePoint for that, **Files Connect** is a strong tool we can use to expose documents stored in SharePoint into Salesforce. However, you need to think about how you will get the documents into SharePoint to begin with.

If you have used Files Connect and are comfortable with its capabilities, then you can design your solutions based on it. Otherwise, pick a solution that you *know works*. Don't try to force every single requirement into a Salesforce feature just because you are doing a Salesforce exam. You need to propose a solution that you know works and rationally justify using it.

In this case, I feel more comfortable to propose updating the tablet app so that it uses both the Salesforce SDK and SharePoint APIs. Then, it can use these APIs to upload the files directly into SharePoint. Files Connect can be used to expose these files in Salesforce later on if needed. We haven't come across this requirement yet. You will need to explain how you are planning to authenticate to SharePoint.

Dedicated mini scenarios for such requirements are provided in *Chapter 6, Formulating a Secure Architecture in Salesforce*. For the time being, you can explain your proposed solution for this paragraph's requirements like so:

> *In order to meet the requirement to store the generated PDF, I am proposing updating the tablet app so that we can use SharePoint APIs to upload the PDF directly into SharePoint. I have assumed that the tablet app can be updated as it is custom developed. I have also assumed that it is a native app to allow the desired UI capabilities. Once the PDFs have been uploaded into SharePoint, they can be exposed to Salesforce using Files Connect. The actual files will continue to be stored in SharePoint, but only while their links are available in Salesforce.*

I am also proposing updating the tablet app so that it uses the Salesforce
SDK in order to retrieve information such as customer name and ID, which
will be required to upload the PDF to the right location. The tablet app will
authenticate to SharePoint and Salesforce using the OpenID Connect user-
agent flow. Each PUB designer will have a user created in both SharePoint
and Salesforce. I am assuming I can use the employee ID as a federation
identifier to map the users across systems

Please note that at this stage, you have no details about the IDP being used by PUB. However, a few requirements ahead, you will notice the following statement:

All existing systems are connected with the corporate Azure Active Directory (AD) for
internal user single sign-on.

You can now update your landscape architecture diagram and integration interfaces accordingly. Keep doing that on an incremental basis. You might need to change and redraw things at this stage. Therefore, it is recommended to start with a scratch paper and then copy the artifacts into their final form so that you can make them look as professional as possible.

Let's move on to the next paragraph/bullet point, which starts with the following line:

PUB has a set of CRMs (not Salesforce, except Italy) that are used to track the project development and sales activities, which are different by nature in each region

This seems aligned with the plan to utilize a multi-org strategy. PUB wants to integrate each of the regional ERPs with the new system, which will be based on Salesforce. Considering that we are proposing a multi-org strategy, it is fair to assume that each of these ERPs will be integrated with its counterpart regional CRM (that is, the regional Salesforce instance).

The next thing that should come to your mind is *how* – how to integrate Salesforce with PUB's ERPs. Going back to the topics we covered in *Chapter 3, Core Architectural Concepts – Integration and Cryptography*, you know that these systems can be integrated in multiple ways. Considering the pros and cons we covered in that chapter about using middleware and considering the different tools we went through previously, you should consider the following options:

- **Utilize an ESB**: Considering that ESBs are more capable of handling complex orchestration requirements

- **Utilize an ETL tool**: Considering that ETL tools are designed for heavy-duty data replication

You should not consider a point-to-point integration here. You are expected to come up with the most suitable solution from a technical perspective. Lean architecture and the ability to scale for an enterprise should always be part of your target; both cannot be achieved with point-to-point integrations.

The solution didn't specify the number of records that are expected to be transferred between the systems. It didn't specify any orchestration requirements, either. You have to make some assumptions here, clearly communicate them, and use them as the base for your proposed solution.

In the review board, you are expected to come up with a *clear recommended solution* based on the communicated requirements, assumptions, and logic. You can mention the other options, but you must *clearly select* and *communicate the one* you recommend.

You can explain your proposed solution for this paragraph's requirements like so:

In order to meet the requirement of integrating the regional ERPs with the new system – which is based on Salesforce – I propose using an ESB as a middleware. There has been no communicated requirement describing the amount of daily data being exchanged between these systems. ETLs are better at handling bulk data replications. Still, I assumed that the number of records is relatively low and therefore preferred to use an ESB, considering its superior capabilities in handling data orchestration requirements, which is likely to be required by the enterprise. Considering that the new solution will be based on a multi-org strategy, each of the ERPs will be integrated with its regional Salesforce instance. I have also assumed that the ESB will be cloud-based and regionally hosted to ensure that data never leaves the region. I am proposing MuleSoft as an ESB because it is one of the leading ESBs in the market with built-in Salesforce connectors

Whenever you are proposing to use a third party, *you must name it*. We've come across two examples so far: we named the proposed PaaS platform, and now we've named the integration middleware. You don't have to pick Salesforce-owned products. You should pick a product that you are familiar with and that you know for sure will fulfill the requirement. Again, remember that you should cover this requirement without unnecessarily losing time. The preceding paragraph can be presented in 60-90 seconds.

Let's move on to the next requirement, which starts with the following line:

PUB has a central system that's used for scheduled maintenance operations

This is a straightforward requirement. PUB wants to replace its legacy scheduled maintenance system with a new one. You don't need to be an expert in field service solutions, but you should be familiar with some of them and understand the capabilities they offer. In this case, your proposed solution could be as follows:

> *In order to fulfill this requirement, I propose using Salesforce Field Service. It can be configured to generate scheduled maintenance work orders, which would increase the efficiency of the field service and maintenance team.*

> **Note**
>
> Remember to add Salesforce Field Service to your diagram. It is a package that gets installed into your org, so make sure your diagram reflects that. Also, don't forget to include the retiring legacy system. Once this diagram is ready, it will help you present your solution engagingly and attractively.

Let's move on to the next requirement, which starts with the following line:

All existing systems are connected with the corporate Azure Active Directory (AD) for internal user single sign-on

We've come across this requirement previously. The scenario is unlikely to clearly mention the system that acts as an identity provider. You should have enough market knowledge to recognize that Azure AD is one of the leading products in this space. Based on the scenario, it must be acting as the identity provider in this landscape. Ensure you include single sign-on interfaces as part of your landscape diagram and integration interfaces list.

Let's move on to the next requirement, which starts with the following line:

Germany has rolled out a mobile application that allows employees to access the German CRM from anywhere in the world, as long as they are connected to the internet

Clearly, this is a mobile application requirement. For such requirements, you should be able to select the right mobile strategy. We provided an example of this earlier with the tablet app. This paragraph doesn't contain enough information to help you select the right mobile strategy, but the next paragraph does. It starts with the following statement:

Customers should be able to download a PUB-branded mobile application to view their online account, raise up tickets against their properties, and update their profile.

You can select a mobile strategy based on the Salesforce mobile app, a native app, a hybrid app, or an HTML5-based app. Considering that the application should be PUB-branded, you might think that the Salesforce mobile app might not be suitable. However, Salesforce has recently launched a new service called *mobile publishers,* which allows us to deliver a branded version of its mobile app to end customers. All possible mobile strategies can provide branding, access to an online profile, and integration with Salesforce. However, the differentiating requirement is the one related to UI. PUB is looking for a sophisticated and bespoke UI that drives a certain user experience. In this case, your best bet would be on a native app. Your proposed solution could be as follows:

> *Considering the requirement of having a bespoke, modern, and sophisticated mobile UI, I propose developing this mobile application as a native app. Perhaps we can utilize the mobile app developed by Germany and update it to use the Salesforce mobile SDK, or simply build it from scratch. Customers would still utilize a customer community license in order to authenticate to Salesforce. The mobile app would utilize the OpenID Connect user-agent flow.*

You need to explain the solution end to end. You can't skip the part explaining how the users would authenticate to Salesforce. Don't leave any loose ends. Your solutions have to be clear and solid end to end. Also, note that for customers, you are proposing using Salesforce as the identity provider. This should be fine, considering that the scenario mentioned that Azure AD is mainly used for internal users.

> **Note**
> Remember to add the customers' native mobile app and its integration interface to your artifacts.

Let's move on to the next requirement, which is as follows:

PUB does little communication with its customers currently. PUB would like to be able to send regular marketing materials to its customers based on their preferences

The question that should come to your mind is: *What is the most suitable solution in the Salesforce ecosystem for such a requirement?* You need significant customizations in core clouds in order to build this capability, and you would still run against different limitations.

An external system is definitely an option, but the most obvious solution and the one that offers the best out-of-the-box integration with the core cloud is **Marketing Cloud**. Marketing Cloud can be used to segment customers based on their preferences. Your proposed solution could be as follows:

> *I am proposing using Marketing Cloud to fulfill this requirement. Marketing Cloud can be used to segment customers based on their preferences. Considering the regulation requirements, there will be a different Marketing Cloud instance per region. The standard Marketing Cloud connector can be used to integrate the regional core cloud with its equivalent Marketing Cloud instance. The contact ID in the core cloud will be used as a subscriber key in the Marketing Cloud.*

There is a continuous growth of cross-cloud architectural concepts. As a CTA, you are expected to have a very solid knowledge of the Salesforce platform (mostly, Force.com, or what is also known as core clouds). However, you still need to have some familiarity with the common tools and technologies from the Salesforce ecosystem and how they interact with each other.

Marketing Cloud is a very common element of today's Salesforce landscape, and you need to have a basic understanding of its capabilities and how it integrates with the core clouds. It's worth mentioning that the Marketing Cloud connector utilizes the **OAuth 2.0 client credentials flow** to authenticate to Marketing Cloud. This particular flow is not supported by the Salesforce platform (to authenticate inbound integrations) while it is supported by Marketing Cloud. You can read more about it and the Marketing Cloud connectors managed package at https://developer.salesforce.com/docs/atlas.en-us.mc-app-development.meta/mc-app-development/integration-s2s-client-credentials.htm.

Let's move on to the next requirement, which starts with the following line:

PUB realizes that the data that's gathered from the sensors in the managed properties could reveal valuable business trends that can help PUB deliver a better and more efficient service

The sensors' data is stored in Heroku's *Postgres database*, as per our proposed solution. PUB wants to make use of this data now in some business intelligence operations. Earlier, we calculated that we would roughly receive 2,880,000,000 messages daily. This number will become even bigger if we are looking to report on data stored in the past 5 years.

Tableau CRM is a solid analytics solution, but it is not designed to handle that amount of data. **Tableau** is. However, before jumping to the conclusion that Tableau is the right solution, you need to analyze the requirement and think about what value we would get from storing that amount of data.

Most of the time, the sensors will simply send the same status message – except when something happens that impacts their readings. It is fair to assume that you can *aggregate* these readings using *custom code*, which would ensure that you are still getting the value of the data but without unnecessarily storing too much of it. You can develop that custom module on Heroku, and then use Tableau CRM on top of it to provide the required business intelligence. Your proposed solution could be as follows:

> *Considering the amount of received data from the sensors, I propose developing a custom module in Heroku to aggregate the received readings and ensure we only keep the data that could represent value to the business. This should reduce the amount of data to report on significantly. We can use a policy to aggregate all the sensors' data that is more than 1 year old. We can then utilize Tableau CRM to provide high-value trending reports to the business.*

Keep in mind that the solutions we are suggesting here are based on assumptions and valid logic. However, that doesn't mean that they are the *only* solutions. There are multiple possible ways to solve these requirements, and they could be accepted by the CTA judges as long as they are based on logical assumptions and rationale.

With that, we have reached the end of the scenario. Congratulations! We have all that we need now in order to fine-tune our artifacts and deliver a ground-breaking presentation.

Let's go back to our actors diagram and try to add the licenses to it. You typically need to understand the business processes and draw the data model before you can determine the exact types of licenses you will need. For this mini scenario, we didn't include requirements about the business processes. The full mock scenarios in *Chapter 12, Practice the Review Board – First Mock*, and *Chapter 14, Practice the Review Board – Second Mock*, will include that. Based on what we have in the scenario, we can assume that the sales process will be implemented using the out-of-the-box opportunity management capabilities that are available, which means that the sales agents would need a Sales Cloud opportunity.

Designers and property development specialists might utilize a set of custom objects to gather customer requirements and deliver the property design. However, they will likely need access to the sales details, which are stored on the opportunity. Therefore, they would also need a sales cloud license. On the other hand, the project manager and engineer would likely work with custom objects only, which means we can utilize a Salesforce platform license for them.

Property supervisor and maintenance specialists would need to deal with cases and entitlements. Therefore, they are assigned a Service Cloud license. On top of this, the maintenance specialist would need a Salesforce Field Service license. The regional director needs to report on sales opportunities, so they would also need a sales cloud license. Moreover, we can assume that they would be using the trending reports from Tableau CRM. The B2C customer and B2B customer agent need access to the Salesforce community. The customer community license should be sufficient for this. In comparison, we can assume that the supplier/contractor would need access to the sold property, as well as any contracts related to it. We can use a partner community license for that and develop a specific partner community as part of the landscape.

Our actors and licenses diagram now looks much more interesting and can help us tell a story about the personas involved in this solution, what they are expected to do, and what kind of licenses they need:

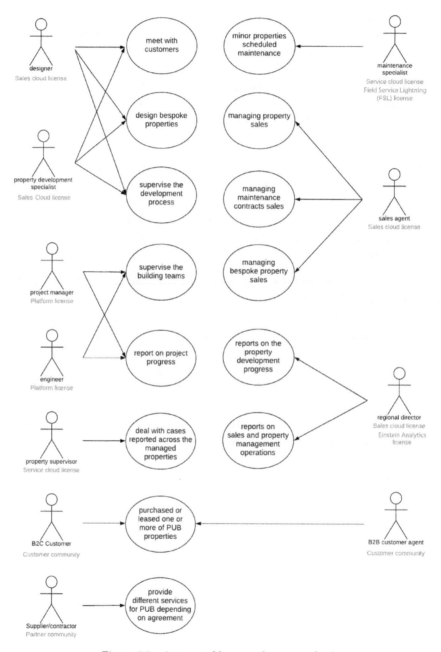

Figure 5.5 – Actors and licenses diagram – final

Now, let's have a look at our landscape architecture diagram and our list of integration interfaces:

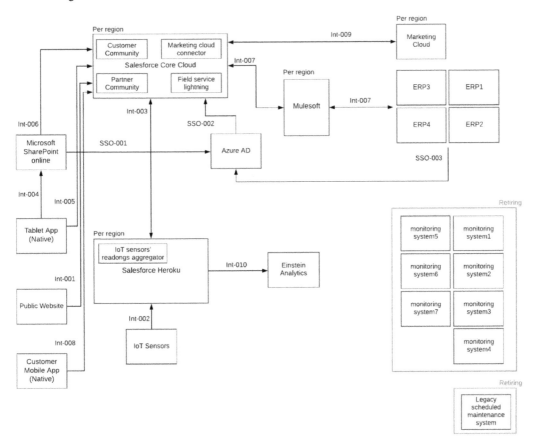

Interface Code	Source / Destination	Integration Layer	Integration Pattern	Description	Security	Authentication
Int-001	Public Website - > Salesforce	Data	Remote Call-In	Using web-to-lead capture leads. Leads contains info such as company information, office addresses, phone numbers, and inquiry forms to prospective customers	HTTPS (one way SSL/TLS)	None, implementing a mechanism to prevent DOS (such as captcha is recommended)
Int-002	IoT sensors -> Heroku	Data	Remote Call-In	Sensors send regular status update to Heroku roughly every 30 seconds	HTTPS (one way SSL/TLS)	oAuth 2.0 asset token flow
Int-003	Salesforce <-> Heroku	Data	Batch Data sync - Asynch	Bi-directional data synch between Salesforce core cloud (force.com) and Heroku using Heroku connect. Assumed objects: Account and cases	HTTPS (one way SSL/TLS)	oAuth 2.0 web-server flow
Int-004	Tablet app -> MS SharePoint Online	Data	Remote Process Invocation— Request and Reply	Upload documents from the tablet app to SharePoint using SharePoint APIs	HTTPS (one way SSL/TLS)	OpenID Connect user-agent flow
Int-005	Tablet app -> Salesforce	Data	Remote Call-In	Pull data from Salesforce such as customer information and ID	HTTPS (one way SSL/TLS)	OpenID Connect user-agent flow
Int-006	MS SharePoint Online -> Salesforce	Data	Batch Data sync - Asynch	Using Files Connect, retrieve links to documents stored in SharePoint and display them in Salesforce	HTTPS (one way SSL/TLS)	OpenID Connect web-server flow
Int-007	Salesforce <-> Mulesoft <-> ERPs	Data	Batch Data sync - Asynch	A scheduled batch job to synch customer and order data from Salesforce to the ERPs. Updates to these records should be synched back from the ERPs to Salesforce. The frequency of the scheduled job is assumed to be 15 minutes	HTTPS (two way SSL/ TLS) between Salesforce and Mulesoft. HTTPS (one way SSL/ TLS) Between Mulesoft and the ERPs	OpenID Connect JWT flow
Int-008	Mobile app -> Salesforce	Data	Remote Process Invocation— Request and Reply	Retrieve and update customer data such as profile using Salesforce REST API	HTTPS (one way SSL/TLS)	OpenID Connect user-agent flow
Int-009	Salesforce <-> Marketing cloud	Data	Batch Data sync - Asynch	Synch data such as contacts and leads from Salesforce to Marketing cloud and vice versa using the marketing cloud connector	HTTPS (one way SSL/TLS)	oAuth 2.0 Client Credentials flow (to authenticate to Marketing cloud) oAuth 2.0 web-server flow (to authenticate to Salesforce)
Int-010	Heroku -> Tableau CRM	Data	Batch Data sync - Asynch	Copy aggregated sensors' readings data from Heroku to Tableau CRM	HTTPS (one way SSL/TLS)	OpenID Connect web-server flow
SSO-001	SSO for MS Share Point using Azure AD as IDP	SSO	SSO – SAML 2.0	SSO using SAML 2.0 with Azure AD as IDP SP initiated flow	HTTPS (one way SSL/TLS)	SAML 2.0 SP initiated flow
SSO-002	SSO for Salesforce using Azure AD as IDP	SSO	SSO – SAML 2.0	SSO using SAML 2.0 with Azure AD as IDP SP initiated flow	HTTPS (one way SSL/TLS)	SAML 2.0 SP initiated flow
SSO-003	SSO for ERP systems using Azure AD as IDP	SSO	SSO – SAML 2.0	SSO using SAML 2.0 with Azure AD as IDP SP initiated flow	HTTPS (one way SSL/TLS)	SAML 2.0 SP initiated flow

Figure 5.6 – Landscape architecture and integration interfaces – final

That concludes our first mini scenario. You can try to re-solve this scenario as many times as needed. I recommend that you do it with no time restrictions for the first time, with an aim to create the best possible artifacts and presentation pitches.

You can then try to add some time restrictions, such as a 90-minute limit, to create your end-to-end solution.

Summary

In this chapter, we dived into the details of the system architecture domain. We learned what is expected from a CTA to cover and at what level of detail. We then tackled a mini hypothetical scenario that focused on system architecture, and we solv it together and created some effective presentation pitches.

We had to make several design decisions during the solution, all while making some assumptions and a lot of justifications. In real-life projects, you need to document all of these design decisions to avoid losing any valuable information in the future.

We then came across the challenge of determining the right org strategy, and we provided a clear, justified recommendation based on the shared requirements. We also tacked the challenge of coming up with a mobile strategy. We provided a clear list of required licenses and explained why we believe they are the most suitable ones for each group of users.

Finally, we tackled some other challenges, such as recommending a DMS solution. We had to deal with the tricky part of determining whether an on-platform or off-platform solution is required to handle a particular requirement, such as mass IoT data consumption.

We are now ready to move on to the next chapter, where we will go through the second domain you need to master: security.

6
Formulating a Secure Architecture in Salesforce

In this chapter, we will continue with other Salesforce-specific knowledge areas required to pass the CTA review board. This time, we will tackle the **security domain**.

Designing a secure system has never been more important than today with the continuous move toward customer-centric solutions and the rise of connected devices.

Salesforce has reshaped our common understanding of CRM. We see more and more enterprises adopting Salesforce as their *central engagement platform*, with dozens of inbound and outbound integrations with different other systems.

As a Salesforce security architect, you are expected to utilize the rich set of Salesforce functionalities available to design a solid security architecture. You are also expected to define the security measures needed to protect the data while being transferred from and to other systems. You have to master the different ways that license types and object relationships impact your data visibility – particularly while dealing with Salesforce communities or complex sharing and visibility requirements.

The security domain is one of the widest domains in Salesforce. It covers many different and diverse functionalities and is also impacted by other domains. We will come across topics related to the security architecture in the other chapters to come, considering the tight relationship it has with other domains such as *data architecture*. In this chapter, we're going to cover the following main topics:

- Understanding what you should be able to do as a security architect

- Introducing the security architecture domain (mini hypothetical scenario) – Packt Innovative Retailers

- Utilizing the appropriate security mechanisms and building your solution and presentation

> **Note**
> You are advised to utilize the cryptography section of *Chapter 3, Core Architectural Concepts – Integration and Cryptography*, and the authentication flows listed in *Chapter 4, Core Architectural Concepts – Identity and Access Management*, as references to help you make the most out of this chapter.

Let's get started!

Understanding what you should be able to do as a security architect

According to Salesforce's online documentation, you should be able to meet a specific set of objectives that can be found at the following link: `https://trailhead.salesforce.com/en/help?article=Salesforce-Certified-Technical-Architect-Exam-Guide&search=release+exam+schedule`.

Let's have a closer look at each of these objectives.

Utilizing the appropriate platform security mechanisms

Salesforce comes with a rich set of functionalities and tools that you can use to manage access to data. These functionalities can be considered stacked up on *multiple levels*. You need to have a good understanding of each of these capabilities, how they work, and what their limitations are. You also need to practice configuring these features in order to get a solid understanding of their behaviors. Using these tools, you can configure security on multiple levels:

- Org
- Object
- Record
- Field levels

The following diagram illustrates these different levels:

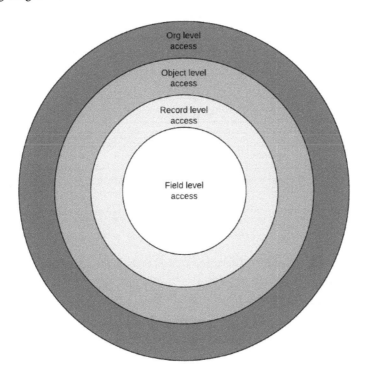

Figure 6.1 – Data access-control level

Object and field levels are sometimes considered one combined level, and it allows you to configure *which objects and fields* the user can have access to and what exactly they will be able to perform over these objects and fields. On the other hand, **record-level** access determines which *records* – out of the objects a user has access to – are visible to that user and if they can *view* it only or also *edit* it.

The record owner always has full access to a record. When you think of the data sharing and visibility architecture, it is always about determining what records the current users *don't own* but still require access to. **Org-level** access is about ensuring the data in your org cannot be accessed by users in other orgs, in addition to different security mechanisms to ensure users can access your org securely.

The tools and functionalities that can help you design and configure the data sharing and visibility architecture are listed in the following diagram:

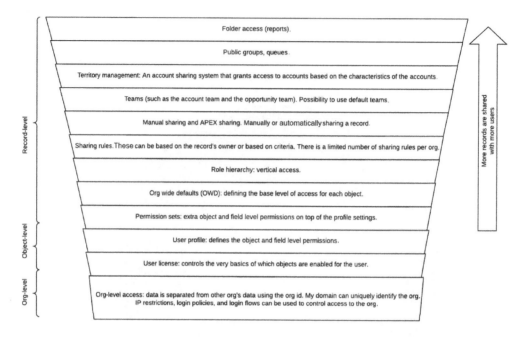

Figure 6.2 – Salesforce data access control tools and functionalities

At the very bottom, you can see the org-level security mechanisms. They ensure that the data of one org is not mixed with data from others. Salesforce is based on a multitenant architecture, which means that data belonging to multiple tenants could be hosted on the same platform. The org ID ensures that users of one org can access the data that belongs to that org only.

The other org-level security functionalities are meant to protect the org itself from unauthorized access.

Moving up, there's the object-level security mechanisms, which start by controlling which objects are accessible for a particular user license. For example, suppose the license granted for a particular user doesn't allow access to the opportunity object. In that case, all the higher-level security mechanisms will adhere to this restriction, which means that you won't be able to grant a user access to the opportunity via profiles or permission sets.

If we continue moving up, we will come across the record-level security mechanisms, which control access to the records of a specific object – assuming that the user has access to the object itself from the lower object-level layer. This starts with the **org wide defaults (OWD)**, which set the default access levels for object records. For example, the OWD of the accounts could be private, public read-only, or public read-write. This defines the users' access level for account records they don't own, assuming they have access to the account object.

Role hierarchies, sharing rules, and other sharing mechanisms can be used to grant users access to more records or higher privilege levels. For example, you can use criteria-based sharing rules to grant users in specific role access to account records that meet certain criteria.

There are other factors that impact these tools and functionalities, such as the structure of the data model and the relationship types between the objects.

Designing a secure portal architecture

The **Salesforce community** functionality allows you to design and expose secure customer and partner portals. The *external apps* license can also help you develop custom applications for your internal employees.

Data can be shared with the partner license and the external app license users using the *standard sharing mechanisms* such as *sharing rules*. Users with the **Customer Community Plus license** can also benefit from this. While you can use *sharing sets* to share data with the customer community users, Salesforce has recently made that functionality available for the Customer Community Plus and partner users as well. You can learn more about the different types of community licenses at the following link: `https://help.salesforce.com/articleView?id=users_license_types_communities.htm&type=5`.

The CTA review board scenarios are *likely* to contain one or more customer requirements that can be solutioned using Salesforce communities. You are strongly encouraged to try out the different types of communities and configure them by hand.

Moreover, you need to familiarize yourself with the *social sign-on* capability that is becoming more popular nowadays. With the rise of social media, most enterprises allow their customers to log into secure portals using their social media credentials. Social media networks normally support **OpenID Connect** and/or **OAuth2.0** standards. Considering that Salesforce is a secure platform that can safely store a consumer secret, the flow that's used for social sign-in is the *web server flow,* which we covered in *Chapter 4, Core Architectural Concepts – Identity and Access Management*.

Salesforce has built-in support for some social networks such as Facebook, LinkedIn, and Twitter.

Controlling record-level security using declarative and/or programmatic features

You need to be familiar with all the declarative record-level security features illustrated in the preceding diagram. Besides these, you need to understand *how* Salesforce sharing works. This will help you determine when it is appropriate to select a declarative versus a programmatic sharing mechanism.

The process of creating and calculating record access data

Every time a user attempts to access a Salesforce record by any means (such as opening a record page, viewing it in list views, running a report, accessing it via an API, or even searching for it using global search), Salesforce checks the security configurations for that record to determine the *access level* allowed for this user. As you can imagine, this process could be very expensive and resource-consuming. This happens, especially while working with a complex environment with millions of records, complex hierarchies, dozens of sharing rules, and several portals. Doing such complex calculations to determine if the user can or can't access these records could take a significantly long time.

That is why Salesforce calculates record access data when – and only when – there is a need to do so, which is normally when the configurations are modified.

Salesforce calculates the record access data and persists it so that it can be quickly accessed and evaluated whenever needed. This ensures optimal system performance and means that you need to consider the impact of changing your data security and sharing mechanisms before making any modifications.

You can share records programmatically, and if your Apex class has been developed to use the *with sharing* keyword, then your class will respect the sharing and visibility rules in your org. Classes with the keyword *without sharing* will ignore sharing settings and retrieve all records from a certain object, even if the currently executing user does not have access to some or all these records. This is a very powerful tool that you should use wisely as it might cause a data leak. It is strongly recommended that you design your APEX classes so that they always use the *with sharing* keyword.

The different types of access grants

Salesforce uses *four* different types of access grants to determine how much access a user or group has to a particular object with a private or public read-only OWD setting. These four grants are as follows:

- **Implicit grants**: This is also known as **built-in sharing**. These are non-configurable special case grants that are built-in within the platform. For example, users who have access to child opportunities can also view their parent account record. The same is also true if the users have access to view the account object, they get access to its related opportunities, cases, and contacts.

- **Explicit grants**: These grants are used when the records are explicitly shared with specific users or groups.

> **Particularly in the following use cases:**
>
> A user becomes the owner of a record.
>
> A queue becomes the owner of a record.
>
> A record is shared – via a sharing rule – to a user, a public group, a queue, a role, or a territory.
>
> A record is shared with a user using an assignment rule.
>
> A record is shared with a territory using a territory assignment rule.
>
> A record is shared manually with another user, a public group, a queue, a role, or a territory.
>
> A user is added to an account, opportunity, or case team.
>
> A record is shared programmatically with a user, a public group, a queue, a role, or a territory.

Behind the scenes, Salesforce creates a *share* record that defines the entities who can access this record and the permitted access level.

- **Inherited grants**: This is specific to hierarchies – particularly when a user, personal or public group, queue, role, or territory inherits access to a record via a role, territory, or group hierarchy.

- **Group membership grants**: These types of grant occurs when a group member (such as a user, public group, queue, role, or territory) gets access to a record because the group itself has been explicitly granted access to the record.

Let's move on.

The impact of object relations on the sharing architecture

The *master/detail relationship* between objects grants access to child records if the user has access to its parent/master record. You need to be particularly careful while designing your data model and ensure that you utilize the master/detail fields correctly. Hiding records using the UI layer should not be a preferred solution. You should aim to exhaust all your options, including programmatic sharing, before going that route as there is always a risk that the user can find a way to bypass the UI and get access to restricted records.

Using the platform security features to control object and field access permissions

You need to understand how you can use a combination of *profiles*, *permissions sets*, and *field-level security* to control object- and field-level access. Be careful not to overlook the requirements that require object-level access control in the scenario. They are usually simple, and therefore many candidates tend to overlook them. This may result in missing the points associated with these requirements. Always keep in mind that the CTA review board is a *point collection exercise*, and you should definitely avoid missing easy points.

You also need to understand when you can propose using the *view all* and *modify all* object-level permissions. These are very powerful permissions that allow your user to bypass the sharing mechanisms and access the records directly. Actually, Salesforce won't even create *share records* for the users with *view all* or *modify all* object permissions as they simply don't need it. This makes the process of accessing a massive amount of data quicker compared to the regular case, where Salesforce needs to query and evaluate the *share records* first. This is why these powerful permissions are considered suitable for *service users* who need quick access to massive amounts of data, such as *integration users*.

The *view all data* and *modify all data* permissions are profile-level permissions that allow the user to have access to all the org's data across all objects. They are even more powerful and risky than the *object-level view all* and *modify all*. Be very careful while suggesting a solution that grants a user such high privileges. Even an integration user should not be granted such a high privilege without a very solid reason. Think of the damage that could be done if such a user account got compromised.

Also, make yourself familiar with the other security settings you can configure at the profile level, such as the *session settings*, *password policies*, and *login policies*. Try all of these features by hand so that you become familiar with them.

Designing an end-to-end identity management solution

By now, you should already know the importance of a solid IAM architecture in your solution. This is especially true in today's modern world, where the customer's experience is the main differentiator of online businesses.

In *Chapter 4, Core Architectural Concepts – Identity and Access Management*, we covered all of these aspects, and we went through some of the key industry standards. We also discussed several authentication flows that are supported by Salesforce. Make sure you are very familiar with each and every one of them. You are strongly advised to practice writing these authentication flows over and over until you know them like the back of your hand.

Most, if not all, the CTA review board scenarios will have at least one IAM requirement. And you are very likely going to be asked about an authentication flow. You should show enough understanding and confidence while going through that.

There is one more authentication flow that you should be aware of. It is Salesforce-specific. That is why it wasn't included in *Chapter 4, Core Architectural Concepts – Identity and Access Management* (where we focused on common and standard flows), and it is called **delegated authentication**.

Salesforce delegated authentication – why and how to use it

Platforms can provide bespoke mechanisms to provide SSO capabilities, in addition to supporting standards such as **OAuth 2.0**, **OpenID Connect**, and **SAML 2.0**. Delegated authentication provides SSO capabilities just like the other mentioned standards but using a different user experience. Here, the system relies on another system to authenticate the user. Sounds familiar, right? The difference here is that this authentication is done in a *blocking* fashion and doesn't rely on tokens. Moreover, if you have multiple systems relying on another system to authenticate their users, then the user would need to log in again every time they try to access one of these systems. Let's take a simple example to explain this better:

- Let's assume that you have three Salesforce instances: instances A, B, and C (each with a different *My domain* name obviously, to uniquely distinguish it).

- All these instances are configured to rely on a remote authentication web service to validate users attempting to log in.

- When a user attempts to log into instance A, they will be presented with the Salesforce login screen (note that the user won't be redirected to a different login page, unlike what happens with standards such as SAML or OAuth). The user types in the credentials known by the remote authentication web service and hits the log in button.

- Salesforce checks the user record, and because the user has the *Is Single Sign-On user* permission enabled, it doesn't validate the credentials itself. Instead, it invokes the remote authentication web service, passes the credentials (plus the IP from where the login attempt has been initiated), and waits for the response.

- If the response was positive, the user is authenticated to instance A, a session cookie is created for instance A's domain, and the user is logged in.

- Now, let's assume that the user is attempting to access instance B. The browser won't detect a valid session cookie for instance B's domain, which is the normal behavior. With standards such as SAML, the user won't need to type in their credentials again (review the *SAML 2.0 SP initiated flow* section of *Chapter 4, Core Architectural Concepts – Identity and Access Management*). However, with delegated authentication, there is no mechanism to log them in automatically (based on the fact that they have previously authenticated themselves against the remote authentication web service). Instead, they will have to input their credentials *again* (the same credentials used before to log into instance A) and get authenticated *again* by the remote web service before they are allowed into instance B.

The following diagram illustrates the sequence of events that occur while logging into instance A:

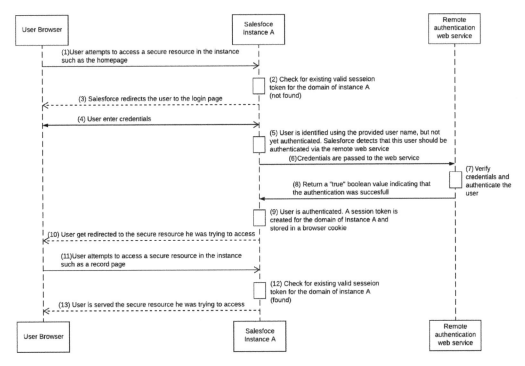

Figure 6.3 – Delegated authentication while logging into a Salesforce instance (instance A)

The following diagram illustrates the sequence of events while logging into instance B after successfully logging into instance A. You'll notice that the same sequence of events is getting repeated:

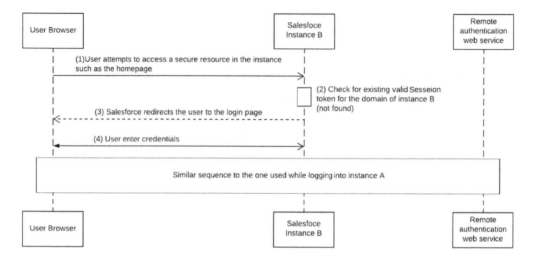

Figure 6.4 – Delegated authentication while logging into a second Salesforce instance (instance B)

You typically use **delegated authentication** when you want to provide SSO functionality by utilizing an identity provider that *doesn't support* any of the standards recognized by Salesforce. You can also use this if the enterprise is using a complex login mechanism (likely, to increase security) that cannot be fulfilled with any of the supported IAM standards.

Now, let's put all this knowledge into action. In the next section, you will be introduced to a mini hypothetical scenario that focuses on the security architecture domain.

Introducing the security architecture domain – Packt Innovative Retailers

The following mini scenario describes a challenge with a particular client. We will go through the scenario and then create a solution, step by step. To make the most out of this scenario, it is recommended that you read each paragraph and try to solve the problems yourself, then come back to this book, go through the suggested solution, and compare and take notes.

Remember that the solutions listed here are not necessarily the *only* possible solutions. Alternate solutions are acceptable as long as they are technically correct and logically justified.

Without further ado, let's proceed to the scenario.

The scenario

Packt Innovative Retailers (**PIR**) is a global digital retailer. They sell computers, computer accessories, and services through multiple channels to both B2B and B2C customers. They also sell via a network of partners/distributors.

Current situation

The organization is structured as two main departments, sales and service. Each report to an **executive vice president** (**EVP**) who, in turn, reports to the CEO. PIR operates mainly in three regions: AMER, EMEA, and APAC. They share a single Salesforce org and currently have a set of global sales and services processed and configured that utilize the account, contact, opportunity, opportunity line item, product, service contract, asset, case, and entitlement objects. The sales department team is currently organized in the following structure:

- EVP for global sales, who require visibility across all sales deals.

- A **senior VP** (**SVP**) covering each of the major three regions: AMER, EMEA, and APAC. SVPs report to the EVP.

- A VP for each country within a region (for example, France, Germany, and so on) reporting to the regional SVP. In total, PIR operates in 100 countries.

- A state/district director of each main territory/state in a country. There can be up to 60 territories per country. The average is 10. State directors report to their country's VP.

- Sales representatives who typically operate in a particular region or city. They report to the state director. Sales reps normally own the sales opportunities and direct customer relationships.

- In addition, there are 5,000 channel representatives (who sell the company's products via the partner/distributor channel). They report directly to the global sales EVP, and they own the direct relationship with the partners.

- In total, there are around 20,000 employees in the sales department.

The service department is organized by two main product lines—hardware and software. This is in addition to the call center agents who operate across both product lines. They are organized in the following structure:

- EVPs for the global service, who require visibility across all reported customer issues, service agreements, and service deals.

- An SVP for each product line that requires visibility across reported customer issues, service agreements, and service deals related to their product lines.

- Each product line has multiple teams of service specialists (which could be up to 25 different teams) who provide support to resolve the raised client tickets and reported issues. They are organized by the different product categories they support, such as software-servers, software-cloud, hardware-desktop, and so on. Specialists can work in more than one team. Teams usually contain around 30 specialists.

- 500 call center agents who answer calls from customers and raise support tickets. They need visibility on all customer records, service agreements, and cases across all product lines.

- In total, there are around 1,000 employees in the service department.

PIR has a concern with their current setup. Several users reported that they could view and edit records that they shouldn't even be able to see. PIR also wants to offer their customers the ability to self-serve as they see this as a crucial part of their future customer-centric services.

Requirements

PIR shared the following requirements:

- Users in the sales department should have access to the accounts owned by them or their subordinates only. This includes both direct and channel sales.

- Reports for direct sales should roll up from the entire sales org up to the global EVP of sales.

- Reports for channel sales should roll up to the global EVP of sales.

- The service department reports should roll up by product line, and then should eventually roll up to the EVP of the service.

- Call center agents can create cases on behalf of customers. These cases could be about specific complaints, inquiries, or requests to service a PIR product they have purchased. Cases are organized by type and subtype, where the type value is aligned with the product line (hardware or software) and the subtype is aligned with the product line category, such as software-servers, software-cloud, hardware-desktop, and so on.

- Specialist teams can work on one or more case subtypes.

- Only the team of specialists working on a case and anyone above them in the hierarchy should be able to view it.

- Once a case is created, it gets assigned to a member of a specialty team based on the case's type and subtype.

- PIR wants to provide its customers with the ability to self-serve themselves by raising different types of cases. They currently have 500k B2B customers with up to 10 contacts each and 1 million individual B2C customers.

- Customers should have access to cases related to their accounts only.

- PIR wants to allow B2C customers to self-register or log in via Facebook. B2B customers must provide their corporate ID and their corporate email address during registration. B2B customers are also expected to provide a second-factor authentication upon logging in for additional security.

- PIR partners should be onboarded by their channel rep. PIR has 20k partners, with an average of 10 users each. Partners should be able to have access to designated customer accounts only, determined by their channel rep. They should also be able to view and collaborate on the different sales and service opportunities for a given customer. They shouldn't be able to access the customer's cases.

- PIR employees in APAC have their credentials and user details defined in APAC's Active Directory. Other regions use a different LDAP provider. PIR wants all its employees to access Salesforce using a unified login mechanism, which also requires the employee to use a mobile application to provide second-factor authentication.

- Once a PIR employee joins the company, a user should be created for that user in Salesforce. Once the employee leaves, their corresponding Salesforce user must be deactivated immediately.

- The call service agents would like to use modern technology to look up the customer account based on the caller number. PIR doesn't want to utilize its existing call center infrastructure and would like suggestions for a more scalable and easy-to-maintain solution.

Utilizing the appropriate security mechanisms and building your solution and presentation

Give yourself some time to quickly skim through the scenario, understand the big picture, and develop some initial thoughts about the solution. Once you've done that, we go through it again, section by section, and incrementally build the solution.

Understanding the current situation

First, let's try to understand the current PIR situation and landscape. We'll start with the paragraph in the preceding scenario that begins with the following line.

The organization is structured as two main departments – sales and service

We gained a lot of information from this paragraph. PIR uses a single org for both the sales and service departments across three regions: AMER, EMEA, and APAC. You need to keep that in mind while reading through the scenario and take notes if you believe they should consider a multi-org strategy.

We also learned that PIR is utilizing a specific set of standard objects. You have to memorize the key standard objects here (such as the sales and service objects). Use the official Salesforce documentation to get full and up-to-date data model diagrams. They are very useful to help you understand the relationships between the different objects in a nutshell. You can use the following link for this: `https://developer.salesforce.com/docs/atlas.en-us.api.meta/api/data_model.htm`.

Based on the standard data model, you can draw your own diagram, which will be useful for the next stages. Your data model diagram may look as follows:

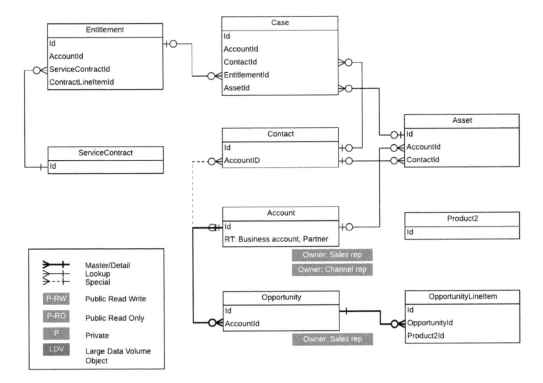

Figure 6.5 – Data model – first draft

By knowing the standard objects that are being used, we can build an early idea of the types of licenses the users would require. Clearly, PIR users are utilizing both sales objects (such as opportunity and opportunity line item) and service objects (such as case and entitlement). Let's keep this in mind while going through the rest of the scenario. You can take these notes on a scratch page.

Next, we have a set of bullet points starting with *EVP for global sales*.

These bullet points describe the organizational structure/org chart of PIR's *sales department*. This section is usually valuable if you wish to get an idea of the potential role hierarchy. But keep in mind that you don't necessarily need to design the role hierarchy so that it matches the org chart. This is a common mistake, actually. The roles in the role hierarchy play a part in defining what data the user will have access to; in particular, what level of data. The user at the top of the role hierarchy gets access to all the records that are visible for their role, plus all the data that's visible to the roles underneath them.

Nevertheless, this part of the scenario gives us a good understanding of the org chart, which can help us develop an early idea of the role hierarchy. The statement *there are 5,000 channel representatives (who sell the company products via the partner/distributor channel)* should be particularly concerning for you because it describes a channel sales model. This means that some of the opportunities could be sold via partners, or at least involving them at certain stages.

This is a good early indication that PIR might need a partner community. This statement also indicates that the channel reps would own the partners' accounts. This is also important considering that the partner roles are set directly underneath the role of the user who owns the partner account.

Remember that you can have up to three levels of partner roles (executive, manager, and user) and that they take the name of the partner account (or the account *ID* value if you enabled shield encryption for the account's name field). For example, if the name of the account record enabled as a partner account is *Test account*, then the partner roles for that account would be *Test account partner executive, Test account partner manager, and Test account partner user*. We still don't have a clear requirement about the partner community, but let's add all these notes to our list. This will help us create the required artifacts eventually.

The channel representatives report directly to the global EVP of sales. Does that mean they should be granted a role directly underneath the EVP's? At this moment, we don't have a clear requirement to direct us. We can add that temporarily and review it later.

At this stage, your draft role hierarchy may look as follows:

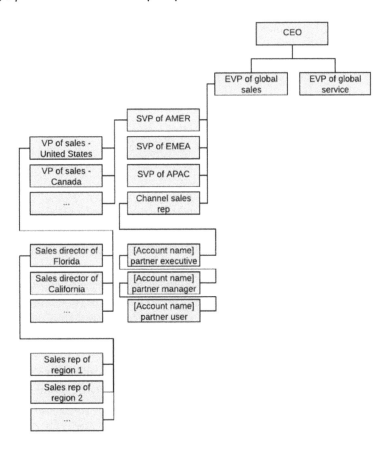

Figure 6.6 – Role hierarchy – first draft

Note that the partner community roles can have three levels max, and they are added right underneath the role of the user owning their account. Your landscape should still be simple and look similar to the following:

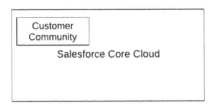

Figure 6.7 – Landscape architecture – first draft

> **Note**
>
> In the landscape architecture diagram, you can also use the term Force.
> com to describe the Salesforce core cloud. The term *Customer 360 platform*
> incorporates more than just the Force.com platform. I personally prefer to use
> the term Salesforce core cloud as we see a continuous increase in the different
> Salesforce clouds and the cross-cloud solutions, and that term sounds more
> precise as a description.

Let's move on to the next paragraph in the preceding scenario, which starts with the
following line.

The service department is organized by two main product lines

This paragraph and the bullet points that follow describe the org chart for the service
department. Update your role hierarchy accordingly. The statement *Each product line has
multiple teams of specialists (which could be up to 25 different teams). They are organized
by the different product categories they support, such as software-servers, software-cloud,
hardware-desktop, and so on. Specialists can work in more than one team. Teams usually
contain around 30 specialists.*, is particularly interesting as it describes a way of working
that is not particularly supported by the role hierarchy. We have users who could belong
to multiple teams. A user can have only one role at a given time. Considering that we are
talking about the *service department* here, it is fair to assume that these users would be
mainly dealing with the case object. There's still no clear requirement at this stage, but the
assumption is logical. Based on that assumption, you can think of two possible out-of-the-b
functionalities that could be useful: case teams and queues. There are other features we could
use, such as public groups, but so far, we don't have enough details about the requirements.

You have to exhaust the configurable potential functionalities before you move on to
programmatic solutions. Let's take note of the features we believe are likely to be used.
Both functionalities are not normally part of the artifacts we covered in *Chapter 1, Starting
Your Journey to CTA*. However, you still need to incorporate that into your presentation,
even as a simple statement. Don't miss any requirements; they all count.

Again, update your notes and draft diagrams according to your latest design. The
statement *500 call center agents who need visibility of all service agreements and cases
across all product lines for a specific region* is also interesting because it clearly describes
the visibility requirements for the call center agents. And this is a good example where the
org chart doesn't match the role hierarchy. In order for the call center agents to see records
across both product lines, they have to belong to a role that sits right below the EVP of
service and above the SVPs of the product lines. In reality, this is unlikely to match the org
chart, but keep in mind that you are trying to sort out record visibility using Salesforce
roles rather than replicating the org chart.

Update your notes and your draft diagrams. Your actors and licenses diagram should look similar to the following:

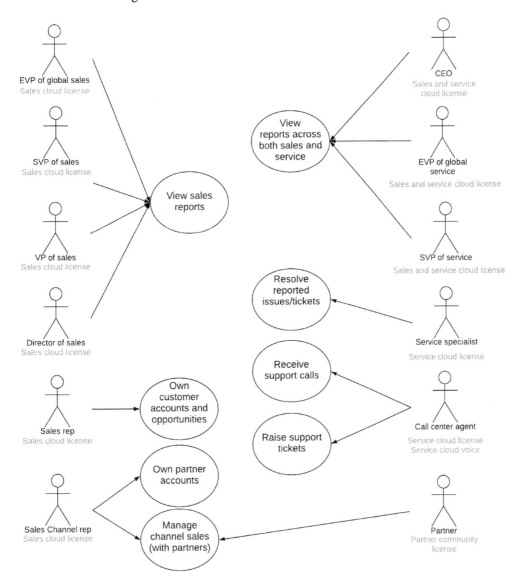

Figure 6.8 – Actors diagram – first draft

Your role hierarchy should look similar to the following:

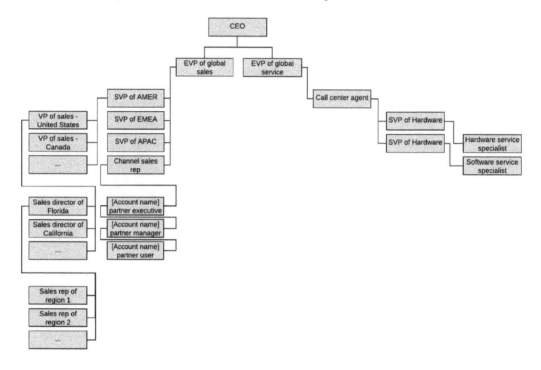

Figure 6.9 – Role hierarchy – second draft

No changes have been made to the landscape architecture diagram here.

Note that although this mini scenario focuses on the security domain in particular, you still need to generate the standard set of artifacts we covered earlier in *Chapter 1, Starting Your Journey to CTA*, to describe your solution end to end.

Let's move on to the next paragraph of the previous scenario, which starts with the following line.

PIR had a concern with their current setup

Here, we get two concrete requirements. PIR expects you, as an architect, to come up with a sharing and visibility architecture that solves their reported issues. They are also planning to offer self-serve to their customers, which is an early indication that you are likely to need a *customer community*.

Take note of that, update your landscape architecture diagram and your actors and licenses diagram, and then proceed to the long list of requirements shared by PIR.

Diving into the shared requirements

PIR shared a set of requirements. We will go through each of them, craft a proposed solution, and update our diagrams accordingly. Let's start with the first requirement.

Users in the sales department should have access to the accounts owned by them or their subordinates only

In order to restrict the visibility of the account records, you need to utilize the **org wide defaults (OWD)**. In this case, accounts should be set to *private*. This ensures the account records are only visible to the user that owns them and anyone above that user in the role hierarchy. Update your data model diagram to indicate that the OWD for the account object is now *private*.

Next, we have the following requirement.

Reports for direct sales should roll up from the entire sales org up to the global EVP of sales. Reports for channel sales should roll up to the global EVP of sales

This is met by the proposed role hierarchy. This means our initial idea of this part of the role hierarchy is correct. There's nothing we need to change on the diagram.

Let's check out what the next requirement is.

The service department reports roll up by product line

This requirement is also met by the role hierarchy. This is a good example where a nice crafted diagram can help you answer the questions you're asking during the presentation quickly.

Let's look at the next requirement:

> **Important**
>
> When you are presenting your solution, use the artifacts you created to tell the story. Your presentation must be engaging and attractive. The artifacts are tools for you to use to deliver your message and tell an engaging story of how you see the solution end to end. Use your diagrams, point at them, and help the audience follow you up and understand your vision. For example, don't just say that this requirement is met by the proposed role hierarchy. Use the diagram while you are doing so, and point right at the branch/path of the role hierarchy that fulfills that requirement.

Call center agents can create cases on behalf of customers

This requirement is fulfilled by granting the call center agents the right license to create cases. Earlier, we assumed that they would be using the Service Cloud license, which fulfills the requirement and allows our users to work with the entitlement object, which is listed as one of the objects used by PIR.

The next set of requirements describe the desired process to assign and handle cases.

Specialist teams can work on one or more case subtypes

To further understand this requirement, we need to go to the next one, which contains the following details: *Only the team of specialists working on a case and anyone above them in the hierarchy should be able to view it. Once a case is created, it gets assigned to a member of a specialty team, based on the case type and subtype.*

These requirements should be considered together before you come up with a solution. The questions you should try to answer now are as follows:

- Is there a declarative feature that can fulfill this requirement?
- Which OWD should be used to restrict the visibility of the cases? And how can we make it visible to the specialist team only?
- What will the case assignment rule look like?

Consider the different possible declarative sharing mechanisms. You can use the case teams and add all the members of a particular specialty team to the case they are working on, but then you would need a mechanism to assign the case to one of the team members who would be owning and closing the case.

Alternatively, you can create queues for each case subtype, add the specialists to these queues, and utilize the case assignment rules to assign the case to one of these queues based on the case subtype (which is also dependent on the case type). Remember that there is likely more than one possible solution. You need to pick a solution that meets all the requirements and is most suitable technically, based on valid logic. Your suggested solution here could be as follows:

> To fulfill these requirements, I propose to set the case object OWD to private. I will create queues for each case subtype and add the specialists to one or more queues, depending on their skillset. I will use the case assignment rules to assign the case to a particular queue based on the case subtype. Once the case has been assigned to a queue, it will be visible to all the specialists in that queue, while other users won't be able to view it due to the OWD settings. This will allow one of the queue members to pick the case and work on it. Any user with a role higher than the user owning the case will also be able to view the case via the proposed role hierarchy.

Remember to use your diagrams and point to the right sections while explaining this topic.

Let's move on to the next requirement, which starts as follows.

PIR wants to provide its customers with the ability to self-serve

The questions you should ask yourself here are as follows:

- What type of community do you need?
- Do you need more than one community?
- Can you utilize the partner community?
- What are the declarative sharing capabilities that you can use to fulfill the desired visibility requirements?

Considering that the requirement here is related to PIR's customers, it makes sense to utilize one of the customer community licenses (customer community or Customer Community Plus). For B2C customers, this requirement can clearly be met by the customer community license. Do you need to assign the Customer Community Plus license for B2B customers?

The advantage you would get from this is the ability to use *sharing rules*. The disadvantage is that you will consume some of the instance's portal roles allowance, which is limited. Moreover, it is a more expensive license that shouldn't be proposed for such use cases unless there is a valid technical reason to do so. There is no shared requirement for the given scenario that cannot be fulfilled using the cheaper and more scalable customer community license. You can find more details about the portal roles at the following link: `https://help.salesforce.com/articleView?id=dev_force_com_system_overview_portal_roles.htm&type=5`.

By default, the customer community license users can only access the account related to their contact records. This automatically fulfills the next requirement: *Customers should only have access to cases related to their accounts.*

Customer Community users don't get an assigned *role*. Therefore, you don't need to update your role hierarchy diagram. However, you do need to update your actors and licenses diagram.

Your proposed solution for this requirement could be as follows:

> *To fulfill this requirement, I propose using customer communities. Each customer, whether B2B or B2C will be utilizing a customer community license to log into the customer community. PIR can consider using either a per-login license or a named user license. This will not have any impact on the technical aspect of the solution. I propose creating a new community for the customer as it is likely to have a completely different look and feel than the partner community. I am assuming that PIR will expose the same set of functionalities for both B2B and B2C customers and offer them the same community look and feel. Therefore, I don't find any reason to go with two different customer communities. The customer community license allows the user to access the account related to the user's contact record by default. I don't see a need to use sharing sets here, and I believe that the standard visibility behavior is sufficient to meet the shared requirements.*

Let's move on to the next requirement, which starts as follows.

PIR wants to allow B2C customers to self-register or log in via Facebook

Your solution could be as follows:

> *In order to fulfill this requirement, I propose to enable self-registration for the customer community. I will customize the registration screen to provide a different set of required fields based on the customer type. When*

the visitor selects to register as a business user, the page will display a set of input fields, including a mandatory field to capture the corporate ID. When the form is submitted, the code will look up the B2B account using the corporate ID and use the website address value stored on the account to validate the email address, to ensure that it belongs to the same domain name and that a contact with the same email address doesn't already exist in Salesforce. If both conditions are met, the code will create a contact and a community user using the provided data, and then link the newly created contact to the corporate account record. Self-registration for B2C customers is straightforward. The code will check if the provided email is unique within Salesforce. If that is met, a person account will be created, along with a community user.

To enable social login/social sign in, I will create a new authentication provider in Salesforce and select Facebook from the list of pre-defined providers. We don't need the consumer ID or the consumer secret because PIR hasn't requested that we customize the Facebook authorization approval screen. Therefore, we also don't need to create a specific app within Facebook. I will then add a button to my community login page to allow users to log in via Facebook. The OpenID Connect web-server flow will be used to facilitate social sign-on. I will create a registration handler class for this authentication provider and set the running user's value to one of the admin users. I am assuming that PIR doesn't want to allow social sign up. Therefore, the registration handler's code will extract the email address from the data that's passed from Facebook and use it to locate a user with the same email address. If no such user is found, login will fail. The code will not auto-create a new user as PIR did not request this.

When a B2B user logs in, a login flow will be used to send the user a request to validate their identity using the Salesforce Authenticator mobile app. B2B users will need to install the mobile app from the Google Play Store or App Store and configure it before it can be used. The login flow will be based on the B2B user profile. The B2C users will have a different profile and, therefore, won't go through the same process.

This way, you're providing an *end-to-end solution* for the shared requirements. Keep an eye on the timer during the presentation; the preceding paragraphs should take no more than 180 seconds to present.

In your solution, you need to mention the proposed *authentication flow*. You don't necessarily need to describe the flow at this stage; you can just mention it. The judges will ask about it in the Q&A stage if they want to test your knowledge. And if they do, be prepared to draw the authentication flow's sequence diagram and explain it in full detail. We explained that flow in *Chapter 4, Core Architectural Concepts – Identity and Access Management*. You can draw the diagram interactively while explaining it or create it at an early stage and simply walk them through it.

This is very similar to the approach you would normally follow in real projects.

Let's move on to the next requirement, which starts as follows.

PIR partners should be onboarded by their channel rep

The solution here could be as follows:

> *The account object's OWD is private. I propose introducing a criteria-based sharing rule to share all accounts with the channel sales rep role. This will ensure that the channel reps get access to all accounts and can share them manually with the partner agents. They can also share them via account teams, or we can introduce a flow to automate this based on specific criteria. I am assuming that manual sharing will be acceptable in this case.*
>
> *In order to restrict access to the case object, I propose controlling this using the profile settings of the partner user and making the case object inaccessible altogether to them. There is no requirement that indicates a need to grant the partners access to the case object.*

Update your diagrams and move on to the next requirement, which starts as follows.

PIR employees in APAC have their credentials and user details defined in APAC's Active Directory

The solution here could be as follows:

> *I propose introducing an identity provider such as Ping Identity to provide a unified login mechanism. This allows Ping to integrate with both Active Directory and LDAP. Ping can be configured to use either Active Directory or LDAP to authenticate the user based on different criteria, such as the IP range. It can also be configured to try a series of identity stores to verify the user's identity in case of failure. For example, it can try to authenticate the user against Active Directory first, and if the user doesn't exist there, it could try the same with LDAP. Ping can integrate with multiple two-factor authentication providers, and it has its own mobile application. I am*

assuming that PIR is fine with its employees using the standard Ping mobile application.

Ping can be centrally configured to request second-factor authentication via the mobile app from all internal users attempting to log in. To enable Salesforce to utilize Ping as an identity provider, PIR will also need to enable the My domain feature in their Salesforce instance. I propose using SAML 2.0 as an authentication standard. Users would be signing into Salesforce using the SP initiated SSO flow.

Again, be prepared to draw the required sequence diagram and explain the SAML 2.0 SP initiated flow, which we covered in detail in *Chapter 4, Core Architectural Concepts – Identity and Access Management.*

The next requirement starts as follows.

Once a PIR employee joins the company, a user should be created for that user in Salesforce

This can be fulfilled as follows:

Internal users provisioning and de-provisioning can be controlled by Ping Identity. Ping can be configured to detect changes in Active Directory and LDAP, such as the creation of a new user or deactivating an existing user. Once that has been detected, Ping can connect to Salesforce and provision or de-provision the user in it either using the Salesforce APIs or the SCIM standard, which is supported by Salesforce.

Finally, we have the last requirement, which starts with the following line.

The call service agents would like to use modern technology to look up the customer account based on the caller's number

Here, your proposed solution could be as follows:

In order to fulfill this requirement, I propose to use Service Cloud Voice. It detects the caller number and looks up the contact record with that number in Salesforce. It can support a fully cloud-based call center, with no need to utilize the existing telephony infrastructure.

Now, let's update all the diagrams and see what they look like.

The landscape architecture diagram should look as follows:

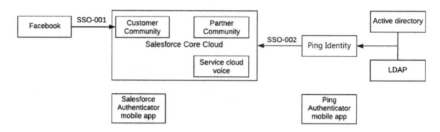

Figure 6.10 – Landscape architecture – final

The list of integration interfaces should be as follows:

Interface Code	Source / Destination	Integration Layer	Integration Pattern	Description	Security	Authentication
SSO-001	Social sign on using Facebook as authorization server	SSO	SSO–OpenID Connect	Social sign on using OpenID Connect with Facebook as an authorization server. Web server authentication flow	HTTPS (one way SSL/TLS)	OpenID Connect web-server flow
SSO-002	SSO for Salesforce using Ping Identity as IDP	SSO	SSO–SAML 2.0	SSO using SAML 2.0 with Ping Identity as IDP and Active Directory and LDAP as identity stores. SP initiated flow	HTTPS (one way SSL/TLS)	SAML 2.0 SP initiated flow

Figure 6.11 – Integration interfaces – final

The actors and licenses diagram should look as follows:

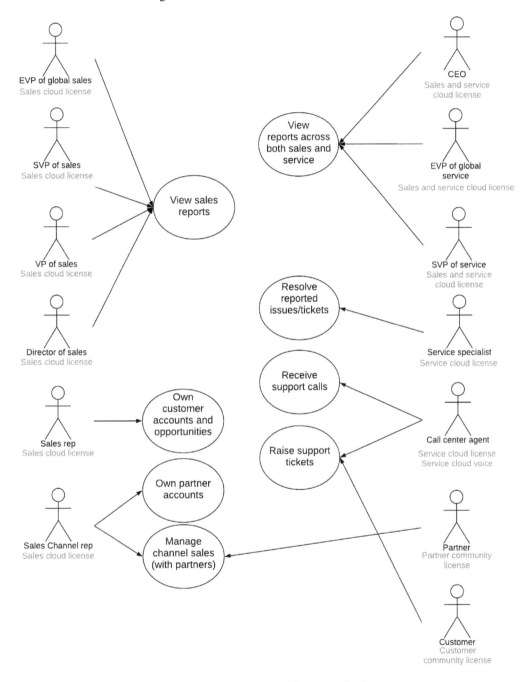

Figure 6.12 – Actors and licenses – final

Finally, the data model diagram should look as follows:

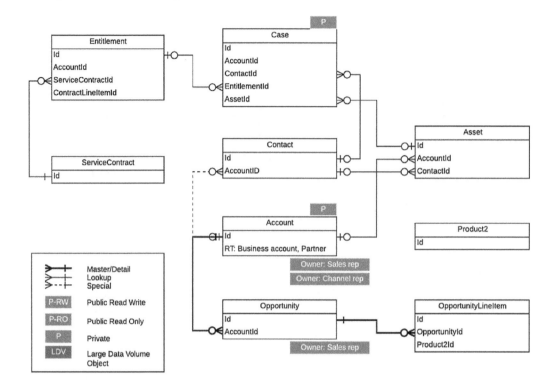

Figure 6.13 – Data model – final

Nothing has changed in the second draft of the role hierarchy. Therefore, it can be considered final.

Summary

In this chapter, we dived into the details of the security architecture domain. We learned what a CTA is expected to cover and at what level of detail. We then discovered how the delegated authentication flow differs from other flows based on standards such as SAML, before digging into the details of some security and data visibility functionalities in Salesforce.

We then tackled a mini hypothetical scenario that focused on security, and we solutioned it together and created some catching presentation pitches. We developed a set of OWDs to restrict records from specific objects to their owners. We then built a complex role hierarchy and a set of sharing mechanisms to allow users to access the right records.

Finally, we worked with multiple types of communities and proposed a secure solution to allow social sign-on via Facebook. We added extra security using second-factor authentication. Then, we explained how to utilize a third-party identity management tool to provide a seamless SSO experience across multiple identity stores.

In the next chapter, we will look at the third domain you need to master: data architecture.

7

Designing a Scalable Salesforce Data Architecture

In this chapter, we will continue looking at other Salesforce-specific knowledge areas that you must know about if you wish to pass the CTA review board. This is the third domain out of the seven mentioned earlier. We will go through the necessary knowledge and preparations for each domain and then complete a hands-on exercise using a mini hypothetical scenario.

The data domain is a broad domain with a lot of interdependencies. It impacts several other domains, and it is impacted, in turn, by several domains. We have come across several design decisions related to data in the previous two chapters already and will continue to come across more of them in the chapters to come.

This is because the data domain is at the center of any Salesforce solution. It involves understanding the key principles of designing your Salesforce data model, which is at the heart of your solution. There are hardly any successful enterprise solutions based on a flawed data model. Arguably, the key to the success of several world-class applications is their well-designed data model.

A successful data architect should also be able to spot potential challenges in a given data model, based on logic and experience, and propose a mitigation strategy as early as possible.

Structuring the data in the right way will allow you to deliver value out of the data you've gathered. As a Salesforce data architect, you need to guide your project's stakeholders through the different tools and techniques to achieve that. You should also advise them on the best approaches to managing the data and migrating it to the target platform.

We already discussed some general data architectural concepts in *Chapter 2*, *Core Architectural Concepts – Data*. This time, we will be diving deeper into more Salesforce-specific topics and architectural principles. In this chapter, we're going to cover the following main topics:

- Understanding what you should be able to do as a Salesforce data architect

- Introducing the data architecture domain mini hypothetical scenario – Packt Online Wizz

- Knowing the data architecture considerations and impact, and building your solution and presentation

Let's get started!

Understanding what you should be able to do as a Salesforce data architect

According to Salesforce's online documentation, the CTA candidate should meet a specific set of objectives, all of which can be found at the following link: `https://trailhead.salesforce.com/en/help?article=Salesforce-Certified-Technical-Architect-Exam-Guide&search=release+exam+schedule`.

Let's have a closer look at each of these objectives.

Describing platform considerations, their impact, and optimization methods while working with LDV objects

First, you need to be able to identify an LDV. I use a simple mathematical method to identify LDVs, where an object has to meet at least one of the following conditions:

- Has more than 5 million records
- Has a growth rate that would lead to creating 5 million new records per year

In addition, some other indicators can point to an LDV use case, such as the following:

- Having an org with thousands of active users who can access the system concurrently.
- Having lookup/parent objects with related/child objects that have more than 10k records.
- The org is using over 100 GB of storage space.

The preceding calculations could be a little bit conservative. Salesforce could be able to perform well with double that amount of records. However, I personally prefer to follow a safer approach and use the previously mentioned figures to identity LDV objects.

Impact of LDVs

LDVs have a wide impact on multiple features, including the following:

- Slow record CRUD operations
- Slows down the standard search functionality
- Slows down SOQL and SOSL queries
- Slows down list views
- Slows down list reports and dashboards
- Impacts the data integration interfaces
- Takes longer to calculate the sharing records
- Impacts the performance of the Salesforce APIs
- Higher chances of hitting the governor limits
- Slows down the **full copy sandboxes** refresh process

It's worth mentioning that not all the transactions on the Salesforce org will get impacted by LDVs. The preceding implications are limited to the LDV objects themselves. In other words, reports involving non-LDV objects will not be impacted because you have some LDVs on your instance. On the other hand, the existence of some LDVs might impact the overall performance of the instance in some specific cases, such as recalculating the sharing records.

There is hardly any full CTA review board scenario that doesn't contain at least one LDV-related requirement. In real life, it pretty much depends on the type and size of the project, as well as the business you are working with.

Mitigating the LDV objects' impact

When you identify an LDV object, you are expected to come up with a crisp and sharp *mitigation strategy*. This is not a mixture of *potential* solutions, but a clearly recommended and justified approach, similar to all the other requirements in the CTA review board.

The following diagram summarizes the different tools and techniques that you can use to create an LDV mitigation strategy:

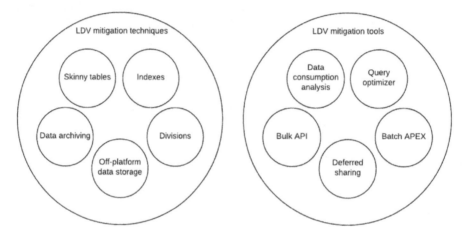

Figure 7.1 – LDV mitigation techniques and tools

Let's briefly go through each of these techniques and tools.

Skinny tables

You can enable **Salesforce skinny tables** on your Salesforce org. A **skinny table** is a special type of read-only custom object that contains a subset of fields from a standard or custom Salesforce object. Skinny tables can significantly boost the speed of Salesforce *reports*, *list views*, and the *SOQL queries* that utilize them.

Behind the scenes, Salesforce stores its standard and custom objects using two separate tables and joins them on the fly whenever a user queries that object. One of these tables is used for *standard fields*, while the other is used for *custom fields*. Skinny tables combine both types of fields on *one table*. This removes the need for joining the two tables and makes skinny tables ideal for reporting. However, due to their nature, they *can't* contain fields from more than one Salesforce object.

The following diagram explains the anatomy of skinny tables:

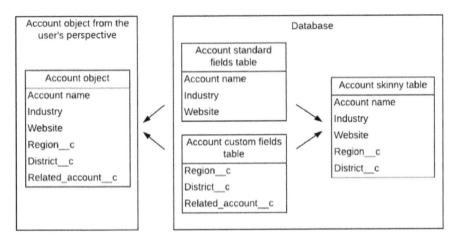

Figure 7.2 – The anatomy of skinny tables

> **Tip**
>
> You can use the following link to learn more about skinny tables:
> `https://developer.salesforce.com/docs/atlas.`
> `en-us.salesforce_large_data_volumes_bp.meta/`
> `salesforce_large_data_volumes_bp/ldv_deployments_`
> `infrastructure_skinny_tables.htm.`
>
> Make sure you fully understand the limitations and use cases of skinny tables.

Standard and custom indexes

Just like any database, you can run much more performant queries if you use indexes in your query criteria. And just like any other databases, primary keys (the object's ID field in Salesforce), foreign keys (the lookup and master/detail relationships in Salesforce), and alternate keys (unique external keys in Salesforce) are indexed by default. In addition, there is a set of standard indexed fields that you can find more details about at the following link: `https://developer.salesforce.com/docs/atlas.en-us.` `salesforce_large_data_volumes_bp.meta/salesforce_large_data_` `volumes_bp/ldv_deployments_infrastructure_indexes.htm`.

You can also request enabling custom indexes on some other fields.

The queries that utilize indexed fields will perform much better as long as the query is returning a specific percentage of records out of the full dataset. More details can be found in the previous link.

Divisions

Divisions act like normal database partitions. They let you segment your Salesforce instance's data into multiple logical partitions. This effectively turns one massive dataset into a subset of smaller datasets, which makes searches, list views, and reports more performant.

Divisions are typically done by geography. Once enabled, they impact several features in Salesforce, such as reports and list views.

You can find out more details about divisions at the following link: `https://help.salesforce.com/articleView?id=admin_division.htm&type=5`.

Off-platform data storage

One of the most effective and efficient mechanisms to handle LDVs is to analyze and re-consider if a specific dataset needs to be stored on-platform (which is the term used to describe storing data on Salesforce core cloud, or what was previously known as Force.com) or off-platform and retrieved on-the-fly whenever it's needed.

There are several mechanisms for fetching data on-the-fly from another data source/application and display in Salesforce, including APIs and mashups.

Data can be stored on a cloud-based or on-premise hosted platform. One of the common platforms to use for this is Heroku. Heroku comes with an out-of-the-box connector to Salesforce core cloud called **Heroku Connect**. This can be used to sync data between the two platforms without consuming any of the Salesforce org's governance limits.

Other platforms include AWS, Microsoft Azure, Google Cloud, Rackspace, and others. Storing some data off-platform could take place as part of a data design decision or as part of a data archiving strategy, which we will explain next.

Data archiving

Archiving is a very effective strategy used to handle LDVs. It relies on identifying data that doesn't necessarily need to be kept on-platform and can be moved to off-platform storage. Sometimes, we can even *expose back* the archived data using tools such as APIs or mashups. Salesforce also provides a tool that's compatible with the **OData** standard called **Salesforce Connect**. It allows you to expose external data tables as **Salesforce external objects**. External objects are very similar to custom objects but with specific limitations and considerations.

You can find out more details about external objects at the following link: `https://developer.salesforce.com/docs/atlas.en-us.object_reference.meta/object_reference/sforce_api_objects_external_objects.htm`.

To develop a solid archiving strategy, you need to get answers to the following key questions:

- How much data/records have to be kept on-platform?
- What is the data retention period for the archived object?
- What other systems are involved in this strategy? Which system would the data flow to?
- Which objects will be archived, and how will that impact child/related objects?

You can archive the data into an off-platform storage container such as Heroku or use **Salesforce Big objects**. Big objects is designed to store billions of records on-platform. But as with any other technology, it has its sweet spots and weak spots. The following summarized table can help you determine the right technology to use:

	Salesforcebigobjects	Off platform storage
Good for	• Store and manage billions of records • Relatively low cost data storage • On platform storage, no need for additional technologies • Less platforms to maintain, as it is part of the Salesforce core cloud	• Store and manage billions of records • Data storage cost is usually low • You can select a target archiving platform that supports both data • archiving and reporting • Several options to choose from, including self hosted solutions • More suitable for larger organizations, particularly when a central • data warehouse is used • Assuming the platform supports oData, the archived data could • be exposed back into Salesforce using Salesforce connect
Considerations	• No out of the box UI. You need to develop a visualforce page or lightning component • No out of the box reporting capability • No out of the box search capability • You need to develop custom code to insert data into big objects • No record level access control capability	• A third party of middleware tool is required to archive and migrate the data periodically from Salesforce to the external system • The data will be distributed on multiple data sources. Building a report that combines all data sources might require an additional tool • An additional platform to maintain • Potentially could lead to additional efforts for compliance due diligence • Record level access control capability requires developing or purchasing specific modules

Figure 7.3 – A comparison between Salesforce Big objects and off-platform storage

You might need to consider several other considerations, depending on the use case, such as the fact that off-platform storage could consume some of your API limits unless you are archiving to Heroku via Heroku Connect.

Let's find out more details about some of the tools that can support us in crafting an LDV mitigation strategy.

LDV mitigation tools

These are a select set of tools that can support you in crafting out your LDV mitigation strategy. Understanding how and when to use these tools is essential if you wish to develop the right end-to-end solution.

Deferred sharing calculations

We mentioned in *Chapter 6*, *Formulating a Secure Architecture in Salesforce*, that Salesforce generates a *share* record in several use cases to grant record access permissions to a particular user or group. Calculating and creating these share records is time-consuming, especially when you're dealing with a massive number of records. **Deferred sharing calculation** is a permission that lets an administrator suspend the sharing calculations, then resume them later to avoid disrupting or impacting any critical business processes.

Deferring the processing of sharing rules can come in handy while you're loading a massive amount of records. You can stop calculating sharing records until you've finished loading the new data or until you've completed a multi-step change of sharing mechanisms across the org. You can find out more about this feature at the following link: `https://help.salesforce.com/articleView?id=security_sharing_ defer_sharing_calculations.htm&type=5`.

The query optimizer

The **query optimizer** is a *transparent tool* that works behind the scenes for you. It evaluates queries (SOQL and SOSL) and routes the queries to the right indexes. Salesforce is a *multi-tenant platform*, and because of that, it has to keep tracking its own statistical information in order to find the best way to retrieve the data. The statistics gathering process takes place *nightly*, with no user interference required.

Bulk API

The **Bulk API** is designed to provide a quick and efficient mechanism for loading a vast amount of data into a Salesforce org.

The Bulk API functionality is available if the Bulk API feature is enabled on your Salesforce org. It is enabled by default for the Performance, Unlimited, Enterprise, and Developer orgs.

You can write a custom application that utilizes the Bulk API or buy ready-made products that do. Most *modern ETL tools* that come with *built-in* Salesforce Connectors support the Bulk API. Some are even built to automatically switch to the Bulk API when they detect that you are about to load a huge amount of data.

You can find out more about the Bulk API at the following link: `https://developer.salesforce.com/docs/atlas.en-us.api_asynch.meta/api_asynch/asynch_api_intro.htm`.

Batch Apex

Batch Apex can be used to develop complex, long-running processes that deal with a huge number of records and therefore require more relaxed *governor rules*.

Batch Apex operates in *batches*, handling one batch of a pre-determined size/number of records at a time. It does this until the entire recordset it's operating on is complete.

You can use Batch Apex to build a data archiving solution that runs at a scheduled time (for example, every week). The code could look for records older than a pre-defined age and archive them in a pre-defined mechanism (for example, move them to an aggregated denormalized table).

You need to remember that this is still an *on-platform* functionality that still adheres to *governor limits*. It is just that the governor limits are a bit more relaxed for Batch Apex. You should continue to consider using a third-party tool (such as an ETL) to do such data archiving activities.

You can find out more about Batch Apex at the following link: `https://developer.salesforce.com/docs/atlas.en-us.apexcode.meta/apexcode/apex_batch.htm`.

Data consumption analysis

One of the techniques that could be very handy to determine the right LDV mitigation strategy is to understand how the data storage is consumed, find out if there are orphan records being created due to poor data governance rules, and analyze the impact the existing data model has on the number of generated/used records.

You can find more details about an instance's data usage using the data usage tool. You can find more details at the following link: `https://help.salesforce.com/articleView?id=admin_monitorresources.htm&type=5`.

Explaining data modeling concepts and their impact on the database's design

Standard Salesforce objects are **normalized**. They store data efficiently in tables with relationships that minimize *redundancy* and ensure data *integrity*.

You can create custom objects that are normalized or denormalized. Due to the nature of Salesforce objects, you can use patterns that are considered sub-optimal in typical database systems, such as defining objects with a huge number of fields.

Records in Salesforce consume around 2 KB of data storage, regardless of the number of fields/columns (with few exceptions).

Creating a denormalized object to store aggregated data is one of the LDV mitigation strategies you can use. It is considered a special case of data archiving.

For more details about normalized and denormalized datasets, review *Chapter 2, Core Architectural Concepts – Data*.

In addition to that, you need to become familiar with some fundamental principles and consider them while designing your data model, as well as while uploading data into that data model. We will briefly cover these principles next.

Account data skew

This is related to specific standard Salesforce objects, such as the account and opportunity. These objects have a *special type* of data relationship between them, allowing access to both parent and child records when the OWD of the account is private.

Account data skew happens when there is a huge number of child records associated with the same parent record. Under these conditions, you could run into a *record lock* when you update a large number of child records (for example, opportunity records) linked to the *same* account in *parallel* (for example, via the Bulk API). Salesforce, in this case, locks the *opportunities* that are being updated, as well as their *parent account*, to ensure data integrity. These locks are held for a very short period of time. Nevertheless, because the parallel update processes are all trying to *lock the same account*, there is a high chance that the update will fail due to the inability to lock an already locked record.

Lookup skew

Lookup skew happens when a large number of records reference a single lookup record. This is applicable to both standard and custom objects. For example, you could have millions of records of a custom object associated with a single account record via a lookup relationship.

Every time a record of that custom object is created and linked to an account record, Salesforce *locks* the target account record until the inserted record is *committed* to the database to ensure *data integrity*.

Again, this takes a very short period of time under normal circumstances, which means you are highly unlikely to experience any issues. However, the time required to execute custom code, sharing records' calculations, and other workflows on an LDV object could slow down the save operation and therefore increase the chance of hitting a *lock exception* (basically, attempting to lock an already locked record), which will cause the operation to fail.

Lookup skews are hard to spot. Reviewing the data model to understand the object relationships then comparing it with the *data usage patterns* and the *record volume* in each object is a good approach to start with.

You typically focus more on objects with a vast number of records and those with a high number of *concurrent* insert and update operations.

Ownership skew

Ownership skew happens when the same user owns a large number of records of the same object type.

All records must have an owner in Salesforce, and sometimes, a business process might *park* records or assign them by default to a single specific user. However, this could have an impact on performance due to the activities required to *calculate the sharing records.*

Ownership changes are considered *very expensive transactions* in Salesforce. Every time a record owner is updated, the system removes all sharing records that belong to the previous owner and parent users in the role hierarchy. In addition, the system removes sharing records associated with other users, which are created by *sharing rules* or other sharing mechanisms, such as *manual sharing*.

You can minimize the risk of ownership skew by *distributing* record ownership to multiple users or by ensuring the assigned owner doesn't have a *role* and, therefore, doesn't belong to the *role hierarchy*.

Determining the data migration approach, tools, and strategy

Data migration is a typical exercise for Salesforce projects. And while it is an extensive topic, you are expected to explain your data migration strategy's high-level details during the CTA review board. You will go into far more detail in real life and include many other factors in your decision-making.

Key topics to consider in your data migration strategy

During the review board, you need to keep an eye on crucial topics such as the following:

- The *record count*; that is, how many objects are you going to migrate, and how many records will be in each object?

- Depending on the migrated datasets' size, you need to come up with a rough *migration plan* that avoids *business disruption*. For example, you can propose doing the full migration in a 4-hour blackout period during the weekend.

- The number and type of *involved systems* and the mechanism of *extracting* the data out of them. You might need to assume that the data will be provided in a specific format and based on a shared template in order to limit the risk from your end.

- You need to determine which data migration *approach* works best for you. The two key approaches are the *big bang* and the *ongoing accumulative approach*.

- You can derive other approaches from the aforementioned key approaches, such as a *local big bang* executed sequentially across different regions/business units, an *ongoing migration* approach where *more than one live system* is maintained and a *delta* of the data is migrated regularly, and so on.

- *Governor limits*, where you need to consider the different governor limits that could be impacted, such as the daily inbound API calls limit.

- Triggers and workflows execute specific logic based on specific criteria. They also take time, CPU power, and consume governor limits while executing, which could be a risk when loading a massive amount of data. As a best practice, you are advised to *turn them off* or provide a mechanism to *bypass them* during the data load.

- Use the **Bulk API** if possible. This could be a simple switch if you are using a modern ETL tool.

- Use the **defer sharing calculation** feature described earlier. Then, activate sharing rule calculation once you've finished loading the data.

- When loading child records, try to group them by their parent ID.

Moreover, you need to propose the right tool based on your assumptions, experience, and logic.

Data backup and restore

Salesforce has announced that effective July 31, 2020, Data Recovery, as a paid feature, will be deprecated and no longer available as a service. Be prepared to explain how your solution will fulfill data backup and restore requirements (if specified in the scenario).

You can review *Chapter 2, Core Architectural Concepts – Data*, to find out more about the different approaches and tools to achieve this.

Introducing the data architecture domain mini hypothetical scenario – Packt Online Wizz

The following mini scenario describes a challenge with a particular client. The scenario has been tuned up to focus on challenges related to *data architecture* specifically. However, this domain is tightly related to the *security domain – sharing and visibility* in particular. Therefore, you will still notice a considerable amount of sharing and visibility requirements. There will be other scenarios in later chapters that also have dependencies on the data architecture domain.

We will go through the scenario and create a solution step by step. To make the most out of this scenario, it is recommended that you read each paragraph, try to solve the situations yourself, then come back to this book, go through the suggested solution, and compare and take notes.

Remember that the solutions listed here are not necessarily the *only* possible solutions. Alternate solutions are acceptable as long as they are technically correct and logically justified.

Without further ado, let's proceed with the scenario.

The scenario

Packt Online Wizz (**POZ**) is an online shopping portal where traders offer different items to consumers. POZ is currently dealing with over 100k different traders. POZ currently estimates that they have over 2 million unique products for sale, organized under 150 different categories. According to their current website traffic, more than 5 million visitors visit their website every day. They place around 150k orders every day. Each order contains an average of five items.

Current situation

The current website allows consumers to place their orders anonymously or as registered users. They currently have 3 million registered users. The website also supports all major online payment methods, such as PayPal and credit cards:

- Once an order has been placed, it can either be fulfilled via POZ or the traders themselves, depending on the preferences provided by the traders for each of their products. Orders are usually fulfilled in no more than 2 weeks.

- POZ stores the bank account details of all its traders. Once the item is shipped to the consumer (either by POZ or the traders), POZ automatically calculates its commission, deducts it from the collected payment amount, and deposits the remainder into the trader's bank account.

POZ has a global support center containing 2,000 support agents and 100 managers operating 24/7 across phone and email channels. POZ shared the following information:

- The support center handles roughly 20,000 cases per day.

- Each support manager is leading a team of 20 support agents. Cases are available for all support teams.

POZ has a global ERP system to handle billing, inventory management, and order returns. They use a bespoke application as an item master and run their custom website on AWS. They utilize MuleSoft as an integration middleware between all systems.

Requirements

POZ has shared the following requirements:

1. The company would like to provide a convenient self-service experience to its consumers, allowing them to raise support tickets and inquiries.

2. POZ would also like to expose a rich set of searchable FAQs to their consumers to help deflect as many cases from their call center as possible.

3. Registered consumers should be able to view their purchase history for up to 4 years.

4. Registered consumers should be able to review an item they have purchased. These reviews should be publicly available to registered and non-registered website visitors.

5. The support agents should have a 360° view of the consumer who raised a specific case. This should include the customer's order history from the past 4 years, other raised cases in the past 4 years, order returns, and any provided product reviews.

6. The support agents should be able to see the overall consumer value indicator, which shows the value of this consumer across their entire history of engagement with POZ. This indicator should take into consideration factors such as purchased products, monthly spending amount, purchased quantities, and the customer's social media influence factor, which is a value POZ gathers and updates daily from three different providers.

7. Traders should be able to view their customer's purchase history for up to 4 years.

8. Traders should be able to log into the POZ trader's portal to view their current pending orders. They should also receive an email notification once a new order is placed. All emails should be sent to a specified corporate email address.

9. Traders should be able to raise support tickets for themselves to resolve issues related to payments and inventory-related queries.

10. POZ top management should be able to run reports and dashboards to track the performance trends of items across different categories. The dashboards should include information such as the number of items sold, returns, and the total weekly value of sold items in a particular period.

11. Historically, POZ used a custom-developed solution to manage the consumers' complaints. POZ is looking to decommission this system and replace it with the new solution. The current system contains more than 200 million records, including some that are still under processing.

POZ is concerned about the system's overall performance and would like to get clear recommendations from you, as an architect, about designing the solution to ensure it has the best possible performance.

Building your solution and presentation

Give yourself time to quickly skim through the scenario, understand the big picture, and develop some initial thoughts about the solution. Once you've done this, you're ready to go through it again, section by section, and incrementally build the solution.

Understanding the current situation

The first paragraph of the preceding scenario contains some general information about POZ's business model. It also contains some interesting figures, such as 5 million daily visitors and 150k orders per day, with an average of five items in each order. Take some notes about these figures. In some scenarios, there are figures that are not necessarily going to impact the solution from a technical perspective. However, they could be mixed up with other figures that you should be very careful writing about.

For example, at first glance, you will notice the huge number of daily visitors, which could impact the governor's limits in many different ways. It is still unclear which governor limit is at risk at this stage, but let's take note of this number and move on. After all, it might simply be a figure impacting an off-platform, third-party solution.

The number of daily orders is also massive. Keep that under your radar too. Start scribbling your data model diagram. You don't know yet if any of these objects would end up in Salesforce, but nevertheless, having that diagram will help you make the right decisions once you go further into the scenario. What we know so far is that we are *likely* going to use the following objects: *account*, *contact*, *product*, *order*, and *order line item*.

The first and second paragraphs are also helpful in building an early understanding of the system landscape. So far, we know that there is a website being used to list, display, and capture orders. There must be an *order fulfillment system*, a *shipment system*, and an *invoicing system*. We don't know exactly which of these functionalities is going to be fulfilled by Salesforce and which is not, but let's capture that and add it to our initial landscape architecture diagram.

Let's move on to the next paragraph.

Once an order is placed, it can either be fulfilled via POZ or the traders themselves, depending on the preferences provided by the traders for each of their products

We can see a clear description of one of the business processes here. The business process diagram is not as essential as the others for the review board, but it is handy for helping you tie back your solution to a business process, which, in turn, will help you present the solution in an engaging way. This diagram is a *must-have* in real-life projects as it can significantly improve the quality of the client requirements you've gathered. Start creating your draft business process diagram. The next paragraph of the preceding scenario completes this picture.

POZ stores the bank account details of all its traders, and once the item is shipped to the consumer (either by POZ or the traders), POZ automatically calculates its commission, deducts it from the collected payment amount, and deposits the remainder into the trader's bank account

We know more about the process now. We don't know which system is going to be used for order fulfillment yet, but let's create the business process diagram to the best of our knowledge and expectations at this stage.

There is potentially a need for one more object that will hold the trader's payment details and the calculated commissions. There is also a need for an application to complete the bank deposit. We are still not sure if that is going to be an *on-* or *off-platform* solution, but let's add it to the landscape diagram anyway and update that later. After updating your diagrams, you may have the following business process diagram:

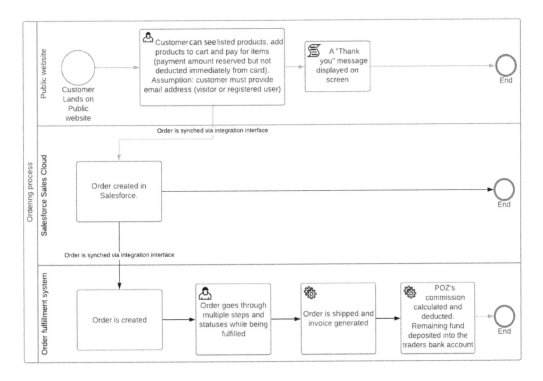

Figure 7.4 – Ordering business process diagram – first draft

Your data model may look as follows:

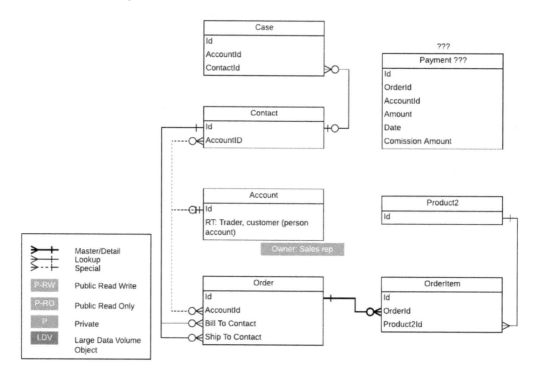

Figure 7.5 - Data model – first draft

Your system landscape diagram may look as follows:

Figure 7.6 – Landscape architecture – first draft

Let's move on to the next paragraph of the previous scenario.

POZ has a global support center containing 2,000 support agents and 100 managers operating 24/7 across phone and email channels

We can now add more actors to our notes or our draft actors and licenses diagram. The scenario doesn't mention any details about the call center infrastructure and how it is integrated with Salesforce. We can assume that the client is using **Service Cloud voice** and **email-to-case** to handle the email support channel.

Let's move on to the next paragraph, which starts with the following line.

POZ has a global ERP system to handle billing, inventory management, and order returns

Adding the ERP system, the item master, and MuleSoft to the landscape will help us complete our landscape architecture. We still haven't gone through the entire set of requirements, but at this stage, we can take another look at some of our early assumptions. The commission calculating module can be closely related to the invoicing process. Also, the process of depositing funds into the trader's bank account is likely going to end up with the ERP system. Let's update the landscape architecture accordingly. Also, take some notes about the number of raised cases. They might indicate that the case is going to be a large data volume object.

Your updated landscape architecture may looks as follows:

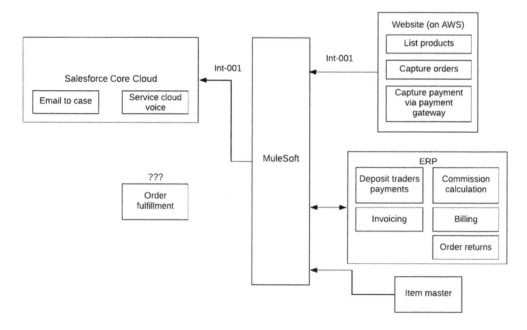

Figure 7.7 – Landscape architecture – second draft

This concludes the first part of the scenario, which is mostly describing the as-is situation. Now, let's move on to the next part of the scenario, which describes POZ's requirements.

Diving into the shared requirements

POZ shares a set of requirements. We will go through each of them, craft a proposed solution, and update our diagrams accordingly. Let's start with the first requirement from the previous scenario.

The company would like to provide a convenient self-service experience to its consumers, allowing them to raise support tickets and inquiries

The consumers are currently placing their orders using the public website, and we know from the scenario that the website allows the consumers to register themselves and log into some sort of portal.

Using the capabilities of the Salesforce Service Cloud, it makes sense to propose that cases should be raised and managed to fulfill this requirement. However, a question that might come to your mind is, should we recommend using **Salesforce communities** or simply build a custom-developed solution on top of the existing portal, then integrate it with Salesforce Service Cloud?

After all, the portal already exists. We can simply develop the functionality of creating, viewing, and updating cases in it, and then integrate that with the Service Cloud using an integration user, right? The answer is *no*. This is another *build-or-buy* decision, and from my personal experience, the *buy* option gives a better *return on investment* in most cases. In this one, though, it is easy to justify why.

In order to build a *secure portal*, you will need to build an entire *user access control* capability on top of the existing portal to ensure that the users can't access cases that they shouldn't. The integration user will likely have access to *all the cases*. A fully custom user access control module is not something that's easy to develop, test, or maintain.

Moreover, utilizing an integration user in that fashion could *breach Salesforce's terms and conditions*, which could lead to a *major data leak* if the portal becomes compromised.

All these reasons are good enough to justify using Salesforce communities instead. They come with a solid user access control module, in addition to configurable pages. Some clients prefer to use their own fully-customized pages instead. In that case, they could end up utilizing the Salesforce Community licenses but not the pages. This is technically a completely acceptable approach.

POZ hasn't shared a requirement indicating that they want the capability of raising support tickets *embedded* within their current portal. We can propose introducing an entire additional new portal based on Salesforce communities. Then, we have the two portals linked via SSO so that the users won't need to log in twice.

Your proposed solution could be as follows:

> *In order to fulfill this requirement, I propose using Salesforce communities.*
> *The consumer would be assigned a Salesforce Customer Community license.*
> *I believe the login-based license could be a better option in this case. I*
> *am assuming that the current portal is utilizing an identity provider that*
> *supports either the SAML 2.0, OAuth 2.0, or OpenID Connect standards.*
> *This will allow POZ to enable SSO between the existing portal and the*
> *Salesforce community.*

Update your actors and licenses diagram, your landscape architecture diagram, and your integration interfaces accordingly. Let's look at the next requirement.

POZ would also like to expose a rich set of searchable FAQs to their consumers to help deflect as many cases from their call center as possible

Salesforce Knowledge is a powerful tool you can use to build an internal or external knowledge base. Community users can be configured to have read access to specific article types using profiles and permission sets. Note that the org must have at least one Salesforce Knowledge license to enable and set up Salesforce Knowledge. Your proposed solution could be as follows:

> *In order to fulfill this requirement, I propose using Salesforce Knowledge. I will control the community user's access to specific article types using profiles and permission sets. This new feature will be part of the new Salesforce Customer Community that we will enable for POZ.*

Update your landscape architecture and move to the next requirement from the scenario, which is as follows.

Registered consumers should be able to view their purchase history for up to 4 years

Let's go back to our notes. According to the scenario, there are 150k daily orders, with an average of five items in each. This means there are nearly 4.5 million orders every month and 22.5 million order line items. In 4 years, those numbers will become massive, at around 216 million orders and more than 1 billion order line items. These two tables are categorized as LDV objects on two fronts: the monthly data growth and the total number of records per year.

We are also still unclear on the system that will be used for order fulfillment. Considering the amount of data, we could propose an off-platform solution, such as using a custom Heroku solution, an extension to the ERP, or a completely new system.

However, according to the scenario, orders are usually fulfilled in no more than *2 weeks*. This means we can use an on-platform order fulfillment solution to handle open orders and use an *archiving mechanism* to move fulfilled orders off the platform. The number of open orders stored on-platform at any given time won't result in creating an LDV object.

There are several order management solutions on AppExchange. Salesforce also has its own solution called *Salesforce Order Management,* which was introduced back in 2019. The scenario itself doesn't dive into the details of *how* the orders will be fulfilled, which means that even if you don't fully know how Salesforce Order Management works, you can still propose it and assume its capabilities are good enough for POZ.

Delivering this functionality using an on-platform solution will allow you to cover other upcoming requirements. This is why it is recommended to *skim* through the scenario at least once before you start the solution. This will help you build an early idea about some key parts of the potential solution.

You can still propose an off-platform solution, but you need to ensure that it can still fulfill all of POZ's requirements.

Be careful of shifting duties to off-platform capabilities more than you should

This could indicate you don't fully understand the platform's value and capabilities, nor the benefits of building your solution on top of a flexible platform such as Force.com, which offers native integration with other CRM functionalities.

In short, when proposing an off-platform solution, make sure it adds value and solves a problem that cannot be optimally fulfilled using on-platform capabilities.

For this requirement, I personally prefer to go with a solution such as the following:

We know that POZ's website is used to capture a massive number of orders every day. I made some calculations and found out that this will be nearly 4.5 million orders and 22.5 million order line items every month. In 4 years, there will be nearly 216 million orders and more than 1 billion order line items. That is a massive amount of data to keep in Salesforce.
I thought of using an off-platform order management solution to handle this, but this would mean we lost a lot of the out-of-the-box functionalities available on the Salesforce platform. We also know that orders are normally fulfilled in no more than 2 weeks. Therefore, I am proposing using Salesforce Order Management to handle order fulfillment requirements. In addition, I propose introducing an archiving mechanism where all fulfilled orders are copied to Heroku and deleted from Salesforce.

I thought of using Heroku Connect for the data sync, but I know that it doesn't provide a mechanism for partially syncing data, and I only need to sync the orders that have been fulfilled. Therefore, I propose using an ETL tool such as Informatica to sync the data. This will run on a scheduled basis, pick all fulfilled orders from Salesforce and copy them to Heroku, and then delete all successfully synced orders. This includes both orders and order line items.

> *We could use MuleSoft for this, but considering the amount of data that needs to be moved, I prefer to use an ETL tool designed for this type of heavy-duty data transfer rather than MuleSoft, which is essentially an ESB. Once the records are in Heroku, I will expose them back to the community users using Salesforce Connect. Users will be authenticated based on a per-user policy, which means that the users will authenticate as themselves to the external Salesforce Connect OData interface, rather than using a named principal/service user. This authentication will be based on the OAuth 2.0 web server flow. I will use named credentials in Salesforce to set up the Salesforce Connect authentication mechanism.*
> *The community users will be able to view the open orders on one page and all previously fulfilled orders on another page.*

Again, remember that this is *one suggested solution* – it is *not the only possible solution*. What you need to deliver is a solution that *works*, *fulfills all requirements*, and is *technically correct*. You also need to justify your solution and explain the rationale behind selecting it. You will need to defend your solution during the Q&A section. This won't be difficult if you are confident in your logic. While explaining such topics, keep an eye on the timer. The preceding statement should be covered in no more than 180 seconds.

Now, update your diagrams, including your data model (so that it includes the external objects), and move on to the next requirement from the scenario, which starts with the following line.

Registered consumers should be able to review an item they have purchased

These reviews should be publicly available to registered and non-registered website visitors.

The data volume here is less. We have nearly 2 million products. We don't have a clear idea of the average number of reviews, so we can make some assumptions. We also don't have additional requirements for the product review capability, apart from the fact that it should be publicly available for registered and unregistered customers.

Typically, product reviews allow other users to rate the review, probably even respond to it. However, POZ hasn't requested such a feature. You are free to make your own assumptions here.

What should come to your mind next is, is there an *out-of-the-box* feature that fulfills this requirement, or do we need to consider a custom solution? And what kind of assumptions do we need to make in order to avoid having an LDV object?

Your proposed solution could be as follows:

> *In order to fulfill this requirement, I propose using Salesforce Chatter. Chatter posts can be made visible to unauthenticated community users via API by setting the value of the Give access flag to public API requests on Chatter (via community preferences) to true. Registered users can post reviews related to a particular product. The product's OWD will be set to public read for external users, including the community's guest user, which is the context user that's used for unauthenticated community visitors. Considering that we have 2 million products, we could end up with many additional Chatter records being created by reviews, likes, comments, and other objects. I am assuming a limit of three reviews per product. I am also assuming that POZ is OK to remove reviews related to products that are not on sale anymore, as well as reviews that are more than 3 years old. We can utilize the ETL tool to run a scheduled cleanup process every week or month to delete additional records. I am also assuming that there is no need to archive these records. If that is required, we can archive them into Heroku's Postgres database.*

> *The user should be able to review purchased products only. To fulfill this, I propose introducing a trigger-based validation rule on the Chatter FeedItem object. This trigger will ensure that the community user can only review a product that they have purchased before.*

Can you think of other potential solutions? You could have created an external reviews object and used it with an unlimited number of reviews. But then, you would need to introduce several more objects to hold data such as likes, comments, and attachments. Again, it is a decision between using an out-of-the-box capability while knowing its limitations or using a customized capability that would require significantly more time and effort to develop but has more capabilities. In this case, I used the former.

Update your data model; the Chatter module contains several objects, and you are not expected to know all of them. You can simply just add the **FeedItem** object to your data model.

Now, let's move on to the next requirement, which starts with the following line.

The support agents should have a 360° view of the consumer who raised a specific case

The requirement here is related to four different data entities, delivered by several systems. Orders are managed in Salesforce, then archived to Heroku once they are fulfilled. Cases are managed in Salesforce as well, but with a *20k* new cases *daily*, we have potential for an LDV object here. This grows to *nearly 600k records every month*, which would lead to roughly *7.2 million new cases annually*.

In 4 years, that number will be nearly *28.8 million records*. This is not very high, but it is still high enough to consider the object an *LDV*. The use case is not as strong and obvious as it was with the order object, but this is still an object that you need to include in your LDV strategy.

Luckily, we already have *Heroku* in the landscape, and we are already utilizing an ETL tool to archive orders and order line items. We can easily extend that to include the case object. We can also archive the orders, order line items, and cases using **big objects**. At this stage, there is no clear requirement that indicates which option would be best between these two. Archiving the data into Heroku allows you to expose it to a customer-facing mobile app via **Heroku Connect**. This is not something that POZ requested, though.

Order returns are handled by the ERP. We have multiple ways to access these records from Salesforce. The scenario didn't mention any details about the ERP system, so you have to make some realistic assumptions. We know that MuleSoft is used to connect the ERP to other POZ systems. It is fair to assume that MuleSoft has access to this data, and it can expose a *REST* service on top of it that allows any *authenticated party* – including Salesforce – to access this data. We can even assume that MuleSoft would expose this REST interface in the *OData standard format*. This allows us to use *Salesforce Connect* to display the data in Salesforce without developing any custom modules, such as *Lightning components*.

Finally, the product reviews are stored as chatter posts, and we can develop a Lightning component that displays all review posts created by a specific user. Let's put all the different elements of this solution together:

> *To give the agents a customer 360° view across these datasets, I will use a combination of different techniques. Orders and order line items can be displayed directly under the customer's record as they are retrieved via Salesforce Connect after being archived in Heroku.*

The number of monthly new cases is roughly 600k, which would create nearly 7.2 million records annually. To ensure we maintain the best platform performance, I propose archiving case records older than 1 year into Heroku using the same mechanism we used for orders. Then, we can expose them back to Salesforce using Salesforce Connect.

I propose developing an OData interface in MuleSoft to expose the order returns data stored in the ERP to Salesforce using Salesforce Connect.

Product reviews are stored as Chatter posts. I propose creating a Lightning component that is used to query and display all four datasets in a combined and organized fashion, to give the support agent the desired customer 360° view in a single location.

Chatter post records and external objects can both be queries in the Lightning component's APEX controller. We can still add the Salesforce Connect external objects to the page layout, but I believe this Lightning component would save time by combining all the datasets in a single view.

Let's move on to the next requirement, which starts with the following line.

The support agents should be able to see the overall consumer value indicator, which shows the value of this consumer across the entire history of engagement with POZ

The questions you should ask yourself are as follows:

- Where will the data for this report be coming from?
- Is there an out-of-the-box feature that can be used to build such a report, considering the amount of data included?
- How can I utilize the data coming from the three social media influence sources?

Such a requirement should point you directly to the need for a **Business Intelligence (BI)** tool. Most of this data resides outside Salesforce core clouds, and the volume of the data should easily tell you this is not something you can achieve with standard Salesforce reports. Building a custom module is too expensive and wouldn't deliver the needed flexibility. This should be an easy *buy* decision.

There are plenty of BI tools available on the market with built-in connectors to Salesforce, Heroku, and other data sources. **Tableau CRM** is one of them, and it is a Salesforce product that provides attractive dashboards that can be easily embedded in the Salesforce core cloud. There could be many other factors to consider in real life when it comes to selecting the right tool for this job, but for this scenario, Tableau CRM sounds like a good solution.

Your solution could be as follows:

> *Considering the required flexibility in this report, the amount of data it covers, and the fact that this data is coming from multiple sources, I propose using a BI tool such as Tableau CRM to fulfill this requirement. Tableau CRM comes with a rich set of connectors that can help it connect to different data sources, such as Salesforce or Heroku. I am assuming that the three social media influence systems are providing their data as a CSV file that I can directly load into Tableau CRM. The result dashboards would then be surfaced in Salesforce, and the support agents would be granted access to it.*

Update your actors and licenses and landscape architecture diagrams, and then move on to the next requirement, which starts as follows.

Traders should be able to view their customers' purchase history for up to 4 years

This one should be straightforward, considering we have that data available in **external objects**.

Your solution could be as follows:

> *Orders and order line items are archived in Heroku and then exposed back to Salesforce by using Salesforce Connect as external objects. We will build a custom page with a Lightning component that queries the external objects to get all the orders that have products belonging to this trader and display them.*

Let's move on to the next requirement, which starts with the following line.

Traders should be able to log into the POZ trader's portal to view their current pending orders

Be careful with such requirements as they might include other minor requirements in them. For example, we have a main requirement here to explain how the trader will get access to the right records, but we also have an embedded requirement that requests sending an email notification upon creating an order. Your solution could be as follows:

Traders will be granted access to Salesforce data using Salesforce Communities. Traders will be assigned a Partner Community license. I believe the Partner Community is more suitable for this use case as we need the ability to share certain records with the traders, such as orders. I am assuming that the trader's account record will be owned by the sales rep who onboarded the trader. I am also assuming that each trader's partner account will have two roles only.

The orders' OWD setting will be set to private, instead of the default controlled by the parent value. This will allow us to share orders with the right trader, without accidentally granting them access to other orders that don't belong to them.

Orders will be shared with the right trader's role using custom APEX sharing. I thought of using criteria-based sharing rules, but there is a limited number of them per object, and we have over 100k traders, each with two roles. I also thought of using Sharing Sets now that they are available for the Partner Community. But considering that this will require making changes to the data model in order to link the orders to the right partner's account record, and considering that it has less flexibility in the ability to control which partner role to share the record with, I decided to use APEX-based sharing. The orders will be shared with the right trader based on the purchased product.

Pending orders will be kept in Salesforce. Fulfilled orders will be archived. Therefore, traders will have access to pending orders by default based on the previously mentioned sharing mechanism.

Each trader has to provide a company email address while being onboarded. This value will be stored on the trader's account record.

When an order is created, I propose using Salesforce Flows to trigger sending an email alert to the trader's email address. We can get the email address value based on the purchased product, as the products will be linked to their trader's account. I propose using Flows over APEX as it is a configurable tool that is easy to edit and modify. I can do the same with Process Builder, but Flows has more capabilities, which might be required in the future.

Don't miss easy points by overlooking easy-to-configure features such as email alerts. Every point counts. Now, update your diagrams, and move on to the next requirement, which starts as follows.

Traders should be able to raise support tickets for themselves to resolve issues related to payments and inventory-related queries

This one should be straightforward; your solution could be as follows:

Traders will get access to the Partner Community, where they can raise cases. We can configure multiple case record types and assign the right ones to the traders and consumers.

Let's move on to the next requirement, which starts with the following line.

POZ top management should be able to run reports and dashboards to track the performance trends of items across the different categories

This is another requirement that should point you straight to proposing a BI tool. You have already proposed one. Your solution could be as follows:

I propose using Tableau CRM for this requirement. The required data is coming from multiple sources; some are external. The requested reports also require analyzing a huge amount of data. Salesforce standard reports and dashboards are not capable of handling such a requirement. We have already proposed using Tableau CRM to cover another requirement, so it makes sense to utilize it here as well.

Update your diagrams and move to the next requirement, which starts with the following line.

Historically, POZ used a custom-developed solution to manage the consumers' complaints

This is a data migration requirement related to one system that is going to be retired. Therefore, there is no need to maintain *parallel running systems*. This could be a *big bang* approach, if not for the huge amount of data that needs to be migrated. Your proposed solution could be as follows:

> *Considering that there is no need to maintain the legacy system running in parallel to the new solution, I propose a staggering big bang data migration approach. I will use the Informatica ETL tool that we already have in our landscape to connect to the legacy complaint management application, extract the data from it, do any required transformations, and then load it into Salesforce core and Heroku.*

> *Informatica ETL has a built-in capability to utilize the Salesforce Bulk API. I propose turning this feature on before loading the data into Salesforce to achieve the best possible performance.*

> *Open complaint tickets will be migrated to the case object in Salesforce core, while closed tickets will be migrated directly to Heroku.*

> *Considering the huge amount of data to migrate, I propose prioritizing migrating open tickets and closed tickets that are less than 6 months old. I am assuming that this can be done during a blackout period, such as during the weekend's night time. This will be followed by migrating the older tickets. Migrating the older tickets doesn't have to take place during a blackout period, as I am assuming it has a lower priority.*

> *While uploading data into Salesforce, all workflows and triggers will be turned off. I propose doing so by assigning a specific custom permission to the data upload user, which is checked in all workflows and triggers.*

> *I will also utilize the deferred sharing calculations to suspend calculating sharing records until the first batch of records is uploaded (the open tickets and those that are less than 6 months old).*

That was the last shared POZ requirement. Now, let's update all the diagrams and see what they look like.

The ordering business process flow diagram should look as follows:

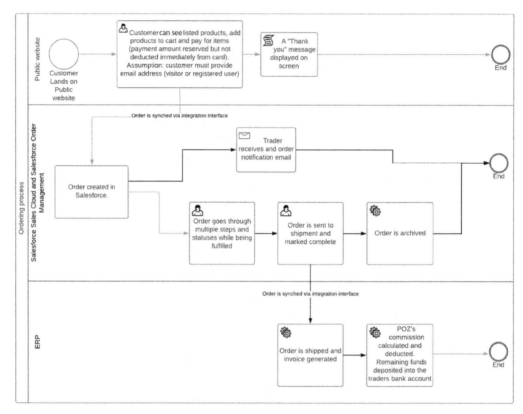

Figure 7.8 – Ordering business process diagram – final

The landscape architecture diagram should look as follows:

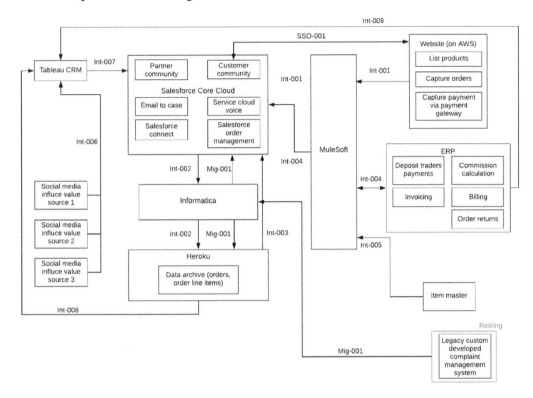

Figure 7.9 – Landscape architecture – final

The list of integration interfaces should be as follows:

Int	Source / Destination	Integration Layer	Integration Pattern	Description	Security	Authentication
Int-001	Website --> Mulesoft --> Salesforce	Data	Remote call in Asynch	Copy order and order line items data from the website to Salesforce via MuleSoft. Data will be sent as soon as possible from the website to Salesforce.	HTTPS (two way SSL/TLS)	Mutual authentication between the website and Mulesoft. OpenID Connect JWT flow between Mulesoft and Salesforce
Int-002	Salesforce --> Informatica --> Heroku	Data	Batch data synch Asynch	A scheduled batch job to archive data from Salesforce into Heroku. Informatica will run every pre defined scheduled period to copy fulfilled orders from Salesforce to Heroku then hard delete the archived records from Salesforce.	HTTPS (one way SSL/TLS)	oAuth 2.0 web-server flow
Int-003	Heroku --> Salesforce	UI	Data Virtualization / Mashup / oData	Archived data is retrieved on demand in Salesforce using Salesforce connect. Retrieved data is not stored in Salesforce	HTTPS (one way SSL/TLS)	oAuth 2.0 web-server flow
Int-004	Salesforce <--> Mulesoft <--> ERP	Data	Batch data synch - Asynch	Orders are copied to the ERP at some stage to proceed with the shipping processes. It is assumed that the orders' shipping status will be synched from the ERP back to Salesforce. This interface can also be used to synch other objects such as accounts. Salesforce and the ERP would send the data to Mulesoft as soon as possible. Salesforce will utilize platform events to send outbound data.	HTTPS (one way SSL/TLS)	oAuth 2.0 web-server flow
Int-005	Item master-> Mulesoft-> Salesforce	Data	Batch data synch - Asynch	An assumed interface to copy data from the item master system to Salesforce using a scheduled Mulesoft batch job	HTTPS (one way SSL/TLS)	oAuth 2.0 web-server flow (assuming supported)

Int	Source / Destination	Integration Layer	Integration Pattern	Description	Security	Authentication
Int-006	Social media sources -> CSV file -> Tableau CRM	Data	Batch data synch - Asynch	The social media sources are assumed to be sending their updated data daily as a CSV file. These files are assumed to be manually retrieved and later on loaded into Tableau CRM	N/A	N/A
Int-007	Tableau CRM-> Salesforce	UI	Data Virtualization / Mashup	Dashboards from Tableau CRM exposed in Salesforce	HTTPS (one way SSL/TLS)	oAuth2.0web-serverflow
Int-008	Heroku -> Tableau CRM	Data	Batch data synch - Asynch	Archived data such as orders are copied from Heroku to Tableau CRM using the standard Tableau CRM' Heroku postgres connector	HTTPS (one way SSL/TLS)	oAuth 2.0 web-serverflow
Int-009	ERP ->Tableau CRM	Data	Batch data synch - Asynch	Data such as order returns are copied from the ERP to Einstein analytic assuming that there is a standard Tableau CRM connector for this ERP	HTTPS (one way SSL/TLS)	oAuth 2.0 web-server flow
Mig-001	Legacy complain management system --> Informatica -->Salesforce and Heroku	Data	Batch data synch - Asynch	Legacy complaint data will be migrated from the legacy complaint management system to Salesforce and Heroku. Archived data to be migrated to Heroku while active and semi active data to be migrated to Salesforce	HTTPS (one way SSL/TLS)	oAuth 2.0 web-server flow
SSO-001	Socialsignon. Auth server isthe orderwebsite	SSO	SSO – OpenID Connect	Single sign on using OpenID Connect and the order website's authorization server as an IDP. Assuming that this authorization server supports OpenID connect	HTTPS (one way SSL/TLS)	OpenID Connect web-server flow

Figure 7.10 – Integration interfaces – final

The actors and licenses diagram should look as follows:

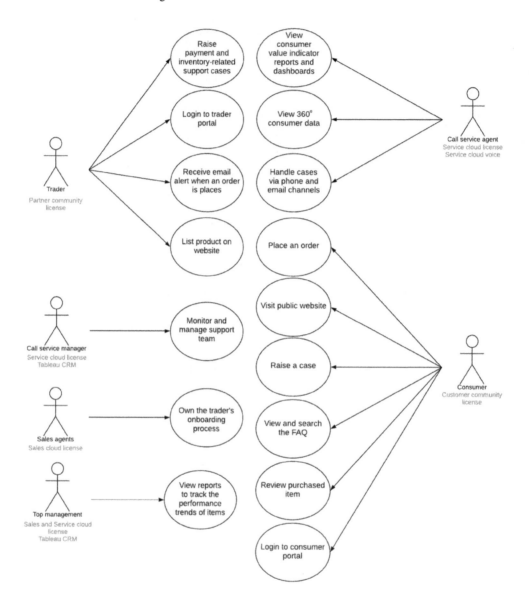

Figure 7.11–Actors and licenses – final

Finally, the data model diagram should look as follows:

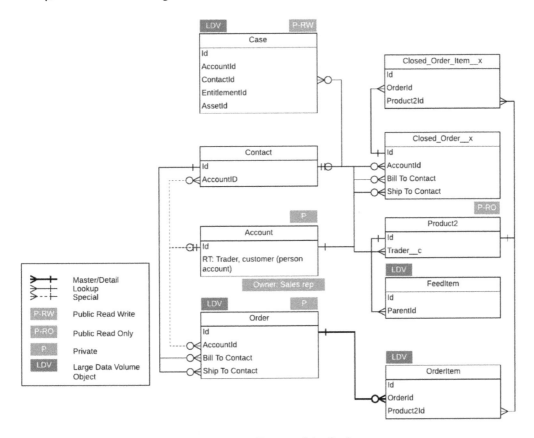

Figure 7.12 – Data model – final

That concludes this scenario. Remember that your diagrams are tools to help you make the end-to-end solution crisp and clear. They are not *targets* themselves, but *tools* that can help you design and document a better solution. They add a lot of value to your presentation.

Summary

In this chapter, we dived into the details of the Salesforce data architecture domain. We learned what a CTA must cover and at what level of detail. We then discovered some interesting principles that a Salesforce data architect needs to master and had an under-the-hood look at the causes, impacts, and mitigation strategies for LDV objects.

We then tackled a mini hypothetical scenario that focused on a data architecture, and we solutioned it together and created some catching presentation pitches. We identified several LDV objects and prepared a comprehensive mitigation strategy based on the business's nature and shared requirements.

If you are now part of a Salesforce implementation project, or you are administrating a running instance, you can practice the process of identifying LDVs. Start by analyzing the data model diagram (or create it if you still don't have one!), and use the tools and techniques we covered in this chapter to identify LDVs. Do your calculations and share your observations, concerns, and the proposed solution with your stakeholders. Remember to make your solution *crisp and clear*; it has to cover the topic from end to end, and it has to logically explain why it is the right solution from your perspective.

We also covered several other topics in the mini scenario, including selecting the right reporting tool and explaining how to get the data into it. We then created a comprehensive data migration strategy based on the shared requirements, ensuring data integrity and minimizing disruption to daily operations.

In the next chapter, we will move on to the fourth domain you need to master: the solution architecture.

8
Creating a Lean Solution Architecture

In this chapter, we will continue with other Salesforce-specific knowledge areas that are required to pass the CTA review board. This is the fourth domain out of seven. We will go through the necessary knowledge and preparations for each domain and then complete a hands-on exercise using a mini hypothetical scenario.

In the digital world, the term *solution architecture* refers to the process of analyzing client needs, understanding the core of their problems, and determining the appropriate solution in order to provide *measurable benefits* to the business.

The solution architect is likely the most business-aware type of architect on a project. In order to pass the CTA review board, you have to possess both the technical skills and the ability to interpret the business needs and craft an end-to-end solution architecture. Your solution has to consider the capabilities and limitations of the platform. This domain is the glue that holds the other domains together.

The detailed principles of lean architecture are beyond the scope of this book. But in short, it is all about eliminating waste by achieving the following:

- Defining and following *standards* to reduce the time wasted in recurring challenges and discussions. This should also aim to reduce overall solution *inconsistencies*.

- Ensuring you are establishing an environment that enables *smooth feature development*. A poorly architected solution could face many difficulties in scalability and extensibility.

- Ensuring that all processes are *creating value for the customer*, reducing wasted time and efforts spent on activities that yield no added value.

- Introducing a well-established mechanism to *document the key solution artifacts*, reducing time and efforts wasted on extensive documentation with low business value.

As a CTA, you are expected to have strong *hands-on experience* with the platform and you are expected to *use* that knowledge while designing a solution. Salesforce is a platform that enables architects to easily *try things out*. This is a powerful capability that should be fully utilized.

> *I always used to say to my mentees: you can't solution from the sky. You have to roll up your sleeves and try things out on the ground. You are lucky to deal with a platform that allows you to try out 70-80% of the features before committing to a proposal.*

We already came across principles and activities related to solution architecture in the past three chapters. That is because, as I mentioned, it is the *glue* that holds the other domains together. This time, we will dive deeper into these principles. In this chapter, we're going to cover the following main topics:

- Understanding what you should be able to do as a Salesforce solution architect

- Introducing the solution architecture domain mini hypothetical scenario – Packt Visiting Angels

- Selecting the appropriate functionalities to build your solution and presentation

Understanding what you should be able to do as a Salesforce solution architect

According to the Salesforce online documentation, the CTA candidate should meet a specific set of objectives that can be found at the following link: `https://trailhead.salesforce.com/en/help?article=Salesforce-Certified-Technical-Architect-Exam-Guide&search=release+exam+schedule`.

Let's have a closer look at each of these objectives.

Selecting the right combination of declarative and programmatic functionalities

It might sound simple, but you need to keep in mind that every suggestion you come up with as a part of your CTA review board solution should be clear and justified. The Salesforce core cloud comes with plenty of different capabilities and out-of-the-box functionalities.

While designing your solution, you should start considering configurable functionalities first. Then, transition to programmatic solutions only when the configurations fall short of meeting the desired functionality.

You might find out that the configurable functionality delivers a sub-optimal user experience or is leaving some questions unanswered. In this case, don't be shy about proposing a programmatic solution. After all, the programmatic capabilities of the platform are there for a reason.

You need to be up to date with the latest capabilities of some of the core platform tools, such as Salesforce flows. Flows have recently evolved and matured well, and they are becoming a very popular tool to build automation with clicks rather than code. But there are still many other functionalities that would require a programmatic solution of some sort: a **Lightning web component** (**LWC**), a Visualforce page, an Apex-based trigger, a batch job, or a custom APEX web service.

To select the right combination of configurable versus programmatic functionalities, you must have deep hands-on experience with the platform's capabilities. You are encouraged to try every single configurable solution that we propose in this book. Make yourself familiar with the key sales, service, and marketing processes. For example, in sales, you need to understand the following:

- The different mechanisms to import leads to the platform including the **import wizard**.

- The different out-of-the-box capabilities for lead *deduplication* and for deduplication in general, regardless of the object.

- Understand how other products could integrate with the core cloud to capture and import leads.

- Understand the typical activities included in lead management business processes, such as *lead auto-responding, lead nurturing, lead assignments*, and more.

- Understand some fundamental principles behind planning and setting up *marketing campaigns*.

- Hands-on experience working with the standard Salesforce sales and marketing object, and familiarity with how to utilize additional products such as **Marketing Cloud** and **Pardot** to execute marketing campaigns.

- Understand how to set up *recurring* and *automatic* tasks related to leads and other objects.

- Practical experience in the entire lead-to-opportunity conversion process, including the details on how the opportunities get assigned upon conversion. Furthermore, you need to understand how a sales rep can use the *opportunity object* and supporting objects such as the *quote* to drive the sales process.

- Understand the process of *opportunity closure* and what activities are typically executed before and after an opportunity closure.

Similarly, you need to fully understand the capabilities offered for service and marketing, in addition to the other supporting general functionalities, such as email alerts, multilingual support, multi-currency support, time-based workflows, profiles, permission sets, app builder, validation rules, and many more.

On the programmatic side, you need to have a good understanding of the platform's available capabilities. Hands-on experience is a huge plus. Make yourself familiar with the structure and some simple examples of Apex classes, triggers, LWCs, and Visualforce pages.

Augmenting your solution with the right external applications

After concluding that the out-of-the-box capabilities are not enough to fulfill the desired functionality, you can consider a programmatic solution or even an external one. In many cases, the decision will be easy to make. In other cases, it may turn out to be a *build* or *buy* decision.

This is a complicated decision to make, and it is very dependent on the use case. You need to consider at least the following:

- **Cost and time-to-value**: The cost of a custom-built solution could become *unpredictable* depending on many factors, including complexity and resource availability. Moreover, a custom-developed solution tends to require much more effort to *design*, *plan*, *test*, and *deploy*. On the other hand, the cost of buying an external solution can be easily calculated. They are easier to deploy and – usually – less error-prone.

- **Maintenance**: Salesforce is a **SaaS**, and it has *three* yearly releases. Each might include updates that impact the custom-developed code. Third-party solutions are *not exempt* from such an impact. However, they have other companies looking after them.

- **Scalability**: The tools are only as good as the people using them. The quality of the custom-developed solution is hugely impacted by the team developing it. I came across hundreds of solutions that operate as expected under normal circumstances but fall apart whenever you expect them to scale up or be extended. Software development houses have systems and processes tailored to deliver high-quality, scalable software products.

- **Quality and peace of mind**: Most enterprises are looking for *battle-tested* solutions, especially for *mission-critical* processes. A product that has been delivered many times to other customers, especially in the same industry, can give a high level of confidence.

It is not an easy task to calculate the total software cost of ownership. You are not expected to do so during the CTA review board, but assuming that *buying* a product is always more expensive than *developing* is a mistake that a CTA should *not* fall into.

On the other hand, don't be shy of proposing a custom solution, using custom objects, and a few customized functionalities here and there, but only when it is more *technically* reasonable to do so than buying a product (then tweak it to meet the desired functionality). Note the following examples:

- Don't propose building a custom CPQ solution. There are plenty of great solutions available in the market, including one from Salesforce (**Salesforce CPQ**).

- Don't be shy to propose building a custom LWC to use as a data entry tool in order to increase users' efficiency.

When you propose an AppExchange or third-party solution, you are still expected to clearly explain how you see it utilized to deliver the desired functionality. We saw some examples in earlier chapters, and we will see some more here.

You are also expected to mention the name of the proposed product. Make sure you are familiar with some popular products from the Salesforce ecosystem.

Introducing the solution architecture domain mini hypothetical scenario – Packt visiting angels

The following mini scenario describes a challenge with a particular client. The scenario is tuned up to focus on challenges related to *solution architecture* specifically. But as you would expect, there are also requirements related to other domains, such as data and security.

As we did in the three previous chapters, we will go through the scenario and create a solution step by step. You are also advised to try the suggested solutions yourself unless you are already familiar with the described feature. You are also encouraged to try different solutions that could fulfill the requirements.

Remember that the solutions listed here are not necessarily the *only* possible solutions. Alternate solutions are acceptable as long as they are technically correct and logically justified.

Without further ado, let's proceed to the scenario.

The scenario

Packt visiting angels (**PVA**) is a home clinical trial company that bridges the gap between **clinical research organizations** (**CROs**) and clinical trial volunteers. PVA provides a different set of services, including home visits and site nurse services. They operate across five different European countries (the UK, France, Germany, Italy, and the Netherlands).

Current situation

PVA has a sales operation team that deals with the CROs. They take over from the marketing team, who gather and qualify information about potential deals via multiple sources.

The sales operations team monitors qualified deals, particularly the high-value deals (with a total amount above 5 million euros). The sales operations team handles various follow-up activities, such as creating quotes, managing contracts, notifications for other internal team members, follow-up tasks, and scheduling wrap-up meetings.

Once the deal is closed, the nurses get assigned to the project. The nurses should follow an optimized schedule to visit as many sites as possible, considering their skills, location, and the shortest possible route.

PVA's business is growing rapidly, and they are looking to introduce more automation to increase their internal teams' efficiency using Salesforce as their central CRM solution.

Requirements

PVA has shared the following requirements:

1. Leads are normally gathered via three channels: web forms, third-party providers, and manually created by the marketing team. PVA wants to ensure that the gathered leads are unique, where no more than one lead per company, per drug, and per country should be open at the same time.

2. Leads that are not created manually should automatically be assigned to a country's marketing team based on the geographic location (country). Leads can have only one associated country.

3. Once the lead is assigned, it goes into multiple stages. At each stage, a set of activities is expected to be completed by the lead owner.

4. Once the lead is qualified, it has to be converted into an opportunity and automatically handed over to the country's sales operations team. One of the team members (a sales operations agent) should pick up the opportunity to develop it further.

5. The sales operations agent will follow up with the deal. The agent should be able to create quotes and negotiate them with the client.

6. Once a quote is accepted, the agent updates the opportunity to the *contracting* stage. Once that is done, the system should automatically generate a contract record using the opportunity information.

7. The agent should censure the contract's data is accurate, select the right terms and conditions, and send the contract to the client for an online signature. The contract should be presented in the local language of the target country.

8. The client should receive a request to sign the document online. Once the document is signed, the contract should be made active, and the opportunity should be updated to closed-won.

9. The agent should update lost opportunities to the **closed-lost** stage manually and set a reason for the loss.

10. Once the opportunity is closed-won, a project that contains key information derived from the opportunity should be created automatically. Only the nurses in the target country and their managers should be able to view the project details.

11. The solution should provide the nurses with their daily optimized visit schedule. This schedule should aim at giving the nurses the opportunity to visit as many sites as possible during their working hours.

12. Once the opportunity is closed, lock all the opportunity fields for all users except the administrator and the opportunity owner.

13. Opportunity line items' fields should also get locked. No products can be added, edited, or deleted once the opportunity is closed.

14. The opportunity owner is allowed to change the value of the description field for up to 7 days after closing the opportunity. However, that is the only field they are allowed to change during that period.

15. After 7 days, all fields should be locked for all users except the administrators.

16. If a high-value deal is closed and lost, send an email to notify the sales agent's manager. The email should include the opportunity name and amount. Create a follow-up task due in 10 days assigned to the sales agent's manager to review the reasons for the loss with the agent.

17. The system should support both the euro and pound sterling currencies with dated exchange rates.

PVA is looking for a proposed solution that can increase their internal teams' efficiency and reduce manual errors using Salesforce.

Selecting the appropriate functionalities to build your solution and presentation

Give yourself time to quickly skim through the scenario, understand the big picture, and develop some initial thoughts about the solution. Then, let's go through it again, section by section, and incrementally build the solution.

Understanding the current situation

The first paragraph has some general information about PVA's business model. It also tells us important information about the different personas that are going to use the system. We now know that they have a marketing team, a sales operations team, and nurses. Each is doing a specific set of activities. Based on that, we can start creating a draft of our actors and licenses diagram. Your diagram could look as follows:

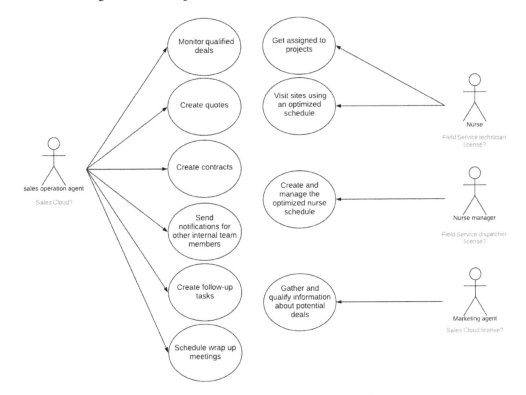

Figure 8.1 – Actors and licenses – first draft

I have included an assumed **Nurse manager** role in anticipation of needing someone to create and manage the nurses' schedule. I assumed a Salesforce **Sales Cloud** license for the marketing and sales agents as they would need to deal with leads, opportunities, and some other objects. At the same time, the nurse and nurse manager would need **Field Service** licenses if we ended up proposing Salesforce Field Service as part of the solution. We might need to change that later.

Even at this stage, we can see some potential requirements, such as creating quotes, contracts, and optimized site visit schedules. You probably also started to build some early understanding of the *likely* functionalities, licenses, and third parties you might need. Let's create a draft landscape architecture diagram using whatever information we have learned and include any assumptions and early ideas we can think of. Your landscape architecture diagram could look as follows:

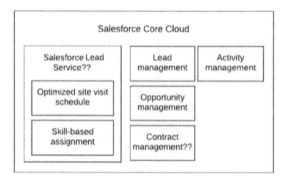

Figure 8.2 – Landscape architecture diagram – first draft

The *optimized scheduling* requirement should immediately trigger in your mind two possible solutions: Salesforce Maps and Salesforce Field Service. There are other third-party solutions as well, but this is a complex topic that you simply shouldn't think of solving with any custom developed solution. It is still too early to determine which solution is a better fit for PVA, but for the time being, the best way to avoid losing this information is by adding it to your draft landscape.

Also, based on the bit of information we know so far, we can create an early version draft data model:

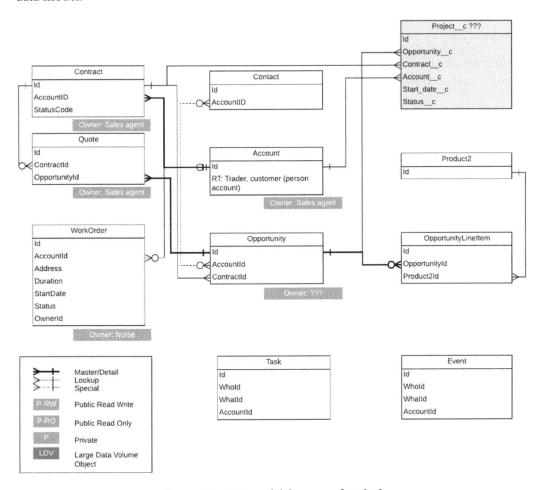

Figure 8.3 – Data model diagram – first draft

PVA's business is growing rapidly, and they are looking to introduce more automation to increase their internal teams' efficiency using Salesforce as their central CRM solution. They shared a lengthy list of requirements, which we are going to cover next.

Diving into the shared requirements

Now, let's go through PVA's requirements, craft a proposed solution for each, and update our diagrams accordingly to help us with the presentation. Let's start with the first requirement, which begins with the following section.

Leads are normally gathered via three different channels

This is a requirement to ensure lead uniqueness across the channels. Open leads are uniquely identified using the company, drug, and country attributes. We can assume that the values of *drug* and *country* are captured using custom fields.

You can use many different ways to ensure the lead record is unique based on the given attributes, such as the following:

- **Using custom-developed Apex code and a trigger**: Custom-developed code gives us ultimate control of the deduplication logic, but it has to be built correctly to ensure optimal performance. Moreover, it is an expensive solution considering the required efforts.

- **Using a third-party solution**: There are several third-party products that can be integrated with Salesforce, including some solutions from AppExchange (such as **Cloudingo** and **RingLead**). They provide advanced configurable capabilities and are optimized for performance. However, they require additional licenses. A good option if there is no *out-of-the-box* Salesforce functionality that can fulfill the requirement.

- **By creating a hidden custom text field and setting it to be a unique external key, then populating it with the concatenated values of the lead attributes**: Considering that the field is unique, it will prevent the creation of other lead records with the same concatenated values. Once the lead is *closed*, we can automatically *empty* this field, which will ensure that other similar leads can be created in the future.

  The performance of this solution is *optimized*. However, it is difficult to change the matching logic because it relies on *persisted data*. For example, to introduce a new field to the set of fields considered for deduplication, we need to update all existing open leads. Moreover, this is always hard deduplication, always preventing new, similar records from being created. And while this is, indeed, the current requirement, fulfilling it in this way *prevents the business* from adopting a different strategy in the future, such as *allowing* duplicate records to be created but *marking* them as duplicates.

- **Using Salesforce duplicate rules**: This is a standard *out-of-the-box* functionality that utilizes configurable *matching rules*. It gives the flexibility to define different actions when a duplicate record is found, such as preventing a new record from being created or allowing it with a prompt. It has its limitations as with any other tool, but it should be good enough to fulfill this requirement.

The order of the aforementioned four potential solutions is intentionally reversed to provide more details on the qualifying logic used for each. You would typically start by considering out-of-the-box configurable functionalities and only venture to other solutions when needed.

Your proposed solution for this requirement could be as follows:

> *In order to fulfill this requirement, I propose using the standard Salesforce deduplication rules. I will create a custom matching rule that relies on the company, drug, country, and lead status fields. I would set the deduplication rule to prevent creating a lead record if a match was found. I don't believe there is a need to use a third-party solution as this requirement can be fulfilled using an out-of-the-box configurable feature. This is also why I have disregarded using a custom Apex-based solution for it. I assume that the leads created via web forms would be using the web-to-lead functionality, and third-party leads are uploaded manually via the import wizard.*

Update your diagrams, and let's move on to the next requirement.

Leads that are not created manually should automatically be assigned to a country's marketing team based on the geographic location (country)

Let's start by asking ourselves a simple question: is there an out-of-the-box configurable functionality that can be used to fulfill this requirement? As a Salesforce solution architect, you are expected to know the details of the standard platform capabilities. In this case, the lead assignment rule can be used in combination with queues. This solution is configurable, optimized, and fulfills the requirement. Moreover, it is also future-embracing, considering that it is based on a standard configurable Salesforce functionality.

I personally prefer to use the term *future-embracing* over *futureproof*. The lean and well-architected solution should *embrace* and *welcome* future changes rather than *prevent* them.

Your proposed solution could be as follows:

> *I will utilize the standard lead assignment functionality to assign the lead to the country's queue based on the country's field value.*

Let's now move on to the next requirement.

Once the lead is assigned, it goes into multiple stages. At each stage, a set of activities is expected to be completed by the lead owner

Starting with the out-of-the-box functionalities, it is easy to recognize that you can utilize the standard lead process functionality to define multiple lead processes, each with different lead statuses. At each stage, we can generate a set of tasks and assign them to the lead owner. This can be achieved using one of the following (in order):

- **Flows**: Salesforce flows can be used to execute complex logic upon creating or updating a record. This is a configurable and scalable tool that is capable of delivering the desired functionality. Moreover, it is a modern tool that Salesforce is actively enhancing with each release. Clearly, it has better chances of receiving more future enhancements than any other tool on this list.

- **Process Builder**: This can be used to execute relatively simple logic. It is still good enough for this requirement, but it is a tool that is less capable and scalable than flows.

- **Workflow rules**: The oldest workflow tool is available on the Force.com platform. Although it can deliver this functionality, it has a less attractive configuration UI compared to the previously mentioned tools. It also doesn't have version management capability and, in general, is less capable and scalable.

- **Custom Apex code**: This gives the ultimate capability and flexibility but with unjustified additional development and maintenance costs.

Your proposed solution could be as follows:

> *I propose utilizing the lead process functionality to define multiple lead processes with different lead statuses. Then, create a Salesforce* **autolaunched flow** *to automatically create tasks and assign them to the lead owner upon updating the lead to a specific status. The flow can be configured to utilize criteria-based branching logic, and this will allow us to create a different set of tasks depending on the lead status.*

Let's now move on to the next requirement, as follows.

Once the lead is qualified, it has to be converted into an opportunity and automatically handed over to the country's sales operations team

This requirement doesn't specify whether the lead conversion should happen automatically or whether it is fine to stick with the manual process. You can make an assumption and base your solution on it.

By default, when the opportunity is created out of lead conversion, it is owned by the same user who owns the converted lead. You need an automation process to assign it to the sales agent's queue of that country. Your proposed solution could be as follows:

> *The scenario didn't specify whether the conversion has to happen automatically; therefore, I am assuming it is done manually by the lead owner. Once the lead is converted into an opportunity, I will utilize a Salesforce* **autolaunched flow** *to update the opportunity ownership and set it to the sales agent's queue of that country.*

Let's now move on to the next requirement.

The sales operations agent will follow up with the deal. The agent should be able to create quotes and negotiate them with the client

This is a standard salesforce functionality; the sales agent has a **Sales Cloud** license and, therefore, can work with the quote object. Your proposed solution could be as simple as the following:

> *The sales agents will be assigned a Sales Cloud license; this allows them to create and update quotes. This is a standard Salesforce functionality.*

Remember to use your diagrams while explaining the solution. The *actors and licenses* diagram is particularly useful in this case.

Let's now move on to the next requirement.

Once a quote is accepted, the agent updates the opportunity to the contracting stage

The main requirement here is to automatically create a contract out of the closed opportunity, which can easily be done using flows, Process Builder, or custom-developed code. The scenario didn't specify any advanced contract creation logic to justify proposing a third-party solution.

There are several **contract life cycle management** (**CLM**) solutions out there in the market, including some available on AppExchange, such as **Apttus Contract Management**, **DocuSign CLM**, and **Conga Contracts**. They provide advanced contract creation and negotiation functionalities. However, that has not been requested in this scenario.

> **Remember**
>
> You need to memorize the names of some common third-party products from the Salesforce ecosystem, such as CPQ tools, integration middleware, identity providers and identity management solutions, e-signature solutions, document generation solutions, advanced lead assignment solutions, CTI, version control, release management, backup and restore, and so on. We are providing examples throughout this book whenever applicable. As a CTA, you should make yourself familiar and keep up to date with what is available on AppExchange.

Your proposed solution could be as follows:

> *There has been no requirement shared about advanced contract creation functionalities. Therefore, I am assuming a simplified solution that utilizes a Salesforce autolaunched flow to automatically create a contract once the opportunity is updated to the mentioned stage.*

Let's now move on to the next requirement.

The agent should ensure the contract's data is accurate, select the right terms and conditions, and send the contract to the client for an online signature

Here, we come across a requirement for an e-signature, a functionality that would require extensive efforts to develop. This is totally unjustified, considering that there are several battle-tested solutions available in the market and via AppExchange, such as **DocuSign**, **HelloSign**, and **Adobe Sign**. These products can also help to fulfill the second part of the requirement, which indicates that the contract should be presented in the CRO's local language. Your proposed solution could be as follows:

> *To fulfill this requirement, I propose using a third-party application from AppExchange, such as DocuSign. This will allow selecting the right contract template with the appropriate language before sending the contract over to the customer. The tool will also allow selecting the suitable terms and conditions to include with the contract.*

Update your landscape architecture diagram, and let's now move on to the next requirement.

The client should receive a request to sign the document online

Once the document is signed, the contract should be made active, and the opportunity should be updated to closed-won.

Luckily, most of this requirement is automatically fulfilled using the third-party e-signature tool we suggested. You still need to explain how that works, though. Your proposed solution could be as follows:

> *This capability is built into the proposed e-signature solution. Using DocuSign, we can update the contract status once the document is signed. Then, we can use a Salesforce autolaunched flow to update the opportunity stage back to closed-won. The flow will kickstart once the contract status is updated.*

Let's now move on to the next requirement, as follows.

The agent should update lost opportunities to the closed lost stage manually and set a reason for the loss

We can assume that the loss reason is captured using a custom field. We then need to introduce a mechanism that ensures this field becomes mandatory when the opportunity is being updated to the given stage. We can utilize *field dependencies* and *validation rules* to ensure that. Your proposed solution could be as follows:

> *To fulfill this requirement, I propose introducing a custom picklist field with predefined values for the possible reasons for losing an opportunity. Then, utilize the standard field dependency feature to make this field dependent on the opportunity stage value. I also propose introducing a custom validation rule to ensure a value is always entered in this field when the opportunity is updated to the closed lost stage, regardless of whether the update took place via the UI, code, or an API call.*

Let's now move on to the next requirement.

Once the opportunity is closed-won, a project that contains key information derived from the opportunity should be created automatically

Don't expect the requirements to be isolated based on their related domain. In many cases, you will come across requirements that cut across different domain knowledge areas, exactly like in real life. In this, we have two requirements: one related to solution architecture and the other to security. Your proposed solution could be as follows:

> In order to fulfill this requirement, I propose to use a custom object to store the project details and use a Salesforce autolaunched flow to create and populate a record of this object once the opportunity is closed. I considered using one of the standard objects, such as the case, to represent a project but decided to use a custom object as there were no shared requirements that justify using the case object, such as SLA requirements or escalations. Moreover, I assumed that the case object might be utilized for customer support-related topics in the future and preferred not to repurpose it.

> The custom object's OWD will be set to private to restrict the record visibility to its owner, which by default will be the sales agent. Considering that the record will be created upon closing the opportunity, which is an action carried out by the sales agent, I assumed that it is acceptable to keep this record visible to the sales agent.

> I propose introducing a role hierarchy to include the nurses and their managers. Then, use criteria-based sharing rules to share the project record with the nurses, granting their managers automatic access.

> **Note**
>
> This scenario doesn't have many specifications for data sharing and visibility and doesn't provide enough details to design a role hierarchy. In this case, you could make some assumptions, such as assuming a role on top of the nurse managers that report to the CEO.

You need to *justify* introducing custom objects to the data model. You should start by trying to *utilize* the standard objects, if possible. But if you decided to use a custom object for any reason (for example, the standard object doesn't fit the requirement or might require significant customizations to be repurposed), then you should clearly justify your rationale. Be *crisp* and *confident*; avoid decisions based on *poor personal experience* that could have been impacted by other non-technical factors.

Always keep an eye on the *time* used during the presentation. Don't waste *valuable time* on further explaining the topics you have already explained. For example, we decided not to use the case object in our solution and provided the key reasons behind that decision. Don't waste the valuable presentation time by trying to list every single minor reason behind your decision. Keep your focus on the *key decision points*.

Your role hierarchy diagram could look as follows:

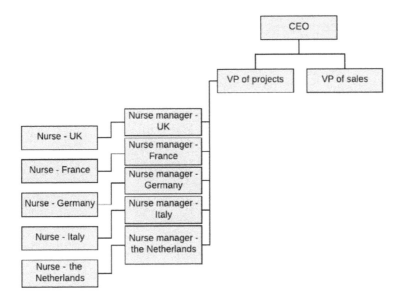

Figure 8.4 – Role hierarchy – first draft

Your data model could look as follows:

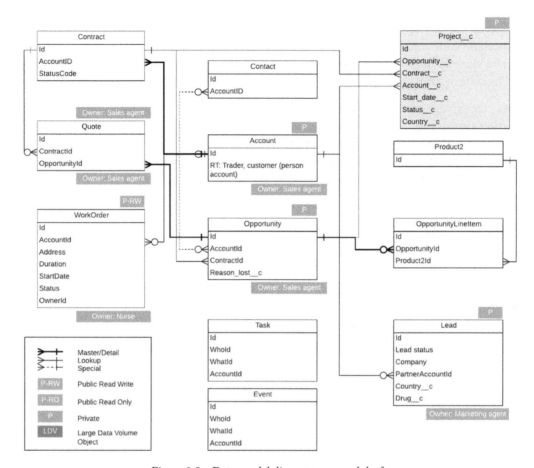

Figure 8.5 – Data model diagram – second draft

Let's now move on to the next requirement.

The solution should provide the nurses with their daily optimized visit schedule

Following the same logic we used for other requirements and using the same order, you should conclude that such a feature requires a specific additional product to deliver it.

Luckily, Salesforce has a product that delivers this functionality, and it is probably one of the most advanced field service scheduling tools available in the market. Salesforce Field Service allows creating optimized site visits for technicians. A technician could be a nurse in this case. The scheduler can consider many factors, such as the different working hours, skillsets, preferred technician, geographic locations, scheduling policies, and many more.

You don't need to become an expert Field Service consultant in order to pass the CTA review board. But you need to be aware of the product, understand when to propose it, and what kind of licenses will be required. It is also recommended to become familiar with its underlying data model.

You can learn more about Salesforce Field Service from the following link: `https://www.salesforce.com/au/products/field-service/overview/`.

You can learn more about the core Field Service data model at the following link: `https://developer.salesforce.com/docs/atlas.en-us.field_service_dev.meta/field_service_dev/fsl_dev_soap_core.htm`.

In your presentation, you are not expected to cover the details of how Salesforce Field Service works (remember the exam's objectives), but you are expected to explain how you are planning to utilize it as part of your overall solution. Your proposed solution could be as follows:

> *In order to fulfill this requirement, I propose using Salesforce Field Service. It provides the ability to create an optimized schedule for nurses based on multiple factors, such as the geographic site location, the required skills, the nurse's work hours, and many more. In the actors and licenses diagram, I assumed that the nurses would be assigned a Field Service technician license. This will allow them to log in to Salesforce and view their optimized scheduled. I also assumed that there would be one or more users managing and creating the optimized nurses scheduled. I called this actor in my diagram a nurse manager. The nurse managers would need a Field Service dispatcher license to use the Field Service scheduler and dispatcher console.*

Update your diagrams, and let's move on to the next requirement.

Once the opportunity is closed, lock all the opportunity fields for all users except the administrator and the opportunity owner

Following the same technique and order we used before, we can think of some potential solutions:

- **Use custom validation rules**. They can be configured to trigger upon attempting to save an edited record. However, they don't prevent the user from attempting to edit the record. They will fire only upon attempting to *save* the record. If you are going to use validation rules, you need to come up with an efficient way to prevent editing the record's fields. You can't simply list each and every single field in your validation rule.

Introducing a new custom `is_locked__c` field and updating it using a flow upon closing the opportunity could be a solution. Your validation rule would then rely on this field alone. However, if you are after a good user experience (and you should be), you need to keep in mind that this solution alone won't prevent the user from *attempting to edit* the record.

- **Update the record type upon closing the opportunity**. A flow can be used for this job too. You can then assign a *page layout* with *read-only fields* to that record type. Some fields cannot be set to read-only, such as *name, currency, closed date, stage,* and some others. This solution also doesn't prevent the record from being edited via code or an API (for example, via a data loader). You should consider this solution as *complementary* to other approaches but not as a comprehensive solution on its own.

- **Use Apex validations in a before-update trigger**. This gives you the ultimate capability and flexibility, but with additional development efforts. This approach will also cause a loss of agility as any future changes would require code edits. You should consider this option only for *sophisticated* use cases.

The requirement here can be completely fulfilled using configurations. There is no justification for using an Apex validation. You can propose a solution based on a combination of the first two approaches.

Before drafting up the end-to-end solution to present, let's also have a look at the next three requirements, which are all related to this.

Opportunity line items' fields should also get locked. No products can be added, edited, or deleted once the opportunity is closed

We understand that the lock should also be extended to the opportunity line item. We can introduce validation rules on the **Opportunity line item** object as well, which relies on its parent opportunity's `is_locked__c` flag. You might want to consider updating the record type as well. The requirement can still be fulfilled using configurable features. Let's explore the next requirement.

The opportunity owner is allowed to change the value of the description field for up to 7 days after closing the opportunity

However, that is the only field they are allowed to change during that period.

The owner should be able to change a single field for a limited time period. Can we still cover this using validation rules? Sure we can. But we need to change our approach a bit. Instead of using a true or false flag, such as is_locked__c, we can instead use a date field such as locked_date__c. The validation rule would then compare this date to the current date and fire on all cases except if the opportunity owner carries out the change, and the value of locked_date__c is less than today's date by no more than 7 days.

Anything more to consider? Let's have a look at the next and final related requirement.

After 7 days, all fields should be locked for all users except the administrators

We need to allow the administrator to edit this record at *any time*. The administrator should also be able to edit *any editable field*. We can update the validation rule to bypass the validation if the executing user's profile equals administrator. This is not very flexible as it includes a *hardcoded* value. A better approach would be to create a **custom permission**, assign it to the administrator, then configure the validation rule to bypass if the currently executing user has this custom permission assigned.

Your proposed solution could be as follows:

> *In order to fulfill this requirement, I propose introducing a custom field to store the opportunity's locked date. A Salesforce autolaunched flow can be used to set the value of that field upon closing the opportunity. I propose using a custom field instead of the standard opportunity close date field because the latter's value could be used for other purposes.*

> *We can then introduce a custom validation rule on the opportunity object. The validation will ensure that no one can modify the opportunity record. An exception is provided for the opportunity owner for up to 7 days and only when attempting to update the description field. This can all be achieved by configuring the right logic in the validation rule.*

I also propose introducing custom permission to bypass this validation and assign it to the administrator. The validation rule will check whether the executing user has that permission or not. This will give us the flexibility to assign this permission to other users in the future if needed.

A similar validation rule will be introduced on the Opportunity line item object, which will check the same custom field on the Opportunity object and have a similar bypass mechanism for administrators.

Finally, I propose using an autolaunched flow to update the opportunity's record type upon opportunity closure. We can assign a page layout with read-only fields to this record type. This will give a better and friendlier user experience.

Let's now move on to the next and final requirement.

The system should support both euro and pound sterling currencies with dated exchange rates

This is a straightforward requirement that can be met with an out-of-the-box feature. Your solution could be as simple as the following:

For this requirement, I propose enabling the advanced currency management feature in Salesforce. Then, enter the suitable dated exchange rates.

That was the last shared PVA requirement. Let's update all the diagrams and see how they look.

The ordering business process flow diagram looks as follows:

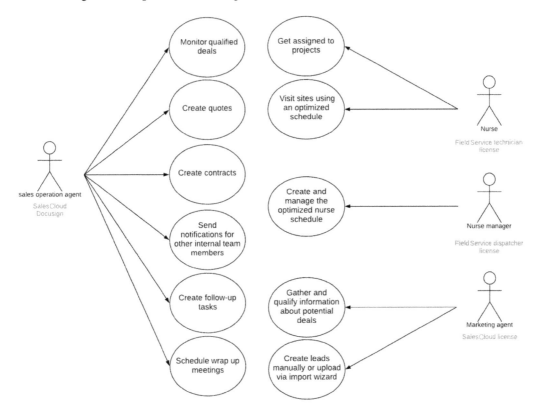

Figure 8.6 – Actors and licenses – final

The landscape architecture diagram looks as follows:

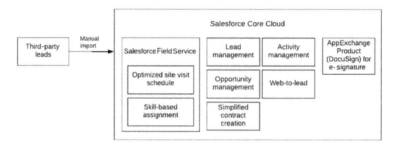

Figure 8.7 – Landscape architecture – final

The data model diagram looks as follows:

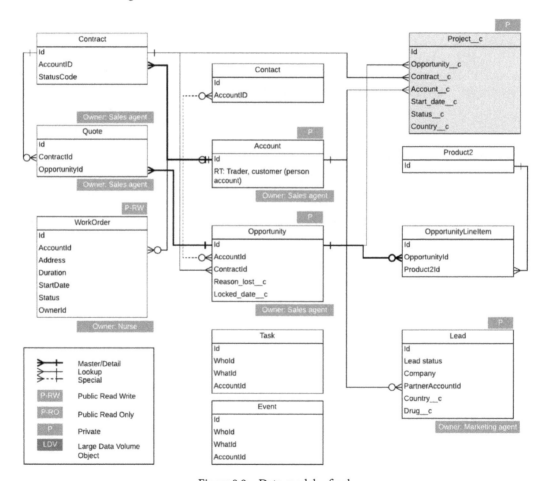

Figure 8.8 – Data model – final

That concludes the scenario. Please note that for some of the mini scenarios, we are not creating all the mandatory diagrams. That is because they are *simplified scenarios*, focusing on a *particular domain*, and we might not need all the diagrams to solve them. This is totally different for full scenarios, where you need to generate *all* the mandatory diagrams.

Summary

In this chapter, we dived into the details of the Salesforce solution architecture domain. We learned what is expected from a CTA to cover and at what level of detail. We discovered the process of selecting the right combination of configurable and programmable features to deliver a requirement, and we discussed some guiding principles in selecting third-party solutions to deliver value in a short time.

We then tackled a mini hypothetical scenario that focuses on solution architecture, and we solved it together and created some catching presentation pitches. We practiced the process of selecting the right feature to deliver functionality, and we learned that it is not enough to simply mention the name of the used feature, but you have to clearly and crisply explain how it is going to be used, end to end, with no gaps and no ambiguity. If it isn't clear for you, then it won't be clear to your client, and then you can't expect your team to be able to deliver it accurately.

We also covered other topics in the mini scenario, including selecting the right third-party solution to deliver value quickly and reduce risks.

In the next chapter, we will move on to the fifth domain that you need to master: integration.

9
Forging an Integrated Solution

In this chapter, we will continue with other Salesforce-specific knowledge areas required to pass the CTA review board. This is the fifth domain out of seven. We will go through the required knowledge and preparations for this domain and then complete a hands-on exercise using a mini hypothetical scenario.

As discussed in *Chapter 3, Core Architectural Concepts – Integration and Cryptography*, the enterprise landscape is continuously growing and becoming more complex. There is hardly an enterprise today that would use Salesforce in isolation from other systems. Distributed solutions are the default nowadays, mostly because integration today is much simpler than before.

Yet, it is still the area with the most significant impact on an implemented solution's success. During more than a decade of working with Salesforce technologies, I had the pleasure of working with clients from all around the world, sometimes as an implementer and other times as an advisor. And the one common area that consistently brought challenges to the teams was integration.

Integration is a complex domain but with a limited number of unique use cases, similar to IAM, where the domain itself was challenging and complex. It is not easy to understand the authentication flows with the required level of detail. However, there is a limited number of them. And if you manage to master them, you will be in a good position for the review board.

There is a limited number of Salesforce integration patterns. Understanding these different patterns, their pros and cons, when to use each of them, and how is vital to pass this domain. They are not easy to grasp, but we will go through each of them and clarify their characteristics and typical use cases.

We've come across some of these patterns in some of the previous scenarios. In this chapter, we will go through each of these patterns, understand when and how to use them, then move on to a mini hypothetical scenario where we put that knowledge into action. In this chapter, we're going to cover the following main topics:

- Understanding what you should be able to do as a Salesforce integration architect

- Introducing the integration architecture domain mini hypothetical scenario – Packt Medical Equipment

- Designing the enterprise integration interfaces to build your connected solution

Understanding what you should be able to do as a Salesforce integration architect

According to the Salesforce online documentation, the CTA candidate should be able to meet a specific set of objectives, which can be found at the following link: `https://trailhead.salesforce.com/en/help?article=Salesforce-Certified-Technical-Architect-Exam-Guide&search=release+exam+schedule`.

Let's have a closer look at each of these objectives.

Recommending the right integration landscape

Integration is a complex domain. Determining the components of an integrated solution includes the following:

- How are they connected?

- How do they securely interact?

- What data is exchanged?
- How does it require an in-depth understanding of the integration principles?

During my time working on Salesforce and non-Salesforce projects, I witnessed cases where a lack of understanding about the technology led to a circle of wasted efforts and fragile solutions.

On one occasion, an integration architect planned to transfer files across integrated enterprise systems using a pub-sub approach, overlooking the impact of the file size on this approach.

On another, the integration architect decided to build an entire middleware on top of core Salesforce, introducing dozens of classes, objects, and components to create an orchestration engine linking between several systems. This was a solution that was never load-tested and soon collapsed under real-world conditions.

Failing to understand a *technology's details* and *why* it has been created the way it has could lead you to bad design decisions. This is the reason I decided to introduce an entire chapter to cover the foundations in *Chapter 3, Core Architectural Concepts – Integration and Cryptography*. Understanding the history behind each integration approach and technology, how they differ from each other, and the right use cases for each will help you determine the exemplary landscape architecture for your integrated solution.

Determining the right enterprise integration architecture technology

Technology is the next topic to consider once you've decided on your integration approach. You need to understand the different tools available in the enterprise landscape. What is an ETL? What is an ESB? How do they differ from each other? And when should you pick one over the other? What is a reverse proxy? And what is an API manager? How can I connect a cloud application to an on-premise application? And more. We covered most of that in *Chapter 3, Core Architectural Concepts – Integration and Cryptography*.

It is recommended to get some hands-on experience with ETL or ESB, or both. This will help you understand the different approaches supported by some tools. For example, in order to integrate with an on-premise/behind firewall application, some tools offer the following:

- The ability to install a *secure client (also known as a secure agent)*. This is a small footprint application (provided by the same company offering the middleware) that can be installed on the secure intranet (behind the firewall). It can connect directly to a local database or API using specific ports. The secure client would then communicate with the cloud-based solution via other ports, such as 80 or 443, which are used for HTTP and HTTPS respectfully, and usually are permitted by the firewall.

- On other occasions, you might need to ask the firewall administrator to allow communications over specific ports for specific addresses, assuming the target application has a unique URI.

The following diagram illustrates how a secure client/secure agent works for a cloud-based ETL solution:

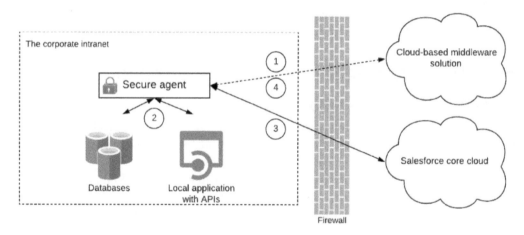

Figure 9.1 – An illustration of a cloud-based middleware using a secure agent app

Let's decrypt the preceding diagram:

1. The secure agent communicates directly with the cloud middleware, typically using ports 443 or 90. These are outbound communications, and therefore, there's no need to adjust or change the firewall rules. The agent downloads the definition of the integration jobs it is supposed to execute and stores them locally (usually encrypted).

2. Based on the downloaded job info, the secure agent executes the planned jobs.

3. The data is extracted, transformed, and transferred directly to the target system (in the diagram, **Salesforce**). Data is not staged in the middleware cloud (which is usually an essential requirement for data privacy regulations).

4. Based on pre-defined schedules, the secure agent would send logging and monitoring data back to the cloud-based middleware.

Understanding these details will help you present the full end-to-end solution during the review board. Let's now look at the next objective a CTA should meet in this domain.

Designing your integration interface using the right integration pattern

Integration patterns describe standard ways to integrate Salesforce with other systems. The principles themselves are not platform-specific, as they can be applied to any other platform. You need to fully understand their purpose, common use cases, and the Salesforce technologies used to implement them. While creating your end-to-end solution, you need to select which pattern to use based on the use case. More details about the patterns can be found at the following link: `https://developer.salesforce. com/docs/atlas.en-us.integration_patterns_and_practices.meta/ integration_patterns_and_practices/integ_pat_pat_summary.htm`.

Let's go through each of these patterns and briefly describe their characteristics.

Remote Process Invocation (RPI) – request and reply

Here is some high-level info about this pattern:

*   **Description**: This pattern is used to invoke a remote web service and wait for its response. During this waiting time, the system is in a *blocking* state. In a classic single-threaded desktop application, you will notice that the application is frozen while waiting for the response. This is not the case with web applications (such as Salesforce), but it is common to see a progress indicator spinning while waiting for a response.

*   **Timing**: This pattern is synchronous, sometimes referred to as *real-time*.

*   **Operational layer**: This pattern operates on both the data layer and the business logic layer, depending on the implementation. I have always found the name of this pattern a bit confusing. RPI integrations operate on the business logic layer, such as invoking a removal of a web service, passing the location and date, and receiving the expected weather forecast for the given date.

But in addition, this pattern can also be used for synchronous integrations on the data level, such as invoking a web service to copy a local record to a remote system and waiting until the transaction is committed and a confirmation is returned. The entire data insertion transaction here is considered an RPI.

- **Key use cases**: Invoke a remote web service, execute an operation, and wait for the result. This could include passing a data structure that gets copied to the remote system.

- **Relevant Salesforce features**: **Callouts** could be considered a relevant feature, such as callouts invoked from a Visualforce page or a Lightning component. This *does not* include an asynchronous callout invoked using **future methods** or similar capabilities.

You can find more details at the following link: `https://developer.salesforce.com/docs/atlas.en-us.integration_patterns_and_practices.meta/integration_patterns_and_practices/integ_pat_remote_process_invocation_state.htm`.

Let's now move on to the next pattern.

Remote Process Invocation (RPI) – fire and forget

Here is some high-level info about this pattern:

- **Description**: This pattern is used to invoke a remote web service and continue with other processes *without* waiting for a response. The system is *not blocked* from doing other operations. In a classic single-threaded desktop application, the application would invoke a remote web service and continue with other operations.

- **Timing**: This pattern is asynchronous. In some cases, it can be considered *near-real-time*.

- **Operational layer:** This pattern operates on both the data layer and the business logic layer, similar to the *RPI request and reply pattern*.

- **Key use cases**: Invoke a remote web service to execute an operation, but don't bother waiting to know the result. This could include passing a data structure that gets copied to the remote system. This pattern can be modified to include a *callback*. In that case, Salesforce would expect the remote system to call back once done processing and send the result. This is a common pattern due to its near-real-time nature, agility, scalability, and small overhead.

- **Relevant Salesforce features**: Several Salesforce features are relevant, such as **outbound messages**, **platform events**, **change data capture** (**CDC**), the **Salesforce streaming API**, callouts using **future methods**, callouts using **queueable classes**, **email notifications**, and **push notifications**.

You can find more details at the following link: `https://developer.salesforce.com/docs/atlas.en-us.integration_patterns_and_practices.meta/integration_patterns_and_practices/integ_pat_remote_process_invocation_fire_forget.htm`.

Let's now move on to the next pattern.

Batch data synchronization

Here is some high-level info about this pattern:

- **Description**: As indicated by its name, this pattern is mainly used to copy a dataset from one system to another. The dataset usually contains a bulk of records to be more efficient.

- **Timing**: This pattern is asynchronous, usually scheduled to run at a certain time and interval. Execution time is normally subject to the size of the copied dataset.

- **Operational layer**: This pattern operates on the data layer.

- **Key use cases**: Copy one dataset from one system to another or sync two datasets on two different systems. This pattern is common due to its efficiency, although it doesn't deliver the desired real-time/near-real-time experience demanded by today's applications. There are many cases where a delayed data sync is acceptable by the business, such as copying invoices from the invoicing system to the data warehouse every 12 hours.

- **Relevant Salesforce features**: The **Salesforce Bulk API** is a relevant feature. Salesforce Batch Apex with callouts could be tempting, but it is a risky pattern that you are encouraged to avoid. Consider using middleware instead.

You can find more details at the following link: `https://developer.salesforce.com/docs/atlas.en-us.integration_patterns_and_practices.meta/integration_patterns_and_practices/integ_pat_batch_data_sync.htm`.

Let's now move on to the next pattern.

Remote call-in

Here is some high-level info about this pattern:

- **Description**: This pattern is used when a remote system wants to invoke a process in Salesforce. From the perspective of the remote system, this will be one of the RPI patterns. From a Salesforce perspective, it is considered a *call-in*.

- **Timing**: This pattern could be synchronous or asynchronous, depending on the implementation.

- **Operational layer**: This pattern operates on both the data layer and the business logic layer, depending on the implementation.

- **Key use cases**: Invoking a standard Salesforce API to **create**, **read**, **update**, or **delete** (**CRUD**) data, or invoking a custom Salesforce web service (SOAP or REST), which returns a specific result.

- **Relevant Salesforce features**: Several Salesforce features are relevant, such as the **Salesforce REST API**, the **Salesforce SOAP API**, the **Salesforce Metadata API**, the **Salesforce Tooling API**, the **Salesforce Bulk API** (for bulk operations), and **Apex** web services.

It's worth mentioning that Apex web services are particularly useful when you want to expose an *atomic* functionality that applies the *all-or-none* transaction principle, for example, to expose a web service that accepts a specific data structure as an input and generates an account, an opportunity, and opportunity line items. Where a failure in creating any record of these objects would result in rolling back the entire transaction, such atomic transactions are essential when data integrity is a concern.

You can find more details at the following link: `https://developer.salesforce.com/docs/atlas.en-us.integration_patterns_and_practices.meta/integration_patterns_and_practices/integ_pat_remote_call_in.htm`.

Let's now move on to the next pattern.

UI update based on changes in data

Here is some high-level info about this pattern:

- **Description**: This is a relatively more recent pattern. You use it when you need to update the Salesforce UI based on some changes in Salesforce data without the need to refresh the entire page.

- **Timing**: This pattern is asynchronous.

- **Operational layer**: This pattern operates on the UI layer.

- **Key use cases**: Building a dynamic page that shows specific values and graphs based on Salesforce data, then update certain elements of that page when the underlying data is changed.

- **Relevant Salesforce features**: Several Salesforce features are relevant, such as the **Salesforce Streaming API**, **push notifications**, **platform events**, and **CDC** (technically based on platform events).

You can find more details at the following link: `https://developer.salesforce. com/docs/atlas.en-us.integration_patterns_and_practices.meta/ integration_patterns_and_practices/integ_pat_ui_updates_from_ data_changes.htm`.

Let's now move on to the next pattern.

Data virtualization

Here is some high-level info about this pattern:

- **Description**: This pattern is used to retrieve and display data stored on a remote system in Salesforce without persisting the data. This is very useful when there is no real need to keep the data in Salesforce. The data will be fetched on the fly and on demand and displayed to the user.

- **Timing**: This pattern is synchronous. However, some techniques, such as **lazy loading**, could turn this into a special case of asynchronous communication.

- **Operational layer**: This pattern operates on the UI layer.

- **Key use cases**: Building UIs that utilize data hosted outside Salesforce, such as archived data. Mashups using remote services such as Google Maps is another valid use case.

- **Relevant Salesforce features**: Custom **Visualforce** pages, **Lightning components**, **Salesforce Connect**, and **Salesforce Canvas** are all relevant features.

You can find more details at the following link: `https://developer.salesforce. com/docs/atlas.en-us.integration_patterns_and_practices. meta/integration_patterns_and_practices/integ_pat_data_ virtualization.htm`.

While designing an integration interface, you need to define the pattern and specify which Salesforce technology to use. This skill is the next you are expected to master in this domain.

Selecting and justifying the right platform-specific integration capabilities

Salesforce comes with a set of out-of-the-box functionalities to facilitate the different integration patterns. You can use the following table as a cheat sheet:

Capability	Description
REST API	Salesforce comes with an out-of-the-box REST API that can be used to interact with Salesforce data. REST APIs, in general, are easy to integrate with, especially from mobiles and JavaScript. It supports simple HTTP calls (GET, POST, PUT, PATCH, and DELETE).
SOAP API	The Salesforce out-of-the-box SOAP API can be used by consuming one of the standard two **Web Services Description Language** (**WSDL**) files. The Enterprise WSDL is strongly typed, making it challenging to maintain but easier to use if the data model rarely changes, while the Partner WSDL is loosely typed, which makes it more dynamic and more fit to be used by partners or by organizations that experience frequent data model changes. The SOAP API can be used to work with Salesforce data similar to the REST API. However, it is more challenging to implement for thin clients, such as mobile devices and JavaScript apps. Moreover, it tends to have a bigger payload and is therefore considered a bit slower than REST.
Bulk API	This API is designed to work with huge chunks of data. Some ETL tools are built to switch automatically to this API when they are used to load a huge amount of data into Salesforce.
Salesforce Connect	A paid feature that allows retrieving data on the fly from an external data source that supports the OData 2.0 or OData 4.0 standards. OData interfaces are REST-based, and you can invoke them using custom code. Salesforce Connect makes that process much more straightforward. External OData tables are automatically represented in Salesforce as external objects, allowing this data to be linked to other Salesforce data and queried using regular SOQL statements.

Capability	Description
Canvas	Salesforce Canvas is a paid feature that enables you to integrate remote web applications within Salesforce. This is typically a UI-level integration, but the Canvas SDK can add more advanced functionalities.
Chatter REST API	Chatter has its own REST API. This API can interact with objects such as Chatter feeds, recommendations, groups, topics, and followers.
Metadata API	This API is unlikely to be used in a data integration scenario. It is mostly used by release management tools. It is used to retrieve, create, update, deploy, or delete salesforce metadata information, such as page layouts and user profiles.
Streaming API	The Streaming API is used to develop modern dynamic pages. It allows your pages/components to receive notifications when Salesforce data is changed, allowing you to update parts of your page/component accordingly. It utilizes the `PushTopic` functionality.
Tooling API	This API is designed to help with building custom development tools that interact with the Salesforce platform.
Apex callouts	This functionality allows invoking a remote web service using Apex. Apex callouts could be synchronous or asynchronous. Asynchronous methods must have the `@future` annotation. You can also utilize the `Queueable` interface to develop Apex classes with asynchronous methods. You can make long-running callouts using the `Continuation` class.
Email	This is an old integration technology. But it is still valid and still has its use cases, for example, while integrating with legacy apps that don't support any of the more recent interfaces. You can utilize the `InboundEmailHandler` interface to develop custom Apex classes to handle inbound emails received by a Salesforce email service.
Outbound messages	A configurable outbound integration capability. It can contain data from one Salesforce object only and is sent using the SOAP standard. This means the consumer must be able to implement a SOAP WSDL. The sent outbound message can include a session ID, enabling the received to do a callback into Salesforce, using the session ID for authentication. Outbound messages have a 24-hour retry mechanism.

Capability	Description
Platform events	Platform events are based on the pub-sub integration approach. You can define the structure of a platform service in a similar way as you do with custom objects. Platform events can be published using Apex, Flow, and Process Builder, and you can subscribe to them using the same tools in addition to CometD clients. Since they can be easily subscribed to using different Salesforce features, they can be utilized to create applications based on event-driven architecture within the Salesforce platform itself, in addition to passing data to external subscribers.
Change Data Capture (CDC)	CDC is a feature built on top of platform events, which means that they share a lot of characteristics. CDC publishes events representing changes to Salesforce records, such as creating a new record, the deletion and updating of existing records, and record undeleting.
External services	External services allow invoking remote web services using Salesforce flows.

Now that you are familiar with this domain's expectations, let's look at a practical example where we use this knowledge to design an integrated, secure, and scalable solution.

Introducing the integration architecture domain mini hypothetical scenario – Packt Medical Equipment

The following mini scenario cdescribes a challenge with a particular client. The scenario is tuned to focus on challenges related to *integration architecture* specifically. But as you would expect, there are also requirements related to other domains, such as data and security.

Before you start, make yourself familiar with the six integration patterns we mentioned earlier in this chapter. In this mini-scenario, you will go through practical examples of some of these patterns. We already came across some of them in earlier chapters. This chapter will focus on the logical design thinking required to design an integration interface.

You are also advised to go through the scenario once to build an initial picture of the required solution. Then, go through the requirements one by one and try to solve it yourself, then compare that with the suggested solution. Try to practice telling the end-to-end solution describing a particular integration interface.

Without further ado, let's proceed to the scenario.

The scenario

Packt Medical Equipment (PME) has been selling medical equipment to health providers worldwide for the past 75 years. PME currently sells more than 20,000 different device models from various brands. PME has experienced massive growth in recent years. They sold nearly 5 million devices last year, and they expect their sales to grow by 10% year on year.

Current situation

PME operates in multiple geographies. Each has a variety of CRM solutions tailored to work with distributors. PME would like to replace all the existing CRM solutions with a Salesforce-based solution. However, they would like to retain two existing systems as they believe they offer a valuable set of tailored services:

- A centralized, browser-based **Enterprise Resource Platform** (**ERP**) system, used by the PME account managers to view the financial details of distributors they own the relationship with. The system is accessible only from within the company's intranet.

- A centralized inventory management system that holds data about the devices available at each location. It includes updated information about the arrival date and time of devices in transit to distributors. Moreover, the system allows for getting information about the devices at distributor locations.

Data is currently entered manually into the inventory management system. The system is not integrated with other systems and does not have any exposed APIs. The system utilizes an MS SQL database to store the data.

The ERP system is also not integrated with other systems. However, it has a rich set of SOAP and REST APIs.

Users are required to authenticate to each of these systems before they can use them. Authentication is currently done separately as each of these systems stores its own user credentials. At the same time, PME uses an LDAP-compatible directory to store all internal and external identities.

The ordering process consists of three stages: negotiation, confirmation, and shipping. Orders are placed quarterly.

PME is looking to modernize its landscape and offer more standardized processes worldwide. Moreover, they are looking to increase the productivity of their users by avoiding double data entry as much as possible.

Requirements

PME shared the following requirements:

1. The PME security team has mandated the use of single sign-on across all the systems used as part of the new solution, including the ERP and the inventory management system.

2. Device orders should be originated in Salesforce.

3. Before the negotiations stage, PME sets a maximum and minimum allocation for each distributor's device type.

4. In the negotiations stage, the distributor should be able to place an order, which contains a list of the device models and quantities.

5. If each model's requested quantity falls within the defined allocation per model, the order is automatically *confirmed*.

6. If each model's requested quantity falls outside the defined allocation per model, the order should be sent to the account manager for approval. The system should automatically retrieve the four values indicating the financial status of the distributor from the ERP.

7. The account manager should utilize the financial health indicator values, in addition to the historical orders for this distributor, to determine the right action.

8. When the order is about to be shipped, the inventory management system may create multiple shipments. For each shipment, a list of the devices and their unique manufacturer IDs are created. The shipments and their line items should be visible to the distributor's fleet managers in Salesforce. The status of each line item should be *in transit*.

9. When the shipment is delivered, the distributor's fleet managers are given 3 days to confirm the shipment's receipt. They should confirm the status of each and every device identified by its unique manufacturer ID. The status of each line item should be *available in stock*.

10. The account manager should be notified if more than 3 days passed without receiving a confirmation.

11. On a regular basis, the distributor's fleet managers update each device's inventory status identified by its manufacturer ID. They should indicate whether the device has been sold, returned, damaged, or is still available in stock. This information should also be updated in the inventory system.

PME is looking for your help to design a scalable integrated solution that meets their requirements and ambitious roadmap.

Designing the enterprise integration interfaces to build your connected solution

Give yourself time to quickly skim through the scenario and understand the big picture and develop some initial thoughts about the solution. This is a must-do step for every scenario. Our approach is to incrementally solve the scenario. However, you still need to understand the big picture first and build some initial ideas, or you might risk losing a lot of time redesigning your solution.

Understanding the current situation

The first paragraph has some general information about PME. We learn from it that PME has some legacy CRM solutions and is looking to consolidate them using Salesforce. Moreover, we get to know that they would like to retain two systems – a legacy ERP system accessible only via the corporate intranet and a centralized inventory management system.

Both systems are disconnected from any other system. The scenario didn't exactly specify where they are hosted, but considering what we know about the ERP solution, it is fair to assume that it is hosted on-premise (or behind a VPN, but this is a less usual scenario). It is also reasonable to assume that the inventory management system is also hosted on-premise.

Even at this stage, you need to start thinking:

> *How can I integrate a cloud-based platform such as Salesforce with an on-premise-hosted application?*

Tip

Don't worry if you are struggling to find the answer. Just flip back to *Chapter 3, Core Architectural Concepts – Integration and Cryptography*, particularly the *Discussing the different integration tools* section, and make sure you are familiar with each of these tools.

In short, you need some sort of middleware to do outbound calls from Salesforce to an on-premise hosted application. We don't know yet what kind of middleware we are going to need. We will find out more while going through the rest of the scenario.

For the time being, let's capture what we learned on a draft landscape diagram. Your diagram could look like the following:

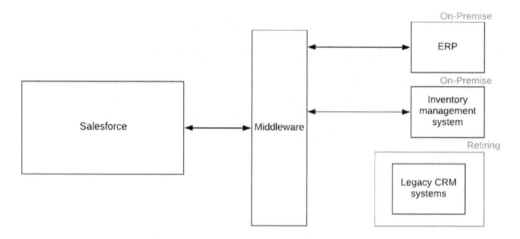

Figure 9.2 – Landscape architecture – first draft

PME wants to modernize its landscape with Salesforce. They also want to integrate it with their legacy applications, and they want that done in the right way to ensure future scalability and extensibility.

They shared a lengthy list of requirements, which we are going to cover next.

Diving into the shared requirements

Now let's go through the requirements shared by PME, craft a proposed solution for each, and update our diagrams accordingly to help us with the presentation. Let's start with the first requirement, which begins with the following line.

The PME security team has mandated the use of single sign-on across all the systems used as part of the new solution, including the ERP and the inventory management system

We know that the ERP and the inventory management systems have their own authentication capabilities. However, there is nothing in the scenario indicating that they don't support standards such as OAuth 2.0, OpenID Connect, or SAML 2.0. You can make that assumption, clearly communicate it, and base your solution on it.

You still need to define an identity provider that can work with all systems. Moreover, you need to explain which system would be holding the user credentials (the identity store).

In my years of coaching CTA candidates, I noticed that this part is often overlooked. They'd also struggle to explain that if it was raised during the Q&A, because they were not prepared for it.

There is a technique that we will learn later, in *Chapter 11, Communicating and Socializing Your Solution*, called **question seeding**. Which, in short, is intentionally leaving some lengthy conversational areas unanswered to draw attention to them during the Q&A. It has to be well understood and used carefully. When you use that technique, you already know the answer to something. You draw the attention of the judges to it but then leave it open, allowing them to ask questions about it during the Q&A.

When you leave some topics open because you are not aware of their importance or don't know the answer, this is more of an attempt to blow a *smokescreen* and hope that the judges won't notice. A strategy that you should avoid at all costs.

When you are proposing an SSO strategy, you need to be crisp and clear about all of its areas unless you are intentionally leaving them open for further conversations. In this scenario, you have to explain your identity management strategy. Your proposed solution could be the following:

> *I am assuming that both the ERP and the inventory management systems support the OpenID Connect standard. I propose introducing an identity provider and identity management tool such as Ping Identity to the landscape. Ping will be utilizing its identity store (PingDirectory) to maintain user credentials.*

> *Currently, user credentials are hosted locally by ERP and inventory management. I propose migrating the user details from these systems to Ping.*

> *I am assuming that it won't be possible to migrate the systems' passwords because only their hashed value was stored. Therefore, we need to send emails to all the migrated customers asking them to set a new password. The email will contain a link with a protected one-time link that allows them to set a new password using a Ping-hosted page.*

> *Ping will handle provisioning and de-provisioning users to all linked SPs. I will utilize a federation ID to uniquely identify the customer across the systems. This could be the employee ID.*

> *When the user is attempting to access the Salesforce instance using the unique MyDomain URL, the system will detect the authentication providers configured for that instance. And if Ping is the only authentication provider, the user will be automatically redirected to Ping's login page. The authentication will take place using the OpenID Connect web server flow.*

Should we stop there or carry on explaining exactly what that flow looks like? It is up to your strategy and how you are planning to utilize the presentation time. If you stopped there, you are effectively *seeding a question*. If the judges are interested in testing your knowledge about that flow, they will come back to it during the Q&A. If they are not (because they believe you already know what it takes to pass the IAM domain), then they won't.

This is the power of that technique. If used wisely, you can avoid losing time explaining areas that you don't necessarily need to.

Are you surprised to see an IAM requirement in a mini-scenario focusing on integration? You shouldn't by now. We discussed earlier that the domains are not isolated and are very much related to each other.

Update your landscape architecture diagram, and let's move on to the next requirement.

Device orders should be originated in Salesforce

This is a short and direct requirement. The orders have to be originated in Salesforce. However, that doesn't mean they will have to stay there for their entire life cycle.

A question that could come to your mind now is: which object can I use for this requirement? The obvious answer is the standard *order* object. However, don't let the word choices used in the scenario dictate your design decisions. If the scenario calls that an *order*, it doesn't mean it has to be translated to the *standard order object*. You can use the opportunity to represent an order in some use cases, mainly when there is a price negotiation process (quotes) or a need to forecast.

You could also decide to use a custom object if any of the standard objects cannot meet the requirements. For the time being, we don't have enough clarity to decide. Let's take some notes and move on to the next requirement.

Before the negotiations stage, PME sets a maximum and minimum allocation for each distributor's device type

How are you planning to organize and offer PME's products to its distributors? One way is to utilize *Pricebooks* (the object is technically called *Pricebook2*). In this case, you can define maximum and minimum allocations as additional fields on the *PricebookEntry*.

Remember that *Pricebooks* work with both the order and the opportunity objects. We still haven't decided which one to use, but while skimming the scenario, we found no requirement that indicates price negotiation or forecasting. We can start assuming that we will use the *Order* object and update that later if required.

Is this the only way to solve this requirement? You know the answer by now. There are multiple ways to solve a problem. Your solution should offer a valid and technically correct solution considering the assumptions you have made.

> **Are the requirements in this scenario good enough to propose using B2B commerce?**
>
> In my opinion, no. But if you decide to propose it, be prepared to clearly explain how you plan to configure it to meet all required functionalities.

Your proposed solution could be the following:

> *I propose using standard Pricebook and PricebookEntry objects to offer products to different distributors. They will allow me to use a different price per distributor based on agreements. I also propose introducing four new fields to the PricebookEntry object to hold maximum and minimum allowed quantity per year and order.*

> **Note**
>
> So far, we don't have any requirement indicating that PME's distributors will have access to Salesforce. Therefore, we can assume that the *Pricebooks* will continue to be accessible to all sales agents. In order to adjust this solution to work with *partner communities*, you need to update the *OWD* of the *Pricebook* object to *no access* or *view only*, then share the right *Pricebook* with the right set of users.

Update your data model diagram, and let's move on to the next requirement.

In the negotiation stage, the distributor should be able to place an order, which contains a list of the device models and quantities

We now have a requirement indicating the need for distributors to access Salesforce. The distributors will need the ability to create *orders*. They will also require a user license that supports record sharing capabilities using *manual sharing* or *sharing rules*. Both the *Partner Community* and the *Customer Community Plus* provide these capabilities. However, it is common to utilize the Partner Community licenses with distributors (after all, they are *business partners*). Let's assume that and adjust later if needed. Your proposed solution could be the following:

> *In order to grant the distributors access to Salesforce to place orders, I propose assigning a Partner Community license to their users. I will update the OWD value of the Pricebook object to no access. The admin will then manually share each distributor's Pricebook with the right partner role for that distributor.*

Update your landscape architecture, data model, role hierarchy, and actors and licenses diagrams. They could now look like this:

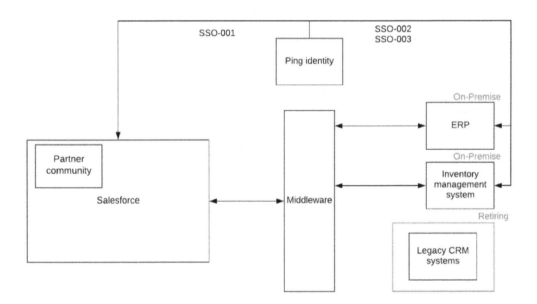

Figure 9.3 – Landscape architecture – second draft

Your data model diagram could look like the following:

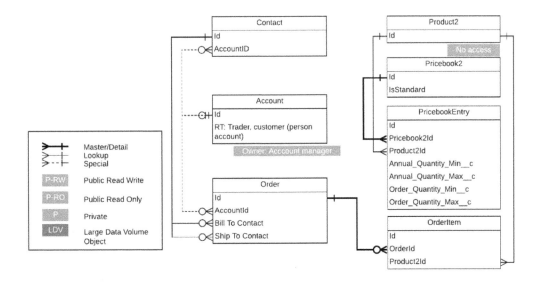

Figure 9.4 – Data model – first draft

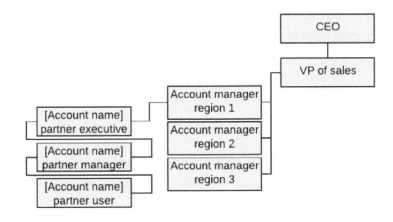

Figure 9.5 – Role hierarchy – first draft

And your actors and licenses diagram could look like the following:

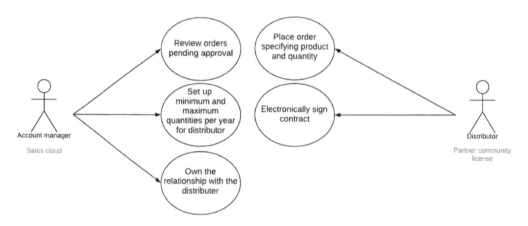

Figure 9.6 – Actors and licenses – first draft

Let's now move on to the next requirement.

If each model's requested quantity falls within the defined allocation per model, the order is automatically confirmed

In order to fully understand this requirement, we need to read the one after. At this stage, you probably should ask yourself: *Is there an out-of-the-box functionality that enables me to check these four fields on the PricebookEntry object upon placing an order?*

Let's check the next requirement.

If each model's requested quantity falls outside the defined allocation per model, the order should be sent to the account manager for approval

We need to introduce a mechanism to check the four values on the *PricebookEntry* object and determine the order's status. In a specific use case, we need to automatically submit the order for approval.

Remember that two of the fields we suggested introducing to the *PricebookEntry* object were annual minimum and maximum quantities. To check these values, you need to query all the specified distributor orders in the current year.

Our early design decisions are affecting the potential solutions available for us at this stage. If you used a different mechanism to introduce the quantity restrictions, you would have ended up with a different challenge at this stage. However, if your solution was technically correct, you are very likely to be able to work around its restrictions. If your earlier solution had serious drawbacks, you might find yourself too restricted at this stage and might need to reconsider your earlier options.

Your proposed solution could be the following:

> *I propose introducing a trigger and an Apex trigger handler class on the OrderItem object, which fires upon inserting or saving a record of that object. The trigger would then retrieve the four quantity restriction values from the related PricebookEntry record and compare them against the OrderItem record's quantity. Moreover, the code would also query all OrderItem records placed by the same distributor for the same product in the current year and determine whether the distributor is still adhering to the annual restricted quantities.*
>
> *Based on that, the Apex code would either set the order status to confirmed or pending approval. And will submit the record for approval if needed.*

The rest of the requirement indicates a need to retrieve four values from the ERP to determine the distributor's financial health.

The system should automatically retrieve the four values indicating the financial status of the distributor from the ERP.

The scenario could give you the impression that this transaction should happen sequentially after submitting the record for approval. But the questions you should ask yourself are: At which integration level will this interface operate? Which pattern should be used? Do we need to copy the data from the ERP, or can we retrieve it on the fly? What is the timing of this interface?

Let's check the next requirement to determine the right integration approach.

The account manager should utilize the financial health indicator values, in addition to the historical orders for this distributor, to determine the right action

The data is retrieved to support the account manager in making a decision. Let's consider the following:

- **Timing**: What is the ideal timing for this interface? The financial status of the distributor could change from one day to another – perhaps even faster, depending on how frequently this data is updated at the ERP. Ideally, this data should be as up to date as possible.

- **The need to host the data in Salesforce**: Do we need to copy the data to Salesforce? What benefit would we gain from that? The data would be reportable, quicker to access, and subject to Salesforce's user access control and data sharing and visibility. Moreover, we could trigger workflows and other automation based on data change. But do we need any of that in this requirement?

  Hosting the data in Salesforce has its challenges too. For example, you might find out that such information has to be encrypted at rest, which will open a host of other restrictions.

  The requirement is simpler than that. Try not to overcomplicate it for yourself. We only want to retrieve these values during the approval process to aid the account manager. This could take place on the fly. There is no need to copy the data or store it in Salesforce.

- **Determining the integration level and the pattern used**: This is going to be easy from here onward. We are looking for a pattern that allows near-real-time data retrieval, where the data is not stored in Salesforce but simply displayed at the UI level. Go through the patterns listed earlier in this chapter, and see which one fits the requirement best.

Your proposed solution could be the following:

> *In order to fulfill this requirement, I considered different integration patterns. I believe that the right pattern to use is data virtualization, where the data is fetched on the fly and on demand and displayed only on the UI level. No data will be kept in Salesforce.*

I will create an Aura app or Visualforce page that initiates a callout to the middleware upon loading. I am going to add a hyperlink field to the standard approval page. Once the link is clicked, a new tab will open with the Visualforce page. The callout will be made to the middleware, which, in turn, will call the ERP system and retrieve the data. The data will then be displayed on the Visualforce page. I will use the continuation class in my Visualforce page controller to ensure that the call from Salesforce to MuleSoft has a long timeout.

I propose using MuleSoft as an integration middleware. It can consume the APIs exposed by the ERP, and it can handle exceptions and retry connecting if needed. I am assuming that the on-premise firewall will be configured to allow MuleSoft to communicate with these APIs.

I will utilize the Named Credentials functionality to authenticate from Salesforce to MuleSoft using a named principal. I am assuming that MuleSoft would authenticate to the ERP using simple authentication. The integration channel will be secured between Salesforce and MuleSoft using two-way TLS.

The page will also retrieve and display the distributor's historical orders. The scenario didn't specify the number of orders created every year by each distributor. I am assuming that is low. I am assuming that there are no more than 100,000 orders generated every year and that PME would archive all orders over 5 years of age. The scenario didn't specify an archiving requirement, so I will not proceed with further details, but I am happy to do so if required.

Once the order is approved, I will utilize a field update to update the status of the order to confirmed.

That provides an end-to-end solution to this requirement. Don't try to over-complicate things for yourself. The scenario didn't specify an archiving requirement. You can add some assumptions and let the judges know that you are willing to explain that if needed, but don't assume that you need to solve something that hasn't been requested and therefore wastes valuable time in your presentation.

> **Tip**
> Remember to use your diagrams while explaining this solution and any other solution, in fact. Your diagrams are tools to help you tell the end-to-end story.

Update your diagrams; you are going to need them to explain the solution to the judges. And let's move on to the next requirement.

When the order is about to be shipped, the inventory management system may create multiple shipments

The questions you should ask yourself at this stage are the following:

- **Timing**: What is the ideal timing for this interface? When is this data going to be required? The shipments and their line items should ideally be available for the fleet managers as soon as possible, but a slight delay of a few minutes is usually acceptable. Shipments take a long time; a delay of 10-15 minutes is hardly going to make a difference.

- **The need to host the data in Salesforce**: Do we need to copy the data to Salesforce? The short answer so far is *no*. There is no benefit of copying this data over to Salesforce.

- **Integration level and pattern**: What is the integration level? We are not sure yet whether this is going to be a UI-level integration or a data-level integration. It will not be a business-process level integration as there is no business process that we need to invoke on either end.

We need more details before we can come up with the right decision. This is very applicable in real life as well. Don't rush to conclusions and assume that every integration is *data synchronization*. I have had the pleasure of working with many clients across many different projects and verticals, and I can assure you that this is a *very common mistake*. Rushing to conclusions and skipping the organized way of design thinking usually leads to the wrong conclusions.

Take this case as an example. We can rush to the conclusion that the data has to be copied to Salesforce. But what would be the justification? Why can't we simply keep this data where it is and retrieve it on the fly (just like we did for the distributor's financial health indicators)? If you don't have a *solid technical reason*, then your solution is missing something. Be prepared to be *challenged* on that during the review board (the judges will know that this is not well justified, so they will probe with questions).

Let's check the next requirement to further understand how this interface should work.

When the shipment is delivered, the distributor's fleet managers are given 3 days to confirm the shipment's receipt

We are now learning about a new requirement. There is a need to invoke a process within Salesforce, depending on the received data.

There are several ways to fulfill this requirement if the data is in Salesforce, such as utilizing time-based workflows, tasks, or scheduled batch jobs (to update the shipment line items with the number of days passed and trigger a notification accordingly). But there is hardly a way to do that if the data is not stored in Salesforce. We would need to modify the inventory management application to introduce this functionality. Updating such a legacy application is a very time-consuming task and typically results in sub-optimal functionality.

Now we have a solid justification for proposing copying the data over to Salesforce. We have an explicit requirement that cannot be easily fulfilled without hosting the data in Salesforce. Your proposed solution could be the following:

In order to fulfill this requirement, I considered different integration patterns. I believe that the right pattern to use is batch data synchronization, where the data is copied from the inventory managing system to Salesforce.

MuleSoft will be configured to run a scheduled batch job every 15 minutes. The job will copy the new shipment and shipment line items records from the inventory system to Salesforce. Ideally, this job should fire whenever a new shipment record is created in the inventory management system. But considering that it is a legacy application, I assumed that it is incapable of notifying MuleSoft of such activity. I also assumed that a delay of 15 minutes is acceptable by the business. If not, the frequency of this job can be increased.

Once the records are created in Salesforce, their status will be set to available in stock. The shipment records will be linked to the order object using a master/details relationship. This will ensure the records are visible to all the distributor users who have access to the order record.

I will use an autolaunched flow to create a task due in three days to update the shipment line item status. The task will be assigned to the distributor's fleet manager's queue.

This is an inbound interface to Salesforce. MuleSoft would authenticate to Salesforce using OpenID Connect web server flow (for the first time, during setup) followed by the refresh token flow afterward using a named principal (integration user). This interface will be secured using two-way TLS.

I also assumed that MuleSoft would use its own connector to MS-SQL to directly access the inventory management database. I assumed that the on-premise firewall would be configured to allow MuleSoft to access the MS-SQL server database. This interface will be secured using one-way TLS. Simple authentication will be used.

I assumed that the number of shipments is relatively low. I assumed earlier that there are 100,000 orders created every year. Therefore, I am assuming two shipments per order. That is 200,000 shipments per year every year. According to the scenario, PME sold 5 million devices last year, with 10% year on year growth. This means that the shipment line item object could become an LDV after a few years.

Therefore, I propose using a MuleSoft scheduled batch job to delete shipments sold by the distributors from more than a year from Salesforce. This assumes that these values will already exist in the inventory management system. Therefore, they won't be completely lost after we delete them from Salesforce. I have considered this as another integration interface in my diagram.

You might think that coming up with all these words during the presentation is too difficult. That is *true* if you are *not utilizing* your *diagrams*. Note that the diagrams will contain all the info about authentication and security. You are simply using your diagrams in your presentation to tell the end-to-end story.

Update your data model, landscape architecture, and your list of integration interfaces. And let's move on to the next requirement.

The account manager should be notified if more than 3 days passed without receiving a confirmation

This is another requirement that can be fulfilled in multiple ways. Your proposed solution could be the following:

> *I will utilize standard reports and dashboards for this. I will create a report showing overdue tasks of a specific type. I am assuming that a report will be created for each account manager, and it will be scheduled to be sent every. This will ensure the account manager is notified. We could have used time-based workflows as well, but I believe reports will be good enough.*

Let's move on to the next requirement.

On a regular basis, the distributor's fleet managers update each device's inventory status, identified by its manufacturer ID

Most of this has been covered already. However, make sure you read the requirement entirely up to the last word. Don't risk skipping a requirement and therefore dropping a valuable point. Your proposed solution here could be the following:

> *The first part of the requirement is already fulfilled using the new custom objects that we introduced. The distributor's fleet managers will be granted read/write access to these objects' status fields using field-level security. Moreover, we already mentioned that the shipment object would be linked to the order using a master/detail relationship. This means the records will be visible to all partner users who have access to the order record.*

> *In order to synchronize these values back to the inventory management system, I will utilize another MuleSoft scheduled batch job. I am assuming that it will run every 1 hour and that this delay is acceptable by the business. The interface will copy the changed shipment line item statuses back to the inventory management system. This will be another interface utilizing the batch data synchronization pattern.*

> *I thought of utilizing platform events or **Change Data Capture** (CDC) to send the changed data from Salesforce to MuleSoft. But preferred the scheduled batch to ensure the consistency of delivering all changes to the inventory management system. Especially that there was no shared requirement indicating a need for near-real-time data synchronization. This interface will also be easier to build, considering that we already have a similar interface operating in the opposite direction.*

The same authorization and security mechanisms used by the shipment
synchronization interface will be used by this one too.

That was the last shared PME requirement. Let's update all the diagrams and see how they look.

Here's the landscape architecture diagram:

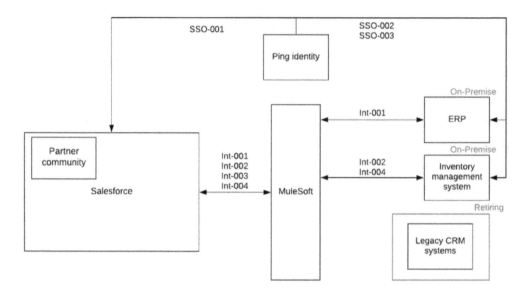

Figure 9.7 – Landscape architecture – final

Here are the integration interfaces:

Interface Code	Source / Destination	Integration Layer	Integration Pattern	Description	Security	Authentication
Int-001	Salesforce --> Mulesoft --> ERP	UI	Mashup / Data virtualization	Retrieve the four financial health indicator values from the ERP system on the fly. Salesforce would invoke a web service exposed by MuleSoft. Which, in turn, would invoke the right API from the ERP system.	HTTPS (two way SSL/TLS) between Salesforce and MuleSoft. HTTPS (one way SSL/TLS) Between MuleSoft and the ERP)	OpenID Connect web server flow (then refresh token flow) with mutual authentication between Salesforce and MuleSoft. Simple authentication between MuleSoft and the ERP
Int-002	MuleSoft (pull from inventory management) --> Salesforce	Data	Batch data synch Asynch	A scheduled MuleSoft batch job to retrieve shipments and shipment line items from the inventory management system and copy them to Salesforce.	HTTPS (two way SSL/TLS) between Salesforce and MuleSoft. HTTPS (one way SSL/TLS) Between MuleSoft and the inventory management system)	OpenID Connect web server flow (then refresh token flow) with mutual authentication between Salesforce and MuleSoft. Simple authentication between MuleSoft and the inventory management system)
Int-003	MuleSoft --> Salesforce	Data	Batch data deletion Asynch	A scheduled MuleSoft batch job to delete shipment line items records which have been sold by the distributor more than one year ago. The job also deletes Shipments without shipment line items.	HTTPS (two way SSL/TLS) between Salesforce and MuleSoft	OpenID Connect web server flow (then refresh token flow) with mutual authentication between Salesforce and MuleSoft
Int-004	MuleSoft (pull from Salesforce) --> inventory management	Data	Batch data synch Asynch	A scheduled MuleSoft batch job to retrieve shipment line items from Salesforce and copy their statuses to the inventory management system.	HTTPS (two way SSL/TLS) between Salesforce and MuleSoft. HTTPS (one way SSL/TLS) Between MuleSoft and the inventory management system)	OpenID Connect web server flow (then refresh token flow) with mutual authentication between Salesforce and MuleSoft. Simple authentication between MuleSoft and the inventory management system)
SSO-001	SSO for Salesforce using Ping Identity as IDP	SSO	SSO - OpenID Connect	SSO using OpenID Connect with Ping Identity as IDP and entity stores. Web server flow	HTTPS (one way SSL/TLS)	OpenID Connect web server flow
SSO-002	SSO for ERP using Ping Identity as IDP	SSO	SSO – OpenID Connect	SSO using OpenID Connect with Ping Identity as IDP and identity stores. Web server flow	HTTPS (one way SSL/TLS)	OpenID Connect web Server flow
SSO-003	SSO for the inventory management system using Ping Identity as IDP	SSO	SSO – OpenID Connect	SSO using OpenID Connect with Ping Identity as IDP and identity stores. Web server flow	HTTPS (one way SSL/TLS)	OpenID Connect web server flow

Figure 9.8 – Integration interfaces – final

And the data model diagram looks like this:

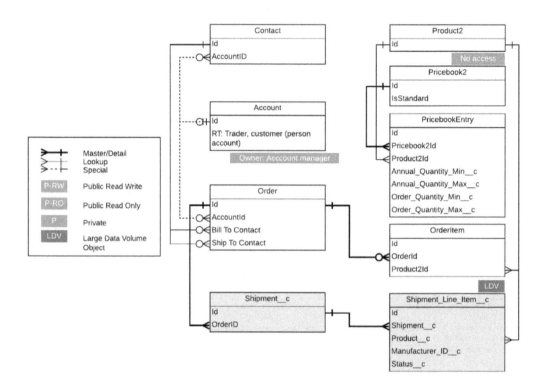

Figure 9.9 – Data model – final

> **Note**
> No changes occurred to the other diagrams.

That concludes the scenario. We will continue to see more integration-related requirements in the chapters to come. But we have now learned about the structured way to determine the right design for an integration interface.

In this scenario, we needed to connect to an on-premise hosted application, therefore, it was easy to justify using a middleware. However, integration middleware adds value in many other use cases. Please ensure you go through the details listed in *Chapter 3, Core Architectural Concepts – Integration and Cryptography*. I have seen a lot of technical debt created in the Salesforce core cloud due to a lack of integration middleware.

Summary

In this chapter, we dived into the details of the Salesforce integration architecture domain. We learned what is expected from a CTA to cover and at what level of detail. We discovered the key Salesforce integration patterns, and we understood their importance and impact on the clarity of the designed solution.

We then tackled a mini hypothetical scenario that focused on integration architecture, and we solutioned it together and created some catching presentation pitches. We learned the structured way of designing an integration interface, and we came up against some interesting design decisions. We came across multiple examples where we used our diagrams to structure an end-to-end solution presented in an easy-to-follow way. We learned the negative impact of rushing to conclusions about the integration interfaces and how to avoid that.

We also covered other topics in the mini-scenario, including migrating users to new identity stores and dealing with partner users, and got a glimpse of a presentation technique known as *question seeding*.

We will now move on to the sixth domain you need to master, development life cycle and deployment planning.

10
Development Life Cycle and Deployment Planning

In this chapter, we will continue looking at other Salesforce-specific knowledge areas required to pass the CTA review board. This is the sixth domain out of seven. We will go through the required knowledge and preparations for this domain and then complete a hands-on exercise using a mini-hypothetical scenario.

In the previous chapters, we covered several domains that contain knowledge required to develop a secure and scalable enterprise solution using the Salesforce platform. In this chapter, we will go through the considerations, capabilities, concepts, techniques, and tools required to set up an enterprise development environment.

Enterprises want to ensure they are making the most out of their Salesforce investment. This can't be achieved without the right level of governance, which supports and guides development activities throughout the program. Project/program governance should ensure the developed solution meets the business requirements in that it is easy to maintain, scalable, can perform well, and is bug-free.

As a CTA, you are expected to provide guidance throughout this process. You should be able to help your client establish the right governing body, as well as guide the development teams to put together the development and release engine, which will ensure Salesforce features are delivered bug-free and in time and budget.

There is usually a whole section full of requirements dedicated to this domain in full review board scenarios. This is one of the domains with a well-defined scope, which means that the challenge typically lies in the *depth* of the knowledge that must be passed. In this chapter, we're going to cover the following main topics:

- Understanding what you should be able to do as a Salesforce development life cycle and deployment architect

- Introducing the development life cycle and deploying a domain mini-hypothetical scenario – Packt Modern Furniture

- Designing the project environment and release strategy

What you should do as a Salesforce development life cycle and deployment architect

According to Salesforce's online documentation, the CTA candidate should be able to meet a specific set of objectives, all of which can be found at the following link: `https://trailhead.salesforce.com/en/help?article=Salesforce-Certified-Technical-Architect-Exam-Guide&search=release+exam+schedule`.

Let's have a closer look at each of these objectives.

Identifying project risks and developing mitigation strategies

The review board scenario is designed to represent a real-world use case. In real projects, you will come across many challenges and risks. Some are related to the platform itself, while others are related to other systems, solutions, or parallel projects.

You are expected to identify these risks and develop a set of mitigation strategies to address them. The risks could be related but not limited to the following:

- Conflicting release cycles
- Conflicting processes
- Low adoption and high resistance

Let's look at each of these in detail.

Conflicting release cycles

You could have multiple projects running in parallel on the Salesforce platform or on another platform related to/integrated with Salesforce. When more than one project/platform has a different release cycle, it is common to get conflicts. You can typically solve this by proposing a combination of the following:

- **A multi-layered environment strategy**: This allows you to test specific functionalities at an early stage. This includes testing cross-system functionalities as part of what is known as **integrated testing**.

- **A governance body**: This includes business and technical members from both teams/projects/streams. This will ensure that functionalities developed by one team are known and approved by the others.

- **A lively release cycle**: This ensures all streams use the latest code base.

More details on each are included later in the *Recommending the right project governance to support technical decision-making* and *Crafting the right environment management strategy while considering the platform's capabilities and limitations* sections. Now, let's explore the next most common risk you might encounter while designing your development life cycle and deployment strategy.

Conflicting processes

One of the key challenges for multi-regional/multi-national projects is the lack of discipline in every region's used processes. Many enterprises will be looking to get some sort of unification across these processes. But this is not an easy task, and you usually address this using a combination of the following:

- **Using the right org strategy**: We covered this topic in *Chapter 5, Developing a Scalable System Architecture*. Selecting the right org strategy is the first step in handling such requirements. Sometimes, the value of having more than one business unit operating on the same org is offset by the challenges that could bring.

- **Using a governance body**: This includes business and technical members from most, if not all, involved regions/countries/business units to help us select the right solution that meets everyone's needs.

- **Using the right delivery methodology**: This embraces change, allows for prototyping, and keeps the client close to the delivery team. This will help us set up expectations and ease any resistance.

More details on the second and third points will be provided in the *Recommending the right project governance to support technical decision-making* section. Now, let's explore the next most common risk you might encounter while designing your development life cycle and deployment strategy.

Low adoption and high resistance

This is another common challenge for any new solution or technology that's introduced for an enterprise. People are the enemies of what they don't know by nature. Some users might find it difficult to leave their comfort zone for a new solution or a totally new platform. Such a challenge requires a comprehensive *change management process*. This is not something a Salesforce architect is expected to lead. However, you are expected to be familiar with some of its principles and the common ways to address it, which generally includes a combination of the following:

- **A comprehensive communication plan**: Before, during, and after the project. Accompanied with a solid training program.

- **A governance body**: This includes business and technical members, including technology champions for each involved department. These champions will act as *ambassadors* for the project within their own departments. They will share their thoughts, challenges, and requirements during the project. They are *included* and *involved* in shaping the solution. This will give them the feeling that they *own* the solution and that they are a part of the team. The champions will then become the *go-to experts* to support other colleagues and ensure adoption once the project is released.

- **The right delivery methodology**: This keeps the client and champions users close to the delivery team. They will know about the solution *while it is being built*. Therefore, they won't be surprised by the end result. They will have all the chances to *rectify* things during the build time and *provide their feedback*. This ensures that the solution is going to be *fit for the needs* of our end users.

Again, we will cover the second and third points during this chapter. Change management goes much more beyond this, though. You are encouraged to read more about this from other sources such as the book *Practical Change Management for IT Projects,* by *Emily Carr.*

Identifying the impact development methodologies have on workstreams

As a Salesforce CTA, you are expected to have strong knowledge and experience with the different development methodologies used in IT, particularly Salesforce projects.

There are three main methodologies:

- **Waterfall**: Activities are broken down into sequential phases (although some could happen in parallel). The output of each phase is considered input for the next. It provides a rigid and strongly controlled delivery model.

- **Agile**: This model relies on discovering requirements and developing their appropriate solution using collaboration between cross-functional team members and the end client. Its principles include embracing change, evolutionary development, early involvement of end users, continuous improvements, and early delivery.

  Product development is broken into small incremental iterations, called **sprints**. Each normally lasts between 1-4 weeks and involves a cross-functional team working on planning, defining, designing, developing, testing, and releasing the different features included in a given sprint.

- **Hybrid**: This contains elements from both previous methodologies. It normally includes a **pre-game/blueprinting** phase at the beginning of the project to define the overall scope and agree on the *right-level* solution design (I am *intentionally* avoiding the word *high-level*, which could wrongly indicate that the details are not important at this stage). This is followed by a set of activities derived from the agile methodology. Here, the functionalities are prioritized, further understood and developed, tested, and delivered using sprints.

It's worth mentioning that the *right-level solution design* is exactly the level of detail you are expected to provide during the CTA review board. You have seen several examples and mini-scenarios already; this is exactly the level you are expected to come up with after the *blueprinting* phase.

The following diagram illustrates the difference between **waterfall** and **agile**:

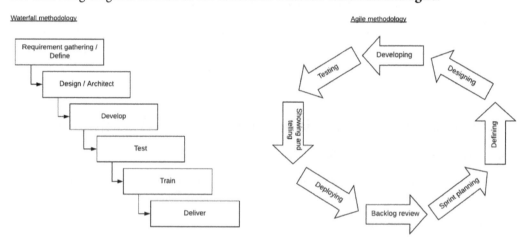

Figure 10.1 – Waterfall and agile delivery methodologies

The following diagram illustrates the hybrid methodology:

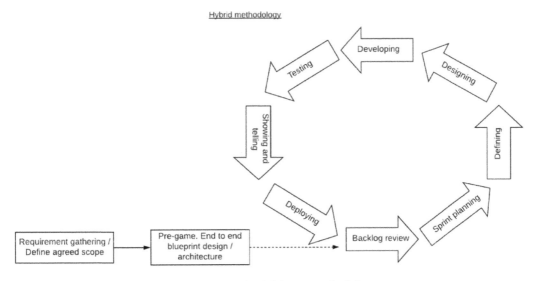

Figure 10.2 – Hybrid delivery methodology

The flexible nature of the Salesforce platform makes it very suitable for the Agile methodology. However, in some cases, continuous design changes create a hard-to-maintain solution due to the lack of early solution vision. This is better addressed in the Hybrid methodology. This is the reason why we can see an increased number of Salesforce projects delivered using a hybrid methodology.

Recommend test strategies to mitigate project risks

Every software solution has to pass a rigorous set of tests to ensure quality. You need to be familiar with the different types of tests and the environments that are most suitable to execute each.

The following table will help clarify this:

Test type	Purpose	Tools
Unit test	This test is used to check your solution's building blocks' validity, such as APEX code and the various different configurations. This is a must-have test. This is not only because of the enforced Salesforce test coverage, but because of the value it provides. It should be considered the first line of defense. Unit tests are executed every time new code is deployed to a particular instance. Again, remember that this could be used to test configured functionalities, not just code.	APEX test classes.
Functional test	This test is used to check the validity of a specific functionality's behavior based on tailor-made test scenarios and use cases. It can be executed manually or automatically using specific tools. Automating these tests ensures that the exact scenario is executed every time they are needed, such as when new functionality is deployed to an environment.	Manual test scripts and automated testing tools such as Selenium and Provar.
Integration test	This test is used to check the validity and confirm that the overall parts of the solution work together as expected. This includes any externally integrated system.	Manual test scripts and automated testing tools.
UAT test	This test is used to check specific UAT scripts/scenarios to ensure that the delivered functionality meets the business requirements. This is usually done side by side with the client.	Manual test scripts.
Load test	This test is used to gauge the system's performance under normal conditions but after loading the environment with a huge dataset. This type of test is particularly crucial for solutions with a potentially large volume of objects.	Manual test scripts and automated testing tools. Data loading is done using ETL tools such as Informatica.
Performance test	This test is used to gauge (and document) the system's performance under both normal and edge conditions. You need to raise a case for Salesforce to plan this test. This test is particularly important for solutions with complex setups.	Raise a case with Salesforce.
Smoke test	This test is used to ensure overall system stability. This test normally validates a set of basic, common, and most frequently used functionalities by running a limited set of tests (typically, this is done in the production environment, but it could take place in other environments as well) for a pre-defined time. The results are then monitored. This is based on the simple test you could execute on a newly bought machine; for example, you turn it on and observe any smoke coming out of it after a specific period of time.	Manual test scripts and automated testing tools.

> **Note**
>
> There are many other types of tests you can perform, such as regression tests, security tests, penetration tests, and more. Regression tests usually include a combination of functional tests, integration tests, and smoke tests. Security and penetration tests are beyond the scope of this book.

We will explain the environments that are most suitable for perform some of these tests shortly in this chapter.

Recommending the right project governance to support technical decision-making

Project governance is essential to the success of any project.

Let's take a simple example where different teams are developing and releasing different features and functionalities. They could overwrite each other's work, redevelop the same functionalities multiple times, create conflicting functionalities, modify the data model and the sharing model to negatively impact performance or security, and create a difficult system to change and maintain. In short, this is total chaos.

Can you imagine a case where the situation is even more complicated? Imagine multiple Salesforce teams (probably from multiple service implementation partners) developing and releasing a series of functionalities and solutions. These solutions involve other integrated applications. One team is building a series of APEX classes to develop point-to-point integration interfaces. Another is using an integration middleware, and a third team has decided to develop their own versions of these APEX classes because they are unaware of the effort that's been made by the first team or because there are time constraints.

When different teams begin to introduce different processes and bring in disparate ways to use Salesforce (probably to meet the same objectives), this will inevitably create confusion within the organization. Moreover, there will likely be a lot of duplicate work, something all enterprises should try to avoid to maintain an efficient setup.

In more than a decade of being the Salesforce business, I can confidently say that this is a very common challenge – not only with complex implementations, but even with more straightforward projects. This is exactly why enterprises create a Salesforce **Center of Excellent (CoE).**

A Salesforce CoE is a central governing body that deals with anything related to Salesforce. The COE is a unified entity responsible for discussing, evaluating, challenging, and deciding on everything associated with Salesforce. It includes both business and technical members from across the enterprise. The CoE is concerned with topics such as the following:

- Are IT and business aligned?
- Does the delivered solution meet business requirements?
- Will the project be delivered on time?
- Will the project be delivered to the budget provided?
- Have the necessary compliance considerations been made?
- Does the design adhere to best practices?
- Does the design reuse the enterprise-wide components?
- Does this project have the right governance model?
- Does the CoE have the right people around the table to make decisions?
- Are there any architectural frameworks that have been defined? Code standards? Best practices?
- Are the different teams and stakeholders communicating efficiently?

The CoE can contain a sub-body that's responsible for challenging and approving every design decision that's made. This is referred to as the **design authority (DA)**.

The following diagram explains the standard structure of a Salesforce CoE:

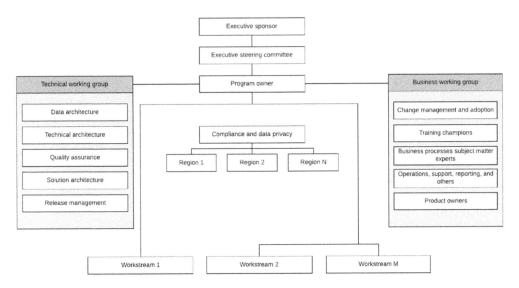

Figure 10.3 – Proposed CoE structure

The actual implementation could vary from one client to the other. This is by no means a one-size-fits-all structure. You need to work out what the right format is with your client. During the review board, you need to come up with a proposal based on the given scenario. The shared diagram is a good base to start from.

The design authority may have the following structure:

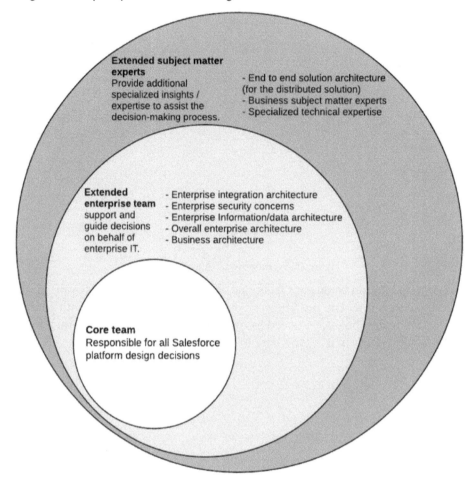

Figure 10.4 – Proposed DA structure

The structure of the DA could also be different from one client to the other.

During the review board, you need to explain the value of a CoE, what kind of roles are involved in it, and what activities and tasks are expected to be accomplished by the group. This all has to be done in the context of the given scenario and should address the scenario's challenges.

Crafting the right environment management strategy while considering the platform's capabilities and limitations

You need to understand the different types of environments that are available in the Salesforce platform/Salesforce core cloud. You should propose an environment management plan that includes the right type of environment, explain each environment's use, and justify the rationale behind the selected environment type.

In organized development environments, the development process contains multiple stages (such as development, QA, UAT, and so on). The activities in each of these stages are accomplished in a different environment. This separation of concerns removes any dependencies and allows other teams to work in parallel. This multi-layered development environment is something very common in Salesforce, mainly because it is easy to create sandboxes. Monolith applications typically have three environments (development, testing, and production). In Salesforce, we can create more layers to provide an even more organized development and release cycle. The typical arrangement is *development, continuous integration environment* (also known as the *build environment*), *QA, staging,* and *production*. Additional layers can be added, depending on the project's nature, such as *integration testing, hotfix,* and a *dedicated training environment*.

The following table can be used to help you select the right combination of environments for each task:

Sandbox type	Developing new features	Testing	Integration testing/ performance testing	Staging and UAT
Scratch	Excellent fit.	Good (unit test, functional tests, UI automated test).	Not a good fit.	Not a good fit
Developer	Excellent fit.	Good (unit test, functional tests, UI automated test).	Not a good fit.	Not a good fit
Developer pro	Good fit.	Excellent fit for feature testing. Data storage can be used for limited regression testing.	Limited usage for integration testing. Not a good fit for performance testing.	Not recommended
Partial copy	Ensure that the data subsets are OK to be shared with the developers.	Excellent fit for feature testing. Data storage can be used for limited regression testing and production debugging (data subset).	Good fit for integration testing (limited data subset). Not a good fit for performance testing.	Good fit (limited data subset)
Full copy	Unusual. Ensure it is OK to share data with the developers.	Best used for production debugging.	Excellent fit for integration testing. Ideal for performance testing (considering that it has the same infrastructure as the production org).	Excellent fit

You can find more details about the different sandbox types at the following link:
`https://help.salesforce.com/articleView?id=create_test_` `instance.htm&type=5`.

The following link contains some information about the capabilities and limitations of the different sandboxes' types: `https://help.salesforce.com/` `articleView?id=data_sandbox_environments.htm&type=`.

The following table can further help you select the right combination of environments for each layer of your environment strategy:

	Scratch	Developer	Developer Pro	Partial copy	Full copy
Development	X	X	X	X	
CI / Build		X	X	X	
QA		X	X	X	
Integration testing				X	X
Training				X	X
UAT				X	X
Load testing					X
Performance testing					X
Staging					X

In the solution for this chapter's mini-scenario, we will find an example of an environment strategy that utilizes some of the aforementioned environment types.

Describing the value of continuous integration (CI) tools and source control in release management

Understanding the value of these two topics is crucial to passing this domain. I have coached many CTA candidates. Some have spent a lot of time supporting DevOps teams in release management. They knew the different tools and technologies available for release management very well. But in some cases, they struggled to explain the value of CI in particular. The multi-layered development environment structure and the automated release management tools have become so popular to the point that some architects are overlooking the *original reason* CI was created. During the review board, you are expected to explain such details. You are expected not only to come up with the proposed release management but also to be ready to explain *why* you are suggesting it, as well as *how* it will solve its shared challenges.

Let's have a quick look at the CI concept:

- CI activities include continuously and frequently *merging the developers' work* into a shared *build environment*. It is preferred if this is automated. But what is the value of that?

  The value is mainly *avoiding conflicts* and *detecting them as early as possible*. Developers work in different environments (except if they use a shared development environment, something you should try to avoid as it makes it difficult to trace the developed functionalities and tie them back to requirements). If they are aware of the changes that have been made by other developers, there will be fewer chances for conflicts. Merging their work regularly and frequently (some practices recommend doing this multiple times a day) ensures that they are aware of the conflicts they have with others as early as possible. This work is typically merged into a specific source control's *build branch* associated with the build environments.

- CI also involves ensuring that the developers are *avoiding conflicts* by working on the *latest code base* (as much as possible). If the developer is working on a 10-day old code base, there is a high chance that another developer has made significant changes to the platform during that period. The chances of that become much less if the code base is simply a few hours old. To do that, the developers are expected to fetch the latest code base, which is usually available in the *build branch*. This could take place in multiple shapes and forms. It could be a manual exercise or automated using a simple script or even using an automation tool. An alternate approach is to build the entire developer sandbox using the code base, which is available either in the source control branch or in the build environment itself.

  Scratch orgs are a good example of the first case, where a new scratch org is created and built using the data stored in source control every time a developer delivers a new feature.

  Sandbox cloning is a good example of the second, where you can clone the build sandbox to create a new development environment with the latest code base.

You need to understand the CI concept and the rationale behind it. It is recommended that you practice this if possible.

CI comes with is sibling, **continuous delivery (CD)**. CD is more straightforward; it complements CI and offers help to bridge the gap between development and operations by automating an application's testing and deployment. Establishing the right multi-layered development environment strategy, selecting the right release management automation tools, and crafting a comprehensive automated test strategy will ensure that you have the right building blocks for CD.

The last ingredient to cover here, which is a crucial part of your CI/CD strategy, is source control. **Source control management (SCM)** (also known as **version control**) provides us with the ability to track and manage code changes in an easy and efficient way. It helps us detect and resolve conflicts, and it provides us with a mechanism to roll back changes to an earlier version if needed. **GitHub**, **Bitbucket**, and **GitLab** are very popular SCM solutions nowadays.

The final part you need to know about and include in your release strategy is versioning. Each time you release a set of functionalities to production, they have to have a version name/number. The version number has three common parts:

- A *major* version number, which changes every major release. This could be a monthly or quarterly release that includes major changes to the solution.

- A *minor* version number, which changes every minor release. This could be a weekly or bi-weekly release with noticeable changes to the solution, but the essential functionalities are still working the same way as they were previously.

- A *patch* version number. This number changes every time you introduce a new patch to the solution, such as a hotfix.

For example, version 2.1.3 can be translated into major version 2, minor version 1, and patch version 3.

Some might add another number that represents a *daily release number*, but this is only applicable for businesses with a very rapid release cycle.

Now that you are familiar with this domain's expectations, let's have a look at a practical example of using this knowledge to design smooth and scalable development and deployment processes.

Introducing the mini-hypothetical scenario – Packt Modern Furniture

The following mini-scenario describes a challenge with a particular client. The scenario has been tuned up to focus on challenges related to the *development life cycle and its deployment* specifically. This is one of the domains that has the least amount of dependency on the others. Despite that, it is vital for the success of any project in real life.

You are advised to go through the scenario once to build an initial picture of the required solution. Then, you should go through the requirements one by one and try to solve this yourself, then compare that with the suggested solution.

Make yourself familiar with the diagrams we provided earlier in this chapter. Many of them can be reused with minor or no changes. Learning them off by heart could save you a lot of valuable time while you're creating your review board's solution.

Without further ado, let's proceed to the scenario.

The scenario

Packt Modern Furniture (**PMF**) is a large furniture retailer operating in the United States. It has been using Salesforce Sales Cloud and Service Cloud for about 5 years. You, as their trusted consultant, have been requested to review their environments, particularly the release process. They are open to suggestions and would like to become more agile and quick to respond to market demands.

During the last 4 years, their release strategy utilized **Visual Studio Code** (**VSC**) as an IDE and a tool to deploy metadata between their different sandboxes and their production environment. From time to time, they also used **Change Sets**, although the developers favor VSC.

Current situation

PMF has the current situation:

- They are mainly organized into two teams. The Sales Cloud team releases a new version of their solution every month, while the Service Cloud team does that every 3 months.

- Half of each team contains code developers. The other half are either administrators or point-and-click developers.

- Currently, each developer (code or point-and-click) is using their own sandbox.

- A senior executive in PMF is a strong supporter of innovation. They often need to create a separate development environment for their team to carry out different initiatives.

PMF investigated their issues internally and defined a set of requirements.

Requirements

PMF has been struggling with many topics recently. Some of them can be traced back to their governance model and release strategy. They shared the following requirements:

- In general, there is a lack of auditable records of the functionalities that have been released in each version.

- Both development teams reported challenges during deployment, such as the inability to predict the result. On many occasions, a piece of functionality would work fine in the sandbox but fail to be deployed.

- The current process is creating several conflicts between the two development teams. On many occasions, they have overwritten each other's work.

- The reported number of bugs in production is high, especially after deployments. This seems to be on the rise.

- The QA team is overwhelmed with tasks. They can't keep up with the developments and are consistently leaking untested bugs. The QA reported that 90% of their test scripts are manual.

- The last deployment took more than 5 hours. The actual deployment time was estimated to be less than 30 minutes. The delay was traced back to the significant number of failures experienced before managing to deploy successfully.

- Currently, a lot of challenges have been made to the existing environment setup. The teams are unsure if they should continue using a developer sandbox per developer or have each team sharing a single sandbox.

PMF is looking for your help to rearchitect their current strategy to allow them to be more agile and responsive to their business needs.

Designing the project environment and release strategy

Give yourself time to quickly skim through the scenario, understand the big picture, and develop some initial thoughts about the solution. This is a must-do step for every scenario. In this scenario in particular, you will find some requirements that are related to each other and can be clubbed together.

Understanding the current situation

We understand that PMF is using two different *clouds*. The scenario didn't specify that both these products are actually in the same environment, but considering the difficulties mentioned in release management, it is fair to assume so. Note that such a challenge would likely not happen with a multi-org setup.

PMF used VSC and **Change Sets** to deploy metadata between environments. What does that information tell us?

It probably indicates that no source control management is included, which means that changes cannot be tracked and tied back to a requirement. Moreover, that could indicate that the environments are likely out of sync. Out-of-sync environments could become a real challenge during deployments. One environment might have some functionalities built that depend on a specific system state and all of its tests have been designed based on that. While releasing to production, the system might be in a different state, which will cause some tests to fail and some functionalities to behave irregularly.

We also learned that there are mainly two teams working for PFM and that they operate in different release cycles. This is something usual in parallel projects but could be a significant risk for the project in the short and long term.

We also learned that each developer is using a separate sandbox. Let's use all of this information to build our landscape architecture and current development life cycle diagram.

Your landscape architecture may look as follows:

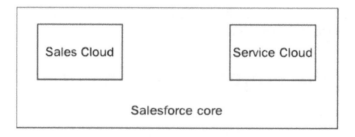

Figure 10.5 – Landscape architecture

On the other hand, your development life cycle diagram may look as follows:

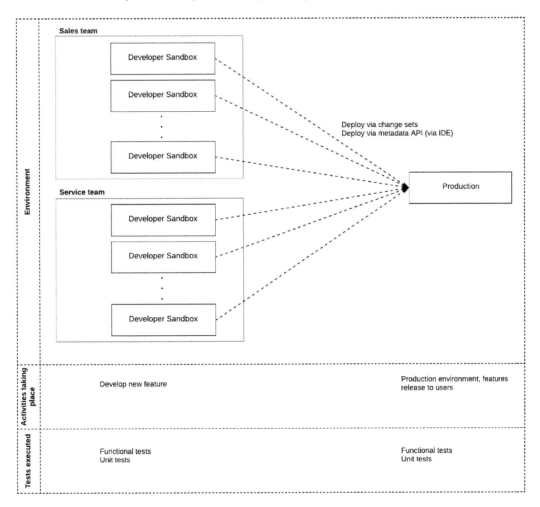

Figure 10.6 – Development life cycle diagram – first draft

Now that we understand the current situation, let's move on and look at the shared requirements.

Diving into the shared requirements

Now, let's go through the requirements shared by PME, craft a proposed solution for each, and update our diagrams accordingly to help us with our presentation. Let's start with the first requirement, which begins with the following.

In general, there is a lack of auditable records of the functionalities released in each version

This requirement should be an assertion of our previous expectations. If the deployments are taking place using change sets and the IDE, they likely lack an auditable record. This can be overcome with a very high level of discipline, of course, but from my experience, that is nearly impossible to achieve.

There is a solution, and it has been battle-tested for years, although in custom software development rather than with Salesforce. That solution is *SCM*. We explained the concept and value of SCM earlier in this chapter. Your proposed solution could be as follows:

> *To resolve this issue, I propose using an SCM solution to track the changes in all trackable metadata in Salesforce. The SCM will give a full history of all developed features. I propose using a tool such as GitHub. We can even tie back the SCM changes to the related user stories in PMF's project management tool, such as JIRA. This will give us the ultimate visibility of any developed feature and will allow us to create a release note containing all the new features of a particular release. The SCM will be part of our overall development and release strategy, which I will explain next.*

Note the relationship between this requirement and the next. You need to go through all of these requirements to come up with a comprehensive solution. You might decide to split up your answer during the presentation and map it to each requirement. However, the proposed solution should consider all of them.

Also, note that you need to explain the value of SCM shortly and concisely. Remember that the audience is supposed to be CXOs from the client company. They know what SCM is, but you need to explain what value you see it adding to your solution.

Now, let's move on to the next requirement.

Both development teams reported challenges during deployment, such as the inability to predict the result

This is another thing we could predict, even without PMF reporting it. It is a common challenge when parallel teams are developing new features in silos. They have no idea what the other team is building, and even if they do, they have no mechanism to ensure that it won't conflict with something else they are developing.

This challenge is the key reason why two of the concepts we explained earlier in this chapter were created: multi-layered development environments and CI.

You need to utilize your proposed development life cycle diagram to explain the proposed solution. Your proposed solution could be as follows:

> *In order to address this requirement, I propose an environment strategy where we utilize additional environments and SCM to detect conflicting functionalities earlier. In my development life cycle diagram, you can see that the development efforts would continue to take place in the developer sandboxes. Once the developer is done building and testing a feature on their local sandbox, they will raise a pull request to merge the new/modified metadata with the CI branch.*

> *The SCM will detect if there are any code conflicts that need to be resolved. And if any exist, the developer will be requested to fix them. When the pull request is approved, an attempt to deploy these changes to the CI environment will take place, which would also run all unit tests. If any of the unit tests are broken, the deployment will fail, and the developer will be requested to resolve the issue. The CI environment will always have the latest code base from both teams, which means that conflicts can be detected much earlier in the release cycle.*

> *Once the changes have been deployed to the CI environment, they can then be promoted to higher environments, as per the agreed time and procedures.*

Your proposed development life cycle diagram may look as follows:

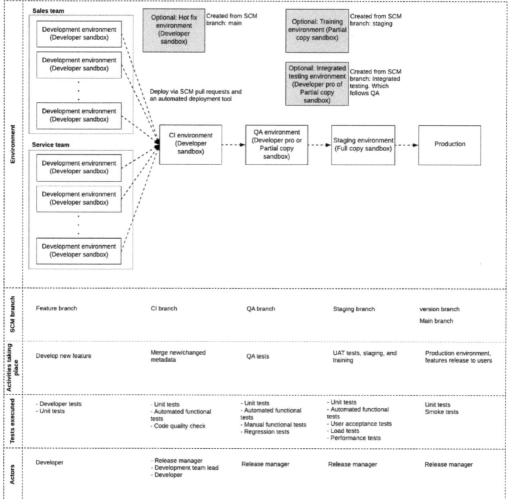

Figure 10.7 – Development life cycle diagram – final

This pretty much answers this requirement. Note that this diagram is almost complete, even at this stage. This diagram is one of those that you would likely build in one go once you have gone through all the related requirements, unlike other diagrams, which you would progressively develop.

Let's continue to the next requirement and continue building our end-to-end development and release management solution.

The current process is creating several conflicts between the two development teams

Your proposed solution could be as follows:

> *As I mentioned earlier, the CI branch and environment will contain the latest code base from both teams. This means that any conflicts are going to be detected and resolved at an early stage. However, to ensure the developers do not create conflicting requirements in the first place, I propose introducing a mechanism to refresh the developer's sandbox once a new feature is merged into the CI environment. This can either be automated or introduced as a manual step that the developer is expected to complete.*

> *In short, the developer will get the latest code base from the CI branch and deploy it to their own environments before they start working on any new requirement. They will need to resolve any merge issues. By the end of this process, they will be developing the new feature on the latest code base, which will reduce the potential of overwriting someone else's code.*

> *We can also utilize scratch orgs instead of sandboxes for developers to make the process even more streamlined. However, we need to trial this out first and ensure that the time required to create a new scratch org is not becoming a hurdle for the overall process.*

Again, remember that it is not enough to know what the ideal setup should be. This is pretty much easy to find out from many online resources. You should also know *why* it has been designed like that in the first place and *defend* the rationale behind it.

Now, let's move on to the next requirement.

The reported number of bugs in production is high, especially after deployments

This requirement could be addressed by introducing a more structured testing mechanism. The multi-layered development environment we proposed should address part of that automatically. But to further improve this process, we can utilize automated testing tools and ensure that the unit tests are used properly. Your proposed solution could be as follows:

> *The newly proposed multi-layered environment strategy should help to address some of these issues. On top of this, I propose using an automated testing tool such as Provar. Release management needs to be automated as much as possible. I also propose using a tool such as Copado to manage my entire release cycle. Copado can be configured to automatically start the Provar testing scripts once the code is merged successfully into a particular environment. This will increase the solution's overall quality and reduce the number of reported issues.*

> *Moreover, the multi-layered environments will ensure that most issues are caught way before they reach production.*

> *In addition to this, I propose further utilizing the APEX unit tests to create a business-logic-level testing layer that is automatically invoked once a particular functionality is released to an environment. APEX tests will include test methods for positive and negative use cases to ensure that we cover as much logic as possible.*

Let's move on to the next requirement, which starts with the following few lines.

The QA team is overwhelmed with tasks. They can't keep up with the developments and are consistently leaking untested bugs

The previous points address most of this. Your proposed solution could be as follows:

> *The previous point already addresses this requirement. Provar would allow us to convert many manual tests into automated tests that can be easily and consistently invoked at various stages. This combination of automated scripts, APEX unit tests, and a structured multi-layered development environment approach would ensure that the QA team's load is eased up.*

Now, let's move on to the next requirement, which starts as follows.

The last deployment took more than 5 hours. The actual deployment time was estimated to be less than 30 minutes

Again, most of this is addressed by the previous points. Your proposed solution could be as follows:

> *Using a combination of multi-layered development environments, source control, automated release management, and automated tests should reduce the number of reported issues and help discover them earlier. This means that the features released to production have been thoroughly tested already. The entire deployment had taken place at an earlier stage when we moved the new features from the QA to the Staging environment, which means there is a very small chance that the deployment to production would fail.*

Let's move in to the next and final requirement, which starts as follows.

Currently, there have been a lot of challenges regarding the existing environment setup

The teams are unsure if they should continue using a developer sandbox per developer or have each team sharing a single sandbox.

This is something we addressed previously, but let's not jump over any requirements. Make sure you cover everything in your presentation. Your proposed solution could be as follows:

> *I propose to continue using a developer sandbox per user. We can also investigate the possibility of using scratch orgs, as we mentioned previously. However, in both cases, I don't see the team members of each team sharing a single development org, as this will make it nearly impossible to track all the changes happening and tie them back to a user story or task. This means we lose the desired transparency, which was one of PMF's main requirements.*

That concludes this scenario. The diagrams we created earlier are still valid. Therefore, we are not going to list them again here.

Summary

In this chapter, we dived into the details of the Salesforce development life cycle and deployment domain. We learned what is expected from a CTA to cover and at what level of detail. We discussed some key principles, such as DevOps, CI/CD, multi-layered development environments, and SCM. Then, we understood their importance and their impact on the development and release cycle.

As you might have already noticed, the scope of this domain is limited. The key challenge with such types of domains is in their depth of knowledge, understanding *why* some best practices are there, and *how* to implement them.

Then, we tackled a mini hypothetical scenario that focused on development life cycle and deployment, and we solutioned it together and created some catchy presentation pitches. We developed a development and release diagram that could be easily reused for other scenarios (with minor changes), and we learned how to present this to an audience to capture their attention and provide them with detailed, but not overwhelming, information and rationale behind our proposal.

In the next chapter, we will move on to the seventh and final domain you need to master: communication.

11
Communicating and Socializing Your Solution

In this chapter, we will continue with another Salesforce-specific knowledge area that is required to pass the CTA review board: communication. This is the seventh and final domain. We will go through the needed knowledge and preparations for this domain and then complete a hands-on exercise using a mini-hypothetical scenario.

Communication skills are crucial for a CTA. These skills allow you to explain your vision in a clear and detailed way, ensuring that your audience fully understands how everything is going to work together. This skill incorporates several sub-skills, such as the ability to create a descriptive diagram that can help you explain your solution and how to handle unexpected changes of scope and adjust your solution accordingly.

We have already practiced creating presentation pitches in the past six chapters. Each time, we ensured we utilized our diagrams to describe the end-to-end solution. We learned that the presentation has to be engaging and captivating; you should be *telling a story* while walking your audience from one point to the next.

In this chapter, we're going to cover the following main topics:

- Understanding what you should be able to do while communicating your solution
- Practicing communicating a mini-hypothetical scenario – Packt Digital
- Articulating your solution and managing objections

By the end of this chapter, we will also have practiced handling objections and adjusting a solution on the fly. You will learn some best practices across the broad domain of communication. We will start by understanding what is expected from a CTA to master in this domain and then move on to our mini-hypothetical scenario, where we will put that knowledge into action.

Understanding what you should be able to do while communicating your solution

According to Salesforce's online documentation, the CTA candidate should be able to meet a specific set of objectives, all of which can be found at the following link: `https://trailhead.salesforce.com/en/help?article=Salesforce-Certified-Technical-Architect-Exam-Guide&search=release+exam+schedule`.

Let's have a closer look at each of these objectives.

Communicating design decisions and considerations

Communication is one of the most critical soft skills needed in a CTA's arsenal. While creating your solution, you will come across several use cases that can be fulfilled in one way or the other. We saw this earlier while developing solutions for the mini-hypothetical scenarios in previous chapters.

During the review board, you have a very limited amount of time and a lot of land to cover. When you present a proposed solution, you should focus on the *considerations* that would *make a difference*. These considerations should steer you away from one design decision to the other.

In the end, you are expected to come up with a *crisp* and *precise* solution for a given requirement, not to list out the available options and take a step back. You are supposed to be the most senior Salesforce expert on a project. You should be the one *confidently guiding* other stakeholders to make decisions.

> **Provide a crisp, clear, and comprehensive solution**
>
> The three CTA judges are very seasoned and experienced architects. They can sense and smell a lack of confidence. Don't bluff or use extensive buzzwords. This is not an audience that will be impressed by buzzwords unless you can match them with solid, in-depth, practical knowledge.

During the presentation, you have to give an end-to-end solution. Think of it as a story to tell. You have to explain how your solution is solving the problem. Take the following requirement as an example:

The sales manager needs to submit the new customer record for a credit check. The manager should be informed about the result as soon as the check is complete and receive an error if the check fails for any reason.

The following statement is an example of a dry, unattractive, and unengaging way of presenting a solution:

I will do the credit check via an APEX callout.

The judges are supposed to be CXOs representing the scenario's client company. You are supposed to guide them, not throw back dry answers to their questions. To help them keep up with your presentation, you can point out or mention the requirement first, then explain your proposed solution. For example, you could start with something like the following:

On page three, paragraph two, we have the following requirement.

Then, you can briefly describe the requirement.

Once you've done that, you proceed with the solution. Your response should explain the *why* and *how* with enough details. For example, the preceding statement could be rephrased like so:

> *To fulfill this requirement, I will implement a Lightning component with a button to submit the customer account for a credit check. The Lightning component will have an APEX controller. I propose using the Remote process invocation – request and reply integration pattern.*
> *The controller will use a callout to invoke a web service exposed by MuleSoft. I will use named credentials to authenticate to the web service. Authentication will occur using the OAuth 2.0 JWT token flow, and the integration channel will be protected using two-way TLS. Once the MuleSoft web service is invoked, MuleSoft will orchestrate the call to the credit check provider, get back the result, and return it to the Lightning component's controller. The component will then display the result to the user.*

If you are doing a virtual review board, it could be a good idea to arrange the requirements and proposed solution in an Excel sheet or a PowerPoint slide, whichever works best for you.

The key thing to keep in mind is that these artifacts are tools that you should use to tell your end-to-end solution. You can't simply go through your sheet and read the solution out; you have to use your diagrams to explain and visualize the solution, which is exactly what the next required objective is all about.

Demonstrating your visualization skills to articulate the solution

The common language for architects is diagrams. Similar to human languages, certain diagrams represent a common language known and understood by peer architects.

In *Chapter 1, Starting Your Journey as a CTA*, we listed the types of diagrams you need to describe an end-to-end solution. We also discussed the level of detail required in each of these diagrams. There are several additional diagrams that an architect can use to explain a solution, including, but not limited to, the following:

- **Flowcharts**: This is a very common way to represent an algorithm. It describes the steps required to solve a particular task. Swimlane can be used to provide a better visual representation of the chart, especially complex processes.

- **Data flow diagrams**: This diagram provides a representation of the flow of data through systems or processes. Do not mix these with ERD diagrams or object diagrams.

- **Wireframes**: This type of diagram represents a visual skeletal framework of the solution's UI.

These additional diagrams could be valuable to explain some aspects of your solution. They are rarely used during the CTA review board but are very valuable in real life.

What you particularly need to avoid are the top three mistakes in creating architectural diagrams. We'll learn about those in the following subsections.

Mixed diagrams

In some cases, the architect might decide to mix multiple diagrams into one. This could be due to one of the following reasons:

- **Underestimating the value of standard diagrams**: The standard diagrams took years to reach the stage they are at. They are known by many architects and represent a common architectural language. Attempting to create a new language simply means that you will be the only one to speak it. Moreover, a newly created type of diagram would likely lack the desired maturity level.

- **Lack of knowledge**: The architect might be unaware of a standard way to create a specific diagram. This could also be due to the confusion created by a lack of standardization.

- **The wrong impression that standard diagrams are too complicated**: Sometimes, the desire to create something simple could mean miscommunicating valuable information. Moreover, the architectural diagrams are not only communication tools; they are frameworks to help the architect shape and refine thoughts. We touched base on some of this in *Chapter 1*, *Starting Your Journey as a CTA*. In short, as an architect, you should use your diagrams to create, validate, and communicate your solution. You don't create the diagrams as an after-thought of some already-delivered job.

The following diagram is an example of a mixed diagram. The architect mixed a **flowchart diagram** with a **landscape architecture diagram**:

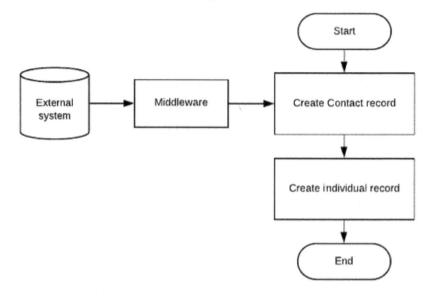

Figure 11.1 – An example of a mixed diagram

Such non-standard diagram mixing will cause confusion at multiple levels, especially with complex processes. It will distract and confuse the reader with unnecessary details. Moreover, it will create a redundant version of information that is likely to exist elsewhere. For example, you will need to maintain the list of integration interfaces across both the landscape architecture diagram and flowcharts. This is a likely cause of outdated information in some diagrams.

Oversimplified diagrams

We mentioned this earlier as a potential reason for mixing diagrams. This is also one of the most common reasons for *information loss* in diagrams. As an architect, *you are responsible* for generating architectural diagrams. This is not the duty of a junior resource or a job that you can offload on someone else. You are *responsible* for the overall solution architecture, which makes you accountable for creating or closely supervising the creation of all the elements that are required to communicate and document the technical solution.

This is precisely what you are expected to develop and communicate during the CTA review board: the end-to-end technical solution design.

The following diagram is an example of an oversimplified data model:

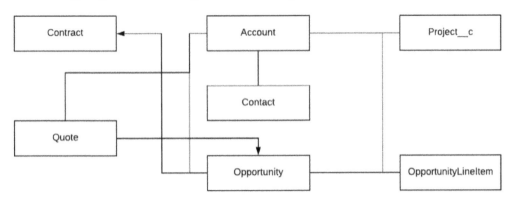

Figure 11.2 – An example of an oversimplified data model

You can quickly tell that this diagram will not help you understand the proposed data sharing and visibility strategy. It won't help you detect LDVs or sub-optimal relationships. It won't even help you understand the nature of the relationships between the objects or their cardinality. The arrows might even communicate the wrong message. This could be an example of oversimplification and a lack of standardization (which is the third and next common mistake we will be covering).

Lack of standardization

The next time you want to create a diagram, try to Google and see whether there is a common standardized version of it. Look for templates and examples provided by purposely built diagramming tools such as **Lucidchart**, **Visio**, or **Gliffy**.

You will likely find a standard diagram that's suitable for your purpose. Don't try to search for something such as a *solution architecture diagram* because that is not just a single diagram. We have mentioned this many times throughout this book. To describe an end-to-end solution architecture, you need multiple diagrams. We listed and explained the value of each in *Chapter 1, Starting Your Journey as a CTA*.

> **Note**
> The practice of creating these diagrams should become part of your daily activities, not something you do temporarily to pass the CTA review board. You need to continuously demonstrate your knowledge, values, and attitude of a CTA day in, day out in real projects. Try to embed the activity of creating these diagrams in your daily work routine. This will help you develop an architectural muscle memory. Drawing these diagrams will become easier and quicker during the review board.

A good architectural diagram can help you organize your thoughts and spot gaps in your solution, answer questions before they are asked, and help you explain your solution in a much more thorough way, as well as handle objection, which is exactly what the next objective is all about.

Handling objection and unexpected roadblocks

We've mentioned several times in this book that there is no *single correct answer*. You need to expect some challenges to your solution. Some of these challenges might drive some solution changes, but you need to defend your solution and not be too stubborn about it. When you figure out that you made the wrong decision, admit it. Don't worry; we all make mistakes. The judges themselves made many mistakes in their careers, just like I did and just like any other architect in this business.

The way you handle an objection is a skill that will be assessed. Showing confidence in defending your solution is as important as showing maturity in receiving feedback and accepting it without losing control. A CTA will come across such circumstances daily. If you made a mistake, show courage in admitting it and demonstrate your skills by rectifying it on the fly.

The judges will also add or change some scenario requirements during the *Q&A* to test your ability to quickly and adequately react to the evolving requirements and *solve on the fly*. When that happens, make sure you understand the requirement first. Don't be shy about asking for explanations (but don't lose much time doing so as well). Take a few seconds to think it through, then confidently present your solution. Trust yourself; if others have managed to do it, then surely you can too.

Now that you are familiar with this domain's expectations, let's take a look at a practical example where we will use this knowledge to create an engaging presentation and handle objections.

Practicing communicating a mini-hypothetical scenario – Packt Digital

The following mini-scenario describes a challenge with a particular client. This scenario is slightly different from the others as it has been tuned to raise tricky challenges that could be subjected to questions from the judges during the Q&A stage. In this scenario, we will not only provide a proposed solution, but we will also defend that solution appropriately during a hypothetical Q&A.

The judges will challenge some of your proposed design decisions. You should expect a different type of challenge from each judge. After all, we are human, and we all have different personalities, strengths, and weaknesses.

The judges will also attempt to change some requirements during the Q&A. They might even introduce some new requirements. This doesn't mean that you did or are doing something wrong. This is all part of the test. To pass this particular domain, you need to be able to handle the objection. This is one of the vital soft skills for a CTA.

Moreover, you need to be able to *solve on the fly*. Some people refer to this as *solving on your feet*. The client might simply throw out a new requirement, and you are expected to understand it, challenge it (if needed), and provide a detailed solution that could fulfill it.

> **Remember**
>
> Don't lose your focus or confidence when/if the judges start to ask questions and dig deeper into requirements. This will be obvious to the judges and will reduce your chances of passing. Don't assume that these questions are being asked because you are not answering correctly or are doing something wrong. The judges could merely be checking whether you have the right soft skills and can handle such difficult situations, which, for sure, you will face in real life.

Similar to the other scenarios, you are also advised to go through the scenario once to build an initial picture of the required solution. Then, you should go through the requirements one by one and try to solve them yourself, then compare them with the suggested solution. Try to practice presenting the end-to-end solution, as well as answering the Q&A challenges.

Without further ado, let's proceed to the scenario.

The scenario

Packt Digital (**PD**) is an innovative software reseller. They sell a broad set of software services, including support services and maintenance. They operate across Europe, and they offer their products directly to their end customers via multiple channels. They have recently started a digital transformation involving Salesforce Marketing Cloud, Salesforce Service Cloud, and eCommerce. They are planning to use Service Cloud as the system of record for customer management.

Current situation

PD has several requirements around customer match, merge, and deduplication. This is considered key to the program's success.

They have multiple back-office applications, including Oracle ERP, a custom-developed order management system, and several other home-grown apps. They are all hosted on-premises.

PD has recently acquired another digital services company that operates in the USA only. The acquired company also uses Salesforce as its main CRM. It has been tuned for their specific business processes.

Requirements

PD shared the following list of requirements:

- All of PD's enterprise apps need to utilize the customers' golden records. They also need to be able to enrich some of the values periodically. PD is looking for your guidance to provide recommendations around the tools and strategies to implement this requirement best, as well as ensure it scales up as more brands are brought into the system.

- PD would like to implement a new sales solution focused on retail execution. The solution should serve all regions using a standardized business process wherever possible, with room for minor localization. The solution should also be integrated with the rest of the enterprise apps, such as the order management system. PD is looking for your help to determine the right org strategy for their plans.

- PD would like to equip their reps in Europe with mobile apps that support offline functionality. This should help the reps operate in all locations and regions. The data that's captured via the mobile application needs to be surfaced in Salesforce and seven other different applications. They are looking for your guidance to determine the right mobile strategy, as well as their integration strategy.

- PD currently maintains invoices in a custom object. They need to share this record with the user specified in a lookup field. This sharing should be maintained even if the record owner is changed and should share the record only with the current user specified in the lookup field.

PD is looking for your help and guidance with all of their shared requirements.

Articulating your solution and managing objections

You might have noticed that this scenario is a little bit light on the details. This is because we want to focus more on the presentation and Q&A activities and handle them in the best way possible.

Give yourself time to quickly skim through the scenario, understand the big picture, and develop some initial thoughts about the solution. Once we've done that, we can go through the scenario step by step and create our solution, similar to what we did in the previous scenarios we covered in this book.

Understanding the current situation

PD is using Salesforce Service Cloud as the primary system of record for customer management. Moreover, they have acquired another company that also uses Salesforce as a CRM. However, it is a heavily customized org tailored to meet specific needs. PD is having issues with data quality, particularly duplicate management. On top of that, they have several other applications that we need to integrate Salesforce with. The PD landscape looks as follows for the time being:

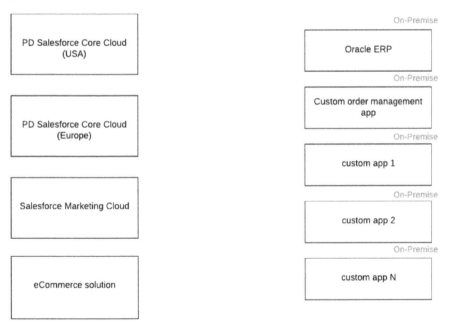

Figure 11.3 – Landscape architecture – first draft

Now that we understand the current situation, let's go through the requirements.

Diving into the shared requirements

We are all set to start tackling PD's requirements, craft a proposed solution for each, and update our diagrams accordingly to help us with the presentation. Let's start with the first requirement.

All of PD's enterprise apps need to utilize the customers' golden records

First, you might consider using Salesforce's native deduplication capabilities using **duplicate rules**. This makes sense because PD specified that they are considering Salesforce Service Cloud as the **system of record (SOR)**. By definition, this is the system that is the *authoritative source of truth* for specific data (customer records, in this case).

However, PD also shared requirements that indicate they have issues detecting and managing duplicates. This could be because their matching algorithm is complex and probably relies on complex fuzzy logic. They also reported that they have concerns with merging duplicates.

Advanced matching and data merging are not capabilities offered out of the box in Salesforce. This is the land of MDM. We covered various MDM concepts and the three different implementation styles for MDM tools in *Chapter 2, Core Architectural Concepts – Data*.

> **Tip**
> As a reminder, the three implementation styles are **Registry**, **Consolidation**, and **Coexistence**. The latter two support the concept of the **golden record**.

To deliver the required PD functionality, we need an MDM tool that supports one of the two MDM implementation styles with the golden record concept. As I've mentioned several times already, you need to familiarize yourself with product names from the Salesforce ecosystem. In this case, we can propose **Informatica MDM**.

Your proposed solution could be as follows:

> *In order to fulfill this requirement, I propose using an MDM tool that supports advanced deduplication and merges processes such as Informatica MDM. Informatica will be linked with Salesforce Service Cloud, which will be the system that's allowed to create new customers. Informatica will use its advanced matching capabilities to detect a duplicate and, if needed, merge it. Then, it will update the data in Service Cloud to ensure that the latest version of the data is always held in Service Cloud. This fulfills PD's requirement to use Service Cloud as a SOR.*

> *The other applications can get access to the golden customer record directly from Informatica. This also allows them to update specific attributes in it. Informatica would then handle any validations required for these values and attempt to replicate the data to Service Cloud. And only upon successful updates to the data in Service Cloud Informatica will the golden record changes be committed.*

> *I thought of using Salesforce duplicate rules to handle this requirement, but I assumed that the mentioned need for advanced deduplication is beyond the out-of-the-box capability. Moreover, Salesforce duplicate rules don't handle record merging if needed.*

This looks good and solid. However, the judges may still want to challenge your proposed solution, either to ensure that you *really understand* the topic (and you haven't merely memorized it) or to test your communication skills and the ability to *solve on the fly*.

A judge might ask you the following:

> *How do you propose handling the existing duplicate data in the Salesforce Service Cloud org? And what would be your strategy considering the newly acquired Salesforce org?*

These questions are normally clear and straightforward, but don't expect to be spoon-fed. If you are continuously failing to spot the question and answer it correctly, they might simply decide not to give you the points. Your answer should be crisp, clear, and to the point. You have very limited time during the Q&A, and you should aim to make the most of it. Your answer could be as follows:

> *Regarding the existing data, I plan to load that into Informatica MDM once the tool is introduced. This will be part of the tool's setup. The MDM will determine duplicates and update or merge the existing records in Service Cloud, including any re-parenting process.*

> *The fact that we have an MDM tool gives us more flexibility with the other Salesforce org. I am going to explain my org strategy in a later requirement. But, in short, we can connect the MDM tool to the other environment as well and utilize it as another SOR.*

Remember, crisp and sharp answers. Don't be nervous. A real CTA enjoys bouncing ideas off others. Consider the Q&A stage as an opportunity to share your thoughts in a limited time slot.

Update your diagrams, and then move on to the next requirement.

PD would like to implement a new sales solution focused on retail execution

The new solution should be used in all regions, and it should introduce a high level of standardization but with some room for minor changes.

But what is the right org strategy for PD to start with? The acquired brand has another Salesforce instance, which is heavily customized to meet their needs. The sales solution could be an extension of what they already have. Of course, you can assume that it is a complete replacement of their existing solution, then build your proposal based on that. The scenarios haven't specified any details. Different assumptions could lead to entirely different logical answers. In any case, your assumption should be reasonable and not too far from what you would see in reality.

Once you've decided on the proposed org strategy, you need to come up with a solution that allows standardization with room for modification. Your proposed solution could be as follows:

> *The Salesforce org of the acquired company is heavily customized. I am assuming that the current functionalities in this org don't include anything for retail execution. Therefore, the new functionality would be extending the existing functionality rather than replacing it.*

> *Based on that, I propose keeping these orgs separate. The USA org has other functionalities that are tailor-made for the region. The new retail execution solution will be developed based on the standard process, and it will be delivered to both orgs as an unmanaged package. This will allow the solution to be centrally managed and updated.*

> *Whenever new functionality is introduced or updated, a new version of the package will be made available. After deploying the unmanaged package, the target org can add or modify it based on their requirements. The features and code will contain hooks to allow an extension and a mechanism to turn some functionalities on or off using metadata configurations.*

> *Both orgs will be connected to the rest of the enterprise applications using an ESB such as MuleSoft. This will enable PD to establish a scalable and reusable integration architecture. MuleSoft will handle all required orchestrations, error handling, queueing, and retry mechanisms. Moreover, it will allow us to integrate a cloud-based solution such as Salesforce with on-premises hosted solutions.*

Your assumption might be sound, but the judges might decide to change it, either because they find it unsatisfactory or because they want to test your skills further.

A judge might ask you the following:

> *What would change in your solution if we assume that the customized solution in the USA org is all about retail execution?*

In this case, the judge is changing the scenario to further check the logic behind your proposed org strategy. In addition, this is a test for your *on-the-fly solving* skills. Your answer could be as follows:

> *This will change the way I think of the org strategy. Previously, the two orgs were serving different regions with two completely different processes. The retail execution processes were something new for both orgs, and I didn't find a reason strong enough to propose an expensive org merge.*
>
> *However, if the new solution is a replacement for the USA org's customized solution, this would be a good opportunity for an org merge. Eventually, both orgs will have an almost identical sales process. Merging both orgs will make it simpler to introduce and manage a unified process. These minor changes can still be accommodated without impacting the solution's quality or stability.*
>
> *In the org merge case, all the USA users and data will be migrated to the unified org. I am also assuming that no regulations are preventing this.*

Remember to keep an eye on the stopwatch. The previous answer should take no more than 90 seconds of your Q&A time. Try to read it and rephrase it using your own words and measure the time it takes you to do so. You might need to repeat this several times until you feel confident about the results.

You could also be asked about the rationale behind selecting the specific middleware. In this case, they are likely testing your integration domain knowledge. You need to explain the difference between an ETL and an ESB (we covered this earlier in *Chapter 3, Core Architectural Concepts – Integration and Cryptography*).

They might even ask you how MuleSoft will be able to communicate with an on-premises hosted application. For MuleSoft, this would require setting up a **virtual private network (VPN)** between MuleSoft **CloudHub** (assuming it is using **CloudHub**) and the client's intranet. This is different from the *secure agent* mechanism we explained in *Chapter 9, Forging an Integrated Solution*, which is used by other ETL tools.

Update your diagrams and move on to the next requirement, which starts with the following line.

PD would like to equip their reps in Europe with mobile apps that support offline functionality

The critical requirement here is to deliver a mobile app with offline capabilities to the agent. The requirement didn't specify any additional information, so you have to make some valid assumptions.

You can assume that the required offline capability is advanced and therefore requires a specific type of mobile application to fulfill it.

Looking back at *Chapter 5, Developing a Scalable System Architecture*, we came to know four different types of mobile applications that we can develop/use with Salesforce:

- **Salesforce mobile app**: The standard app that's developed and maintained by Salesforce. It provides a rich set of configurable functionalities and a modern UI. However, it has limited offline capabilities. You can find out more about the offline capabilities of the Salesforce mobile app at the following link: `https://help.salesforce.com/articleView?id=salesforce_app_offline.htm&type=5`.

  It's worth mentioning that the Salesforce mobile app can be branded using the **Salesforce Mobile Publisher** functionality.

- **Hybrid apps**: Custom-developed cross-platform mobile applications. They typically have limited offline capability.

- **HTML5 apps**: Cross-platform mobile apps developed using HTML5. They have a very limited offline capability by nature.

- **Native apps**: Custom-developed mobile apps, targeted at specific platforms such as iOS and Android using specific programming languages. You can develop native mobile applications with advanced offline capabilities. This includes the ability to cache a considerable number of records, store them safely in encrypted storage, and sync them back to Salesforce whenever the connection to the internet is restored.

Based on your assumption, you can propose a native app. Alternatively, you could have assumed that the standard Salesforce mobile capabilities are enough for this use case. However, in my opinion, it is a safer option to go with the former approach as the limitations of the Salesforce mobile app could be easily challenged by complex businesses, such as PD.

This will answer half of the requirement. The rest of the requirement indicates a need to surface the data captured via the mobile application into Salesforce and seven other systems. This is another example where you might have more than one potential solution. The approach you choose will determine the challenges you might face during the Q&A stage. The following two possible options explain this:

- The mobile application can communicate directly with an API layer exposed by MuleSoft. This, in turn, would communicate with Salesforce and the seven other systems. This could happen in a parallel or sequential manner, where the changes are pushed to the other seven systems only after being accepted and committed in Salesforce.

  Proposing this approach could raise several questions, including *How can we authenticate to MuleSoft APIs? Is there an alternative approach that avoids caching data in MuleSoft?* Besides, the required customizations in MuleSoft to achieve this are substantial, which could raise a few more questions and challenges.

- The mobile application can communicate directly with Salesforce. Once the data has been committed to Salesforce, it can be replicated to the other applications in many different ways, such as batch sync using MuleSoft, asynchronous **platform events**, or **CDC**.

  Proposing this approach could raise a different set of questions. The judges might be curious to know why you picked this approach over an **API-led** approach utilizing MuleSoft, which promises a more reusable interface. They might also change the requirement to include the USA instance, which will push you toward the first approach.

The following diagram illustrates both approaches:

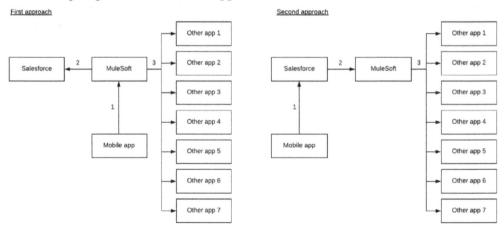

Figure 11.4 – An illustrative diagram showing two different approaches for the mobile application

I am always in favor of a simple architecture. The simpler the architecture is, the less likely things could go wrong, unless the architecture is unable to deliver the desired functionality or produces a sub-optimal variation of it.

> **Note**
>
> The mobile application is going to deal with data coming from Salesforce only. The mobile app is not supposed to retrieve data from other applications or commit data to them directly, so assuming a need for an API that does complex orchestrations could be exaggerated.

The requirement to surface the captured data in other systems could be simply interpreted as a need to replicate this data to other systems once it has been committed to Salesforce. Avoid unnecessarily complicating things for yourself.

Your proposed solution could be as follows:

> *I am assuming that the desired offline capabilities are beyond what the Salesforce mobile app can offer. Hybrid and HTML 5 mobile app offline capabilities are also limited. Therefore, I propose developing a native mobile application with advanced offline capabilities. The mobile app will allow reps to create and update data offline and sync back to Salesforce once the connection to the internet is restored. The app will also manage conflicts and will notify the user if any are found.*

> *Once the data passes all server-side validations and is committed to Salesforce, I will use a data replication mechanism to copy this data to the other seven applications via MuleSoft. The scenario didn't specify any timing requirements, so I am assuming a delay of 1 hour is acceptable. I propose using a batch data synchronization pattern where a scheduled batch job is initiated in MuleSoft. The job pulls the new data from Salesforce and replicates it to the other applications.*

The batch data synchronization approach is more straightforward than the near-real-time *fire-and-forget pattern*. Think about it: when offline users go back online, they would be synchronizing dozens of records. These records should be committed to Salesforce in the right order. However, committing a large number of records would fire several platform events from Salesforce.

Ideally, they should all go into the event queue in the right order, sent to MuleSoft (or other subscribers) in the correct order, and should all be delivered with nothing missing. However, you can see that several areas could go wrong in this approach. Unless a near-real-time data sync is essential, this will be an unnecessary complexity.

The choice is yours, as long as you can justify it. Now, let's move on to the next requirement, which starts with the following.

PD currently maintains invoices in a custom object

They have a requirement to share this record with the user specified in a lookup field. This sharing should be maintained even if the record owner is changed, and they should only share the record with the current user specified in the lookup field.

Similar to what we've done several times already, we will start by considering configurable functionalities. We will only move on to a custom developed solution when we have concluded that the standard functionalities are incapable of delivering the requirements.

This requirement cannot be met with configurable platform functionalities. However, we know that the record owner can share the record manually with the target user. We can also automate this process and create *share* records using APEX. In this case, the APEX class will create an `invoice__share` record automatically to share the record with the target user. Your proposed solution could be as follows:

> *The desired functionality cannot be met using the configurable sharing mechanisms; therefore, I propose to create the invoice__share records automatically using APEX. When the record is created or updated, a trigger will delete all the invoice__share records associated with users other than the user specified on the lookup field. The trigger would then create an invoice__share record and associate it with the user specified on the lookup field if such a record doesn't already exist.*

Good enough? The answer is *no*.

One of the common challenges I observed while coaching over a dozen and a half CTA candidates is the accidental *jump* over requirements. The candidate is under pressure to deliver the solution in time. In such circumstances, the candidate might *miss* or *jump over* requirements and fail to identify them.

In some cases, it might be a simple requirement with low or no impact on the solution. In other cases, it may have a significant impact. This may lead to the *domino effect*, where one hesitant solution change will cause other elements to fall apart. In my opinion, this is one of the most critical risks a candidate could face in the review board.

The best way to avoid it is by making sure you don't miss any requirements. Let's continue with our proposed solution. Such an incomplete solution would definitely draw some questions from the judges, such as the following:

The requirement indicated that sharing should be maintained even if the record owner is changed. How would you achieve this using your solution?

This is a requirement we failed to spot. It came back to bite us. A hesitant answer could be as follows:

The trigger will fire even on the change of the record owner. In this case, the code will continue to run, as described earlier.

A hesitant answer is usually much longer than that, I am afraid, and this means that you are losing some valuable Q&A time. However, this answer made things worse. The judges might now get the impression that you are unaware of the standard behavior associated with the record owner's change.

When a record owner is modified, the manual sharing records are automatically deleted. You might know that already, but the provided answer doesn't reflect this knowledge. Moreover, relying on the trigger to unnecessarily create share records is a suboptimal solution, especially when there is a standard way to meet the desired requirement.

I am not going to proceed further with the different conversations that incorrect or incomplete answers might spark. However, I have seen candidates losing more than 5 precious minutes in such cases.

A good answer, which would likely grant you the points associated with the requirement, could be as follows:

I plan to define a custom sharing reason on the Invoice object and then use this sharing reason in the APEX sharing. I am aware that manual sharing records will get automatically deleted upon changing a record owner. However, APEX-managed sharing records with custom sharing reasons are maintained across record owner changes.

It would have been ideal if you included that statement in your original proposed solution. This would have saved you 30+ seconds lost from your precious Q&A time.

> **Remember, please!**
>
> I've mentioned this several times already and will repeat it here again. The Q&A stage is your friend. The judges will try to ask you questions to fill in any gaps and missed requirements. They will also ask questions that help them determine whether you have what it takes to pass the exam. This time is very precious, so don't waste it.
>
> Some of my mentees were dreading the Q&A. They considered it the most challenging stage of the review board and looked at it as a tough time to survive. It actually isn't. This is a time given to you to close any gaps and prove that you've got what it takes to pass the exam.

That was the last shared PD requirement. Let's update all the diagrams and see what they look like. The following is the landscape architecture diagram:

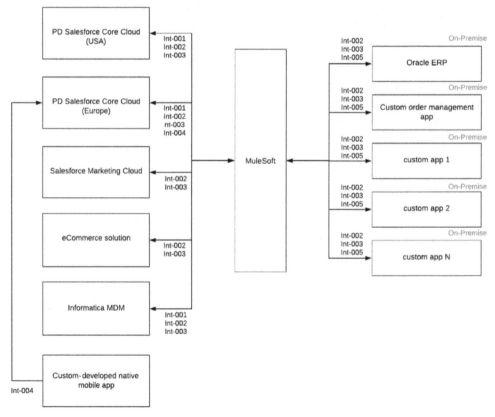

Figure 11.5 – Landscape architecture – final

The following are the integration interfaces:

Interface Code	Source / Destination	Integration Layer	Integration Pattern	Description	Security	Authentication
Int-001	Salesforce --> MuleSoft --> Informatica MDM	Data	Batch data synch-Asynch	Customer data from Salesforce is ingested by Informatica MDM. This is initiated on demand by Informatica MDM. Duplicate and advanced matching rules are executed to create the golden record.	HTTPS (two way SSL/ TLS) between Salesforce and MuleSoft. HTTPS (one way SSL/ TLS) Between MuleSoft and Informatica MDM.	OpenID Connect web server flow (then refresh token flow) with mutual authentication between Salesforce and MuleSoft. Same is also used between MuleSoft and Informatica MDM
Int-002	Informatica MDM --> MuleSoft --> All applications	Data	Batch data synch-Asynch	Golden record customer data from Informatica MDM is replicated to other systems by Informatica MDM. The data is retrieved on demand by the system requesting the data.	HTTPS (two way SSL/ TLS) between Salesforce and MuleSoft. HTTPS (one way SSL/ TLS) Between MuleSoft and Informatica MDM.	OpenID Connect web server flow (then refresh token flow) with mutual authentication between Salesforce and MuleSoft. Same is also used between MuleSoft and Informatica MDM
Int-003	All applications--> MuleSoft --> Informatica MDM	Data	Remote Process Invocation-Request and Reply	All applications can change specific attributes on the golden record. This assumed to be a real time synchronous process.	HTTPS (two way SSL/ TLS) between Salesforce and MuleSoft. HTTPS (one way SSL/ TLS) Between MuleSoft and Informatica MDM.	OpenID Connect web server flow (then refresh token flow) with mutual authentication between Salesforce and MuleSoft. Same is also used between MuleSoft and Informatica MDM
Int-004	Mobile app--> Salesforce (Europe)	Data	Batch data synch-Asynch	Replicate all offline changes from the mobile app to Salesforce once the connection to the internet is restored.	HTTPS (one way SSL/TLS)	OpenID Connect User agent flow (then refresh token
Int-005	Salesforce (Europe)- -> MuleSoft --> Seven applications	Data	Batch data synch-Asynch	A scheduled MuleSoft batch job runs every specific time to pull changed records from Salesforce and replicate them to seven other applications	HTTPS (two way SSL/ TLS) between Salesforce and MuleSoft. HTTPS (one way SSL/ TLS) Between MuleSoft and the seven applications.	OpenID Connect web server flow (then refresh token flow) with mutual authentication between Salesforce and MuleSoft. Simple authentication between MuleSoft and the seven applications

Figure 11.6 – Integration interfaces – final

That concludes this scenario. You may have noticed that we only had a few diagrams for this scenario. This is only because it is a mini-scenario with a particular focus on communication. Things will look different for a full scenario.

Summary

In this chapter, we dived into the details of the Salesforce communication domain. We learned what is expected for a CTA to cover and at what level of detail. We went through some practical examples of ways to present a particular solution, and we also understood the importance of standard diagrams and the common types of diagrams you are likely to encounter.

We then tackled a mini-hypothetical scenario, and we included a hypothetical Q&A stage to practice handling objections. We solved the scenario together, handled specific challenges, and asked questions. We also learned about some pitfalls to avoid and how to leave the right professional impression during the CTA review board, as well as in real life.

After that, we explored multiple potential ways to handle a particular requirement. We learned how one path can lead you to a completely different set of potential challenges and how to prepare for them. We also learned how to avoid difficult situations by merely striving for a simple solution where fewer things can go wrong.

This concludes the seven knowledge domains you need to master. In the next chapter, we will start with our first full hypothetical scenario. You will be introduced to a full-size scenario that we need to solve using all the knowledge and techniques we've learned so far. Buckle up and get ready!

Section 3:
Putting It All
Together

This section will put all the knowledge we have accumulated from the previous sections into action. We will tackle two full CTA review board scenarios. We will learn the structure of the full review board scenarios and learn some of the best practices to deal with them. We will come across challenging design decisions and learn how to select and justify the most suitable one. We will create a comprehensive end-to-end solution for each scenario and practice presenting and defending parts of it. This section will give you practical, hands-on experience to help you prepare for the CTA review board exam.

This section has the following topics:

- *Chapter 12, Practice the Review Board – First Mock*

- *Chapter 13, Present and Defend – First Mock*

- *Chapter 14, Practice the Review Board – Second Mock*

- *Chapter 15, Present and Defend – Second Mock*

12
Practice the Review Board – First Mock

In this chapter, we will put all the knowledge we accumulatively learned from the past chapters into action. We will be introduced to our first full mock scenario, which is very close to a real scenario you may encounter in the review board.

After reading this chapter and the next ones, you are advised to reread the scenario and try to come up with a solution to it on your own.

You can do that as many times as needed until you feel comfortable enough. Try to stick to the *three-hour solving window*. We will learn some handy time management techniques in *Appendix, Tips and Tricks, and the Way Forward*.

In this chapter, we're going to cover the following main topics:

- Introducing the full mock scenario – Packt Pioneer Auto
- Analyzing the requirements and creating a draft end-to-end solution

By the end of this chapter, you will be familiar with the shape, size, and complexity of a full mock scenario. You will also have learned how to create an end-to-end solution for the business processes in a scenario. Without further ado, let's have a look at our first full mock scenario.

Introducing the full mock scenario – Packt Pioneer Auto

Packt Pioneer Auto (**PPA**) is a global car rental company that provides services to end customers in AMER, EMEA, and APAC. PPA operates in 50 major cities across 10 different countries, including Italy, Spain, France, Australia, Japan, the USA, and the UK. In each city, there is an average of 5,000 cars available for rental through the PPA offices. Each city has an average of 10 offices.

PPA allows its customers to pre-book their car rental up to 3 months upfront. Historically, they used their call center to handle customer bookings, but they are looking to modernize their services. Customers can also walk into any of PPA's offices to rent an available car directly.

PPA has around 1 million registered users globally, with an average of 10 million car rentals every year.

PPA works with a network of partners to clean, repair, and maintain their fleet of cars. Each car is fitted with a modern GPS tracking device able to send the car's location periodically in addition to other sets of services, such as detecting harsh braking and going over the speed limit.

PPA's offices are staffed by sales and support teams responsible for managing customers and their relationship with partners. Currently, each country has a bespoke solution for tracking customer and rental information. These solutions are known to be bug-prone and difficult to maintain.

PPA recently decided to use Salesforce as the central CRM solution for unified customer, rental, and partner processes.

Project overview

There are five types of employees who require access to the system:

- **Sales agents**: They are responsible for staffing the regional offices, help walk-in customers to register, and book car rentals. They are also accountable for inspecting returned cars for any damages and provide the final customer invoice.

- **Support agents**: They are responsible for supporting registered customers and resolving reported issues with the rental or the car itself. They also support car reservations via the call center. Support agents work from a single support office in each region (AMER, EMEA, and APAC).

- **Office technicians**: They ensure returned cars are fully functional; they closely inspect the vehicles and provide maintenance reports to the office manager.

- **Office managers**: Each office has a manager responsible for running the businesses from end to end, including managing the relationships with the partners.

- **Regional executive team**: They are responsible for analyzing the customer and rental data across the AMER, EMEA, and APAC regions.

There are two types of external system users:

- **Registered customers**, who need access to a whole new set of modern services.

- **Partners**, who should have access to the system to receive and update maintenance requests. Some partners are open to utilizing PPA's solution, while others have expressed their interest in using their own systems and only integrating with PPA's solution.

PPA has the following landscape.

Current landscape

PPA is currently using the following systems:

- **Regional ERPs**: The regional ERPs are used to manage the partners' accounting and payments. Each ERP is based on different technology, and they are hosted on-premises.

- **Global tracking system**: This is a cloud-based solution used to control car tracking devices remotely. The solution is very expensive to change or modify and has a limited capability to configure or extend any logic beyond its standard features.

- **Customer and rental management applications**: PPA has over five different applications used across the globe for customer and rental management. Historically, these systems had a lot of redundant and duplicate data. PPA is planning to replace them all with a new solution.

- **Violation databases**: PPA purchased a subscription-based service from a global provider specializing in collecting vehicle violation data. As a part of this subscription, PPA gets access to a database containing all received violations, penalties, and tickets for their cars in a particular region. PPA has access to three AWS-hosted Oracle databases across the AMER, EMEA, and APAC regions.

- **Global car rental calculator**: PPA has developed an in-house application to calculate car rental costs based on multiple factors, such as location, start and end dates, car model, car specs, and many more. The application has a built-in REST API and is hosted on AWS.

- **PPA uses LDAP to authenticate all its employees**: PPA would like to keep using LDAP for the foreseeable future.

PPA has shared the following business process requirements.

Business process requirements

The following subsections explain the business processes that PPA expects to have in their new system.

Customer registration

PPA requires specific information to be captured for all its customers regardless of the channel used to rent the car. The new system must support the following processes:

- Customers should be able to self-register using an online portal and a mobile application.

- Sales agents can also register new customers who walk into a PPA office.

- The following information must be captured while registering a customer:

Full customer name

Email address

Mobile number

Preferred language

Driving license number

- The customer must also accept PPA's privacy terms and conditions. The customer can optionally opt-in to receive marketing materials via email, phone, or mail.

- The driving license validity must be checked in real time using the national driver and vehicle licensing agency services.

PPA has shared the following requirements for the reservation process.

Car reservation

Customers should be able to reserve cars up to 3 months upfront either by using the online services (portal and mobile application) or by calling the national customer services number. The online process should use the following steps:

1. The customer should be able to enter the pickup location (city) and start and end date. The system should show a list of cars available at that location and point in time.

2. The system should calculate and display the price for renting each car. The price could differ by date and the total number of reserved days. PPA has a pricing policy that reduces the daily cost if the customer is reserving the car for extended periods.

3. Customers should select the desired car and proceed to online payment. The solution should support PayPal as well as all major credit cards.

4. Once the payment is collected, the transaction is considered complete. An email confirmation should be sent to the customer with a specific activation code. The car should immediately become unavailable for the reserved date.

The reservation process is very similar when using the call center, with slight differences:

1. The support agent should be able to search for available cars in a particular location (city) using the start and end date.

2. The support agent can then verbally inform the customer of the available cars and the associated price. The price calculation rules are consistent across all channels.

3. Once the customer confirms the car selection, the agent should capture the customer's payment details and confirm the reservation.

4. Once the payment is collected, the transaction is considered complete. An email confirmation should be sent to the customer with a specific activation code. The car should immediately become unavailable for the reserved date.

PPA has shared the following requirements for the car check-in process.

Car check-in

PPA wants to automate its processes as much as possible. The check-in process should look like the following:

1. Each office has multiple tablets with a particular application to allow customers to *check in* using the activation code they received during reservation. Once the code is entered, the application should validate the code, booking location, and date. If the validation is successful, a confirmation message will be displayed on the screen, and the reservation record is updated to indicate the customer has checked in for collection. All tablets are connected to the internet.

2. Once the customer checks in, a sales agent can hand over the car keys and update the reservation status to indicate that they collected the keys.

PPA has shared the following requirements for the car check-out process.

Car check-out

The check-out process should look like the following:

1. When the customer returns the car, the sales agent should collect the keys and quickly inspect the vehicle. The sales agent should enter any notes related to changes in the car's condition, such as dents or scratches. If major damage is detected, the office technicians should be informed and asked to further investigate the car's condition.

2. This information should be sent to the ERP, which generates a customer invoice after 72 hours.

3. Once an invoice is generated, a notification will be sent to the client with the invoice amount and instructions to settle any remaining balance.

4. The sales agent updates the reservation status to closed once the inspection is done.

PPA has shared the following requirements for the car status update.

Car status update and penalty settlement

As mentioned before, all cars are fitted with a GPS tracking device. The following details describe the car status update and penalty settlement process:

- All tracking devices can communicate over 4G and 3G. They send the car's location every 30 seconds. For security reasons, this continues to happen even if the car is turned off.

- PPA would like to gather information that describes the behavior of drivers, including going over speed limits and harsh braking. That should all be analyzed for PPA to calculate driving patterns during specific dates and times of the year.

- PPA would like to use GPS tracking devices to detect possible vehicle theft. If the device is reporting a change in the car's location while the car is turned off, this could be a possible theft incident that the support team should be notified about within no more than 15 minutes.

- Every day, the violation databases should be checked. If they contain a violation record for a PPA car on a given date, the system should look up the car's driver details for the given date, then transfer the penalty amount to the ERP to calculate a new invoice and send it to the customer.

PPA has shared the following data migration requirements.

Data migration requirements

Considering the previously shared information about the current landscape, PPA has shared the following data migration requirements:

- PPA would like to migrate the data from all its current customer and rental management applications to the new system.

- PPA is aware that the current data contains many redundancies and duplicates and is looking for your guidance to deal with the situation and achieve high data quality in the target system.

- PPA has around 50 million rental records in each of its current rental management applications. Most of them are stored for historical purposes as PPA wants to keep rental records for at least 10 years. PPA would like to continue allowing its sales and support agents to access these records in the new system.

PPA has shared the following accessibility requirements.

Accessibility and security requirements

PPA is looking for guidance to design a secure solution; they shared the following requirements:

- Customer accounts should be visible to the office managers, sales, and service agents worldwide. However, technicians should only see customers for their specific country.

- Support incidents should be visible to support agents and their managers only.

- Only office technicians can update the car status to indicate that it is out of service and requires repairs.

- Office technicians should not be able to view the customer's driving license number.

- Once a theft incident is detected, only the support agents trained for such type of incidents, their managers, and regional executives should be able to view the incident's details.

- The regional executive team should have access to all regional data, including drivers' behavior, such as harsh braking.

- Office managers should be able to see the details of the partner accounts in their own country only.

- Partners should be able to log in to Salesforce using Salesforce-managed credentials only.

- Customers can self-register to the online portal and mobile application.

- Customers should also be able to log in to the online portal and the mobile application using their Facebook accounts.

- PPA employees who are logged in to the corporate network should be able to automatically log in to Salesforce without the need to provide their credentials again.

- PPA employees can log in to Salesforce from outside the corporate network using the LDAP credentials. However, if they log in from outside the network, they should provide a second-factor authentication, such as a text message received on their mobile phone.

PPA has shared the following reporting requirements.

Reporting requirements

PPA has requested a rich set of reporting capabilities, including the following:

- The regional executive team would like a report that shows the relationship between customers' driving behavior and particular times of year across the past 10 years.

- The regional executive team would like a trending monthly report that shows the pickup and drop off locations of each rental in order to determine the appropriate distribution of cars across their offices.

- Customers should be able to view a full history of their rental bookings, including bookings from the past 3 years.

- Customers should also be able to view their full trip history for each completed rental.

- Partners should be able to view a monthly report showing the repair jobs completed for PPA.

PPA has shared the following project development requirements.

Project development requirements

Considering the complexity of PPA's program, they have requested the following project development requirements:

- PPA plans to have three different **service implementers** (**SIs**), delivering different functionalities across parallel projects. PPA would like to avoid conflicts across the teams, such as code overwriting or breaking each other's logic. PPA requires your help to define a way to manage the code base to avoid such conflicts and reduce the chances of breaking existing functionalities.

- Historically, SIs used to follow their own coding standards while dealing with other platforms. On many occasions, they introduced duplicate functionalities. PPA would like to understand how to control and avoid this situation in Salesforce and enable better code reuse.

- PPA has a new platform owner who joined from another company that also used Salesforce. She reported that on several occasions, bugs were fixed in UAT but then showed up again in production. PPA would like to understand the likely cause of such an incident and how to avoid it in their program.

- PPA would like to release the solution to Italy first, then roll out the same solution to other countries based on a pre-agreed schedule. Each region country may have country-specific requirements that need to be defined and accommodated in the solution. PPA is looking for your support to determine the right development methodology and governance to achieve that.

PPA has also shared the following other requirements.

Other requirements

PPA would like to know the best practices to manage their customer consent. They have shared the following requirement:

- PPA wants to ensure that data in development environments is always anonymized.

That concludes the hypothetical scenario. Ensure you have gone through all the pages and requirements of your hypothetical scenario before proceeding further.

We will now start identifying requirements and create our draft solution following the same methodology we used in previous scenarios.

Analyze the requirements and creating a draft end-to-end solution

Give yourself enough time to go through the scenario and understand the big picture. You can even start adding notes with potential solutions. If you plan to do the in-person review board, you can add the notes on a separate piece of paper or on the printed scenario itself, while you can use Excel sheets for the virtual review board. You can use a combination of the two for both experiences; it depends on your preference and what you feel comfortable with.

We will cover two ways to prepare and play your presentation in *Appendix, Tips and Tricks, and the Way Forward*. We will also see an example of a time plan for the solution and presentation phases, where you allocate a specific period to do pre-planned activities.

Considering the size of the full scenarios and the number of shared requirements, we will split the finding of a solution and the presentation creation over two chapters. We will cover most of the scenario's requirements in this chapter. In *Chapter 13, Present and Defend – First Mock*, we will continue with the remaining requirements and create the presentation pitch.

We will continue to follow the same method we are now familiar with, incremental solution development. Let's start by understanding the current landscape and create our first draft of the diagrams.

Understanding the current situation

Starting with the first set of paragraphs of the preceding scenario, we see a description of PPA's activities and geographical presence. By going through the requirements for the first time, we see several incidents for accessibility requirements that indicated granting access to users and *their managers*.

This should point you directly to a potential need for role hierarchies. Moreover, you should expect a likely need for role hierarchies and/or territory management once you see a description of multiple geographical locations.

Let's create a draft role hierarchy based on what we know so far. We know that PPA operates in AMER, EMEA, and APAC. They cover 50 cities in 10 countries. We will adjust the diagram later once we learn more about the requirements.

Let's also create an initial draft for our actors and license diagram. We have sales agents, support agents, office technicians, office managers, and regional executives. We also have customers and partners. The scenario has also provided an initial description of the actors' activities. Please note that we might figure out more activities while going through the scenario. This is where we need to go back and adjust our diagram accordingly.

We can even start allocating potential licenses to different actors. We can always adjust that if needed. Let's add them now, as that is the best way to ensure we don't miss any requirements.

Your role hierarchy diagram could look like the following:

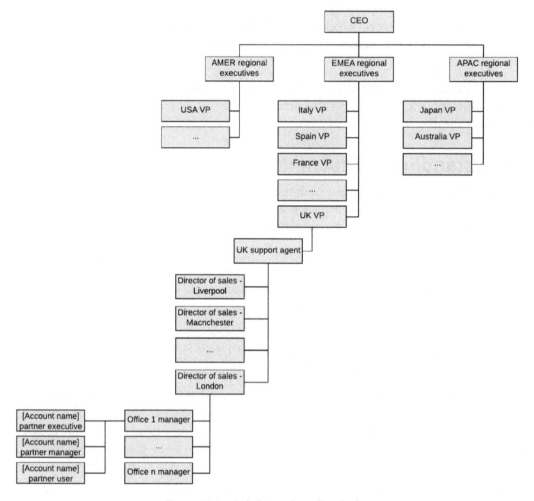

Figure 12.1 – Role hierarchy – first draft

Your actors and licenses diagram could look similar to the following:

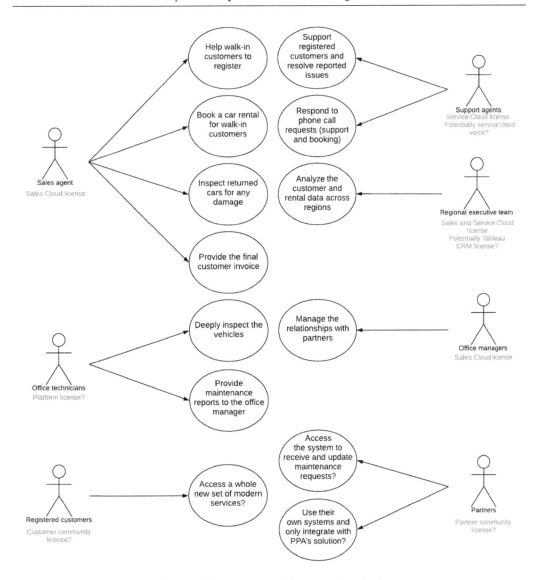

Figure 12.2 – Actors and licenses – first draft

I usually leave question marks on the diagram for the not-very-clear topics at this stage. This helps me identify any gaps later on.

The scenario also provided some interesting figures, such as *5,000 cars, 10 offices per city, 1 million registered users globally*, and an *average of 10 million car rentals annually*. Pay attention to these numbers because they typically would lead to some data challenges, such as LDV objects. Take a note of these numbers, keep them at the top of your paper, notes, or sheets, and keep checking them while designing your solution.

I have never come across a CTA review board scenario that doesn't have a requirement related to LDV. If you don't manage to identify one in your scenario, I would strongly recommend you go through it again and ensure you fully understand the requirements and the scope.

Let's now move on to the current landscape description. We can use the provided details to create our draft landscape architecture diagram. Remember that we need to indicate all involved systems in it, including those being retired.

Your landscape architecture could look like the following:

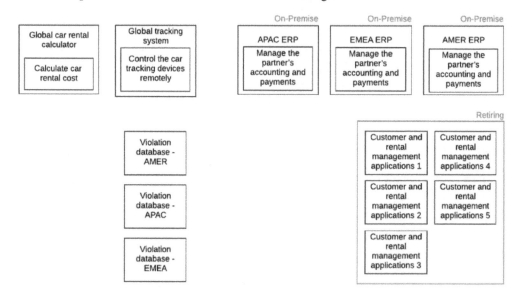

Figure 12.3 – Landscape architecture – first draft

The full scenarios are typically structured in a specific way, where there is a section for each related set of requirements. Sections such as the *business process requirements* contain subsections explaining all the key business processes in this scenario.

In *Appendix, Tips and Tricks, and the Way Forward*, we will better understand a full scenario's typical structure. For the time being, let's proceed with analyzing and working on a solution for the shared requirements.

Analyzing the business process requirements

PPA has shared five key business processes: customer registration, car reservation, car check-in, car check-out, and car status update and penalty settlement. This part of the scenario usually contains the most significant chunk of the requirements. You are strongly advised to create a business process diagram for each of these processes. This will help you spot the tricky parts of the solution and would also give you an engaging and attractive tool to use during your presentation.

Let's start with the first shared business process.

Customer registration

PPA has shared five key requirements for the customer registration process. Perhaps you have already noticed this, but some requirements in the *Accessibility and security requirements* section might add a few more requirements to this process. This is why the *incremental solution development* processes are particularly useful to ensure you don't accidentally miss any requirements.

Let's start with the first requirement for this process.

Customers should be able to self-register using an online portal and a mobile application

Self-registration can be easily enabled on Salesforce communities. But the two main questions this requirement raises are the following:

- What type of community license is required?
- What is the right strategy for the mobile app?

This is a customer-related requirement, so you should be choosing between the Customer Community and the Customer Community Plus licenses. So far, we haven't come across any accessibility requirements that would direct us toward the Customer Community Plus license. Therefore, it is better to stick with the Customer Community license for the time being and adjust if needed.

The Customer Community license is more optimized to handle a vast number of end customers, unlike the Customer Community Plus license, which is more suitable for use cases that require complex sharing mechanisms.

You should also specify whether you are going to use named users or per-login licenses. We don't have a requirement to help us decide, so we need to assume. For example, we can assume that the customers won't be logging in frequently, and therefore a Salesforce Customer Community login license should be an ideal fit.

That sorts out the first half of the requirement. Now, we need to figure out the right mobile strategy. There are not that many different options. As we discussed earlier in *Chapter 5, Developing a Scalable System Architecture*, the possibilities are the Salesforce mobile app (with or without Mobile Publisher), native app, hybrid app, or HTML5 app.

The requirements we are aware of so far can be fulfilled using all of these options, so let's assume the easiest to develop and deploy, that is, the option that allows us to save development efforts and focus on delivering value to the customer. Salesforce Mobile Publisher can be used to create and deploy a branded mobile app of your Salesforce community.

Is it the most cost-efficient option? If you don't consider the time-to-market and the return-of-investment calculations, then the answer will probably be *no*. At the review board, you should be looking for the *best* technical solution (based on best practices and expert judgment). In this case, it makes sense to recommend using Salesforce Mobile Publisher.

Update your landscape architecture and actors and licenses diagrams, then let's move on to the next requirement.

Sales agents can also register new customers who walk into a PPA office

This is an out-of-the-box capability in Salesforce. Sales agents can simply create a **person account** for the customer (or a separate account and contact; however, a person account is more suitable in our case), then enable a Customer Community user for it. This is an easy-to-collect point; don't fail to identify or solve such requirements in your presentation.

Let's move on to the next requirement.

The following information must be captured while registering a customer

Again, this is an easy-to-collect point. You just need to mention that you will be capturing these fields upon registration and that you will be making them mandatory to ensure we always capture a value in them. There is no standard field on the contact object to hold the driving license value, so you need to introduce it as a custom field.

You need to mention that this field will be custom; this is how you ensure you capture this question's points. Imagine how bad would it be to lose such an easy point!

I tend to add all custom fields to the data model. This is not what you usually have on your data model's logical level, but I find this useful, particularly for the review board. This will ensure I still get the points even if I fail to mention the custom fields in my presentation. My diagram will answer the question for me.

Create or update your data model diagram, and let's move on to the next requirement, as follows.

The customer must also accept PPAs privacy terms and conditions

Salesforce introduced the *Individual* object as part of a rich set of consent management objects. When you come across a consent management requirement, you need to think about utilizing the standard objects to fulfill it. In most cases, you won't need to introduce any additional custom object or field. You just need to make sure you are familiar with the use of each of the standard consent management objects. A full description can be found at the following link: `https://help.salesforce.com/articleView?id=consent_mgmt_fields.htm&type=5`.

In this case, I will use the *Individual*, *Contact point type consent*, and *Data use purpose* objects.

Update your data model diagram, and let's move on to the next requirement.

The driving license validity must be checked in real time using the national driver and vehicle licensing agency services

This requirement contains two challenges:

- How do you achieve the desired functionality as part of the customer's self-registering process?

- How do you achieve the desired functionality for sales agents registering walk-in customers?

To fulfill this requirement, you need to design an integration interface with the relevant national agency services. You can assume that the agency has publicly accessible APIs. Still, you need to decide which integration pattern to use, how that interface would work, whether there is a need for middleware, and how the authentication and data security will be handled.

The word *real time* should give you a hint. The desired pattern should invoke logic in a remote system, get the result in real time, and return it to the caller. Sounds familiar? It should, because that is precisely what the *Remote Process Invocation – Request and Reply* pattern is all about.

We know that this pattern needs to be triggered by the caller and then wait for the response. In the online self-registration form, this can be achieved in multiple ways, such as invoking the remote service upon clicking on the submit button. We will have to use a custom registration page, giving us control over all its behaviors.

We need to introduce a different mechanism for the sales agents as they will be using the standard Salesforce UI. We can introduce a custom *validate driving license* action that triggers a **Salesforce flow**. In turn, the flow can use **Salesforce External Services** to invoke a remote web service and get back the result.

The middleware can add value even for such simple requirements, as it can handle any required retry mechanisms. Moreover, it provides a unified interface for Salesforce to communicate with. Behind the scenes, it communicates with the *right* national agency depending on the issuing country of the driving license. We can assume that this middleware is MuleSoft.

Authentication from Salesforce to MuleSoft should always use one of the common authentication standards, such as **OAuth 2.0**. We can use either the **web server authentication flow** (for the first time, followed by a **refresh token flow**) or the **JWT flow**. In both cases, data will be protected in transit using **one-way TLS**.

Authentication from the middleware to the agency's web services depends on the agency itself. You can assume that they only support simple authentication (username/password).

Update your landscape architecture diagram and your list of integration interfaces. At this stage, you should also create your first business process diagram. It will help you significantly during the presentation. It could look like the following:

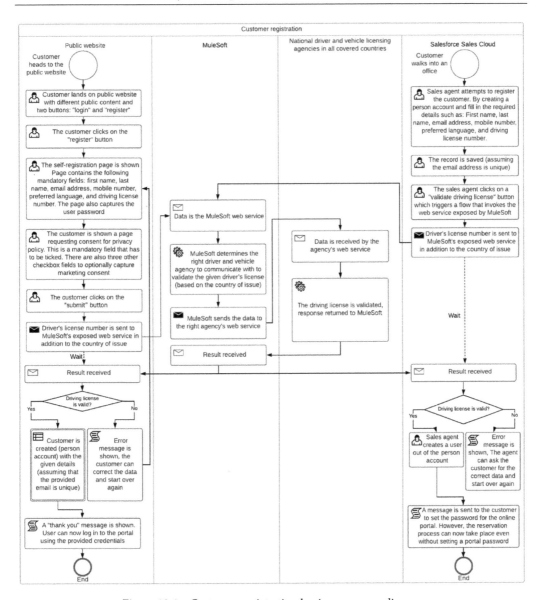

Figure 12.4 – Customer registration business process diagram

You can add as much detail to the process flow as you see appropriate. Just remember that this will be your tool to *tell the story* during the presentation. In real life, this diagram is likely to get more detailed.

Now that we have solved the first business process, let's move on to the second.

Car reservation

PPA has shared two flavors of the car reservation process: one via the online portal and the other via the call center. You can assume a third use case where a walk-in customer is looking to reserve a car. PPA hasn't shared such a requirement, though. Therefore, you don't have to answer that part. It could be a part that the judges might add during the Q&A. If that happens, you will need to explain how the system will handle it.

Let's start with the first requirement for this process.

The customer should be able to enter the pickup location (city) and start and end date

The system should show a list of cars available at that location and point of time.

This will require a custom Visualforce page or Lightning component. The page would query the available cars based on the given parameters and displays the results. Are we missing anything here? Of course we are.

You need to think of the end-to-end solution; there is no one else who will. It is *your responsibility* as the lead architect on this project. You need to consider the following challenges:

- Which object is going to be used to represent a car?
- How do we maintain the availability of cars?
- How are we going to organize the cars per location?
- What are the accessibility settings required to allow customers to view cars?

Clarification

Some colleagues and CTA candidates have asked me whether the right way to prepare for the CTA review board is to engage with more pre-sales activities. In my opinion, that is only half the answer. Pre-sales activities would significantly enhance your communication skills, but that is not enough.

While engaged in pre-sales activities, you rarely dive into the level of details we are demonstrating in this scenario. That level of detail is a must to pass the CTA review board. You need to have the breadth of knowledge, the consultant mindset, the hard-core technical depth, and a wealth of soft skills. Combining both pre-sales activities with hard core day-to-day implementation work would significantly boost your learning curve.

Can we use any standard object to represent the cars? The `Product` object is an obvious candidate considering that it is also related to the `Order` object we might use for the car reservation. You can utilize the `PriceBook` object to group cars by location.

The pricing is going to be handled by PPA's global calculator application anyway (more on that in the next requirement). You can also use a custom object, but you might need to make some adjustments to the `Order` object in that case.

Your products and price books have to be visible to your customers. Products don't have **OWD** settings as they are controlled by price books. `PriceBook` has special OWD settings and sharing mechanisms. You can share it manually from the `PriceBook` page (currently only supported on Classic) with all portal users.

Finally, the page would need to use `Order`'s `Order Start Date` (`EffectiveDate`) and `Order End Date` (`EndDate`) fields to determine cars' availability in the provided period.

Update your data model diagram, and let's move on to the next requirement, as follows.

The system should calculate and display the price for renting each car

PPA already has a specific application to calculate the price of each car based on the given parameters. We need to integrate with that solution, pass the right arguments, and then display the results in the Visualforce page/Lightning component.

This is a new integration interface. We are now familiar with the details required for every integration interface in our solution. The pattern is *Remote Process Invocation – Request and Reply* as we need the response back before we can proceed to the next step (which is displaying the results to the customer).

What will be your strategy if the judges decided to take the calculator application out of the landscape? How would you handle this requirement? Be prepared for such challenges as they could be raised during the Q&A.

For now, update your landscape architecture diagram and your list of interfaces, then let's move on to the next requirement, as follows.

Customers should select the desired car and proceed to online payment

You can build an integration to a payment gateway or use a product that provides that capability out of the box. The latter is the right solution technically as it saves you time and effort. Moreover, a battle-tested product is usually more reliable than a custom solution.

You still need to explain how the product works (at a high level) and how it would collect the payment details in a PCI-compliant manner. After all, this would be the first point your client would ask about in a real-life scenario.

Try to memorize the names of some ISV products that provide this functionality, such as **Bluefin** and **Chargent**.

Update your landscape architecture diagram, then let's move on to the next requirement, as follows.

Once the payment is collected, the transaction is considered complete

Once the payment is collected, **Bluefin** can create a payment record (custom object) related to the order. This, in turn, can trigger a **Salesforce flow** that updates the order status to *complete* and sends an email notification to the customer.

The order *start date* and *end date* will be used to determine the car's availability.

Have we covered all the requirements? We have missed a minor one, actually. You are the lead architect, and you are expected to provide the end-to-end solution with all the required details. You need to explain how the activation code will be created and included in the email notification.

This could simply be a custom field on the order object, with a **Globally Unique Identifier (GUID)** value that is generated and populated using an **APEX** trigger before updating the order status to *complete*.

Once the value is populated into that field, you can use **merge fields** to include the field's value in your email notification. The created order will be linked to the customer's **person account**, where the rest of the email notification values (such as first name, last name, and so on) can be fetched from.

Update your data model; it should look like the following:

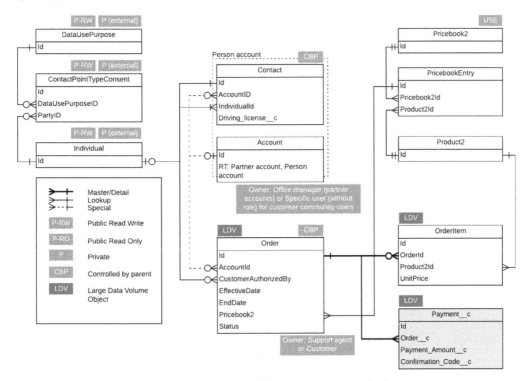

Figure 12.5 – Data model diagram – second draft

At this stage, you might have noticed that we have labeled some objects as **LDV**. This is based on the figures we took note of at the beginning and still at the initial state. You need to do the math to confirm that these objects can indeed be considered LDVs. I usually do that after drafting the solution for the business processes.

Also, at this stage, your landscape architecture diagram should look similar to the following:

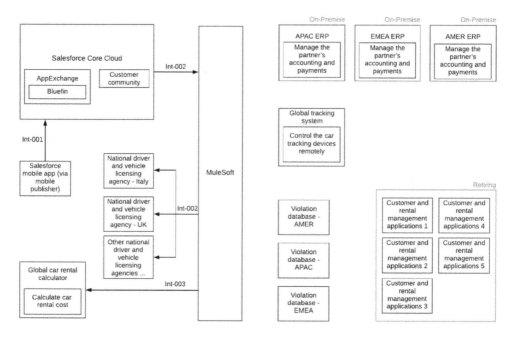

Figure 12.6 – Landscape architecture – second draft

The next set of requirements describes the same process executed by a different actor (the support agents). Let's start with the first requirement.

The support agent should be able to search for available cars in a particular location (city) using the start and end date

We can assume that the Visualforce page/Lightning component created for the customers is also available for the support agents. The new Lightning component can be easily embedded into a tab in Salesforce. We can assume that the component has design-time properties that control its capabilities. For example, a property could be set to indicate that the internal team will use it. This property controls the visibility of a specific part of the page where the customer's person account can be selected.

You can create a wireframe for the page if you wish. I consider this an extra mile that you can cover if you have enough time. What is important is to explain how the pre-built **Visualforce** page or **Lightning component** can be repurposed for the usage of internal users.

Let's now move on to the next requirement.

The support agent can then verbally inform the customer of the available cars and the associated price

This requirement is automatically fulfilled as the support agents would be using the same car search and reservation page exposed to customers. The page is constantly communicating with PPA's calculator via MuleSoft and should return consistent pricing across the channels.

Let's move on to the next requirement.

An email confirmation should be sent to the customer with a specific activation code

This is the same requirement requested before for a different actor (customer). It is automatically fulfilled as the support agents use the same car search and reservation page exposed to customers, which should execute the same logic, including sending the email notification.

The business process diagram for this process might look like the following:

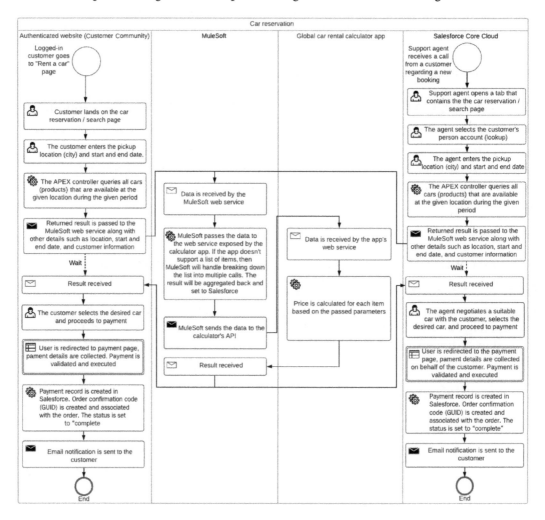

Figure 12.7 – Car reservation business process diagram

Now that we have solved the second business process, let's move on to the third.

Car check-in

PPA has shared two requirements for this process. Let's start with the first.

Each office has multiple tablets with a particular application to allow customers to check in using the activation code they received during reservation

The customer is expected to interact with the tablets in the office by entering the activation code. The application installed on the tablet should authenticate to Salesforce, look up the order record using the activation code, then update its status (or sub status) to indicate the customer has checked in. There will probably be a validation in place to prevent early check-in.

In your solution, you need to explain the integration pattern used (**remote call-in**), the authentication mechanism (**OpenID Connect User-Agent Flow**), and the security measurements to protect data in transit.

> **Caution**
>
> Authentication on its own doesn't protect data in transit (mutual authentication is an exception). Most authentication standards require a secure HTTPS connection. However, this is not mandatory for simple authentication. If a simple authentication took place over a non-secure HTTP connection, there would be no security measurements to protect the data in transit. Your data will be transferred in plain text format, and attackers can sniff the traffic and get access to your data. The most common way to protect data in transit is using one-way or two-way TLS.

Take a moment to think of the potential changes that could be introduced to this requirement during the Q&A. How can we enhance this process? A possible addition could be to send a push notification to the sales agents in the current office shift to inform them of the check-in. This will make the process more streamlined. This is not a shared requirement at the moment but be prepared for such additions/changes during the Q&A.

Update your landscape architecture diagram, your list of integration interfaces, and your data model (adding any new fields required, such as a sub status), then let's move on to the next requirement.

Once the customer checks in, a sales agent can hand over the car keys and update the reservation status to indicate that they collected the keys

We can assume that this will happen manually. The agent will search for the reservation, validate the order's sub status, then hand over the keys and manually update the order again.

Further automation could be requested during the Q&A. Again, be prepared for that.

The business process diagram for this process can look like the following:

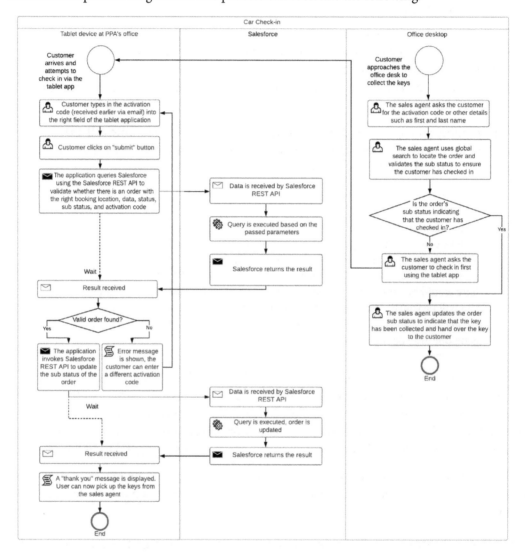

Figure 12.8 – Car check-in business process diagram

Now that we have solved the third business process, let's move on to the fourth.

Car check-out

The process of returning the car to the leasing office is more straightforward. It can only be done in person by the client. Let's have a look at the first requirement, as follows.

When the customer returns the car, the sales agent should collect the keys and quickly inspect the vehicle

The sales agent can look up the order related to this particular rental using the activation code or customer information. But where can we store the inspection details? And how can we inform the technicians about major damage to follow up with?

This is where you need to demonstrate your understanding of the platform's capabilities. You can propose a solution based on a set of custom fields and workflow rules with email notifications. But then you will find yourself trying to solve other future challenges, such as the following:

- How can you send an email notification to an entire team? I strongly discourage you from proposing any solution that is based on a *shared email inbox* pattern. That pattern was acceptable a few decades ago, but today's enterprises want something far more traceable and auditable.

- How can you ensure that the technicians are acting against the incident? If they don't act, the right invoice won't be generated. This will impact the main process you are solving.

- If you are planning to introduce a set of new fields on the order object, how could that impact the user experience? If you are planning to introduce a whole new custom object for this, have you considered the standard objects that might deliver the desired functionality?

Considering that you are looking for the *best solution technically*, you should consider using the `Case` object whenever you detect a need for a well-governed incident management process, for requirements such as reporting, assigning, progress tracking, and eventually resolving an incident.

For this requirement, the sales agent can create a case (the Sales Cloud license permits that), link it with the customer's order, and use it to provide structured feedback. If specific criteria are met, the case can be automatically assigned to the technicians' queue of that office. Once the case is assigned to the queue, all queue members will be notified by an email alert (this feature can be turned on or off).

The queue assignment can also grant the technicians access and visibility to the case records. You could configure escalation rules to ensure that the case can be reported to higher management if the technician took no action during a specified period.

This is a scalable and flexible solution. The judges can challenge you and change some requirements on the fly, but your solution is flexible enough to handle these changes.

Your proposed approach must deliver *value* to your customer that other approaches won't. You have to *believe* in this. You are not a salesperson who is mainly focusing on hitting a sales target. You are the client's *trusted advisor*; when you propose a solution, you must believe in it and clearly articulate its value. Otherwise, it will show you up during the presentation and Q&A, and you won't radiate the confidence expected from a CTA.

This information should be sent to the ERP, which generates a customer invoice after 72 hours

We have three ERPs hosted on-premise, probably in entirely different physical locations. How can we transfer the data from Salesforce to the *right* ERP system in order to generate the invoice? How can we connect a cloud-based application such as Salesforce to an on-premise application?

If your answer is anything but *middleware*, then you are likely stepping into a minefield. Proposing a point-to-point approach here would very likely result in a failure in the integration domain. The very first challenge would simply be: how would Salesforce connect to a system protected behind a firewall?

Coming up with unreasonable assumptions such as moving the ERP to a DMZ (which means it is pretty much exposed to the outer world) will open a can of worms that you don't want to deal with. And that's not even mentioning the associated cost of such an activity.

You already have MuleSoft in your landscape; use it. If you don't have it yet, this is a solid reason to propose it. You can suggest other middleware as well. Considering that this requirement would need a system capable of orchestrating the call with multiple systems, and considering that this interface is not meant to deal with a massive amount of data, an ESB is a reasonable option.

You can propose any ESB tool you feel comfortable with. You don't have to stick with MuleSoft just because it is a Salesforce product. Remember, you have to believe in the value of your solution. We are proposing MuleSoft because it is a leading middleware, according to many credible sources. Moreover, I am personally more comfortable with it. But feel free to propose whatever you believe can deliver a similar functionality and that you are more familiar with.

You still need to specify the integration pattern, authentication mechanism, and how you will protect your data in transit. You might need to explain how MuleSoft will communicate with an on-premise solution during the presentation. We did something similar in *Chapter 11, Communicating and Socializing Your Solution*.

When you select the pattern, you need to consider the object(s) you plan to copy over to the ERP.

Based on our proposed data model, you would likely need to synch the `Order`, `OrderItem`, and `Case` objects, assuming that the `Account` and `Contact` tables are already synced along with lookup tables such as `Product`.

Which pattern would serve you best here? Which Salesforce functionality can be used to sync all three objects with as little technical burden as possible? You can think of the following functionalities and tools:

- **Outbound messages**: Outbound messages can only contain data from one object. However, we can send the lead object (such as `Order` in this case) to MuleSoft, request MuleSoft to do a callback to retrieve the rest of the objects, and then transfer them to the ERPs. This is a good option that you should shortlist, although it requires a bit of custom development in MuleSoft.

- **Platform events**: They can be designed to contain data from multiple objects. However, we are dealing with an object that has one-to-many relations here. You can't model a single platform event that combines data from the parent and the child records except if you go with non-standard solutions such as defining a long text field with JSON content. You are discouraged from proposing such an approach due to the associated technical challenges (creating the JSON structure, populating it, and parsing it at the other end) unless it is unavoidable.

- **Future methods**: You can develop an APEX callout to invoke a remote service exposed by MuleSoft, and pass the data. Considering that this needs to happen in an asynchronous fashion, you would need to use future methods (or queueable interfaces). You are discouraged from proposing such an approach due to the associated technical challenges (additional custom development, retry mechanism, logging mechanism, and so on) unless it is unavoidable.

- **Salesforce flows**: Using flows, you can invoke the remote web service using a configurable point-and-click functionality. Sounds good, but you still need to consider the required supporting functionalities, such as retry and logging mechanisms.

- **Batch data synch**: This might sound old-fashioned, but it is effortless to put in place and, on many occasions, good enough for the business. You can configure a batch job in MuleSoft to run every hour, pick the relevant records from all target objects, then send them over to the ERP in the right order. This is likely to be the most cost-efficient option too.

Our evaluation of the preceding functionalities depends on the use case we are trying to solve. For example, in other use cases, you might find that platform events are optimal.

Once the data is synced to the ERP, we can assume that the ERP has all that is needed to generate the invoice in the given timeframe.

Update your landscape architecture diagram and your list of integration interfaces, then let's move on to the next requirement.

Once an invoice is generated, a notification would be sent to the client with the invoice amount and instructions to settle any remaining balance

You can solve this requirement in multiple ways. You can assume that the whole process is going to take place off-platform. The ERP generates the invoice and the email, then sends them across to the client.

Alternatively, you can go with a total on-platform solution, where the ERP generates the invoice and its line items, MuleSoft replicates that to Salesforce, then fires an email notification from Salesforce containing the invoice and its detailed line item. However, in this case, you would need to deal with at least 10 million invoices every year and at least an equal number of invoice line items with a potential to go up by 50% (assuming half the invoices will contain two line items). This means you will need to consider the new invoice and invoice line item objects in your LDV strategy.

However, if you follow the scenario's requirement carefully, you will notice that the requirement is to share the invoice amount only, probably with an invoice number, issue date, due date, and a few other attributes, which are usually included in the invoice header.

You can either store this information in a custom object related to Order or as attributes on Order itself. Both options are fair as long as you can clearly communicate why you chose one over the other.

A related custom object will allow you to store multiple invoices if needed, such as a provisional and a final invoice. It adds one LDV to your data model, but that is fine as long as you are articulating the value of this approach accurately and including this object in your LDV mitigation strategy.

Remember, there is no *one correct answer*. There are many ways to solve a problem, but you just have to rationally justify your approach and back it up with a solid technical understanding of the associated pros and cons.

I will introduce a new custom object to the data model to hold the invoice header details. We will also require a new integration interface between the ERPs and Salesforce to copy the data. As usual, you need to provide all required information to describe the interface.

Update your data model, list of integration interfaces, and landscape architecture diagram, and let's move on to the next requirement.

The sales agent updates the reservation status to closed once the inspection is done

This event chronologically precedes the ones mentioned in the last two requirements. However, that is not an issue here because this requirement can easily be fulfilled. We just need to ensure we draw the right chronological order in our diagrams. The agent is expected to update `Sub_Status__c` on `Order` to closed. Don't miss such easy points.

The business process diagram for this process can look like the following:

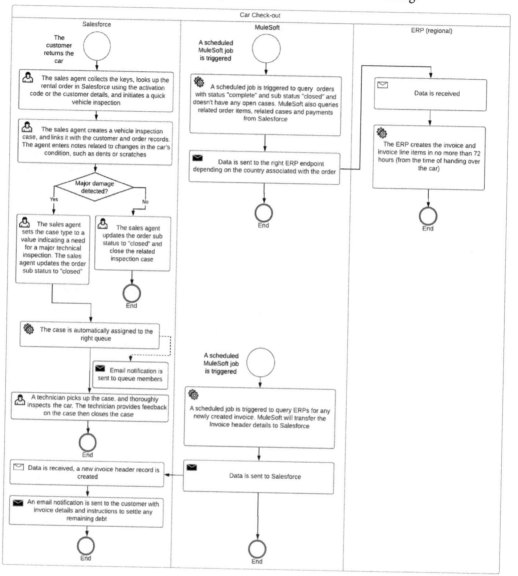

Figure 12.9 – Car check-out business process diagram

Now that we have solved the fourth business process, let's move on to the fifth and final one.

Car status update and penalty settlement

PPA has tracking devices in its cars; they are used to track the car's location by periodically sending its GPS coordinates. The devices also send additional information such as incidents of harsh braking or speeding.

What do we call devices equipped with sensors and other technologies that can communicate with other devices and services over the internet to exchange data? Correct, **Internet of Things (IoT)** devices.

There are specific authentication flows explicitly designed for IoT devices, such as the **device flow** and the **asset token flow** (which is more suitable for IoT devices that are not equipped with a screen). We covered both in *Chapter 4, Core Architectural Concepts – Identity and Access Management*.

IoT devices tend to send small chunks of data at a high frequency. This typically results in generating a massive amount of data considering the number of connected IoT devices at any given time.

As a rule of thumb, Salesforce core cloud (also known as Force.com) is not an ideal platform to receive such a massive number of inbound communications, nor the best place to store the retrieved data over a long period.

In some scenarios, you might still be able to pitch Salesforce core for this role. But in that case, you need to carefully calculate the expected inbound calls and compare them with the likely governor limit at the target org. A safer approach would be to utilize an off-platform solution to receive and aggregate the result. **Salesforce Heroku** is an excellent fit for such scenarios, especially with some add-on products such as **Apache Kafka on Heroku**, **Postgres**, and **Redis**.

Let's go through the shared requirements and start crafting our solution. The first requirement is as follows.

All tracking devices can communicate over 4G and 3G. They send the car's location every 30 seconds

PPA has 5,000 cars (and it is fair to assume that this number will grow). The tracking devices send a message every 30 seconds; this takes place day and night for security reasons.

That means 2 messages every minute, 120 every hour, and 2,880 every day.

In total, that would be 14,400,000 daily messages from all cars. That is over 430 million messages every month.

Clearly, Salesforce core is not the ideal platform for such a massive number of call-ins or create/update operations. But you still have to do the math to justify your rationale. This is precisely what you are expected to do in your real-life project.

You are an architect, and you can't simply assume that *there will be many call-ins, and based on that, I propose the following solution.* Make your reasonable assumptions and do the required math; numbers are the best way to deliver an unquestionable message.

We also need to keep in mind that PPA already has a global tracking system. It is used to *control* the car tracking devices remotely. This means it can be used to configure the devices remotely, a functionality that we would likely want to retain. However, the global tracking system is very expensive to change or modify and cannot be extended via configurations.

So far, we haven't come across a use case where we need to extend it. We can still utilize the global tracking system to receive the messages from the car. But let's proceed further with this process requirements and see whether that will change. The next requirement is as follows.

PPA would like to gather information that describes the behavior of drivers

This requirement indicates a need to store a vast amount of data. In addition, there is also a need to analyze this data to create meaningful reports and dashboards. PPA's global tracking system doesn't have such capability. It is likely capable of storing the required amount of data but doesn't have the right capabilities to create such reports and dashboards. We need a BI tool such as Microsoft Power BI, Tableau, or Tableau CRM.

You are unlikely to dive into the details of each of these tools' capabilities during the review board. This is something you would do differently in a real project, but then you have much more time to conduct a proper comparison, probably combined with some proofs of concept.

For the time being, we know that we need one of these tools added to our landscape. Feel free to propose other similar tools as well. We still don't have a clear answer on the platform that will store this data, but the next requirement will help us make up our minds. It starts as follows.

PPA would like to use the GPS tracking devices to detect possible vehicle theft

This requirement describes a business process based on the received IoT data. A common use of IoT data is to analyze data and detect patterns, but it can also be used to trigger specific actions based on pre-determined conditions and machine states. It can even go further to enable **machine-to-machine** (**M2M**) processes, where one machine determines, based on specific logic, that it is time to communicate with another machine to trigger a remote transaction.

This requirement doesn't go that far. But there is still a need to introduce custom logic. Which platform would be best suited for such logic? You can probably think of four options:

- **Salesforce core cloud**: Considering the amount of communicated data, this option will be disregarded.

- **MuleSoft**: MuleSoft can receive the messages and process them based on custom logic. However, it is not the best platform to handle such complex logic, which requires machine-state handling. Moreover, it is also not a platform with a rich UI that is user friendly. This option will be disregarded.

- **PPA's global tracking system**: It can be modified to accommodate this logic. However, PPA have clearly communicated that this is a very expensive activity. This option is suboptimal.

- **A custom-developed app hosted on a scalable PaaS platform**: This could be a custom-developed app hosted on AWS, or, more reasonably, on Heroku (considering that Heroku has out-of-the-box connectors to the Salesforce core cloud and Tableau CRM). Heroku can become the platform that receives all the messages sent by the IoT devices. The custom-developed app can add the capabilities of handling the theft detection use case. It can also be extended to handle other use cases in the future, and it can do that in a scalable and reliable manner. Moreover, **Heroku Connect** can easily synchronize data between Heroku and Salesforce. This allows us to create cases in Salesforce once a theft incident is detected. The case can then be assigned to the right queue, which, in turn, would send an email notification to the queue members. This solution sounds optimal, considering all the factors.

We can now also assume using Tableau CRM for the previous requirement and make use of the standard connector to transfer the data from Heroku to Tableau CRM. Let's add all of that to our landscape architecture, update our integration interfaces list, and move on to the next requirement, as follows.

Every day, the violation databases should be checked

We have three violation databases. We need to check each and execute a unified logic based on their data. Which tool can help us achieve this?

The option of developing an APEX batch job to do this overnight would put you in a very tricky situation during the Q&A. You will be cornered, and even if you managed to rectify the solution, you would likely still lose some points. This option is mainly proposing a suboptimal pattern that requires extensive custom development (always keep in mind the need for exception handling, logging, and retry mechanisms, and also keep in mind that you will be connecting to three different endpoints), ignoring the fact that you already have middleware capable of doing this job in a much better way in your landscape.

Such a mistake will show a lack of understanding of the value of middleware. This is not going to be a fun topic to be challenged on during your Q&A.

Use your middleware. You can schedule a MuleSoft batch job to run every night, retrieve records from the three databases, execute the desired filtering and lookup logic, and transfer the data to the ERP to generate a new invoice.

Remember to describe any new integration interfaces fully. Also, update your landscape diagram to reflect the latest changes.

I have split the business process diagram for this process into two diagrams as this will make them more readable in this book. Feel free to combine them. The car status update process diagram looks like the following:

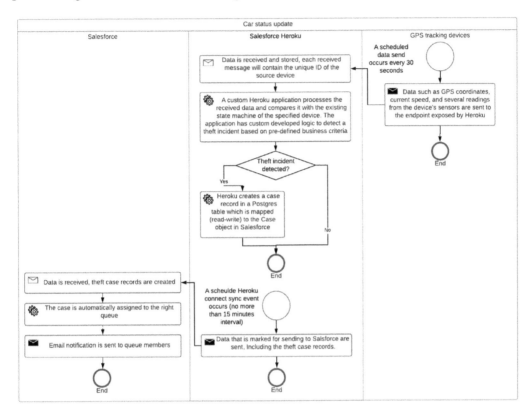

Figure 12.10 – Car status update business process diagram

The penalty settlement diagram looks like the following:

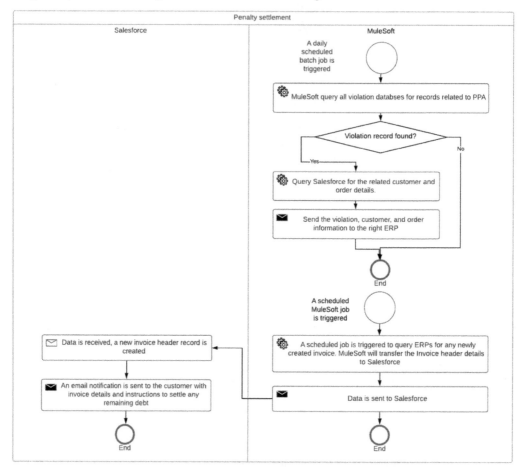

Figure 12.11 – Penalty settlement business process diagram

Remember that you can add more details to these diagrams if you wish. That is fine as long as you have enough time.

This concludes the fifth and last business process. Let's have a look at our diagrams after all these updates.

The landscape architecture diagram looks as follows:

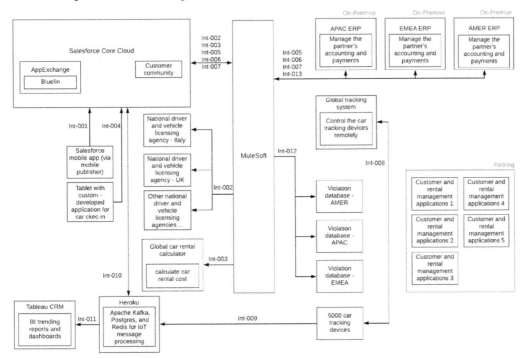

Figure 12.12 – Landscape architecture – third draft

The integration interfaces look as follows:

Interface Code	Source / Destination	Integration Layer	Integration Pattern	Description	Security	Authentication
Int-001	Salesforce mobile app (via mobile publisher) -> Salesforce	Data	Remote Call-In	Customer registration and interaction with all services available on the customer community. Data is retrieved using Salesforce REST API	HTTPS (one way SSL/TLS)	OpenID Connect user-agent flow
Int-002	Salesforce -> MuleSoft -> National driver and vehicle licensing agency of a given country	Business logic	Remote process invocation - request and reply - Blocking	Validate a customer's driving license. This interface is triggered in real time/blocking mode. The sales agent clicks on a button that starts the transaction, invoking a webservice exposed by MuleSoft. MuleSoft would then determine the right licensing agency to call, then call the right endpoint and return results back. The same process is triggered by the customer during self-registration.	HTTPS (two way SSL/TLS) between Salesforce and MuleSoft. HTTPS (one way SSL/TLS) Between MuleSoft and the licensing agency / Global car rental calculator	oAuth 2.0 web-server flow (then refresh token flow) with mutual authentication between Salesforce and MuleSoft. Simple authentication between MuleSoft and the national licensing agency / Global car rental calculator
Int-003	Salesforce -> MuleSoft -> Global car rental calculator			Calculate the rental price based on a set of parameters. The interface is invoked in blocking mode when searching and displaying the available cars.		
Int-004	Tablet app -> Salesforce	Data	Remote Call-In	Check in for car collection. The tablet accepts a text input (activation code) and invokes the Salesforce REST API to validate it. The tablet will also update the order status if the validation was successful	HTTPS (one way SSL/TLS)	OpenID Connect user-agent flow

Interface Code	Source / Destination	Integration Layer	Integration Pattern	Description	Security	Authentication
Int-005	Salesforce <-> MuleSoft <-> ERPs	Data	Batch Data Synchronization - Asynch	A scheduled MuleSoft batch job to sync customer details from Salesforce to ERP. This also includes several other lookup/master tables such as Product. The frequency of the scheduled job is assumed to be 15 minutes	HTTPS (two way SSL/TLS) between Salesforce and MuleSoft. HTTPS (one way SSL/TLS) Between MuleSoft and the ERPs	oAuth 2.0 web-server flow (then refresh token flow) with mutual authentication between Salesforce and MuleSoft. Simple authentication between MuleSoft and the ERPs
Int-006				A scheduled MuleSoft batch job to synch order, order items, and payments from Salesforce to ERP. The frequency of the scheduled job is assumed to be 15 minutes		
Int-007				A scheduled MuleSoft batch job to sync invoice headers from the ERPs to Salesforce. The frequency of the scheduled job is assumed to be 1 hour		
Int-008	Global tracking system -> Tracking devices	Business logic	Remote process invocation - request and reply - Blocking	Configure the tracking devices remotely	HTTPS (one way SSL/TLS)	oAuth 2.0 asset token flow
Int-009	Tracking devices -> Heroku	Data		Data such as the car's GPS coordinates and speed is sent from the tracking devices to Heroku.		
Int-010	Heroku <-> Salesforce	Data	Batch Data Synchronization - Asynch	Bi-directional data synch between Salesforce core cloud (force.com) and Heroku using Heroku connect. Assumed objects: Account and cases. This interface is used to transfer the theft incidents from Heroku to Salesforce	HTTPS (one way SSL/TLS)	oAuth 2.0 web-server flow
Int-011	Heroku -> Tableau CRM			Copy aggregated sensors' readings data from Heroku to Tableau CRM		

Interface Code	Source / Destination	Integration Layer	Integration Pattern	Description	Security	Authentication
Int-012	Violation databases -> MuleSoft -> ERPs	Data	Batch Data Synchro- nization - Asynch	A scheduled MuleSoft batch job to query the violation databases for any new data related to PPA then transfer that data to the ERPs to calculate new invoices. The frequency of the scheduled job is assumed to be 15 minutes	HTTPS (one way SSL/TLS)	Simple authentication between MuleSoft and ERPs and between MuleSoft and the violation databases
Int-013	Salesforce <-> MuleSoft <-> ERPs	Data	Batch Data Synchro- nization - Asynch	A scheduled MuleSoft batch job to sync the penalty invoice headers from the ERPs to Salesforce. The frequency of the scheduled job is assumed to be 1 hour	HTTPS (two way SSL/TLS) between Salesforce and MuleSoft. HTTPS (one way SSL/TLS) Between MuleSoft and the ERPs	oAuth 2.0 web-server flow (then refresh token flow) with mutual authentication between Salesforce and MuleSoft. Simple authentication between MuleSoft and the ERPs

Figure 12.13 – Integration interfaces – first draft

The data model diagram looks like this:

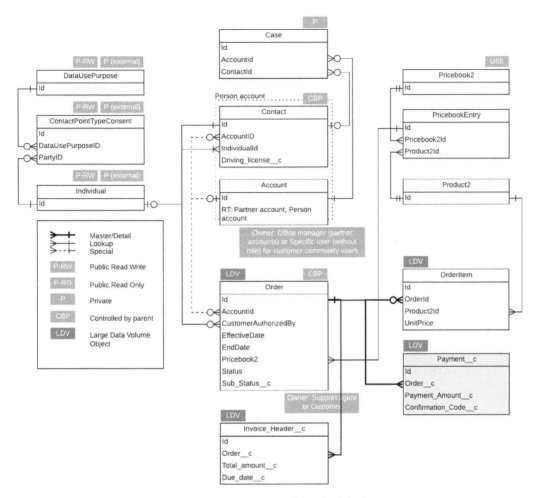

Figure 12.14 – Data model – third draft

We have now covered all the requirements related to the business processes. This section is usually the meatiest part of any scenario, so it should be no surprise that we needed an entire chapter of this book to cover it.

At this stage, we have solved nearly 60–70% of the scenario's requirements. This will be the base of our next chapter, where we will continue to solve the rest of PPA's requirements, then create our presentation pitch.

Summary

In this chapter, we were introduced to the first full mock scenario in this book. Full scenarios are naturally longer, more thorough, and contain many more challenges and requirements than the mini-scenarios. Yet we learned that the incremental solution methodology is the best way to avoid missing any requirements.

In this chapter, we tackled the first part of the scenario. The business processes are the heart and soul of any digital solution. It should be no surprise that creating a comprehensive solution starts with understanding each business process, dividing it into digestible chunks, then solving it as a whole.

We came across exciting use cases and design decisions, and we logically selected the right approach knowing that there are other alternatives. We prepared for some potential questions with ready answers, and we picked simple yet scalable architecture that would give us room to change if needed.

We created several business process diagrams that will help us a lot during the presentation by visualizing our solution.

In the next chapter, we will continue solving the scenario and then put together our presentation pitch. We covered a lot of ground in this chapter, but we still have plenty more to cover in the next.

13
Present and Defend – First Mock

In this chapter, we will continue creating an end-to-end solution for our first full mock scenario. We have covered most of the scenario already in *Chapter 12, Practice the Review Board – First Mock*, but we still have plenty of topics to cover. We will continue analyzing and solutioning each of the shared requirements and then practice creating some presentation pitches.

We will follow the same sequence that you will go through in the real exam. After the presentation, we will move on to Q&A and practice defending and changing our solution based on the judges' feedback.

After reading this chapter, you are advised to reread the scenario and try to solution it on your own.

In this chapter, we're going to cover the following main topics:

- Continuing to analyze requirements and creating an end-to-end solution
- Presenting and justifying your solution

By the end of this chapter, you will have completed your first mock scenario. You will be more familiar with the full mock scenarios' complexity and better prepared for the exam. You will also learn how to present your solution in the limited time given and justify it during the Q&A.

Continuing to analyze requirements and creating an end-to-end solution

We covered the business process requirements earlier. By the end of that, we had a very good understanding of the potential data model and landscape. We have already marked some objects as potential LDVs.

Next, we have a set of data migration requirements that we need to solve. Once we complete them, we will have an even better understanding of the potential data volumes. We can then create our LDV mitigation strategy.

Let's start with the data migration requirements first.

Analyzing the data migration requirements

This section's requirements might impact some of your diagrams, such as the landscape architecture diagram or the data model.

Some candidates prefer to create some diagrams to explain the data migration strategy. These are optional diagrams; therefore, we will not be creating them in this book. Feel free to use any additional diagrams if they help you organize your thoughts.

Let's now start with the first shared data migration requirement.

PPA would like to migrate the data from all its current customer and rental management applications to the new system

This is a very predictable requirement, especially considering that PPA already expressed their intention to retire all five legacy rental management applications. But keep in mind that these five applications might be based on different technology, using different database types, and belong to various generations. The next requirements contain more details.

PPA is aware that the current data contains many redundancies and duplicates and is looking for your guidance to deal with the situation

PPA has struggled with the quality of its data, especially redundancies. How can we help them to achieve the following?

- Dedupe their existing data

- Give a quality score to each record to help identify records of poor quality (such as fractured address details or a non-standard phone format)

- Prevent deduplicates from happening in the future

Salesforce native **duplicate rules** can help to prevent the creation of duplicate records. They have their limitations but are a decent tool for simple and moderate-complexity scenarios.

However, that doesn't answer the first two requirements. Deduplicating can get very complicated, especially in the absence of strong attributes (such as an email address or phone number in a specific format). Data such as addresses and names are considered weak because they can be provided in multiple formats. Moreover, names can be spelled in various ways and can contain non-Latin characters.

In such cases, you need a tool capable of executing fuzzy-logic matching rather than exact matching (Salesforce duplicate rules provide a limited level of that). You might also need to have weights given for each attribute to help with the merge logic.

Moreover, you need a tool capable of reparenting any related records to the merged customer record. In our case, this is very relevant to historical rental records. If multiple customer records are merged into one, you need all their related rental records to point out to the newly created golden record.

Calculating each record's quality might also require some complex logic as it involves comparing multiple records against pre-defined criteria and updating some records accordingly. The criteria could be as simple as a pre-defined phone format and as complex as an entire sub-process.

All these capabilities can be custom developed, assuming you have the time and budget, or simply purchased and configured. This would generally save a lot of money (considering the overall ROI calculation).

As a CTA, you are expected to come up with the most technically accurate solution. In this case, it makes no sense to delay the entire program for 9-18 months until the tool is custom developed and tested. It makes a lot of sense to propose a battle-tested MDM tool that can be configured to meet all these requirements.

You are expected to name the proposed product during the review board, just like what you would normally do in real life. So, let's suggest a tool such as **Informatica** (you don't necessarily need to specify the exact sub-product name as they change very often).

Update your landscape architecture diagram and your integration interfaces to indicate the new migration interface, then let's move on to the next requirement.

PPA has around 50 million rental records in each of its current rental management applications

Most of them are stored for historical purposes as PPA wants to keep rental records for at least 10 years. PPA would like to continue allowing its sales and support agents to access these records in the new system.

PPA has around *50 million x 5 = 250 million rental records* across its 5 legacy systems. Migrating all that data to Salesforce will definitely turn the *Order* object into an LDV. Not mentioning the *Order* Item object, which will at least contain an equal number of records.

It is fair to assume that most of these rental records are closed and are kept only to comply with PPA's policy. Therefore, we can migrate the active Order and Order Item objects to Salesforce while migrating any historical records to Heroku.

PPA would still like its sales and support agents to access the historical records. Yet, instead of copying them to Salesforce, we can simply retrieve them on the fly using **Salesforce Connect** and **external objects**.

We need to add the external objects to our data model. We also need to update the landscape architecture diagram and the integration interfaces list to indicate the new migration interface and the new integration interface between Heroku and Salesforce.

Update your diagrams. Your data model should look like this:

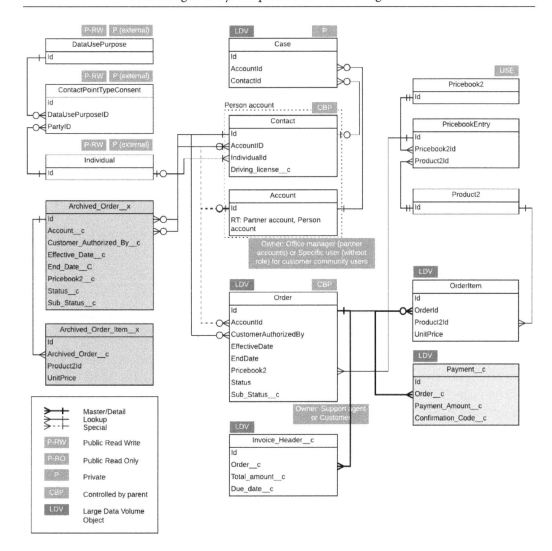

Figure 13.1 – Data model – third draft

This requirement didn't particularly request explaining your data migration strategy. But this is something you need to do nevertheless. You need to explain the following:

- How are you planning to get the data from their data sources?

- How would you eventually load them into Salesforce? What are the considerations that the client needs to be aware of and how can potential risks be mitigated? For example, who is going to own the newly migrated records? How can you ensure that all records have been migrated successfully? How can you ensure you don't violate any governor limits during the migration?

- What is the proposed migration plan?
- What is your migrated approach (big bang versus on-going accumulative approach)? And why?

We came across a similar challenge in *Chapter 7, Designing a Scalable Salesforce Data Architecture*. We need to formulate a comprehensive data migration pitch to include in our presentation that answers all of the preceding questions crisply and clearly. We will do that later on in this chapter.

But before that, we need to review our LDV mitigation strategy. We have penciled several objects as potential LDVs, but we still need to do the math to confirm it. Once we do, we need to craft a mitigation strategy. Let's tackle this challenge next.

Reviewing identified LDVs and developing a mitigation strategy

Have a look at the penciled LDVs in our data model (*Figure 13.1*), and let's validate whether they indeed qualify for that description.

We know that PPA has around 1 million registered users globally. And an average of 10 million car rentals every year. This means that the Order object will grow by 10 million records annually. The object qualifies to be considered an LDV. Moreover, the OrderItem object will have at least 10 million more records. Reasonably, it may contain even more, assuming that 50% of rentals would include an additional line item besides the car rental itself, such as an insurance add-on.

This means 15+ million new records every year. On top of that, the `Payment__c` object will contain at least one record per order. And `Invoice_Header__c` will also contain a minimum of one record per order (some rentals might get more than one invoice due to penalties or required car maintenance). We will also have at least one *Case* record created per rental (for the inspection feedback).

A large number of `Order`, `OrderItem`, `Case`, `Payment__c`, and `Invoice_Header__c` records could impact the speed of CRUD operations. They are all considered LDVs, and therefore we need a mitigation strategy.

Considering that the challenge we are dealing with is related to CRUD efficiency, a solution such as skinny tables won't add much value. Custom indexes would help with the read operations only. Divisions could help, but they would add unnecessary complexity. In comparison, the most suitable option here is to offload some of the non-essential data to off-platform storage.

Archiving data in that way ensures that these four objects remain as slim as possible. Your archiving strategy could include all closed Order and Case records.

You can archive your data to **Salesforce big objects**, external storage such as a data warehouse, or to a platform capable of handling a massive number of records such as **AWS** or **Heroku**. We already have Heroku in our landscape. The decision should be easy in this case. We can utilize Heroku Connect to transfer the data.

Update your landscape diagram and add another integration interface between Heroku and Salesforce. Your landscape architecture diagram should look like the following:

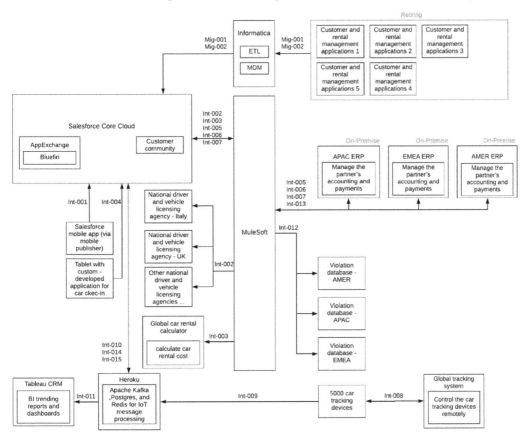

Figure 13.2 – Landscape architecture – fourth draft

Update your list of integration interfaces, and let's move on to the next set of requirements, which are related to accessibility and security.

Analyzing the accessibility and security requirements

The accessibility and security section requirements are usually the second most difficult to tackle after the business processes requirements. In contrast to the business process requirements, they don't tend to be lengthy, but rather more technically challenging.

You might need to adjust your data model, role hierarchy, and possibly your actors and licenses diagram. The good news is that there is a limited number of possible sharing functionalities available. You have a small pool of tools to choose from. However, you have to know each of these tools well in order to select the correct combination.

Let's start with the first shared requirement, which begins with the following.

Customer accounts should be visible to the office managers, sales, and service agents worldwide

You should take enough time thinking about such requirements. They could sound easy at first glance, but if you didn't thoroughly consider all possible challenges, you could easily find yourself stuck with a solution that violates the governor limits. Changing such solutions on the fly during the Q&A is challenging. Think about these requirements thoroughly to avoid that.

Considering that the requirement indicates that some records will be visible to some users but not others, the OWD of the `Account` object should be `Private`.

This will restrict access to accounts not owned by the user. We then need to figure out a mechanism to share all accounts with the mentioned user set (which is literally all internal users except technicians) while allowing the technicians to access customer accounts in their country only.

There are multiple ways to solve this. You need to select something easy to maintain, scalable, and that doesn't pose a threat to governor limits.

Based on the role hierarchy we developed in *Chapter 12*, *Practice the Review Board – First Mock*, we can come up with the following solution:

1. We can introduce two roles underneath the office manager, representing the sales reps and technicians working in that office.

2. Owner-based sharing rules rely on the account owner. Customer accounts might be owned by different users in different roles. Criteria-based sharing rules are more suitable for this requirement. We can configure a set of criteria-based sharing rules to share all accounts with sales agents that will automatically grant all users higher than them in the hierarchy role access to the customer accounts.

3. We can configure another set of criteria-based sharing rules to share the customer accounts with technicians from a particular country.

Sounds good? Not really.

We have a limited number of criteria-based sharing rules that can be defined for any object, a maximum of 50 per object. You can view the latest limitations at this link: `https://help.salesforce.com/articleView?id=security_about_ sharing_rules.htm`.

PPA operates across 10 countries only. However, we have multiple cities covered in each country and various offices in each city. The number of sharing rules required to share customer accounts with the sales agent role could easily go beyond 50.

You can do the math, but even if the number falls a bit short of 50, you are still creating a solution at the edge of the governor limit. This can't be considered a scalable solution.

However, you have another tool that you can utilize in addition to role hierarchy and sharing rules to solve this challenge. You can create a public group for all sales agents. This will be hard to maintain if you choose to add all the sales agent users to the group (imagine the efforts associated with adding/removing users upon joining or leaving the company). However, you can add roles instead.

By selecting and adding all the sales agent roles to the group and ensuring that the checkbox **Grant Access Using Hierarchies** for that group is checked, you'll have an easy to maintain, scalable solution. Now you need just one criteria-based sharing rule to share all customer account records with this public group. This will ensure all sales agents and anyone above them in the role hierarchy has access to these accounts.

We can follow a similar approach for technicians, except that we would need 10 different public groups, one per country, and 10 criteria-based sharing rules. This is not very scalable, but it is well below the governor's limit. You can also highlight that you might need to switch to APEX-based sharing if the company continues expanding to other countries.

Update your role hierarchy; it should now look like this:

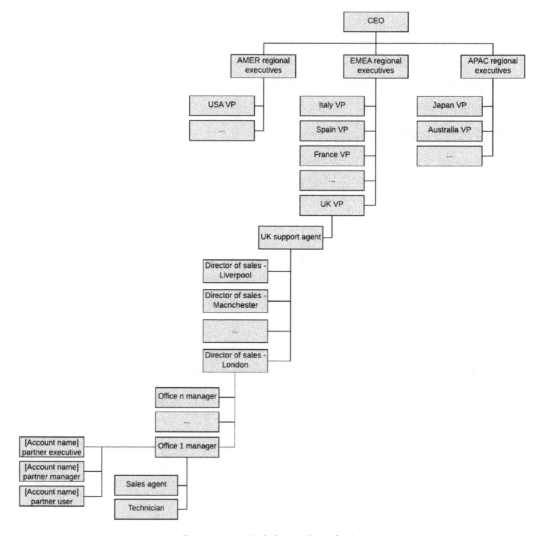

Figure 13.3 – Role hierarchy – final

Let's now move on to the next requirement.

Support incidents should be visible to support agents and their managers only

We can follow an approach similar to the one we used in the previous requirement. We can create a public group, ensure the **Grant Access Using Hierarchies** checkbox is checked, and add all support agent roles to the group. We will also need to set the case's OWD to **Private**, then create a criteria-based sharing rule to share **Case** records of a specific type with this public group.

This will grant access to the cases to the support agents and their managers and everyone on top of them in the role hierarchy. However, by looking at our diagram, we can see that there are only two roles on top of the country's VP role, which are the regional executives and the CEO. There is a requirement later on in this section that requests access to all regional data for regional executives. Therefore, there is no need to adjust the solution further.

If we had multiple other roles between the regional execs and the country's VP, we would likely need to disable the **Grant Access Using Hierarchies** checkbox and utilize a different public group for support agents and their managers.

Let's now move on to the next requirement.

Only office technicians can update the car status to indicate that it is out of service and requires repairs

We have utilized the `Product` object to model cars. In this case, we need to add a custom field to indicate the car status; we can call it `Car_status__c`. We can then set the **Field Level Security (FLS)** of that field to *read-only* for all profiles except the technicians, who will be granted this *edit* privilege.

This is an easy point to collect. However, none of our diagrams shows FLS settings. Therefore, you need to ensure you call the solution out during the presentation.

Update your data model diagram, and let's move on to the next requirement.

Office technicians should not be able to view the customer's driving license number

This is another requirement that can be solved using FLS. This time, we need to make the `Driving_license__c` field on the Contact completely inaccessible/invisible to users with the technician profile.

Let's move on to the next requirement.

Once a theft incident is detected, only the support agents trained for that type of incident, their managers, and regional executives can view the incident's details

We remember that we used the Case object to model the theft incident. How can we assign Cases to the right teams based on skills?

Salesforce **Omni-Channel** provides a **skills-based routing** capability. You can also define a specific queue for theft incidents then add all trained support agents to that queue. We can then use standard **Case Assignment Rules** to assign Cases of a particular type to this queue.

So which approach should you follow? Both would serve the purpose; however, you need to show that you know the most appropriate tool to use from your toolbox. As a simple rule of thumb, these two are different in the following way:

- **Queues** are suitable to represent a single skill. If you needed to represent multiple skills, you would need to define multiple **queues**. Users can be assigned to multiple **queues**, but the **case** would only be assigned to one of these **queues**.

- **Skills-based routing** would consider all skills required to fulfill a particular **case**. It then identifies the users who possess these skills and assigns the **case** to one of them.

The former approach is simpler to set up. Moreover, it is good enough to fulfill this requirement. Let's use **queue-based** assignment to solve this requirement. Users higher in the role hierarchy will get access to these records by default due to our role hierarchy's setup. Let's now move on to the next requirement.

The regional executive team should have access to all regional data, including the driver's behavior, such as harsh braking

The regional executive team will, by default, get access to all data in their region due to the proposed role hierarchy.

The driver's behavior data resides in Heroku and Tableau CRM. The regional executives would require the Tableau CRM license. We penciled that earlier, on our actors and licenses diagram. Now, we've confirmed it. Update your actors and licenses diagram, and let's move on to the next requirement.

Office managers should be able to see the details of the partner accounts in their own country only

Office managers own partner accounts. They can see the records they own regardless of the **OWD** settings. However, the requirement here indicates that they should be able to view all partner accounts in their country, even if a different office manager owns them.

We can utilize country-based public groups just like we did with other previous requirements and add all that country's office manager roles to it. The only difference here is that we can utilize owner-based sharing rules as the partner accounts will always be owned by an office manager.

This owner-based sharing rule will be simple. Share all account records owned by a member of this public group with all the group members. We will end up with 10 owner-based sharing rules, which is way below the governor limit.

Let's now move on to the next requirement.

Partners should be able to log in to Salesforce using Salesforce-managed credentials only

We can use a single community for customers and partners, but that is an unusual setup. They would very likely expect a completely different UI, services, and user experience.

We can propose a separate community for partners, which does not have an external authentication provider. This will ensure that partners will be able to log in to Salesforce using the Salesforce-managed credentials only. Requirement fulfilled.

Update your landscape architecture diagram to include a partner community, and let's move on to the next requirement.

Customers can self-register on the online portal and mobile application

We went through the entire customer registration business process in *Chapter 12, Practice the Review Board – First Mock*. To enable customer self-registration, you have to turn that setting on in the community setup.

Again, this is a straightforward point to collect. It could be easily missed as well, considering its simplicity. Let's move on to the next requirement.

Customers should also be able to log in to the online portal and the mobile application using their Facebook accounts

Customers and partners will have two separate communities. The customer community can be configured to have Facebook as an **authentication provider** (the exact name of Salesforce's functionality is **Auth. Provider**). You have to be clear in describing your social sign-on solution and mention the name of the functionality. You also need to explain how you can use the **registration handler** to manage user provisioning, updating, and linking with existing Salesforce users.

The registration handler is an APEX class that implements the `RegistrationHandler` interface. When the user is authenticated by the authentication provider (for example, Facebook), a data structure containing several values is passed back to Salesforce and received by the registration handler class associated with the authentication provider.

The class can then parse this payload and execute APEX logic to determine whether a new user needs to be provisioned or an existing user needs to be updated. The *email address* is a common attribute to uniquely identify the user (in this case, it is equal to a *federated identifier* for your community users). However, the scenario might ask to utilize a different attribute, such as the phone number. You should expect such requirements during the Q&A too.

This is why you need to practice creating a registration handler and try these scenarios out. The payload you receive from an authentication provider contains several standard attributes, but it can also include custom attributes. These attributes can be used to enrich the user definition in Salesforce. In some cases, one of these attributes could be the desired *federated identifier* for a given enterprise.

Needless to say, you should be prepared to draw the sequence diagram for this authentication flow. We explained the OAuth 2.0/OpenID connect web server flow earlier in *Chapter 4, Core Architectural Concepts – Identity and Access Management.*

Update your landscape diagram and your integration interfaces by adding a new SSO interface, then let's move on to the next requirement.

PPA employees who are logged into the corporate network should be able to automatically log in into Salesforce without the need to provide their credentials again

This requirement should point you directly to an authentication protocol we came across in *Chapter 4, Core Architectural Concepts – Identity and Access Management,* which is used over networks (such as a local enterprise network) to provide single sign-on capabilities. We are referring here to **Kerberos**.

Once a user logs into the corporate network (basically, this is what an employee would do first thing in the morning when they open their laptop/desktop and sign into the domain), the following simplified steps take place:

1. A ticket/token is issued by a **Key Distribution Center (KDC)** once the user logs into the domain from their laptop/desktop. This token is issued transparently without any user interaction and stored on the user's machine (in a specific cache).

2. This cached token is then used by the browser whenever there is a need to authenticate to any other system. You need to update some settings in the browser itself to enable this (such as **enabling Integrated Windows Authentication**). These configurations are not in the scope of this book.

3. To clarify what a **KDC** is, in a Windows-based network, the KDC is actually the **Domain Controller (DC)**.

Identity providers such as **Ping Identity** have *adapters* for Kerberos, which allows them to facilitate the request, recipient, and validation of a Kerberos token (the term ticket and token is used interchangeably in Kerberos). For example, **PingFederate IDP** (the name of the product from Ping Identity) operates in the following way:

1. When the client starts an SP-initiated SSO by clicking on a deep link (or bookmark) or starts an IDP-initiated SSO by clicking on a link from a specific page, an authentication request is sent to PingFederate.

2. Using the Kerberos adapter, PingFederate redirects the user back to the browser with the response `HTTP 401 Unauthorized`.

3. The browser (if configured correctly) will return the Kerberos token to Ping.

4. Once Ping receives the token, its domain is validated against the settings stored in Ping's adapter.

5. Upon successful validation, Ping extracts the **security identifiers (SIDs)**, domain, and username from the ticket, generates a SAML assertion, and then passes it to the SP.

6. The SP (Salesforce in this case) receives the assertion and authenticates the user based on it.

It's worth mentioning that Ping would be integrated with **LDAP**, which is the identity store for PPA as per the scenario. You could have used **ADFS** or **Salesforce Identity Connect** if PPA is using **Active Directory (AD)**. However, these products don't currently support LDAP.

The following sequence diagram (a modified version of the SAML SP-initiated flow we saw earlier, in *Chapter 4, Core Architectural Concepts – Identity and Access Management*) explains this flow. Please note that this diagram is simplified and doesn't describe in detail the way Kerberos works:

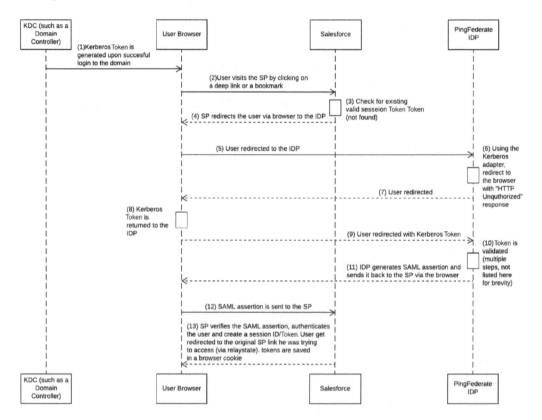

Figure 13.4 – SAML SP-initiated flow with Kerberos

Be prepared to draw and explain this sequence diagram, similar to any other authentication flow we covered in *Chapter 4, Core Architectural Concepts – Identity and Access Management*.

Update your landscape diagram and your integration interfaces by adding another SSO interface, then let's move on to the next requirement, which starts with the following.

PPA employees can log in to Salesforce from outside the corporate network using the LDAP credentials

The good news is that both these requested features are supported by tools such as Ping Identity. Ping has a feature called *adaptive authentication and authorization*, which delivers a set of functionalities, including reading the user's IP address to determine whether the user is inside or outside the corporate network and drive different behavior accordingly.

We can configure Ping to request a **Multi-Factor Authentication** (**MFA**) if the user is logging in from an IP outside the corporate network range. The following simple flowchart illustrates this logic:

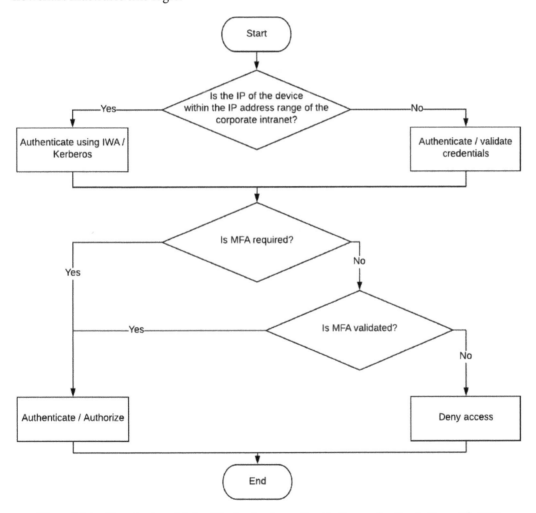

Figure 13.4 – Flowchart explaining Ping's adaptive authentication and authorization with MFA

We can use a mobile application such as **PingID** to receive and resolve the second-factor authentication (for example, a text message). Add the mobile application to your landscape. You don't need to add a new integration interface for it as it will communicate with PingFederate rather than with Salesforce.

This concludes the accessibility and security section requirements. Congratulations! You have nearly covered 85% of the scenario (complexity-wise). We still have a few more requirements to solve, but we have passed most of the tricky topics. Let's continue pushing forward. Our next target is reporting requirements.

Analyzing the reporting requirements

The reporting requirements could occasionally impact your data model, particularly when deciding to adopt a denormalized data model to reduce the number of generated records. Reporting could also drive the need for additional integration interfaces or raise the need for some specific licenses. Let's go through the requirements shared by PPA and solve them one at a time.

The regional executive team would like a report that shows relations between customers' driving behavior and particular times of the year across the past 10 years

This report needs to deal with a vast amount of data. The raw data for drivers' behavior is in Heroku. You can use a tool such as Tableau CRM to create the desired report. We already have it in our landscape architecture. The integration interface Int-011 can be used to transfer data from Heroku to Tableau CRM. We can then expose dashboards within the Salesforce core if needed.

Let's move on to the next requirement, which starts with the following.

The regional executive team would like a trending monthly report that shows the pickup and drop off locations of each rental

Reporting requirements that indicate a need for trending reports should point you towards one of these capabilities:

- **Reporting snapshots**: A functionality within the Salesforce core cloud enables users to report on historical data stored on the platform. Users can save standard report results into a custom object, then schedule a job to run the specific reports and populate the mapped fields on the custom object with data. Once that is done, the user can report on the custom object that contains the report results rather than on the original data.

- **Analytics / Business intelligence tools**: These tools are designed to work with enormous datasets. They provide more flexibility to drill into the details and analyze their patterns. Moreover, these tools are capable of dealing with data on and off the Salesforce platform.

Which one would you pick for this requirement?

If you picked reporting snapshots, then be prepared to adjust your solution if a judge decides to raise the challenge during Q&A and ask you to provide more capabilities to drill into the data or augment the data stored in Salesforce with data archived on Heroku.

A better, more scalable, and safer option would be to pick an analytics tool, such as Tableau CRM.

Again, we already have Tableau CRM in our landscape and a list of interfaces. We can confirm now that the regional executive team members will need the Tableau CRM license. Update your actors and license diagram, if you haven't done it already, then let's move on to the next requirement.

Customers should be able to view a full history of their rental bookings, including bookings from the past 3 years

The data required for this report exists mostly outside the platform. As a reminder, open orders will be in Salesforce while completed orders will be archived to Heroku.

Try not to complicate things for yourself and think of a custom solution that mixes data from both sources to display it in a single interface. Go with the simple, out-of-the-box functionalities.

You can simply display two different lists: one with open orders and another with completed orders. The first is retrieved directly from Salesforce, while the other is retrieved using **external objects** (**Salesforce Connect**). The integration interface Int-014 can be utilized for this.

One more thing to consider: so far, we were planning to use a principal user to authenticate to Heroku for the Int-014 interface. That means all data that the principal user can access will be returned, which is normally all data available.

In order to expose such an interface to end customers, you need to follow one of these two approaches:

- Switch the authentication policy to per-user. This will shift the responsibility of controlling who sees what to Heroku. Heroku must have a comprehensive module to determine the fields, objects, and records each user can see/retrieve from its database. The approach is achievable but would require custom development as Heroku doesn't come with an advanced sharing and visibility module similar to the one in Salesforce core.

- Develop a custom Lightning component on top of the external objects to filter the retrieved records using the current user's ID. This will ensure the user can only view the records that they are supposed to see. However, this a not a very secure approach as a bug in the Lightning component could reveal records that shouldn't be displayed.

- Moreover, considering that the security measures are applied by the UI layer rather than the data layer, there is a chance that an experienced hacker could find a way to get access to records that they are not allowed to.

You can propose the second option as long as you can communicate the associated risks and considerations. This is the approach we will use for this scenario. You will also need to explain why you preferred that over the first option (for example, to save the development efforts on Heroku).

Let's now move on to the next requirement.

Customers should also be able to view their full trip history for each completed rental

This is a challenge similar to the one in the previous requirement. This is good news because we can propose a similar solution.

The full trip history data is also stored on Heroku. We can assume that we will develop a Lightning component that is displayed when the user clicks on a **Display Trip** button next to a particular rental record. When the component is displayed, it retrieves the external objects' data, filters them by the user ID, and displays them on the UI.

Remember that you have to explain all of that during your presentation. It is not enough to simply say that you will develop a Lightning component that fulfills this requirement. You have to explain how it is going to be used and how it will operate. After all, this is what your client would expect from you in reality.

Let's now move on to the next and final reporting requirement.

Partners should be able to view a monthly report showing the repair jobs completed for PPA

This is an easy and straightforward requirement. The repair jobs are represented as Cases. The partner users can simply use standard reports and dashboards to display data in the Cases they have access to, which are the Cases assigned to one of their users.

That concludes the requirements of the reporting section. We are getting there now. The last part of the scenario normally lists requirements related to the governance and development lifecycle. Keep your foot on the gas pedal, and let's tackle the next set of requirements.

Analyzing the project development requirements

This part of the scenario would generally focus on the tools and techniques used to govern the development and release process in a Salesforce project. Previously, we created some nice artifacts, in *Chapter 10, Development Lifecycle and Deployment Planning*, such as *Figure 10.3 – Proposed CoE structure, Figure 10.4 – Proposed DA structure*, and *Figure 10.7 – Development lifecycle diagram – final*.

These artifacts will become very handy at this stage. Try to memorize them and become very familiar with drawing and explaining them. We will now go through the different requirements shared by PPA and see how we can put these artifacts into action to resolve some of the raised challenges. Let's start with the first requirement, which begins with the following.

PPA is planning to have three different service implementers (SIs), delivering different functionalities across parallel projects

The best mechanism to resolve such situations is by implementing source code-driven development using a multi-layered development environment. CI/CD would also reduce the chances of having conflicts by ensuring all developers are working on the latest possible code base (it might not be the very latest, but it is the closest possible).

In *Chapter 10, Development Lifecycle and Deployment Planning*, we discussed the rationale and benefits of this setup. Keep in mind that this is something you need to explain during your presentation. It is not enough to draw the diagram or throw buzzwords around without showing enough practical knowledge about them.

We also saw a sample development lifecycle diagram, *Figure 10.7 – Development lifecycle diagram – final*. This can be the base to use for scenarios such as this. We have three different SIs here, so it makes sense to have three different threads/teams in the diagram.

Your diagram could look like the following:

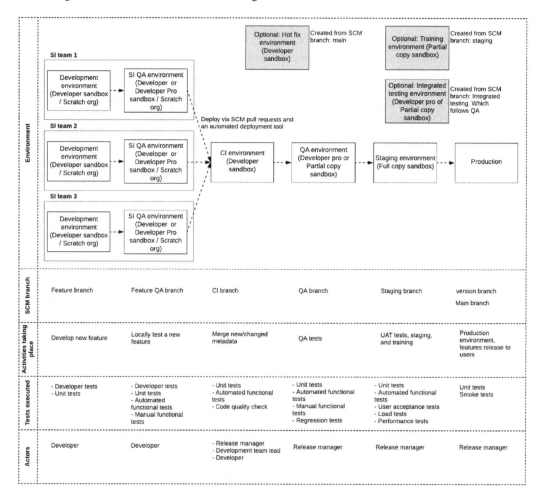

Figure 13.5 – Development lifecycle diagram – final

You would also need an automated build and deployment tool. There are open source solutions such as **Jenkins** and tools built specifically for Salesforce environments such as **Copado** and **AutoRABIT**. Select one and add it to your landscape. Also, remember to add an automated testing tool such as **Selenium** or **Provar**.

Let's now move on to the next requirement, which begins with the following.

Historically, SIs used to follow their own coding standards while dealing with other platforms

This is an interesting requirement. The challenge here is related to the lack of standardization and communication across the different SI teams.

Would CI/CD solve this? Not really. It can improve things a bit with automated code scanning and controlled merging, but to significantly improve standardization, communication, reuse, and the overall quality, you need to introduce a Salesforce COE.

Bringing together functional and technical resources, you can even introduce a design authority as another organizational structure to ensure every single requirement is discussed in detail, validated, and approved before starting any development efforts.

In *Chapter 10*, *Development Lifecycle and Deployment Planning*, we explained the value and structure of each of these. *Figure 10.3 – Proposed CoE structure* and *Figure 10.4 – Proposed DA structure* can also be handy to visualize the two structures.

You are unlikely to be asked to draw the CoE or the DA structures, but you are very likely to be asked about their value and the challenges they address. If you are already on a project that has both, that is excellent news. Otherwise, don't be shy to propose this to your stakeholders. This structure brings tangible benefits to the project and, at the same time, helps develop the skills of its members. It is a win-win for everyone.

Let's now move on to the next requirement

PPA has a new platform owner who joined from another company that also used Salesforce

Such a sad experience impacts many people's judgment on the platform's agility and ability to adopt modern release management concepts. Usually, it ends up being a bad adaptation of a sound concept. On other occasions, such as this one, apparently, it is due to a poor environment management strategy and release cycle.

When a bug is fixed in UAT, UAT's code base becomes unaligned with the code base in lower environments. The next time a feature is promoted from lower-level environments (such as development environments), it could easily overwrite the changes made previously in UAT. Eventually, when this is pushed to production, the once-fixed bugs are brought back to life.

You could have simply said that this symptom is happening because the client didn't use a proper CI/CD release management strategy and probably relied on mechanisms such as **change sets**. That is not a good enough answer, though. You are not expected to throw up buzzwords. You are expected to explain, educate, and justify in detail. This is what a CTA should do during the review and in real life.

This issue could be resolved in one of three ways:

- After fixing the UAT bug, every lower environment should refresh its code base to get this new change. This requires a high level of discipline and organization.

- Upon promoting the lower environment's code, avoid overwriting existing and conflicting features in UAT. Attempt to resolve that with the development team. This is not always easy and can become very difficult when dealing with point-and-click features such as Salesforce flows.

- Fix the bug on a hotfix branch and environment, merge the branch into UAT, then promote it to production. The hotfix branch is also used to refresh all lower-level environment branches. This option sounds very similar to the first, but the difference is that it is more trackable and easier to govern. You still need an adequate level of discipline and organization.

Release management tools such as **Copado** make this process easier than usual using **graphical user interface (GUI)** and point-and-click features rather than a pure **command-line interface (CLI)**.

You have to answer such requirements with enough details, but don't get carried away. Keep an eye on the timer and ensure you leave enough time to cover other topics, whether this is taking place during the presentation or Q&A.

Let's now move on to the final requirement in this section, which starts with the following.

PPA would like to release the solution in Italy first, then roll the same solution out in other countries based on a pre-agreed schedule

We have already explained the value of the COE structure in these situations. It is the best organizational structure to ensure everyone is involved, sharing their ideas and feedback, and aware of the planned features and roadmap. This is where conflicting business requirements are detected and resolved. The COE will aim to create a *unified process* across all countries.

However, in addition to that, you need the right delivery methodology to ensure the smooth rollout of the solution. The COE and DA will ensure that requirements are gathered, validated, and solutioned in the right way to guarantee high quality. Moreover, they will also ensure that the features are developed to accommodate the slight process variation between countries. A 100% unified global process is a hard target to aim for. Your solution should be designed to *accommodate* and *embrace* slight variations in a *scalable manner*.

Consider the following when choosing the right delivery methodology:

- A rigid **waterfall methodology** will ensure a clear scope with a detailed end-to-end solution. However, it will also drive a great distance between the development team and business, who would eventually use the solution. Moreover, it has a longer value realization curve.

- An **Agile methodology** ensures that the business is closer to the developed solution. This increases adoption and enables quick feedback. However, without a clear vision, this could easily create a solution that is a perfect fit for one country but unfit for others. This would be very difficult to maintain even in the short term.

- A **hybrid methodology** ensures you get the best of both worlds with minor compromises. You get a relatively clear scope during the blueprinting phase with an end-to-end solution covering 70%-80% of the scope. It is not as rigid and well-defined as you would get in a waterfall methodology, but it mitigates many risks from day one.

The solution gets further clarified during the sprints' refinement activities. With the DA structure in place, we ensure that every user story's solution is challenged and technically validated by the right people before we start delivering it.

Again, keep an eye while explaining such requirements. I coached many candidates who got carried away while explaining this part, mostly describing personal experiences. However, remember that you have a very limited time. Your primary target is to pass the review board.

I also noticed that other candidates ran out of steam at this stage of the presentation, which is totally understandable considering the mental and emotional efforts required to reach this far. However, you need to keep your composure. You are very close to becoming a CTA. Don't lose your grip on the steering wheel just yet.

That concludes the requirements of the project development section. The next section is usually limited and contains other general topics and challenges. Let's maintain our momentum and continue to the next set of requirements.

Analyzing the other requirements

The *other requirements* section in a full mock scenario could contain further requirements about anything else that has not yet been covered by the other sections. There are usually a limited number of requirements in this section.

Your experience and broad knowledge about the Salesforce platform and its ecosystem will play a vital role at this stage. Let's explore the shared requirement.

PPA wants to ensure that data in development environments is always anonymized

This is an essential requirement today, considering all the data privacy regulations. As a CTA, you should not only be ready to answer this question but even proactively raise it with your client.

Not all users would or should have access to production data. Even if some have access, it is likely restricted to a specific set of records. While developing new features or fixing bugs in the different development sandboxes, it is crucial to ensure that the data used by developers and testers is test data. Even when dealing with staging environments (where the data is supposed to be as close as possible to production), you still need to ensure that the data is **anonymized**, **pseudonymized**, or even deleted. Here is a brief description of these three:

- **Anonymization**: Works by changing and scrambling the contents of fields, so they become useless. For example, a contact with the name John Doe could become `hA73Hns#d$`. An email address such as `JohnD@gmail.com` could become an unreadable value such as `JA7ehK23`.

- **Pseudonymization**: Converts a field into readable values unrelated to the original value. For example, a contact with the name John Doe could become Mark Bates. An email address such as `JohnD@gmail.com` could become `MarkBates@SomeDomain.com`.

- **Deletion**: This is more obvious; this approach simply empties the target field.

Developer and Developer Pro sandboxes contain a copy of your production org's metadata, but not the data. However, partial copy sandboxes contain the metadata and a selected set of data that you define. Full copy sandboxes contain a copy of all your production data and metadata.

Your strategy here could be to do the following:

- Ensure that data used in the developer and developer pro sandboxes are always purposely created test data.

- Ensure that any data in partial or full copy sandboxes is anonymized or pseudonymized. You can achieve that using tools such as **Salesforce Data Mask** (which is a managed package), custom developed ETL jobs, custom-developed APEX code, or third-party tools such as **Odaseva** and **OQCT**.

You can find out more details about Salesforce Data Mask at the following link:
`https://www.salesforce.com/blog/data-mask-secure-sandbox/`.

Let's propose using that for PPA. Add Data Mask to your landscape architecture diagram. Your landscape architecture diagram should look like the following:

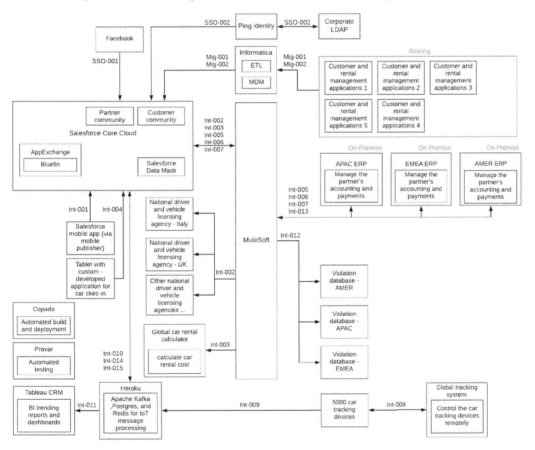

Figure 13.6 – Landscape architecture – final

Your list of integration interfaces should look like this:

Interface Code	Source / Destination	Integration Layer	Integration Pattern	Description	Security	Authentication
Int-001	Salesforce mobile app (via mobile publisher) -> Salesforce	Data	Remote Call-In	Customer registration and interaction with all services available on the customer community. Data is retrieved using Salesforce REST API	HTTPS (one way SSL/TLS)	OpenID Connect user-agent flow
Int-002	Salesforce -> MuleSoft -> National driver and vehicle licensing agency of a given country	Business logic	Remote process invocation - request and reply - Blocking	Validate a customer's driving license. This interface is triggered in real time/blocking mode. The sales agent clicks on a button that starts the transaction, invoking a webservice exposed by MuleSoft. MuleSoft would then determine the right licensing agency to call, then call the right endpoint and return results back. The same process is triggered by the customer during self-registration.	HTTPS (two way SSL/TLS) between Salesforce and MuleSoft. HTTPS (one way SSL/TLS) Between MuleSoft and the licensing agency / Global car rental calculator	oAuth 2.0 web-server flow (then refresh token flow) with mutual authentication between Salesforce and MuleSoft. Simple authentication between MuleSoft and the national licensing agency / Global car rental calculator
Int-003	Salesforce -> MuleSoft -> Global car rental calculator			Calculate the rental price based on a set of parameters. The interface is invoked in blocking mode when searching and displaying the available cars.		
Int-004	Tablet app -> Salesforce	Data	Remote Call-In	Check in for car collection. The tablet accepts a text input (activation code) and invokes the Salesforce REST API to validate it. The tablet will also update the order status if the validation was successful	HTTPS (one way SSL/TLS)	OpenID Connect user-agent flow

Interface Code	Source / Destination	Integration Layer	Integration Pattern	Description	Security	Authentication
Int-004	Tablet app -> Salesforce	Data	Remote Call-In	Check in for car collection. The tablet accepts a text input (activation code) and invokes the Salesforce REST API to validate it. The tablet will also update the order status if the validation was successful	HTTPS (one way SSL/TLS)	OpenID Connect user-agent flow
Int-005	Salesforce <-> MuleSoft <-> ERPs	Data	Batch Data Synchroniza tion - Asynch	A scheduled MuleSoft batch job to sync customer details from Salesforce to ERP. This also includes several other lookup/master tables such as Product. The frequency of the scheduled job is assumed to be 15 minutes	HTTPS (two way SSL/TLS) between Salesforce and MuleSoft. HTTPS (one way SSL/TLS) Between MuleSoft and the ERPs	oAuth 2.0 web-server flow (then refresh token flow) with mutual authentication between Salesforce and MuleSoft. Simple authentication between MuleSoft and the ERPs
Int-006				A scheduled MuleSoft batch job to synch order, order items, and payments from Salesforce to ERP. The frequency of the scheduled job is assumed to be 15 minutes		
Int-007				A scheduled MuleSoft batch job to sync invoice headers from the ERPs to Salesforce. The frequency of the scheduled job is assumed to be 1 hour		
Int-008	Global tracking system -> Tracking devices	Business logic	Remote process invocation - request and reply - Blocking	Configure the tracking devices remotely	HTTPS (one way SSL/TLS)	oAuth 2.0 asset token flow
Int-009	Tracking devices -> Heroku	Data		Data such as the car's GPS coordinates and speed is sent from the tracking devices to Heroku.		
Int-010	Heroku <-> Salesforce	Data	Batch Data Synchroniza tion - Asynch	Bi-directional data synch between Salesforce core cloud (force.com) and Heroku using Heroku connect. Assumed objects: Account and cases. This interface is used to transfer the theft incidents from Heroku to Salesforce	HTTPS (one way SSL/TLS)	oAuth 2.0 web-server flow (then refresh token flow)
Int-011	Heroku -> Tableau CRM			Copy aggregated sensors' readings data from Heroku to Tableau CRM		

Interface Code	Source / Destination	Integration Layer	Integration Pattern	Description	Security	Authentication
Int-012	Violation databases -> MuleSoft -> ERPs	Data	Batch Data Synchroniza tion - Asynch	A scheduled MuleSoft batch job to query the violation databases for any new data related to PPA then transfer that data to the ERPs to calculate new invoices. The frequency of the scheduled job is assumed to be 15 minutes	HTTPS (one way SSL/TLS)	Simple authentication between MuleSoft and ERPs and between MuleSoft and the violation databases
Int-013	Salesforce <-> MuleSoft <-> ERPs	Data	Batch Data Synchroniza tion - Asynch	A scheduled MuleSoft batch job to sync the penalty invoice headers from the ERPs to Salesforce. The frequency of the scheduled job is assumed to be 1 hour	HTTPS (two way SSL/TLS) between Salesforce and MuleSoft. HTTPS (one way SSL/TLS) Between MuleSoft and the ERPs	oAuth 2.0 web-server flow (then refresh token flow) with mutual authentication between Salesforce and MuleSoft. Simple authentication between MuleSoft and the ERPs
Int-014	Heroku -> Salesforce	UI	Data Virtualizatio n / Mashup / oData	Archived data is retrieved on-demand in Salesforce using Salesforce connect. Retrieved data is not stored in Salesforce	HTTPS (one way SSL/TLS)	oAuth 2.0 web-server flow (then refresh token flow)
Int-015	Salesforce -> Heroku	Data	Batch Data Synchroniza tion - Asynch	Single-directional data synch from Salesforce core cloud (force.com) and Heroku using Heroku connect. Assumed objects: Order, OrderItem, Payment_c, Invoice_Header_c, and Cases. This interface is used to archive closed orders and their related records (such as OrderItem) from Salesforce to Heroku then remove the record in Salesforce. This archiving process is to mitigate the impact of these LDVs in Salesforce	HTTPS (one way SSL/TLS)	oAuth 2.0 web-server flow (then refresh token flow)

Interface Code	Source / Destination	Integration Layer	Integration Pattern	Description	Security	Authentication
Mig-001	Legacy rental management apps -> Informatica -> Salesforce and Heroku	Data	Batch data synch - Asynch	Customer data will be migrated from the legacy rental management applications to Informatica MDM where they get deduplicated based on complex fuzzy logic. Once that is accomplished, deduplicated customer records will be migrated to Salesforce	HTTPS (one way SSL/TLS)	oAuth 2.0 web-server flow
Mig-002	Legacy rental management apps -> Informatica -> Salesforce	Data	Batch data synch - Asynch	Legacy rental data will be migrated from the legacy rental management applications to Salesforce and Heroku. Archived data to be migrated to Heroku while open rental orders will be migrated to Salesforce	HTTPS (one way SSL/TLS)	oAuth 2.0 web-server flow
SSO-001	SSO (social sign on) for Salesforce customer community using Facebook as IDP	SSO	SSO – OpenID Connect	SSO using OpenID Connect with Facebook as the authorization server and identity stores. Web-server flow	HTTPS (one way SSL/TLS)	OpenID Connect web-server flow
SSO-002	SSO for Salesforce using Ping Identity as IDP and LDAP as identity store	SSO	SSO – SAML 2.0	SSO using SAML 2.0 with Ping Identity as IDP and LDAP as identity store SP initiated flow	HTTPS (one way SSL/TLS)	SAML 2.0 SP initiated flow

Figure 13.7 – Integration interfaces – final

While your data model diagram should look like the following:

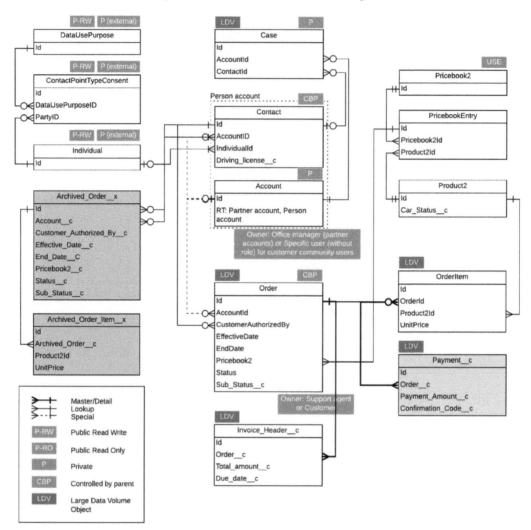

Figure 13.8 – Data model – final

Finally, your actors and licenses diagram should look like the following:

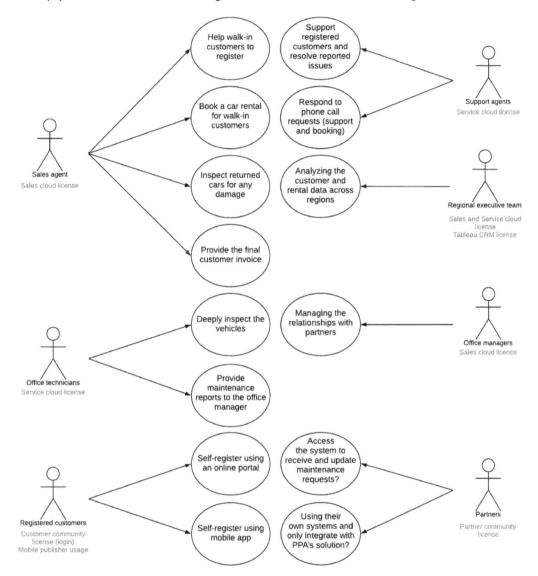

Figure 13.8 - Actors and licenses – final

Note that we have updated some of the penciled licenses for some actors, and we upgraded the technician license from the Salesforce Platform license to Salesforce Service Cloud to allow technicians to create and work with **Cases**.

Congratulations! You managed to complete the scenario and create a scalable and secure end-to-end solution. We need to pair that now with a strong, engaging, and attractive presentation to nail down as many marks as possible and leave the Q&A stage to close down a few gaps only.

Ready for the next stage? Let's do it.

Presenting and justifying your solution

It is now time to create your presentation. This is something you will have to do on the go during the review board as you will likely consume all 3 hours in creating the solution and supporting artifacts.

This is why you need to develop your presentation and time management skills to ensure you describe the solution with enough details in the given timeframe. We will discuss some time keeping techniques in *Appendix, Tips and Tricks, and the Way Forward.*

In the previous chapters, we saw several examples of presentation pitches that dived into the *right level* of detail. This time, we will focus on shaping an actual review board presentation. We will also create presentation pitches for the following topics: the overall solution and artifact introduction, one of the business processes, and the data migration and LDV mitigation strategy. We will pick the customer registration process as it is the most complex and lengthy.

We will then hold our ground and defend and justify our solution, knowing that we might need to adjust our solution based on newly introduced challenges.

Let's start by understanding the structure and strategy of our presentation.

Understanding the presentation structure

During the review board presentation, you need to engage and captivate your audience. In addition, you need to help them keep up with you.

You could create a fantastic pitch (using slides or other tools) that describes the solution end to end, mixing business processes with accessibility requirements and data migration, and present it in an engaging but not very organized way, firing out a solution whenever the related topic comes to your mind.

This will make it very challenging for the judges to keep up with you. You will play out a solution for a requirement on page 7, followed by a solution for a requirement on page 3, then two more from page 5. It is indeed the judge's responsibility to give you points for the solutions you provide, but I always tell my mentees to *help the judges* by being more organized. After all, the ability to walk an audience in an organized fashion is a real soft skill that you need in real life.

I recommend dividing your presentation into two main parts:

- **The structured part**: In this part, you describe specific pre-planned elements of your solution. You usually start by introducing the overall solution and the artifacts you created. Then you move on to describe the proposed solution for the business processes, followed by an explanation of your LDV mitigation and your data migration strategies. You can add more elements to this part as you see appropriate. You need to plan which elements and requirements you will be covering in this part before you start your presentation. This will help you budget time for it and ensure you have enough left for the next part.

- **The catch-all part**: This is where you go through the requirements one by one and call out those that you haven't covered in the first part. This will ensure you don't miss any points, particularly the easy ones.

In the following sections, we will be creating sample presentation pitches for the structured part. Let's start with an overall introduction of the solution and artifacts.

Introducing the overall solution and artifacts

Start by introducing yourself; this shouldn't be more than a single paragraph. It should be as simple as:

> *My name is [your name], and I am here today to present the proposed solution for [the company's name in the scenario].*

Then proceed with another short paragraph that briefly describes the company's business. This will help *you* to get into presentation mode and break the ice. You can simply utilize a shortened version of the first paragraph in the scenario, such as:

> *PPA is a global car rental company that provides services to end customers in AMER, EMEA, and APAC. PPA operates in 50 major cities across 10 different countries. There is an average of 5,000 cars available for rental through PPA offices. Each city has an average of 10 offices.*

You shouldn't use more than a minute to present yourself and set the scene. Now you can start explaining the key need of PPA using a short and brief paragraph. At this stage, you should be utilizing your landscape architecture diagram. Remember to *use your diagrams*. I can't stress the importance of that enough.

At this stage, you should be pointing out the relevant sections of your diagrams to help the judges visualize your solution. An image will speak a thousand words. Even if you are doing this using a PowerPoint presentation, use your mouse cursor and flip between the slides. Don't be under the impression that a professional presentation should go in one direction only. That does not apply to this kind of presentation. Your pitch could be as follows:

> *PPA is looking to modernize its CRM solution by utilizing a Salesforce-centric solution. They currently have regional ERPs in APAC, EMEA, and AMER [point them out on the diagram] hosted on-premises.*

> *PPA also has 5 different customer and rental management applications used across the. These applications will be replaced with the new Salesforce-centralized solution.*

> *The new solution will utilize Salesforce Sales and Service Cloud as a core system to handle customer registration and bookings. Two Salesforce communities will be part of the solution, a customer community and a partner community. Moreover, I will make use of an AppExchange product to handle online payments.*

> *The solution will also include Heroku as a platform to receive and handle the massive amount of data received from the tracking devices, and MuleSoft, which will be the middleware used to integrate Salesforce with the other external and internal applications.*

> *I have chosen MuleSoft because several requirements are shared that require a middleware capable of orchestrating a process, such as determining the target ERP system and invoking it accordingly. Also, the integration interfaces utilizing MuleSoft won't be transferring a massive amount of data. This is what pointed out to me the need for an ESB rather than an ETL. However, I am also proposing an ETL to handle the data migration.*

> *I am also proposing introducing an IDP capable of handling the SSO requirement shared by PPA and that works with LDAP [point at Ping Identity on the diagram]. It will also handle the provisioning and de-provisioning of the internal users and supports MFA requirements. I will explain these processes shortly.*

That should be enough as a high-level introduction to the solution. You have introduced the problem, the key elements of the solution, and given some teasers for what is coming.

Now you have the audience's attention. You are showing them that you are not here to *answer a question* but to give them a presentation on *the solution they will be investing in*. Remember, they are PPA's CXOs today.

Remember to call out your org-strategy (and the rationale behind it) during your presentation. You can then proceed by explaining the licenses they need to invest in. Switch to the actors and licenses diagram. If you are doing the presentation in person, move around, don't just stand in one place. You should radiate confidence. Moving around always does the trick. Your presentation could be as follows:

> *I have identified the following six actors. They will need different types of licenses based on their expected roles. For example, the office managers and sales agents [point at them on the diagram] will need a Sales Cloud license because they need to review bookings and inspect returned cars. They need to create cases, which, in my proposal, represent the inspection reports. They could utilize either the Sales or Service Cloud licenses, but I assumed the Sales Cloud license considering their role and the potential need to deal with leads.*

> *The office technicians will utilize a Service Cloud license as they need to work with the Case object during the inspection process. This is not supported by the Platform License. Support agents would also utilize the Service Cloud license as they need to work with different types of cases.*

> *Regional executives will need full Service Cloud and Sales Cloud licenses as they will need access to all the data in the org. They will also need a Tableau CRM license as they will use this tool for trending reports and some other advanced analytics.*

> *Finally, we have customers and partners. The former will be utilizing a Salesforce Customer Community Login license, while the latter will use a Salesforce Partner Community license. The Customer Community Login license will be a good fit for the 1 million PPA customers, considering that it is tailored for a vast number of users. Moreover, I am confident we can manage their accessibility requirements using functionalities such as sharing sets.*

> *While PPA partners will need a Partner Community license because they need to access PriceBooks, Products, Orders, Cases, and Reports. Moreover, we need sharing rules to control their record visibility. Furthermore, I assumed they will need access to leads, which is a typical requirement for partners.*

That concludes the overall high-level solution presentation. This part should take no more than 5 minutes to cover end to end.

Now let's move on to the most significant part of your presentation, where you will explain how your solution will solve the shared business processes.

Presenting the business processes' end-to-end solution

We are still in the *structured* part of your presentation. For each business process, you will use the relevant business process diagram we created. In addition, you will be using the landscape architecture diagram, the data model, and the list of interfaces to explain your solution's details. You can start this part with a short intro such as this:

> *PPA shared five business processes. I will go through each and explain how the solution fulfills it.*

We will create a sample presentation for the first business process.

Customer registration

We have already planned a solution for this process and created a business process diagram. Check *Figure 12.4 – Customer registration business process diagram*. You will use this diagram to *tell the story* and explain this process's end-to-end solution. Your pitch could be:

> *I will start with customer registration. This process can be triggered via two channels, either online or via the call center. Typically, PPA would be looking for a unified experience across channels.*
>
> *I propose using Salesforce communities to develop a customer portal. I will configure the customer community to allow users to self-register. When the customer attempts to access the community, they will be directed to a login page with a link at its bottom to register a new account. When that link is clicked, the user will be redirected to the registration page.*
>
> *The registration page will contain a Lightning component with input fields such as first name, last name, email, password, and driving license number. Moreover, the client will be shown a section to provide consent for the privacy policy. If all mandatory fields are populated, the user can submit the page.*

When the submit button is clicked, I will initiate a synchronous blocking web service call to a REST web service exposed by MuleSoft and pass the driving license number. MuleSoft will, in turn, call the right national driver and vehicle licensing agency and get back the result.

If the received result is positive, the Lightning component will create a Person Account and a Community User for the customer. The Person Account will be owned by a user outside the role hierarchy to avoid ownership skew. We can use a nightly batch job to assign this account to another user at a later stage.

The Lightning component will also create Individual and Contact Point Type Consent records to hold the captured consent. I am aware that we will need to use Future methods or Queueable APEX to avoid the mixed DML exception. Once the Community User is created, the customer will receive a notification email confirming the registration and can log in using the password set.

The same experience will also be provided to the call center's support agents. However, they will be using a different UI. The support agents will use the standard Salesforce UI to create the Person Account, Individual, and Contact Point Type Consent. Once all the data is in place, the agent will click on a button to validate the driving license. This button will invoke the exact same synchronous interface described earlier. Once the positive result is returned, the agent can proceed with creating the Community User.

The integration interface is described with all the details in my list of interfaces. It will follow the Remote process invocation – request and reply pattern. Authentication will be achieved using the OAuth 2.0 web server flow followed by the Refresh Token flow. The data will be protected in transit using two-way TLS between Salesforce and MuleSoft and one-way TLS between MuleSoft and the national agency systems.

Needless to say, you should be pointing at the right integration interface on your list, the objects in your data model, and the other different elements in your Landscape Architecture Diagram such as MuleSoft and the national driver and vehicle licensing agency systems.

You can be a bit creative with your presentation and bring forward a requirement from the accessibility and security requirement section. You could add the following:

> *Later on, there is a requirement to allow users to sign in using their Facebook credentials. To enable that, I will define a new authentication provider in Salesforce. I will set that to Facebook and define a registration handler class. I will need the registration handler to determine whether the user already exists or there is a need to provision it. Once I finish setting up the authentication provider, I will configure my community to use it on its login page.*

> *Once that is done, a new button will show on the community's login page with the title Login with Facebook. When the user clicks the button, an OpenID connect web server authentication flow will be initiated. The user will be redirected to Facebook to authenticate. Once that is done, a screen will display a message to the user asking for permission to access personal data. The page will have approve and reject buttons. Once the user clicks on the approve button, the user will be redirected back to the Salesforce community.*

> *The registration handler will receive a payload containing data such as first name, last name, and email address. It will use that to determine whether the user already exists or needs to be created. If the user already exists, the user will be automatically logged into the community. Otherwise, the registration handler will create the user.*

> *However, before the user can proceed further, we need to capture the driving license. This is not a value that we will receive from Facebook. Therefore, we need to use a Custom Login Flow to prevent community users with no value in their driving license field from logging into the community, and instead display a custom VisualForce page that captures the driving license.*

> *The page will have a button. Once the button is clicked, it will invoke the validation web service explained earlier to validate the driving license and return the result. If the result is positive, the user will be allowed into the community.*

You have seeded some questions, such as the full description of the OAuth 2.0 web server flow. If the judges feel a need to get more details, they will come back to this point during the Q&A.

This is a lengthy business process, but presenting its solution should not take more than 5 minutes. The other business processes should take less time. Practice the presentation using your own words and keep practicing until you are comfortable with delivering a similar pitch in no more than 5 minutes. Time management is crucial for this exam.

Let's now move on to the next element of our structured presentation.

Presenting the LDV mitigation strategy

After presenting the business processes, the next set of requirements in the scenario are related to data migration. Before proceeding with that, let's prepare our pitch for the LDV objects mitigation strategy:

> *We are aware that PPA has an average of 10 million car rentals every year. That means the Order object will grow by 10 million records every year. The OrderItem, Payment__c, Case, and Invoice_Header__c objects will also grow, at least, at a similar rate. This means that they are all considered LDVs.*

> *LDVs impact the performance of many functionalities in the system. The most concerning impact, in this case, is the CRUD efficiency. I thought of using divisions, but I believe that archiving data to Heroku is simpler and easier to implement. Also, this approach won't impact any of the existing functionalities.*

> *Closed orders will be synchronized to Heroku and removed from Salesforce, all alone with their related OrderItem, Payment__c, Case, and Invoice_Header__c records.*

> *I will then utilize Salesforce Connect to expose these records back to Salesforce via external objects. This means that historical rental records will be available for internal and community users. I will ensure that the data is visible to the Community Users via a Lightning component only, which will filter the received results based on the current user ID. This will ensure that the user can see only what they are allowed to see. I thought of using a per-user authentication policy but preferred this approach as it is easier and quicker to implement.*

> *I don't think that skinny tables would help with this requirement as the main challenge is with CRUD operations rather than reporting. Also, with this archival strategy, we will ensure that these five objects contain as few records as possible. I don't think we need to introduce any custom indexes.*

That explains your LDV mitigation strategy and rationale. Let's now proceed with explaining the data migration strategy.

Presenting the data migration strategy

Let's stick with the four points listed earlier to explain our data migration strategy. We need to explain how we will get the migration data, how to load it into Salesforce, what our plan looks like, and our migration approach. Let's start to put that together for our scenario:

PPA has around 50 million rental records in each of its retiring 5 rental management systems. That is a total of approximately 250 million records. Many of them are historical records that should ideally be migrated to Heroku rather than Salesforce.

I propose using a staggering big bang approach. We will migrate each retiring rental management system's records using a big bang approach then proceed to the next retiring system. The migration activities will occur during weekends, when the entire system will be shut down to all users except those performing the migration.

We will execute a migration dry-run on the full copy Sandbox 3 days before the migration to production to spot potential issues. Before migrating the data, we will disable all workflows, flows, and other automation.

We will use Informatica to do the data migration. It is optimized to use the Bulk API, which should speed up the migration process. We can connect Informatica directly with the source systems to retrieve data from the source database. But the type of databases is unclear. Therefore, I am assuming that PPA would extract the data as CSV files based on a template shared with them.

All newly migrated records will be owned by a user who doesn't have a role. This will mitigate the ownership skew. Later on, we will assign the migrated records to their rightful owners based on a planned schedule. This process will take place gradually every night to avoid impacting the platform performance by calculating a huge number of sharing records.

After completing the migration for each region, we will run some tests to ensure that we have all migrated records in the target systems. Again, the migration will be done using Informatica to both Salesforce and Heroku, where open rental records will be migrated to Salesforce and closed ones will be migrated to Heroku.

That covers our data migration strategy and plan. You have to mention these details to collect this domain's points. Again, remember to keep an eye on the timing. You should not consume more than 30-35 minutes of your valuable 45 minutes to cover the *structured* part of your presentation. This will leave you with 10-15 minutes for the *catch-all* part, which is very important to avoid losing any easy points. Let's now proceed to that part and see how it works.

Going through the scenario and catching all remaining requirements

At this part of the presentation, we will go through the requirements one by one and ensure we covered each one.

If you are doing an in-person review board, you will receive a printed version of the scenario. You will also have access to a set of pens and markers. When you read and solution the scenario, highlight or underline the requirements. If you have a solution in mind, write it next to it. This will help you during the *catch-all* part of the scenario.

If you are doing a virtual review board, you will get access to a digital version of the scenario. You'll have access to MS PowerPoint and Excel, and you'll be able to copy requirements to your slides/sheets then use that during the presentation. The *catch-all* part of the presentation is not attractive, as it feels like you are going through questions and answering them. But it is a pragmatic and effective way to ensure you never miss a point.

Also, remember to help the judges keep up with you. Let's take two examples from the accessibility and security requirements section.

Support incidents should be visible to support agents and their managers only

We have already created a solution for this requirement. Let's see how we can present it. First, we need to help the judges keep up with us by calling out the location of the requirement:

> *On page [mention the page number], and underneath the accessibility and security requirements section, the second bullet point explains a visibility requirement for support incidents.*

You don't need to do that for every requirement. Just do it whenever you feel the need or when you move to a new set of requirements.

Let's proceed with the presentation as usual:

> *I propose using the Case object to model support incidents. The Case object's OWD will be private to allow controlling the records' visibility.*
>
> *I will create a public group for support agents and ensure the Grant Access Using Hierarchies checkbox is checked. Then I will add all support agent roles to this group. I will then create a criteria-based sharing rule to share case records of the specific type with this public group.*
>
> *I am aware that a limited number of criteria-based sharing rules can be created for any object. I have chosen this approach to ensure I stay within the limits and leave some room for future flexibility.*
>
> *The cases will also be visible to the support agents' managers and anyone above them in the role hierarchy. However, according to the proposed role hierarchy, we can see that the only two roles above are the regional executives and the CEO, who should have access to all of the data org anyway.*

We can create a public group, ensure the checkbox is checked, and add all support agent roles to the group. We will also need to set the Case's OWD to Private, then create a criteria-based sharing rule to share Case records of a specific type with this public group.

Remember that you still need to explain the solution end to end, with enough details, and using your diagrams. Being in the *catch-all* part doesn't mean you skip that. Let's take another example.

Only office technicians can update a car's status to indicate that it is out of service and requires repairs

You should explain the solution for such requirements in less than 15-20 seconds. It can be as simple as this:

> *I have used the Product object to model cars. I will add a custom field to capture the car status and use FLS to ensure that this field is read-only for all profiles except the technicians, who will be granted the edit privilege.*

Use your own words, but keep it short and crisp.

The *catch-all* part will ensure you never miss a requirement. For example, I have intentionally left one requirement without a solution. Have you spotted it?

It was mentioned at the beginning of the scenario – easy to miss. But this approach will ensure we don't even miss those. Let's create a solution for it now.

Some partners are open to utilizing PPA's solution, while others expressed their interest in using their own systems and only integrating with PPA's solution

The solution can be straightforward:

> *Partners will be accessing the new solution via the partner community. Partners who prefer using their own systems and integrating with Salesforce can utilize Salesforce APIs such as the REST API to communicate directly with Salesforce. They will still be authenticated using their partner community users, which means data accessibility, sharing, and visibility will still be enforced by Salesforce.*
>
> *I am assuming that the standard REST API will be enough to fulfill all their requirements. Alternatively, we can expose a set of new APIs via MuleSoft.*

That concludes our presentation. The next part is the Q&A – the stage where the judges will ask questions to fill in any gaps that you have missed or not clearly explained during the presentation.

Justifying and defending your solution

We'll now move on to the Q&A – the stage that should be your friend. Relax and be proud of what you have achieved so far. You are very close to achieving your dream.

During the Q&A, you should also expect the judges to change some requirements to test your ability to solution *on the fly*. This is all part of the exam. Let's see some example questions and answers.

The judges might decide to probe for more details on one topic, such as the proposed solution for IoT. The question could be as follows:

> *In your proposal, the tracking devices would send their data to Heroku. You also proposed developing a custom solution on top of Heroku to handle the theft incident. Can you further explain the rationale behind this, and will your solution change if you know that PPA has a plan to introduce logic for several other incident types, such as geofencing or reaching a particular mileage limit.*

Don't lose your composure and assume the worst straight away. The judge could have simply missed parts of your presentation and wanted to make sure you understand the platform limitations. Or, they could be simply trying to put you under pressure and see how you respond.

Ensure that you fully understand the question. If you don't, ask them to repeat the question. Take a few seconds to organize your thoughts if needed. Your answer could be as follows:

> *PPA has 5,000 cars, each with an always-on tracking device. The device sends a message every 30 seconds. That is around 14 million messages per day. Salesforce has governor limits for both the number of concurrent calls (although that is mainly for calls with a duration of 20 seconds or more) and the number of API calls per day.*

> *In addition, considering that Salesforce is a shared tenancy SaaS platform, an excessive number of* **DML (Data Manipulation Language)** *operations could result in degradation in the overall org-wide processing performance.*

> *I thought of extending the existing PPA global tracking system, but it was reported to be very difficult and expensive to change. Therefore, I thought of using a PaaS platform that can scale to that huge API demand. I preferred to use Heroku over AWS because I wanted to use Heroku Connect, which doesn't consume Salesforce's API limits.*

> *I understand your concerns regarding developing a custom solution on Heroku. If I had enough time, I would have searched for an existing application with the desired capabilities that can be hosted on Heroku. But I am confident that custom developed solutions can be created with enough flexibility to accommodate future use cases.*

Assuming that the audience *knows the limitations* (because they are all CTAs), and therefore you don't need to bring that up, is a common *killing mistake*. We've repeated many times that *you should consider yourself presenting to the client's CXOs*, not to CTA judges from Salesforce.

You don't want to bother the CXOs with the exact number of allowed APIs per day. But you should clearly communicate the limits a solution could potentially violate and explain how your solution will honor those limits.

Let's explore another question raised by the judges:

> *You mentioned that Ping Identity would allow SSO for users logging in from within PPA's intranet or from outside. How will Ping communicate with LDAP knowing that the LDAP user store is hosted on-premise?*

On some occasions, you might lack the knowledge on how to set up a particular third-party product. But you still have your broad general architectural knowledge, and you will be able to rationally think of a valid answer.

In *Chapter 3, Core Architectural Concepts – Integration and Cryptography*, we discussed a similar challenge with ETL tools, while in *Chapter 11, Communicating and Socializing Your Solution*, we came across that challenge again for MuleSoft.

The same principle can be extended to IDPs such as **Ping** or **Okta**. Connecting them via a VPN or an agent application are valid options (depending on each product's finer details). Also, some of these tools offer a **password sync agent** that can synchronize password changes from LDAP (or AD) to the tool's own database (remember, passwords are always hashed). Your answer could be:

This needs to be further validated with the vendor. In general, similar tools can be connected to an on-premise LDAP using specific agent applications provided by the vendor or via a VPN. In some cases, the vendor could also offer a password sync agent application that can replicate the password from LDAP or AD to the IDP.

You don't need to worry that you don't know how to configure Ping or the firewall. You are not expected to know how to configure all the tools under the sun. But you are expected to know that a cloud application can't communicate directly with an application hosted behind a firewall without specific arrangements and tools. We covered that in detail in *Chapter 3, Core Architectural Concepts – Integration and Cryptography*.

Let's explore another question raised by the judges:

You mentioned that MuleSoft would be using the OAuth 2.0 web server flow followed by the Refresh Token flow to authenticate to Salesforce. Can you walk us through that process?

This is an expected question. How are you planning to handle it? If you want to ensure that you collect all points, you have to draw the sequence diagram and explain it. We explained these two flows in detail in *Chapter 4, Core Architectural Concepts –Identity and Access Management*. We are not going to repeat the diagram here. You are expected to know all the authentication flows we covered in this book by heart.

Let's explore one last question raised by the judges:

PPA wants to change the registration process a bit. They want to include a copy of the driving license with the online registration request. The request should be assigned to one of the support agents to validate the driving license's image. The customer can access the community after the support agent approves the registration request. How would you adjust your solution to meet this requirement?

This is one of the requirements that tests your ability to *solution on the fly*. And at the same time, tests your platform knowledge. Your answer could be as follows:

> *I will introduce an additional mandatory step during the customer registration process to request uploading the driving license image. I will also change the code of the registration's Lightning component so that it creates a case of a specific type in addition to the community user and person account. The code will also associate the case with the newly created Person Account.*
>
> *I am aware that I need to use a Future or a Queueable class to avoid the mixed DML exception while creating the Case record. The case will be automatically assigned to the right queue based on the configured Case Assignment Rules.*
>
> *Once the case is resolved/approved, I will update a flag on the community user's record to indicate that it has been validated. I will utilize a Custom Login Flow to prevent the newly created community users from logging in until they get that flag set to true.*

That concludes the Q&A stage. You experienced different types of questions that could be raised and confidently defended your solution or adjusted it if needed. Try to keep your answers short, crisp, and to the point. This will give more time for the judges to cover topics that you might have missed.

Summary

In this chapter, we continued developing the solution for our first full mock scenario. We explored more challenging accessibility and security requirements. And we created comprehensive LDV mitigation and data migration strategies. We tackled challenges with reporting and had a good look at the release management process and its supporting governance model.

We then picked up specific topics and created an engagement presentation pitch that describes the proposed solution end to end. We used our diagrams to help us explain the architecture more thoroughly, and practiced the Q&A stage using various potential questions.

In the next chapter, we will get to know our second full mock scenario. You will get the chance to practice solving another challenging set of requirements, and you will get even more familiar with the structure of full scenarios.

In the next chapter, we will tackle our second full mock scenario. It is as challenging as the first, but it has a slightly more tricky data model. We will experience a new set of challenges and learn how to overcome them. Nothing prepares you better than a good exercise, and we will have plenty up next.

14
Practice the Review Board – Second Mock

In this chapter, we will put all the knowledge we have accumulated in the previous chapters into action. We will be introduced to our second full mock scenario, which is very much like a real scenario you may encounter in the review board.

After reading this chapter and the next ones, you are advised to reread the scenario and try to solution it on your own.

You can do that as many times as needed until you feel comfortable enough. Try to stick to the *three-hour solutioning window*. We will learn some handy time management techniques in *Appendix, Tips and Tricks, and the Way Forward*.

In this chapter, we're going to cover the following main topics:

- Introducing the full mock scenario – Packt Lightning Utilities
- Analyzing the requirements and creating a draft end-to-end solution

By the end of this chapter, you will be even more familiar with the shape, size, and complexity of a full mock scenario. You will also have learned how to create an end-to-end solution for complex business processes. Without further ado, let's have a look at our second full mock scenario.

Introducing the full mock scenario – Packt Lightning Utilities

Packt Lightning Utilities (**PLU**) is a European utility company that serves cities across Germany, Italy, France, Portugal, Belgium, and the UK. PLU operates in 40 cities. PLU offers services to both B2C customers (residential) and small and medium B2B customers. They offer a wide range of services related to electricity and natural gas distribution. They currently serve more than 6 million households and over 700,000 small business accounts.

PLU has been struggling with its existing CRM solutions for many years, and as a new strategic movement, has decided to switch to Salesforce. PLU is looking to use its new CRM to launch a new set of unified global sales and service processes. This is part of a bigger digital transformation that PLU is undertaking to become a more customer-centric organization.

The new services should offer the most modern customer experience and maintain an overall low-cost-to-serve operating model. They also plan to use the new CRM to manage a close and special relationship with their most valued B2B customers and as a way to boost the performance of their field sales and field service teams.

PLU has a centralized service support center that offers multilingual support for all countries covered. However, the cost to serve has historically been too high in the last 3 years and PLU would like to explore the possibility of introducing additional modern service channels.

Project overview

There are multiple types of employees who require access to the system:

* **Key customer managers**: They manage the relationship with the key B2B customers and are organized by region. Each country contains multiple regions. The key customer managers report to the country's VP of key customers, who, in turn, reports to the global **Senior Vice President** (**SVP**) of key customers.

- **Support agents**: They operate from a central call center. They serve both residential and business customers. Agents are organized into teams depending on the languages they support. Some agents are multilingual. They all report to the global SVP of service.

- **Field sales**: They operate in specific regions in each country and are mainly responsible for developing the B2B business. They regularly visit existing and potential customer sites and try to generate new and renewal deals for PLU. They report to the region's director of sales, who, in turn, reports to the country's VP of sales.

- **Field service**: They operate in specific regions in each country and are responsible for collecting meter readings and fixing reported minor issues with residential and business customers. They report to the country's VP of service, who, in turn, reports to the global SVP of service.

- **Marketing team**: They are responsible for generating more leads by executing marketing campaigns to attract and retain B2C and B2B customers. They segment customers and send mass marketing emails. There is a marketing team in each of the countries covered that reports to its VP of marketing. Marketing and sales VPs report to the global SVP of sales and marketing.

- **Maintenance partners**: PLU works with a network of over 500 maintenance partners across Europe. They handle fixing incidents related to energy supply. Each partner is associated with one or more regions within a country.

Residential customers can have up to *two contacts per property* and be related to more than one property. On average, residential customers are subscribed to 1.5 different services per account/property. Business customers can have up to *five contacts per account* and typically have several related properties. More than 80% of business customers are subscribed to both electricity and gas.

PLU has historically received an average of three service requests per customer annually. Legally, they should keep 2 years' worth of data such as meter readings and service requests.

PLU is expecting its future system to support the local language of operating countries. PLU has the following landscape.

Current landscape

PLU is currently using the following systems:

- **Country ERP**: PLU uses a different ERP system for each country. All these systems except Belgium's ERP have SOAP-based APIs. Belgium's ERP is very old and is based on a flat-file database. It doesn't offer any APIs and doesn't support any database adapters. However, it can connect to SMTP servers. PLU would like to retain all ERPs and integrate the new CRM with them.

- **Power Sales**: This is a heavily customized third-party solution. It is currently used to calculate the tariffs, discounts, and bundles for electricity and gas offers. This system offers a poor API, which is difficult to modify. However, PLU still plans to use it for the coming 5 years. It has recently signed a maintenance contract with the vendor.

- **Radar reader**: This is a device that is used to read older-generation meters remotely. It operates within a range of 20 meters and sends a wake-up radio signal to the meter to instruct it to power up and transmit its data. This device supports corded and Bluetooth communications. PLU would like to continue using these devices to read older-generation meters.

- **Smart meters**: These are the new version of meters. They can transmit their readings directly to a centralized server. In addition, they can also receive data and signals from the server. PLU deals with four different smart meter vendors; each provides its own SaaS cloud-based solution to manage smart meters remotely. All smart meter platforms have REST APIs.

- **Legacy CRM**: PLU has a different CRM per country. One of them is based on a legacy XML file storage system with very poor data quality. The others are all based on MS SQL Server. However, they have different data models and are developed by different vendors. PLU is looking to retire all of these systems and replace them with a unified Salesforce-based solution.

- **PDF Generator**: This is a third-party application that is used to generate PDF versions of invoices. It has bespoke PDF-generating capabilities and offers a rich API. Generated PDFs will be stored temporarily at a related **SSH File Transfer Protocol (SFTP)**. The application automatically deletes files that have been stored on the SFTP for more than 24 hours.

PLU shared the following business process requirements.

Business process requirements

The following sections explain the business processes that PLU expects to have in its new system.

Key customer management

PLU needs to maintain a special relationship with its key business customers. The new system must meet the following requirements:

- Key customers are small or medium businesses that consume more than 50,000 kWh of electricity annually at one of their sites. Key business customers usually have between 5 and 15 sites/properties across the country.

- PLU would like the system to regularly identify new key customers and enroll them automatically into a special nurturing program. If any site is consuming more than 5,000 kWh for 3 months in a year, the enrollment team should be notified. The enrollment team consists of the country's VP of key customers and the relevant regions' key customer managers.

- The enrollment team should start the enrollment process. The first stage is to define a leading key customer manager to start the negotiations with the customer. Multiple tailored tariffs and offers could be shared with the customer. These offers should be generated by Power Sales. PLU would like to get a recommendation for the best way to facilitate this without impacting its employees' efficiency.

- By the end of this process, the customer could be switched to a different, more business-oriented tariff, and a new contract should be signed.

- PLU would like to streamline the process by introducing a digital signature. Once the document is signed, the contract is updated, and the process of switching the customer to the new tariff should start.

- The new contract details are sent to the country's ERP, which facilitates the switching process. This can take up to 48 hours. Once the process is done, the customer and key account managers of the relevant regions should be notified.

PLU shared the following requirements for the customer service process.

Customer service

PLU is looking to expand the number of support channels. Furthermore, they are looking to introduce a more governed and standardized way of handling their customers. The new system must meet the following requirements:

- All customers should be able to create inquiries or complaints using a self-serve customer portal or by calling the call center. These requests should be assigned to the right agent based on multiple factors, including language, incident type, and customer type.

- If a complaint is not resolved within 7 days, the SVP of service should be notified.

- The system should automatically generate a forecasted meter reading for the next month based on the previous month's reading.

- Forecasted and actual electricity and gas consumption for every site should be displayed in the customer portal. The data should cover the last 24 months. Customers should also be able to view their past invoices and payments and should be able to view a PDF version of their invoices.

- If an energy failure is reported, a critical incident should be created and assigned to the right maintenance partner based on the property's address. All customers in the impacted region should receive an SMS and email messages upon incident creation, status update, and incident resolution.

PLU shared the following requirements for the scheduled manual meter reading process.

Scheduled manual meter reading

The manual meter reading process is still required for the older meter models. PLU shared the following requirements:

- Manual readings are expected to be taken every quarter. In some countries, this has to happen every month due to regulations. The field service agents drive or walk by the residential house or the business establishment and use the radar reader devices to identify nearby compatible readers served by PLU.

- The radar reader device has a screen that displays the meter ID of nearby PLU-served meters. The device can communicate with the meters to get their readings. The radar reader is not connected to the internet. However, it can be paired with a nearby Bluetooth device.

- PLU would like the radar reader devices to be paired with the field service agent's mobile phone, then use the phone to send the reading data to Salesforce.

- PLU is looking to optimize the visiting time and travel costs for their field service agents.

- At any given time, PLU would like to track the location of its field service technicians.

PLU shared the following requirements for the scheduled automatic meter reading process.

Scheduled automatic meter reading

The automatic meter reading process is the most commonly used. PLU shared the following requirements:

- Smart meters are widely used across the countries covered. However, PLU has worked with four different vendors during the past 3 years. Each provided and installed their own smart meter devices. Each vendor has a different cloud-based platform used to control and communicate with the meters. The last 3 months' meter readings are also stored on these platforms. PLU currently has subscriptions to all these four cloud-based platforms.

- Smart readers must be read on a monthly basis. Two of the device models can push data periodically to a server. All models support *pull* operations. PLU is looking to unify the way it retrieves the smart meter data from all of its vendors. All four platforms offer a rich set of SOAP and REST APIs. They all offer web services that can be used to pull the meter readings from a smart meter. In addition, two of them also offer a pub/sub interface that allows a real-time recipient of meter readings.

PLU shared the following requirements for the customer registration process.

Customer registration

The customer portal represents a significant part of PLU's strategy to modernize customer service. They shared the following requirements for customer registration:

- Customers can't self-register in the community except via invitation. The B2C customer's access to the portal should be generated after signing up for a PLU service.

- PLU would like to expose its products to unauthenticated users via a public website. The users can subscribe online to PLU's service by providing information such as the number of households, expected power consumption, and address details. The system should automatically determine and display the right tariff for the customer. PLU is expecting this to happen via integration with *Power Sales*. The UI should be responsive to both browsers and mobile phones.

- The customer should be able to confirm the tariff. This should generate the necessary objects in Salesforce to store the customer and contract details. Furthermore, user access to the customer portal should be created.

- Upon the creation of the user access, the customer should receive an email notification to set a password. The password must meet strict complexity requirements.

- Once logged in, the customer should be able to view their contact and contract details. Customers should be able to log into the portal using a PLU-branded mobile application as well.

- Customers should be able to invite one more contact to the portal to co-manage a particular property and contract.

PLU shared the following requirements for the field sales process.

Field sales

The field sales process is essential to develop the B2B business. PLU shared the following requirements:

- The field sales agent visits a potential B2B lead and walks them through the different offers available using a handheld tablet. PLU would like to track all activities done with the client, even if the client decided not to use PLU's services.

- Three days after completing the visit, an email survey should be sent to the B2B customer's primary contact. Two different survey templates should be used, one for successfully signed deals and another for lost deals. If the field sales agent's score is below 3 out of 10, a case should be automatically created and assigned to the field sales agent's manager.

PLU shared the following data migration requirements.

Data migration requirements

Considering the previously shared information about the current landscape, PLU shared the following data migration requirements:

- PLU has over 80 million customers in its legacy CRMs. The data is expected to contain a significant number of duplicates. The number of unique active customers is likely to be in the range of 6 million. PLU would like to migrate active customers only to Salesforce. PLU would like to understand how they can deduplicate the migrated records and link them with their corresponding ERP records, knowing that the same duplication also exists in the ERPs. There is no plan to do any significant data cleanup in the ERP.

- The legacy CRMs have details for over 200 million meters. The vast number of records is due to significant record redundancy. The actual number of meters to migrate is expected to be less than 10 million. PLU would like to clean up the data and maintain a single record for each meter to develop a 360-asset-view.

PLU shared the following accessibility requirements.

Accessibility and security requirements

PLU is looking for guidance to design a secure solution; they shared the
following requirements:

- Key customers and their meter readings are only visible to the key customer
  manager, who manages that customer and their managers, except for support
  agents, who can view all accounts in the org.

- The key customer manager should be able to delegate the visibility of a customer
  account to another manager for a specific period. Once that period is up, the record
  should not be visible to the delegated manager anymore.

- A complaint is only visible to the agent who is managing it and their manager. PLU
  would also like to define a set of super users who can view all complaints in
  the system.

- Inquiries should be visible to all support agents.

- The maintenance partner records should be visible to the support agents only.
  However, they should be editable only to the support agent who manages the direct
  relationship with that partner.

- B2B customers should be able to manage all properties and meters related to
  their account.

- B2C customers should be able to manage all their related properties. It is common
  to have a B2C customer associated with more than one property.

PLU shared the following reporting requirements.

Reporting requirements

PLU requested a rich set of reporting capabilities, including the following:

- The global SVP of service would like a report showing service requests handled by
  the maintenance partners for a given year compared to data from 4 other years.

- The global SVP of service would like a dashboard showing the number of inquiries
  and complaints received and resolved broken down by country and region. The
  dashboard should indicate the number of incidents resolved within the target
  timeframe versus those that ran over.

- Key customer managers would like a set of business intelligence reports showing business improvements gained by switching the key customers from the previous tariffs to new tariffs.

- PLU would like to offer their customers a dashboard showing the change in their consumption across the past 2 years.

PLU shared the following project development requirements.

Project development requirements

Considering the complexity of PLU's program, they have requested the following project development requirements:

- PLU would like to start realizing value quickly and get Salesforce functionalities as soon as possible.

- The team maintaining the ERPs work in a 6-month release cycle, and they are unable to modify their timeline to suit this project.

- Historically, the customer support team is used for high-productivity systems, and they have a regulatory requirement to handle calls in no more than 10 minutes. They desire a similar experience in Salesforce.

- PLU would like to get support in identifying potential project risks.

- PLU would like to have a clear, traceable way to track features developed throughout the project "life cycle".

- PLU is looking for recommendations for the right environment management strategy to ensure the proper tests are executed at each stage. PLU is keen to understand how to ensure the reliability of its integration interfaces.

- PLU is looking for an appropriate methodology to manage the project delivery and ensure proper technical governance.

PLU also shared the following other requirements.

Other requirements

PLU's business is growing, and they are looking to expand to the renewable energy business. They shared the following requirement:

- PLU has recently acquired a company working in renewable energy. They manufacture and install solar panels as well as electric batteries. The acquired company is also utilizing Salesforce as their central CRM. PLU would like to know if they should plan to merge this Salesforce instance with theirs or keep it separate and are looking for your support with this decision.

That concludes the hypothetical scenario. Ensure you have gone through all the pages and requirements of your real hypothetical scenario before proceeding further.

We will now start identifying requirements and create our draft solution following the same methodology we used in previous scenarios.

Analyzing the requirements and creating a draft end-to-end solution

Give yourself enough time to go through the scenario and understand the big picture. You can even start adding notes with potential solutions.

Similar to what we did in *Chapter 12*, *Practice the Review Board – First Mock*, and *Chapter 13*, *Present and Defend – First Mock*, we will split the solutioning and the presentation creation over two chapters. This is due to the size of the full scenarios and the number of shared requirements. We will cover the business process requirements in this chapter. Then, in the next chapter, we will continue with the remaining requirements and create the presentation pitch.

As we did in all previous mocks, let's start by understanding the current landscape and creating our first draft of the diagrams.

Understanding the current situation

Starting with the first set of paragraphs, we see a description of PLU's activities and geographical presence. We also see a description of the actors, their activities, and who they report to.

By merely following the description in this section, you can understand the potential role hierarchy.

You might also consider using *Enterprise Territory Management*. However, I find it simpler to use a role hierarchy for this scenario. Try not to complicate things for yourself.

You can learn more about **Enterprise Territory Management** at the following link: `https://help.salesforce.com/articleView?id=tm2_intro.htm&type=5`.

You can learn more about using a **Role Hierarchy** at the following link: `https://help.salesforce.com/articleView?id=admin_roles.htm&type=5`.

At this stage, we might be able to create the following draft role hierarchy:

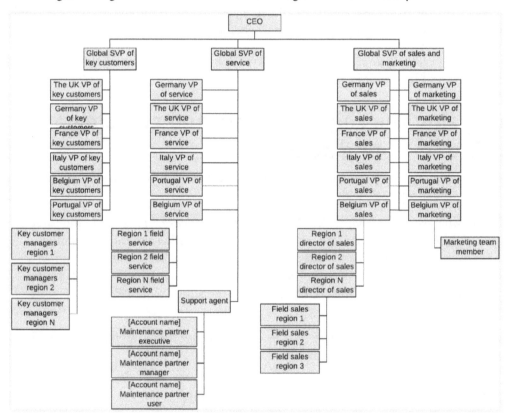

Figure 14.1 – Role hierarchy – first draft

Considering the shared info, we can also plan some targeted licenses for our actors. The following section explains that.

Determining the actors and licenses

PLU shared a brief description of the foreseen actors and their activities. We can use that to generate an early draft of their required licenses. During the presentation, you will also need to explain the rationale behind the suggested licenses. For this scenario, this could be something like the following:

- **Field sales**: Considering they need to deal with B2B customers and create new and renewal deals, they would likely need to work with the **Account**, **Opportunity**, and **Contract** objects. The **Sales Cloud** license seems like a good fit.

- **Support agents**: Considering they need to handle different incidents, and considering that we would likely end up using the **Case** object to model an incident, they might need a **Service Cloud** license. In fact, many other licenses can work with the Case object. However, the scenario also mentioned that support agents are divided into teams based on their skills. This could be achieved using either **Queues** or **Omni Channel**. The support agents will need the **Service Cloud** license if we end up utilizing **Omni Channel**. Therefore, let's assume this license for the time being. Call centers might also require some CTI capabilities. Let's pencil in the **Service Cloud Voice** license for the support agents.

- **SVP of Service**: These actors will likely need the same license as the support agents, considering that they need access to the same objects.

- **Marketing team**: Considering they need to generate and nurture leads, they need a **Sales Cloud** license. They also need to segment customers and send them mass emails. The ability to mass email 6 million customers is not a capability you should solve using **Salesforce Core**. There are several other mass email tools. One of them, in particular, integrates very well with **Salesforce Core Cloud**. I am referring to **Salesforce Marketing Cloud**, of course. Let's assume a **Marketing Cloud** license for the marketing team members as well.

- **SVP for sales and marketing**: There are not many details about the activities of this role. But assuming this role will need access to the same objects and tools used by the sales and marketing teams, we can assume that it will need a **Sales Cloud** and **Marketing Cloud** license.

- **Key customer manager**: Considering that this actor needs to interact with B2B customers and generate new deals with them, there will likely be a need to interact with the **Opportunity** object. The **Sales Cloud** license seems like a good fit.

- **SVP of key customers**: Assuming this role will need access to the same objects used by the key customer manager, we can assume it will also need the **Sales Cloud** license.

- **Field Service**: This actor needs to collect readings and fix minor issues. Issues here could be another name for incidents, which we are likely to use the **Case** object with. Let's assume they'll need the **Service Cloud** license. You should also pay attention to the *field* actors as they might indicate a need for additional solutions to help them execute their field visits, such as **Salesforce Field Service**. Let's pencil in that license for this actor and adjust it later if needed.

- **Maintenance partners**: Partners do not use any of the internal Salesforce licenses usually. In most cases, they would need a **Partner** or a **Customer Community Plus** license. At this stage, we can't determine which one would be more suitable. Let's assume the **Partner** license for the time being.

- **Customers**: Customers need access to an online portal where they can manage their account details. Considering that we have around 6 million customers, you should have no second thoughts about the required license. This actor will definitely use a **Customer Community** license, whether it is the login-based or the named-user license.

Your actors and licenses diagram could look like the following:

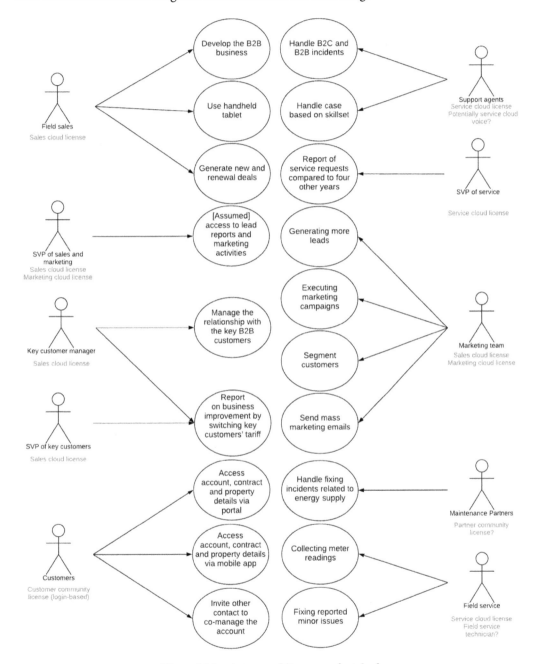

Figure 14.2 – Actors and licenses – first draft

We have a good idea of some of the objects that we might end up using. Let's use that to create our draft data model.

Creating the draft data model

PLU shared an interesting statement, suggesting a need for a complex account model to achieve such behavior. The statement starts with the following:

Residential customers can have up to two contacts per property and be related to more than one property.

This indicates that the same customer can be linked to multiple properties. Moreover, up to two customers can also be related to the same **Property**. Knowing that we are planning to use the **Customer Community** license and understanding its limited sharing capabilities, we have the following challenges:

- How are we going to model the **Property**? Will we use the **Account** object or a **Custom** object?

- How are we going to model the customers? It is easy to assume that we will be using **Person Accounts**, but how can we relate multiple-person accounts to multiple **Properties**?

- How can we ensure that we can control user visibility using **Sharing Sets** (the sharing mechanism available for the **Customer Community** license)? We haven't reached that requirement yet, but it is obvious that the customers should only be able to see the **Properties** they are related to.

- How can we model other data such as the **Contract**, **Meters**, and **Meter readings** so that they are visible to the user who has access to the **Property** record?

Some of these questions can impact the potential ways you solve others.

This is a critical requirement. One of those that could cause a lot of trouble if not solved right in the first place.

Salesforce has made a lot of improvements in the past few years to support such use cases. It introduced the object **AccountContactRelation**, which allows contacts to be linked with multiple accounts. It also updated Sharing Sets to allow record sharing based on the **AccountContactRelation** object. This was a massive boost to the communities' sharing model at that time.

Based on that, we can model our data to utilize **Person Accounts**, **AccountContactRelation**, and a custom record type of the **Account** object to represent a **Property**. This will allow us to use the **Contract** and **Asset** objects to describe a particular deal with the customer and the related enabled services (for example, electricity).

The following diagram represents a data example of how the account structure would look for B2C customers:

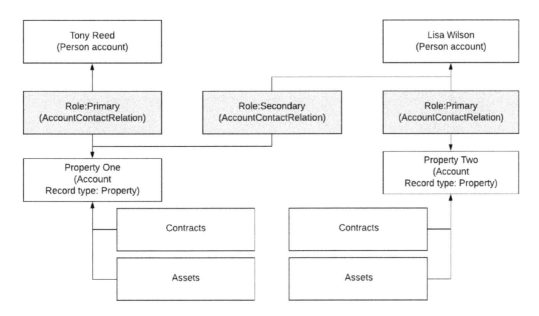

Figure 14.3 – B2C account structure data example

When you come across such a crucial data-modeling requirement, don't hesitate to check the *Accessibility and security requirement* section to ensure your model will fulfill the requirements related to Community users.

In that section, you will also notice a need for B2B customers to manage multiple properties. Following the same principles, we can come up with the following data example of the proposed account structure for B2B users:

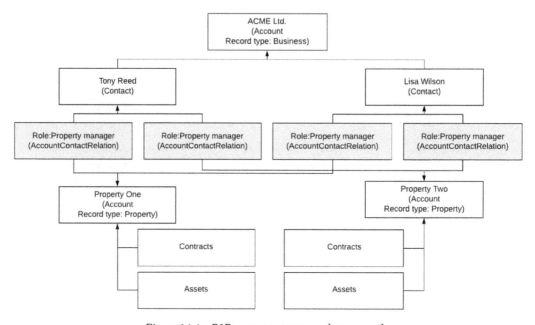

Figure 14.4 – B2B account structure data example

Don't feel shy about creating such supporting diagrams for your presentation. You can create whatever diagrams will help you further explain your solution. Try to stick to standards while creating any additional diagrams. The data example diagrams could help you put your thoughts in order and imagine how the solution will actually look.

Now that we have arranged our thoughts, let's create a draft data model using the objects we plan to use:

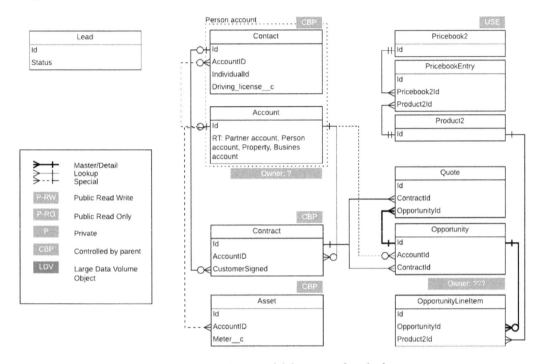

Figure 14.5 – Data model diagram – first draft

At this stage, you are just creating sketches and drafts. Don't worry about the look of your diagrams. You can tidy that up later on.

One other interesting paragraph starts with this:

On average, residential customers are subscribed to 1.5 different services per account/ property.

> **Tip**
> Take notes of these numbers, and keep an eye on them. By now, you should know the importance of such numbers in a scenario.

Finally, let's have a look at the landscape architecture.

Compiling the current landscape architecture

This part is straightforward. PLU shared a set of systems that are used today. We know that **Salesforce Core Cloud** (also known as Force.com platform) will be at the center of the proposed solution. If we put all of that together, we get the following diagram:

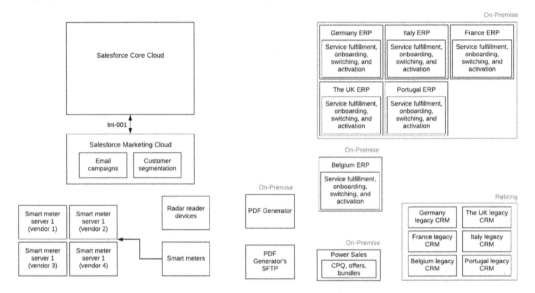

Figure 14.6 – Landscape architecture – first draft

Now that we have developed an understanding of the current situation and potential solution, let's proceed with analyzing and solutioning the shared requirements.

Analyzing the business process requirements

PLU shared six key business processes. This part of the scenario usually contains the most significant chunk of requirements. You are strongly advised to create a business process diagram for each of these processes. This will help you spot the tricky parts of the solution and will also give you an engaging and attractive tool to use during your presentation.

Let's start with the first shared business process.

Key Customer Management

PLU shared five key requirements for the **Key Customer Management** process as the first bullet point is just a definition of this type of customer. We will go through each of the shared requirements, analyze, and solution them. By the end of this exercise, we will have a business process diagram that can help us explain our end-to-end solution.

Let's start with the first requirement.

PLU would like the system to regularly identify new key customers and enroll them automatically into a special nurturing program

The three questions that might immediately come to your mind are as follows:

1. How can we execute a process to scan and evaluate customer consumption regularly?

2. How do we model the monthly consumption considering that we have 6 million B2C customers and 700,000 B2B customers? We don't know how many **Properties** we have for each group, but we know that **Key Customers** have between five and fifteen sites/properties.

3. What would the *enrollment* process look like? What objects would they use?

The first question is the easiest, as you can simply use a **Batch APEX** class or a **Schedule-Triggered Flow**. However, depending on how you model your data, even a **Batch APEX** could perform poorly with such an amount of data.

The second question is critical. It is another example of a data model-related design decision that could impact many other things. Pay extra attention to such requirements. Let's explore the common and most straightforward option of modeling monthly consumption as a normalized 3NF (third normal form). As a reminder, we covered the three primary normal forms in *Chapter 2, Core Architectural Concepts – Data*. The following diagram is an illustrated data example:

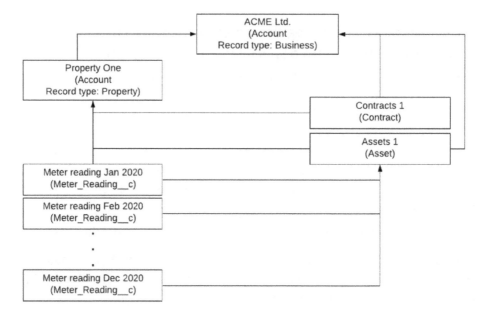

Figure 14.7 – Modeling meter readings using the 3NF

You can see that using the 3NF here will create 12 records every year for every asset. Now let's do some math.

We have 6 million B2C customers. On average, 1.5 of them have subscriptions to both electricity and gas. This is 9 million potential assets (based on our plans to use the asset object to represent a customer's subscription to a service via a meter).

We also have 700,000 B2B customers. We don't know how many of them are Key Customers, so we need to assume a reasonable percentage. Let's assume that 25% of the B2B customers are Key Customers, that is 175,000.

We know that 80% of B2B customers are signed up for both electricity and gas. Moreover, we know that **Key Customers** will have an average of 10 properties. That means we have around 3,150,000 assets used for B2B (around 945,000 for regular B2B customers and 2,205,000 for B2B **Key Customers**). In total, we have approximately 12,150,000 assets.

In a 3NF, you will get 12 records annually per asset. That is nearly 146 million records. Around 38 million of them belong to B2B customers. Any batch job that attempts to deal with this number of records would experience performance challenges.

A potential solution would be to shift all the meter reading data to an external platform such as Heroku and develop the logic that triggers the enrollment process there as well. But then you will come across other challenges related to data visibility and access management.

An alternate solution would be to use a denormalized object to store each meter's monthly readings (or even for multiple meters if the business has a maximum limit). The following diagram is an illustrated data example:

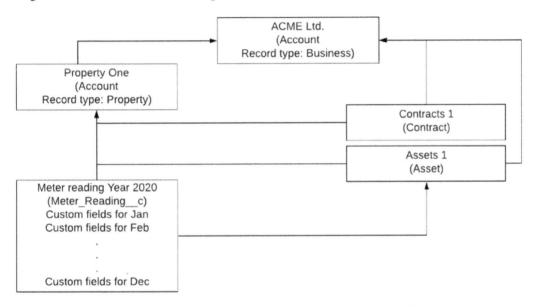

Figure 14.8 – Modeling the meter readings using a denormalized object

You can even extend the Asset objects with these additional fields unless you want to keep more than one-year's worth of data in Salesforce, which is the case here (there is a requirement to keep up to 2 years' worth of data in the system). You can even make the batch query simpler by introducing a formula field on the Meter_Reading__c object that determines if any three meter readings in the year are above the given threshold or not.

Denormalized objects have their limitations and challenges, but they have their strengths and useful use cases as well. Don't feel shy about proposing such an approach if you have a reasonable justification.

We finally come to the third question: how can we model an enrollment process?

Is there a standard object in Salesforce that allows us to run a sales process with our existing clients that involves multiple stages and activities? An object that enables a set of sales-related capabilities, such as **sales teams**, **reports**, and **forecasts**?

You guessed right: we can use an **Opportunity** to model such sales processes.

If we put this solution together, we are planning to use a batch job to query our new denormalized `Meter_Reading__c` custom object. If certain conditions are met, create an **Opportunity**, and assign the right **Opportunity team members** to it based on the relevant regions. This task looks too complicated for a **Flow**, so let's use a **Batch APEX** (the complexity justifies it).

Update your data model and business process diagrams, then let's move on to the next requirement, which starts with the following.

The enrollment team should start the enrollment process

Determining the leading Key Customer Manager can take place manually. And by the end of it, that user would own the customer account record.

The requirement also indicates a need to negotiate different offers and tariffs with the customer. This is a common use case for the **Quote** object, and the entire requirement is ideal for **Configure, Price, Quote (CPQ)**. The challenge here is that PLU insists on using Power Sales as the CPQ engine.

During the review board, you can't assume that you will convince PLU to use a different CPQ. Mainly, because the scenario clearly indicated PLU's intention to continue using Power Sales.

PLU is looking for a recommendation for the best way to facilitate using Power Sales by its users without impacting their efficiency.

You can generally suggest one of the following approaches:

- Establish **SSO** between Salesforce and Power Sales. The users are expected to *swivel their chairs* and jump from one system to another to complete the task.

- Use **Salesforce Canvas** to view the Power Sales UI from within Salesforce. This simplifies the chair-swiveling process, but you still need to handle authentication.

- Develop full integration with Power Sales and build a custom UI on top of it.

The third option is most appealing, but it usually has associated high costs. Building a totally new UI on top of another system's business logic is not an easy task and should never be underestimated.

If this were the only requirement related to Power Sales, then I would have recommended one of the first two approaches. However, we will come across multiple other requirements later on in the scenario where there is a need to integrate with Power Sales and develop a custom UI on top of, such as the requirements in the **Customer Registration** business process. Therefore, it makes sense to use the same integration interfaces and UIs for this process as well. The custom UI can be a set of Lightning components.

Before we can wrap this requirement's solution up, we need to sort out the challenge of integrating with Power Sales. We already know that it offers a poor API, which is difficult to modify. We can't develop custom UIs based on such poor APIs. We need a way to connect directly to Power Sales' database, in addition to its APIs, and create a granular set of APIs on top of them.

This is a perfect use case for a middleware such as MuleSoft. There are several more requirements in the scenario that justify the need for an ESB, such as orchestrating communications with multiple on-premise ERP systems.

So, let's put this solution together. We will develop a custom UI on top of integration with Power Sales using MuleSoft. We will use that interface to generate and populate the **Quote** object in Salesforce. The **Quote** object can then be shared with the customer.

Defining the leading Key Account Manager will be a manual process that ends up assigning the account ownership to the selected user.

Update your landscape architecture diagram, your data model, and your integration list, then let's move on to the next requirement, which starts with the following.

By the end of this process, the customer could be switched to a different, more business-oriented, tariff and a new contract should be signed

This is a common requirement. Once the **Opportunity** is closed-won, you can automatically use its data to create a Contract. You can use Salesforce flows to achieve that. The **Contract** status will be draft and pending for the client's signature.

It's worth mentioning that the **Contract** object doesn't have an out-of-the-box relationship with the **Asset** object. The **Service Contract** object does (via the confusingly-named ContractLineItem object). The **Service Contract** object is not available for **Customer Community** users, though. This is why we need to extend the **Contract** object with a custom object that enables relating it to **Assets**.

Assets would represent a relationship with a meter rather than the meter itself. The reason behind that is to facilitate the usage of the same meter by multiple customers, for example, in a rented property, without losing track of previous customers. This forms the asset 360 view, which is usually desired by utility companies.

We will introduce two custom objects: the `Meter__c` and `Contract_Linte_Item__c` objects.

It's worth mentioning that you can use the Utilities data model from Salesforce Industries (formerly **Vlocity**) as long as you can explain its objects, their use, and how to identify and mitigate any LDV objects. Similarly, if you plan to use other Vlocity-based functionalities, such as **OmniScript**, **DataRaptor**, or **FlexCards**, then be prepared to explain how they work and justify their usage.

> **Note**
>
> If you don't have enough experience with a Salesforce vertical product, just stick with a solution you know would work. This extends to specialized solutions such as Salesforce Field Service.
> In short, if you are planning to use any of these products, you better have a fair amount of knowledge about it, why it is used, how to use it (high-level), what its data model is, and what the pitfalls to be aware of are.
> Salesforce Field Service is increasingly becoming one of the products that a CTA should be aware of.

Update your data model, and let's move on to the next requirement, which starts with the following.

PLU would like to streamline the process by introducing a digital signature

There are plenty of third-party products that enable capturing a digital signature. Most of them can also trigger logic in Salesforce or update records.

We can propose using a product such as **DocuSign**. Once the signature is captured, DocuSign can update the **Contract** status, which initiates the switching process. Update your landscape architecture diagram to include DocuSign.
According to the next requirement, the switching process is fulfilled by the ERP. Let's move on to the following requirement and clarify that further.

The new contract details are sent to the country's ERP, which facilitates the switching process

This can take up to 48 hours. Once the process is done, the customer and key account managers of relevant regions should be notified.

The requirement didn't specify the expected timeframe to send the contract details to the ERP. We can assume that this can be fulfilled using a batch sync job from MuleSoft. We can also utilize a functionality such as **Platform Events** to send a near-real-time payload to MuleSoft, which, in turn, sends it across to the right ERP. We can also utilize an **outbound message** for the same purpose considering that we are only sending details from one object (the Contract).

Platform events offer an excellent added capability that is usually overlooked. As their name indicates, they fire an event that the **Platform** itself can subscribe to. This allows us to develop a loosely coupled, scalable, event-driven architecture within the platform.

You might ask yourself: Can signing be considered an event that I want to execute specific platform logic based on, such as creating a chatter post or updating some fields on other objects? If the answer is *yes* or *possibly in the near future*, then **platform events** are a great choice to hit two birds with one stone. They fire platform-based events that can be subscribed to from inside or outside the platform.

In this case, this could be a valuable feature considering that the utility business relies heavily on the status of their contracts with their customers. Firing a platform event upon signing a contract could help us accommodate several other future requirements. This will be our rationale to use it to solve this requirement.

Once the ERP does the switching process, it will initiate an inbound call to Salesforce to update the Contract status again. Once that is done, we can launch a **flow** to create a **Chatter** post to notify the key account managers who are part of the **Opportunity** team and an email alert to inform the customer.

To make it more readable, we have split the business process diagram into two. The first could look like the following:

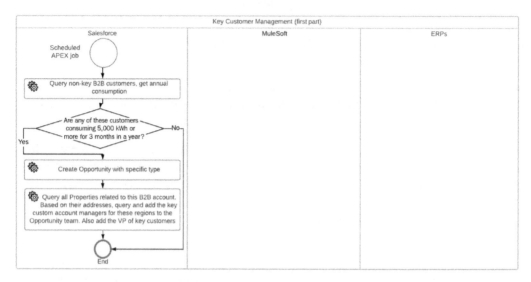

Figure 14.9 – Key Customer Management business process diagram – Part one

The second part explains the lengthier part of the process and could look like the following:

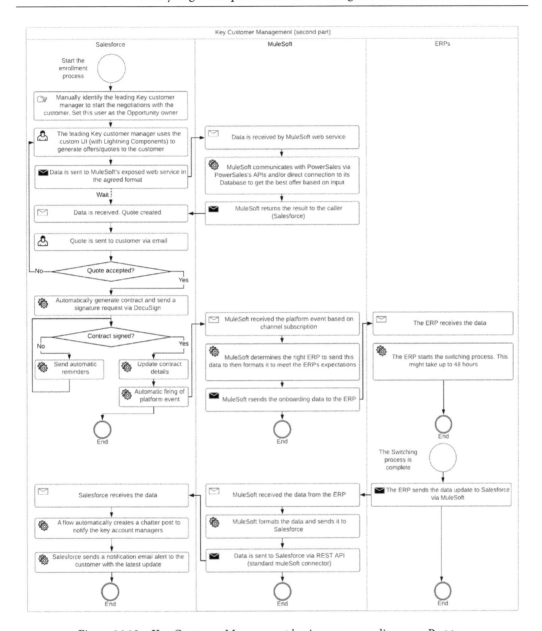

Figure 14.10 – Key Customer Management business process diagram – Part two

One interesting challenge would be the integration with the Belgium ERP. We know that it doesn't offer any APIs, it is based on a flat-file database, and it doesn't support a database adapter.

MuleSoft can connect and communicate with flat files. They are generally simple text or XML based. Writing to it should not be a challenge. However, the Belgium ERP is a legacy system that is incapable of consuming APIs. But it can communicate with a **Simple Mail Transfer Protocol (SMTP)** server. This way, it can send an email once the switching process is complete. We can develop a custom **APEX Email Service** to receive the emails, parse them, then update the relevant records accordingly.

That concludes the first business process. Update your landscape architecture diagram and your list of integration interfaces, then let's move on to the next business process.

Customer service

PLU shared five key requirements for the customer service process. We will go through each of the shared requirements and analyze and solution them. Let's start with the first requirement, which begins with the following.

All customers should be able to create inquiries or complaints using a self-serve customer portal or by calling the call center

Customers will be able to raise inquiries and complaints using the Customer Community. We can utilize the **Case** object with multiple record types to represent inquiries and complaints.

The scenario didn't specify whether PLU is looking to modernize its call center with **SoftPhone** and CTI capability, but let's assume that and add **Service Cloud Voice** to our landscape.

We discussed the difference between **Queues** and **Salesforce Omni-Channel** in *Chapter 13, Present and Defend – First Mock*, and explained that Queues are suitable to represent a single skill. This requirement requires implementing **skills-based routing** that will consider all necessary skills to fulfill a particular case, something that is offered by **Salesforce Omni-Channel**.

Update your landscape architecture diagram to include both the **Customer Community** and **Omni-Channel**, then let's move on to the next requirement.

If a complaint is not resolved within 7 days, the SVP of the service should be notified

This requirement can be met using **Case Escalation Rules**. You can configure the escalation rules to send an email to the SVP of the service when the mentioned conditions are met.

Let's move on to the next requirement.

The system should automatically generate a forecasted meter reading for the next month based on the previous month's reading

We modeled annual meter readings using a denormalized custom object. This requirement can be met by introducing 12 more fields to represent the forecasted monthly readings for a given year.

In *Chapter 2, Core Architectural Concepts – Data*, we explained some of the differences between classic RDBMSes and Salesforce, including the fact that in Salesforce, it is acceptable to create an object (table) with many fields (columns) for specific use cases.

We can then have a scheduled flow to populate the right forecasted field every month automatically. Alternatively, we can use a **Before-Save Flow** to update the forecasted field value upon updating the actual reading value. For example, the flow could automatically populate the `Feb_Forecasted__c` field's value once the `Jan_Actual__c` field is updated. This will be more efficient considering the vast number of `Meter_Reading__c` records we will have in the system.

Update your data model, and let's move on to the next requirement, which starts with the following.

The forecasted and actual electricity and gas consumption for every site should be displayed in the customer portal

The data should cover the last 24 months. Customers should also be able to view their past invoices and payments and be able to view a PDF version of their invoices.

According to this requirement, the `Meter_Reading__c` object should be visible to the Customer Community users of a particular account. We can achieve that by linking the `Meter_Reading__c` object to the Asset object using a master-detail relationship. This way, any user who has access to the Asset record will be able to view its related `Meter_Reading__c`. Customer community users will get access to the Assets related to the Accounts records they have access to, including any Properties.

This is the first time we have come across requirements related to invoices and payments in this scenario. It is fair to assume that these objects will exist in the ERPs. We can then expose them in Salesforce using **Salesforce Connect**.

> **Note**
> You will end up with six external Invoice objects if you use a direct connection with the ERPs. Moreover, some of the ERPs are legacy and unable to provide an **oData-compatible** interface.

You can use MuleSoft to connect to all the ERPs, retrieve the invoices, and aggregate and expose them as an **oData** interface that Salesforce can subscribe to. Let's also assume that we would be retrieving the invoice headers, line items, and payments as separate external objects.

Update your data model to include the new external objects.

PLU's PDF Generator application should generate PDFs. The application receives input data and generates a PDF that is stored on an SFTP. This means it won't provide an interactive user experience where the PDF is generated on the fly. The PDFs need to be generated upfront and stored in a place accessible to Community Users.

PLU doesn't have a DMS. You can either propose they start using one or use Salesforce Files. This option is decent enough, considering that these files' content will not change after they are generated. No advanced document management capabilities are required.

To generate these PDFs, we can assume a batch MuleSoft job that runs every month, retrieves the invoice details from the ERPs, and passes them to the PDG Generator system to generate PDFs. MuleSoft would then retrieve all files stored on the SFTP and transfer them to Salesforce. We can use a specific file naming convention that includes the account ID. This will allow MuleSoft to attach the files to the correct Account record.

Add the `Content Document` object to your data model. Your data model could now look like the following:

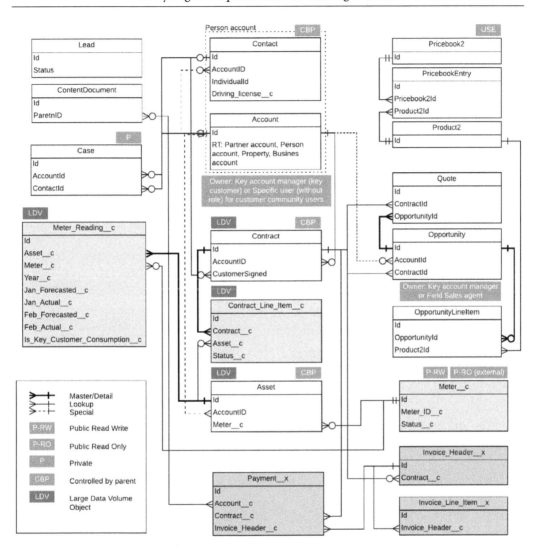

Figure 14.11 – Data model – second draft

Your landscape architecture diagram could look like the following:

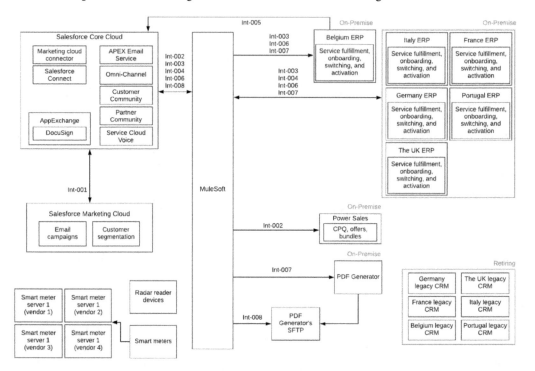

Figure 14.12 – Landscape architecture – second draft

Your list of interfaces could look like the following:

Interface Code	Source / Destination	Integration Layer	Integration Pattern	Description	Security	Authentication
Int-001	Salesforce <-> Marketing cloud	Data	Batch Data Synchronization - Asynch	Synch data such as contacts and leads from Salesforce to Marketing cloud and vice versa using the marketing cloud connector	HTTPS (one way SSL/TLS)	oAuth 2.0 Client Credentials flow (to authenticate to Marketing cloud) oAuth 2.0 web-server flow (to authenticate to Salesforce)
Int-002	Salesforce -> MuleSoft -> Power Sales	Business logic	Remote process invocation - request and reply - Blocking	Invoke multiple methods and get back quote details from Power Cloud. The APIs can be invoked using buttons within a custom UI in Salesforce. Once the button is clicked, an APEX controller would invoke the MuleSoft API. Once invoked, MuleSoft will determine if it is going to call one of Power Sales APIs or connect directly to its database to execute the logic (such as creating a quote). Once the result is returned, the APEX controller creates a Salesforce Quote record and link it to the relevant Opportunity	HTTPS (two way SSL/TLS) between Salesforce and MuleSoft. HTTPS (one way SSL/TLS) Between MuleSoft and Power Sales	oAuth 2.0 web-server flow (then refresh token flow) with mutual authentication between Salesforce and MuleSoft. Simple authentication between MuleSoft and Power Sales
Int-003	Salesforce -> MuleSoft -> The right ERP	Data	Remote Process Invocation—Fire and Forget	Fire a platform event from Salesforce. This will be subscribed to by MuleSoft. MuleSoft will use the data in the Platform Event to determine the right ERP to send the data to.	HTTPS (one way SSL/TLS)	oAuth 2.0 JWT bearer token flow

Interface Code	Source / Destination	Integration Layer	Integration Pattern	Description	Security	Authentication
Int-004	ERPs (except Belgium's) -> MuleSoft -> Salesforce	Data	Remote Call-In	The ERPs will send a message to MuleSoft to indicate the completion of the Switching process. MuleSoft would then invoke the standard Salesforce REST API to update the relevant record.	HTTPS (two way SSL/TLS) between Salesforce and MuleSoft. HTTPS (one way SSL/TLS) Between MuleSoft and the ERPs	oAuth 2.0 web-server flow (then refresh token flow) with mutual authentication between Salesforce and MuleSoft. Simple authentication between MuleSoft and the ERPs
Int-005	Belgium ERP -> Salesforce	Data	Remote Call-In (Email)	An email sent by the Belgium ERP using an SMTP server and received by a Salesforce custom APEX Email Service	HTTPS (one way SSL/TLS)	None (to Salesforce). Simple authentication with the SMTP server.
Int-006	MuleSoft -> Salesforce	UI	Data Virtualization / Mashup / oData	Invoices, invoice line items, and Payments are displayed in Salesforce using Salesforce Connect. MuleSoft fetches the data from the relevant ERPs and aggregate them using an oData interface.	HTTPS (one way SSL/TLS)	oAuth 2.0 web-server flow (then refresh token flow)
Int-007	MuleSoft -> ERPs MuleSoft -> PDF generator	Business logic	Remote process invocation - request and reply - Blocking	A scheduled MuleSoft job retrieves new invoice data and pass them to the PDF Generator to generate PDF invoices.	HTTPS (one way SSL/TLS)	Simple authentication
Int-008	MuleSoft -> SFTP MuleSoft -> Salesforce	Data	Batch Data Synchronization - Asynch	A scheduled MuleSoft job retrieves PDF invoices from the SFTP and transfers them to Salesforce	HTTPS (two way SSL/TLS) between Salesforce and MuleSoft. HTTPS (one way SSL/TLS) Between MuleSoft and SFTP	oAuth 2.0 web-server flow (then refresh token flow) with mutual authentication between Salesforce and MuleSoft. Simple authentication between MuleSoft and the SFTP

Figure 14.13 – Integration interfaces – first draft

Let's now move on to the next and final requirement in this business process, which starts with the following.

If an energy failure is reported, a critical incident should be created and assigned to the right maintenance partner based on the property's address

All customers in the impacted region should receive an SMS and email messages upon incident creation, status update, and incident resolution.

A critical incident could be another **Case** record type. We can use **Case Assignment Rules** to assign it to the right **Partner user** or **Queue**, assuming we have a field that indicates the relevant Case region.

We can use a **Before-Save Flow** to set the value of that field based on the related **Property** (**Account**) details.

Once that is done, we need to identify all customers relevant to that particular region and send them all an SMS notification. This is a mass SMS send, a capability not available out of the box on the Salesforce Platform. You can use a third party such as **SMS-Magic** or utilize **Marketing Cloud** itself, assuming PLU has the required licenses.

You can send transaction emails and SMS using the **Marketing Cloud Transactional Messaging API**. This is a REST-based API that can be used to send immediate, non-promotional messages. It is very suitable for this use case.

This API cannot be invoked using the connector. There is a need to execute the following logic:

- Based on the reported critical **Case**, create a unique list of customers that needs to be notified based on the address of their properties.

- Use this data to invoke the **Marketing Cloud Transactional Messaging API**.

How can you achieve both?

You always need to be aware of *all the tools* that you have. Don't try to solve everything using Salesforce Core alone. We saw many examples where we used other platforms, such as Heroku and MuleSoft.

In this case, you can use MuleSoft to handle both tasks. We can fire a **platform event** from Salesforce to MuleSoft with the necessary **Case** details. MuleSoft can then query Salesforce to find out the relevant customers, then invoke the **Transactional Messaging API**. MuleSoft can orchestrate the entire process in a scalable and performant way. If you choose to develop that using custom APEX, you should expect many challenges during the Q&A.

Update your landscape architecture diagram and your list of integration interfaces. We will not create a business process diagram for this process as it is simple enough to be explained without it.

That concludes the second business process. Let's now move on to the next business process.

Scheduled manual meter reading

PLU shared three key requirements for the Scheduled Manual Meter Reading process as the first two bullet points just explain the business process and the technology used. Let's go through each and analyze and solution them, starting with the first requirement.

PLU would like the radar reader devices to be paired with the field service agent's mobile phone, then use the phone to send the reading data to Salesforce

The mobile app with the field service technician has to be able to communicate with the radar reader via Bluetooth. This requirement should help you decide on your mobile strategy. This capability is unlikely to be supported by a hybrid app; a native app is required. But before we reach a final decision, let's have a look at the next two requirements.

PLU is looking to optimize the visiting time and travel costs for their field service agents

You have two out-of-the-box capabilities in Salesforce to optimize the visiting time and travel costs. **Salesforce Maps** and **Salesforce Field Service**. The latter has more advanced capabilities and is more geared towards field service requirements and activities, such as skills-based assignments, shift management, and crew management.

Let's select that to cover this requirement. You need to add the relevant **Field Service** objects to your data model. Make yourself familiar with the standard **Field Service** objects, and be prepared to explain how they are used. You can find more details at the following link: `https://developer.salesforce.com/docs/atlas.en-us.field_service_dev.meta/field_service_dev/fsl_dev_soap_core.htm`.

We will add `WorkOrder` and the `ServiceAppointment` to our data model to keep things simple.

Update your data model and landscape architecture, then let's move on to the next requirement.

At any given time, PLU would like to track the location of its field service technicians

We know that **Salesforce Field Service** has a specific mobile app that offers this feature out of the box. This requirement can be fulfilled with that. But can we extend the Salesforce mobile application to communicate with the radar reader over Bluetooth?

You can change some configurations on the mobile app currently. Still, even if you don't know the app's full limitations, it is risky to assume that it can be extended to cover such sophisticated requirements.

You can propose developing another native mobile application to handle the communications with the radar reader. In your presentation, you can explain that this is an approach that you know works and that you would investigate this further for a real project.

Update your landscape architecture and the list of integrations. We are not going to create a business process diagram for this process, considering its simplicity.

Let's now move on to the next business process.

Scheduled automatic meter reading

PLU shared two key requirements for the Scheduled Automatic Meter Reading process. Let's go through each of them and analyze and solution them.

Let's start with the first requirement, which begins with the following.

Smart meters are widely used across the countries covered

This paragraph doesn't contain a clear requirement on its own. But it describes a situation where you need some sort of harmonization in the way you interact with the four different cloud-based platforms. Does that ring any bells? Sounds like MuleSoft's turf. Let's move on to the next requirement to be more precise.

Smart readers must be read on a monthly basis

The key point in this requirement is PLU's desire for unification. They are after a unified mechanism to get meter readings. The only jointly supported integration capability in these systems is the web services that enable *pulling* the meter readings.

We can propose developing a scheduled job in MuleSoft that runs every month, pulls the meter readings from all these different platforms, combines them, then updates Salesforce with the combined dataset.

Once that is developed, you can extend the solution by introducing a MuleSoft web service that enables on-demand data pulling. This is not required now, but it is good to have a flexible and extendible design to cover today's and tomorrow's requirements.

We are not going to create a business process diagram for this process due to its simplicity. Update your landscape architecture diagram and list of interfaces, then let's move on to the next business process.

Customer registration

PLU shared six key requirements for the customer registration process. Let's go through each of them and analyze and solution them.

Let's start with the first requirement, which begins with the following.

Customers can't self-register in the community except via invitation. The B2C customer's access to the portal should be generated after they sign up for a PLU service

The first part of the requirement is a bit confusing. What is meant here by invitation? There is no standard invitation process in Salesforce. Is the question perhaps referring to the manual process of enabling **Contacts** into **Community users**?

This part is unclear, and it will continue to be so until you read the sixth requirement of this business process. Real scenarios might have such questions; this is why we have repeatedly highlighted the importance of reading the scenario at least once at the beginning before starting with accumulative solutioning.

Let's proceed with the rest of the requirements. We find a need to autogenerate the B2C customer's portal user once they sign up for a PLU service. This can easily be automated using the **Contract** trigger. Once the trigger is active, we can check whether the related customer already has a community user. If none are found, we create a user.

Does that sound good? Take another look at the described process and identify the potential challenges you could face while handling a happy scenario (a scenario where all required data is provided, and the process is expected to work correctly). Did you spot something missing or that could go wrong?

Correct! **Data manipulation language (DML)** operations on Salesforce setup objects (such as **User**) can't be mixed up, in the same transactions, with DML operations on other objects (such as **Account**, **Contact**, **Contract**, and so on).

In other words, you can't create a User record in the same transaction where you are updating a **Contract** record. Your solution will fail in its current condition. This is a point that the judges will notice and pick up on during the Q&A. They would ask more questions to understand whether you missed mentioning that point or were totally unaware of the challenge.

You can overcome this challenge by separating the transaction into a synchronous and asynchronous part. You can launch a future/queueable method that creates the **Customer Community** user in the **Contract** trigger. In your presentation, ensure that you highlight that this solution will help you avoid the *mixed DML exception*.

Let's now move on to the next requirement, which starts with the following.

PLU would like to expose its products to unauthenticated users via a public website

This requirement is all about exposing your CPQ solution to the public. We have already proposed developing a custom UI (based on Lightning components) on top of a MuleSoft-exposed API that communicates with Power Sales. We can extend the usage of this component to the public **Community**. The responsiveness can be guaranteed using **Salesforce Lightning Design System (SLDS)**.

Let's move on to the next requirement, which starts with the following.

The customer should be able to confirm the tariff

This means the Lightning component that we expose to the public should be able to create all the necessary objects in Salesforce to start the customer's **Contract**. We can ensure that using the right user permissions. It's worth mentioning here that this component would be operating under the **Guest** user context for unauthenticated users. You can grant the guest user access to fields and objects, but ensure you follow *minimal data access principles*.

Let's move on to the next requirement, which starts with the following.

Upon the creation of the user access, the customer should receive an email notification to set a password

This is standard functionality. You can create a Community User associated with a Person Account using the `Site.createPersonAccountPortalUser` method. You can find more details about this method at the following link: `https://developer.salesforce.com/docs/atlas.en-us.apexcode.meta/apexcode/apex_classes_sites.htm?search_text=createPersonAccountPortalUser`.

The user will receive an autogenerated password that has to be changed upon the first login. You can enforce strict password complexity rules using the Profile settings. You can set the value of the **Password complexity requirement** field on the Customer Community user's profile to the desired value, such as *Must include 3 of the following: numbers, uppercase letters, lowercase letters, special characters.*

Let's move on to the next requirement, which starts with the following.

Once logged in, the customer should be able to view their contact and contract details

This will be fulfilled using the proposed data accessibility and sharing model. **Sharing sets** will ensure the community user has access to the relevant **Property Account**. The visibility of **Contracts** is *controlled by parent* (the parent **Property Account** record). This means record-level accessibility is covered. We need to ensure the community user has the right object-level and field-level permissions to view all required fields. This can be controlled using **Profiles** and **Permission Sets**.

PLU also requested to allow its customers to log in to the community using a branded mobile application. We can propose using **Salesforce Mobile Publisher**. It is a quick and easy way to turn a Salesforce Lightning community into a mobile application. You can learn more about **Mobile Publisher** at the following link: `https://help.salesforce.com/articleView?id=s1_branded_apps.htm&type=5`.

> **Note**
> we don't have any advanced capabilities that justify a native app or even a hybrid app. Of course, you can develop your fully branded mobile app using both, but that will cost much more time and effort. Always think of the client's ROI.

Update your landscape architecture and list of interfaces, then let's move on to the next and final requirement.

Customers should be able to invite one more contact to the portal to co-manage a particular property and contract

Here, we come back to the *invitation* requirement mentioned earlier, in the first requirement of this business process.

We can configure Customer Community Users to create other **Contact** records, but they can't convert them into users. Moreover, our data model is based on **Person Accounts** for B2C, which are related to **Properties** (another **Account** record type) via the **AccountContactRelation** object.

These requirements indicate that we need to customize this functionality, keeping in mind the first requirement, which suggests that **Community Users** can't self-register unless *invited*.

We can solve this using a new custom object, which contains all information required to send a unique invitation to an email address. Moreover, the custom object should also include all the necessary information to link the newly created **Community User** with the correct **Property** record once created.

We can configure the **Community User's Profile** to allow the creation of the invitation custom object `Community_Invitation__c`. We can control the number of allowed records to be created via a custom validation in a trigger or use custom validation rules that rely on the value of a custom **Rollup-Summary** field. We will choose the first option (despite the fact it is based on code) to avoid consuming one of the limited numbers of rollup-summary fields that we can introduce into a sensitive object, such as **Account** (representing a **Property** in this case).

The invitation process could look like the following:

1. The logged-in, existing Community User creates a `Community_Invitation__c` record and sets the required values, such as email address and related **Property**.

2. Once the `Community_Invitation__c` record is created, we send an email alert using Flows or Process Builder. The email alert's template will contain the unique invitation code (this could simply be the `Community_Invitation__c` record ID) and a link to follow to self-register in the community.

3. The link itself will have the invitation code as a parameter. When the user clicks that link, they will be redirected to the community's self-registration page with a **Lightning component**. The invitation number will be passed to the page as a parameter, allowing the page to display the number in a field to the customer and other usual fields such as first name, last name, and email address.

4. Once the customer hits the submit button, the Lightning component's APEX controller validates the invitation number. If that was successful, it creates a Customer Community user and launches an asynchronous queueable job to create the required additional records such as `AccountContactRelation` to enable this user to access the **Property** details.

5. The newly created user won't be able to view the related **Property** details until the asynchronous job is concluded. We can't guarantee how long that will take but can communicate upfront that this will take up to several minutes.

Update your data model diagram. Let's create a business process diagram for this requirement, only because the solution will be easier to explain using a diagram. Your diagram could look like the following:

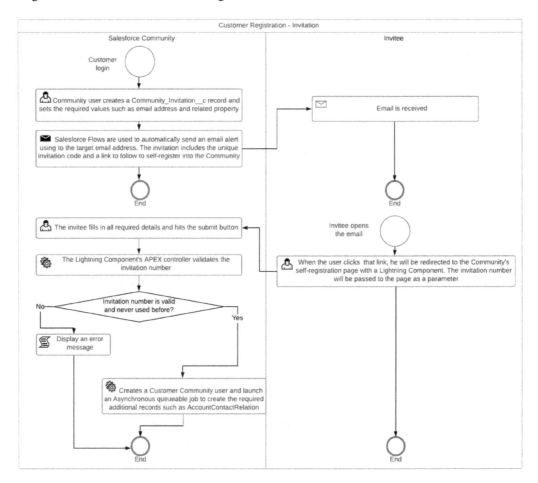

Figure 14.14 – Customer Registration business process diagram – the invitation sub-process

That concludes this business process. Let's now move on to the sixth and last business process.

Field sales

PLU shared two key requirements for the field sales process. Let's go through each of them and analyze and solution them.

Let's start with the first requirement, which begins with the following.

The field sales agent visits a potential B2B lead and walks them through the different offers

We came across a similar requirement before, but the channel was different. We decided to develop a custom UI on top of APIs exposed by MuleSoft, which are integrated with Power Sales. The UI is basically a set of **Lightning components**.

The **Field Sales** agents can use the same components on their tablets. Assuming they are using the **Salesforce mobile app**. The new Salesforce mobile app supports Lightning app pages, which we can logically assume our custom UI will use.

Update your landscape architecture diagram and list of interfaces, and let's move on to the next requirement, which starts with the following.

Three days after completing the visit, an email survey should be sent to the B2B customer's primary contact

Two different survey templates should be used, one for successfully signed deals and another for lost deals. If the score of the **Field Sales** agent is below 3 out of 10, a **Case** should be automatically created and assigned to the field sales agent's manager.

This requirement is becoming more common nowadays as more companies are trying to get closer to their clients and show them that their opinion matters. You have three potential ways to solve this requirement:

- Develop a custom survey module based on custom objects and automation.
- Use a third-party tool such as **SurveyMonkey**.
- Use **Salesforce Surveys**.

Salesforce products come with the regular Salesforce promise: they will be updated regularly, and new features will continuously be included. Furthermore, they are Salesforce products designed for Salesforce. They integrate with the platform in a more straightforward way than others, and they usually simplify other non-functional requirements such as data residency.

On some occasions, the Salesforce product will lack certain functionalities, which justifies considering a third party instead. This is not the case here. This requirement can be fulfilled using Salesforce Surveys.

Similar to other extension products (such as **Salesforce Field Service**, **Vlocity**, and so on), you need to know how the product works and have a good understanding of its components. The most common element you need to be familiar with is the data model.

We will add the key objects we plan to use from the Salesforce Survey to our data model diagram. You can find more information at the following link: `https://developer.salesforce.com/docs/atlas.en-us.api.meta/api/sforce_api_objects_salesforce_surveys_object_model.htm`.

We will still need to add some customizations to deliver certain functionalities, such as scheduling sending the survey, linking the sent surveys to the right object (**Lead** in this case), and processing feedback to determine whether a **Case** needs to be created and assigned to the field sales agent's manager (If the score of the field sales agent is below 3 out of 10).

This automation can get complex if developed using flows. Therefore, we will propose using APEX.

> **Note**
> This might sound weird, but in my opinion, complex logic is better delivered using APEX rather than flows. I have seen some extremely complex flows, which are harder to debug or read than APEX. Flows are still great to solve many other challenges, but are still not a full APEX replacement.

Update your data model diagram.

Your landscape architecture diagram could now look like the following:

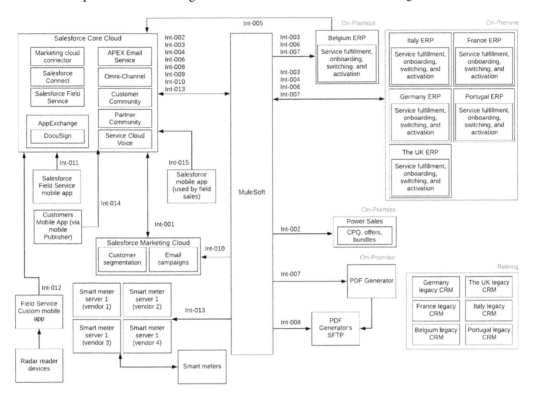

Figure 14.15 – Landscape architecture – third draft

Your list of integration interfaces could look like the following:

Interface Code	Source / Destination	Integration Layer	Integration Pattern	Description	Security	Authentication
Int-001	Salesforce <-> Marketing cloud	Data	Batch Data Synchronization - Asynch	Synch data such as contacts and leads from Salesforce to Marketing cloud and vice versa using the marketing cloud connector	HTTPS (one way SSL/ TLS)	oAuth 2.0 Client Credentials flow (to authenticate to Marketing cloud) oAuth 2.0 web-server flow (to authenticate to Salesforce)
Int-002	Salesforce -> MuleSoft -> Power Sales	Business logic	Remote process invocation - request and reply - Blocking	Invoke multiple methods and get back quote details from Power Cloud. The APIs can be invoked using buttons within a custom UI in Salesforce. Once the button is clicked, an APEX controller would invoke the MuleSoft API. Once invoked, MuleSoft will determine if it is going to call one of Power Sales APIs or connect directly to its database to execute the logic (such as creating a quote). Once the result is returned, the APEX controller creates a Salesforce Quote record and link it to the relevant Opportunity	HTTPS (two way SSL/TLS) between Salesforce and MuleSoft. HTTPS (one way SSL/TLS) Between MuleSoft and Power Sales	oAuth 2.0 web-server flow (then refresh token flow) with mutual authentication between Salesforce and MuleSoft. Simple authentication between MuleSoft and Power Sales
Int-003	Salesforce -> MuleSoft -> The right ERP	Data	Remote Process Invocation—Fire and Forget	Fire a platform event from Salesforce. This will be subscribed to by MuleSoft. MuleSoft will use the data in the Platform Event to determine the right ERP to send the data to.	HTTPS (one way SSL/ TLS)	oAuth 2.0 JWT bearer token flow

Interface Code	Source / Destination	Integration Layer	Integration Pattern	Description	Security	Authentication
Int-004	ERPs (except Belgium's) -> MuleSoft -> Salesforce	Data	Remote Call-In	The ERPs will send a message to MuleSoft to indicate the completion of the Switching process. MuleSoft would then invoke the standard Salesforce REST API to update the relevant record.	HTTPS (two way SSL/TLS) between Salesforce and MuleSoft. HTTPS (one way SSL/TLS) Between MuleSoft and the ERPs	oAuth 2.0 web-server flow (then refresh token flow) with mutual authentication between Salesforce and MuleSoft. Simple authentication between MuleSoft and the ERPs
Int-005	Belgium ERP -> Salesforce	Data	Remote Call-In (Email)	An email sent by the Belgium ERP using an SMTP server and received by a Salesforce custom APEX Email Service	HTTPS (one way SSL/TLS)	None (to Salesforce). Simple authentication with the SMTP server.
Int-006	MuleSoft -> Salesforce	UI	Data Virtualization / Mashup / oData	Invoices, invoice line items, and Payments are displayed in Salesforce using Salesforce Connect. MuleSoft fetches the data from the relevant ERPs and aggregate them using an oData interface.	HTTPS (one way SSL/TLS)	oAuth 2.0 web-server flow (then refresh token flow)
Int-007	MuleSoft -> ERPs MuleSoft -> PDF generator	Business logic	Remote process invocation - request and reply - Blocking	A scheduled MuleSoft job retrieves new invoice data and pass them to the PDF Generator to generate PDF invoices.	HTTPS (one way SSL/TLS)	Simple authentication

Interface Code	Source / Destination	Integration Layer	Integration Pattern	Description	Security	Authentication
Int-008	MuleSoft -> SFTP MuleSoft -> Salesforce	Data	Batch Data Synchronization - Asynch	A scheduled MuleSoft job retrieves PDF invoices from the SFTP and transfers them to Salesforce	HTTPS (two way SSL/TLS) between Salesforce and MuleSoft. HTTPS (one way SSL/TLS) Between MuleSoft and SFTP	oAuth 2.0 web-server flow (then refresh token flow) with mutual authentication between Salesforce and MuleSoft. Simple authentication between MuleSoft and the SFTP
Int-009	Salesforce -> MuleSoft	Data	Remote Process Invocation—Fire and Forget	Fire a platform event from Salesforce for any newly created Critical Incident (Case). This will be subscribed to by MuleSoft. MuleSoft will use the data in the Platform Event to query back Salesforce for additional details	HTTPS (one way SSL/ TLS)	oAuth 2.0 JWT bearer token flow
Int-010	MuleSoft -> Salesforce MuleSoft -> Marketing Cloud	Business logic	Remote process invocation - request and reply - Blocking	MuleSoft queries Salesforce for Customer records that are impacted by a critical Incident (Case). Then invokes the Marketing Cloud Transactional Messaging API to send SMS notifications to these customers	HTTPS (two way SSL/TLS) between Salesforce and MuleSoft. HTTPS (one way SSL/TLS) Between MuleSoft and Marketing Cloud	oAuth 2.0 web-server flow (then refresh token flow)
Int-011	Salesforce Field Service mobile app <-> Salesforce	Data	Remote Call-In	The mobile application will invoke the REST API to query, create, or update records	HTTPS (one way SSL/ TLS)	OpenID connect flow (then refresh token flow)

Interface Code	Source / Destination	Integration Layer	Integration Pattern	Description	Security	Authentication
Int-012	Custom mobile app <-> Salesforce	Data	Remote Call-In	The mobile application communicate with the Radar reader via Bluetooth, read values, cache them locally, then transfer them to Salesforce using the REST API	HTTPS (one way SSL/TLS)	OpenID connect flow (then refresh token flow)
Int-013	MuleSoft -> Smart meter platforms MuleSoft -> Salesforce	Data	Remote Call-In	A scheduled MuleSoft job that retrieves meter readings from the different platforms. The data is then transformed to a unified structure and combined together. The combined data set is then used to update Salesforce.	HTTPS (two way SSL/TLS) between Salesforce and MuleSoft. HTTPS (one way SSL/TLS) Between MuleSoft and the Platforms	oAuth 2.0 web-server flow (then refresh token flow) with mutual authentication between Salesforce and MuleSoft. Simple authentication between MuleSoft and the Platforms
Int-014	Salesforce Mobile app (via Mobile publisher) -> Salesforce	Data	Remote Call-In	The mobile application will invoke the REST API to query, create, or update records	HTTPS (one way SSL/TLS)	OpenID connect flow (then refresh token flow)
Int-015	Salesforce Mobile app -> Salesforce	Data	Remote Call-In	The mobile application will invoke the REST API to query, create, or update records"	HTTPS (one way SSL/TLS)	OpenID connect flow (then refresh token flow)

Figure 14.16 – Integration interfaces – second draft

And your data model diagram could look like the following:

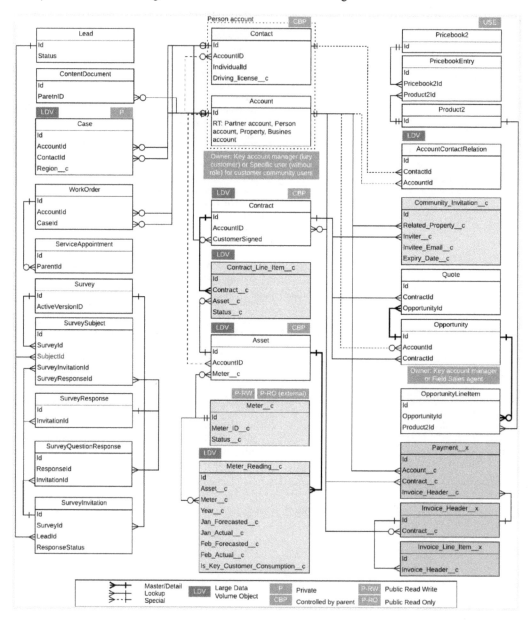

Figure 14.17 – Data model – third draft

At this stage, we have nearly solutioned 60-70% of the scenario's requirements. This will be the basis of our next chapter, where we'll continue to solution the rest of PLU's requirements, then create our presentation pitch.

Summary

In this chapter, we were introduced to our second full mock scenario. You are now more familiar with the nature of full scenarios. They are longer, more thorough, and contain many more challenges than mini-scenarios.

In this chapter, we tackled the first part of the scenario. The business process requirements are usually the meatiest part of a scenario. This part is also where you start creating your comprehensive solution. You start by understanding each business process, then dividing it into digestible chunks and solving it as a whole.

We came across compelling use cases and design decisions, including a complex data model that supports both B2B and B2C. We created several business process diagrams that will help us a lot during the presentation by visualizing our solution.

In the next chapter, we will continue to solution the scenario and then put together our presentation pitch. We covered a lot of land in this chapter, and we still have plenty more to cover in the next.

15
Present and Defend – Second Mock

In this chapter, we will continue to create an end-to-end solution for our second full mock scenario. We have covered most of the scenario already in *Chapter 14*, *Practice the Review Board – Second Mock*, but we still have plenty of topics to cover. We will continue analyzing and solving each of the shared requirements and then practice creating some presentation pitches.

We will follow the same sequence that you will go through in the real exam. After the presentation, we will move on to the Q&A and practice defending and changing our solution based on the judges' feedback.

After reading this chapter, you are advised to reread the scenario and try to solve it on your own.

In this chapter, we're going to cover the following main topics:

- Continuing with analyzing the requirements and creating an end-to-end solution
- Present and justify your solution

By the end of this chapter, you will have completed your second mock scenario. You will have become more familiar with the full mock scenario's complexity and be better prepared for the exam. You will also learn how to present your solution in the limited time given and justify it during the Q&A.

Continuing with analyzing the requirements and creating an end-to-end solution

We covered the business process requirements earlier. By the end, we had a very good understanding of the potential data model and landscape. We have already marked some objects as potential LDVs.

Next, we have a set of data migration requirements that we need to solve. Once we complete them, we will have an even better understanding of the potential data volumes. We can then create our LDV mitigation strategy.

Let's start with the data migration requirements first.

Analyzing the data migration requirements

This section's requirements might impact some of your diagrams, such as the landscape architecture diagram or the data model.

Let's now start with the first shared data migration requirement.

PLU has over 80 million customers in its legacy CRMs. The data is expected to contain a significant number of duplicates

If we analyze this requirement, we can identify the following needs:

- Deduplicate customers in the legacy CRMs so that we end up with one record to represent each.

- Migrate active customers only. The resulting dataset is expected to contain nearly 6 million customers.

- Link the migrated active unique customers with their relevant records in the ERP. This has to be done *without* significant changes to the ERP's data.

Always remember *all the tools* that you can use to solve your client's needs. We can read the preceding three requirements as the following:

- There is a need to deduplicate the legacy CRM customers and create a *golden record* for all PLU customers.

- There is a need to select a *subset* of these customers (active customers only).

- There is a need to identify the customers in the ERPs and *build a relationship* between their records and the unique customer golden record. This will ensure that we can create a customer 360° view across all systems despite all ERPs' redundancies.

In *Chapter 2, Core Architectural Concepts – Data*, we came across three different MDM implementation styles:

- **Registry style**: This style spots duplicates in various connected systems by running a match, cleansing algorithms, and assigning unique global identifiers to matched records.

- **Consolidation style**: In this style, the data is usually gathered from multiple sources and consolidated in a hub to create a single version of the truth, which is sometimes referred to as the **golden record**.

- **Coexistence style**: This style is similar to the consolidation style in the sense that it creates a golden record, but the master data changes can take place either in the MDM hub or in the data source systems.

Now that you have been reminded of these three MDM styles, take a moment to think of your data strategy again in light of the shared requirements. Keep in mind that you *can* combine multiple MDM styles, probably in phases.

Did you create a plan in your mind? OK, let's cross-check it together.

Deduplicating source records to create a consolidated, unique, golden record can be achieved using an MDM tool that implements the consolidation style. Considering that deduplicating can get very complicated, especially with the absence of strong attributes (such as an email address or phone number in a specific format), we need a tool capable of executing fuzzy-logic matching rather than exact matching.

Does that sound familiar? We came across the same challenge in *Chapter 13, Present and Defend – First Mock*. For this part of the solution, we can propose using **Informatica MDM**.

Informatica's ETL capabilities will also be useful to help us identify and select the *active customers* that we will be migrating to Salesforce.

We finally come to the last part of the requirement, where we need to link the unique customers with the duplicated and redundant customer records in the ERPs. For that, you need an MDM tool that supports the **registry style**.

This tool will have its own fuzzy-logic matching. It will use that to identify the different representations of the customer across all ERPs. Then, instead of merging records to create a golden number, it will simply generate a **global ID** and assign it to the customer records on all relevant systems. Once that is done, you can get a 360° view of the customer across all systems using the **global ID**, despite data redundancies. Salesforce Customer 360 Data Manager is an example of such a tool.

> **Remember**
>
> Do not attempt to propose new products just because they are new and therefore you assume that they will solve all problems and challenges. Many challenges can be addressed using tools that have been in the market for years. Propose tools that you know would work based on your knowledge and experience.

The following example diagram illustrates the difference between the **consolidation** and **registry MDM** styles:

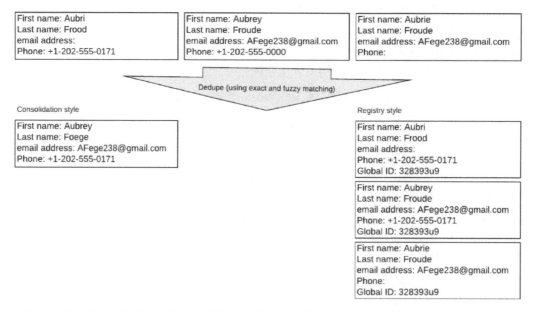

Figure 15.1 – Example illustrating the difference between the MDM consolidation and registry styles

We are now clear on our proposed solution. To help make this even easier to communicate, you can create a simple diagram such as the following:

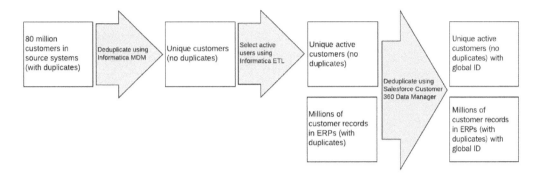

Figure 15.2 – Proposed data migration stages

Diagrams will make it easier for you to present the solution and make it more comfortable for the audience to understand it. Feel free to add other details to your diagram, such as the expected input (for example, CSV files). We still need to explain our migration approach, plan, and considerations. But let's go through the next requirement first to get a better understanding of the scope.

The legacy CRMs have details for over 200 million meters. The vast number of records is due to significant record redundancy

The actual number of meters to migrate is expected to be less than 10 million. PLU would like to clean up the data and maintain a single record for each meter to develop a 360° asset view.

Here is another deduplication requirement. However, it is a bit different because meters are always strongly identified using a meter ID. The MDM tool still needs to consolidate the input records to create a unique golden record for each meter.

Luckily, we already have an MDM tool capable of delivering MDM consolidation. Let's update our landscape architecture diagram to include the migration interfaces. Let's also update our list of interfaces.

Your landscape architecture diagram could look like the following:

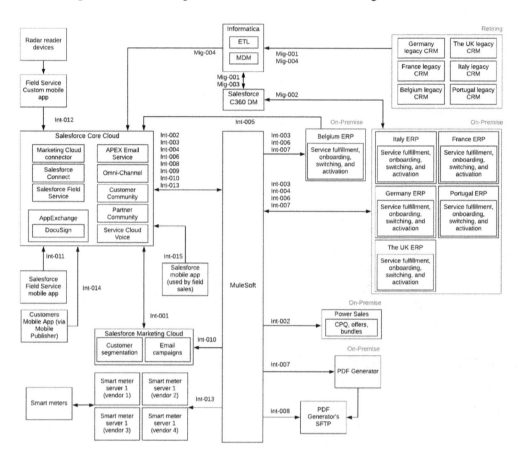

Figure 15.3 – Landscape architecture – fourth draft

The list of data migration interfaces would look like the following:

Interface Code	Source / Destination	Integration Layer	Integration Pattern	Description	Security	Authentication
Mig-001	Legacy CRM apps -> Informatica -> C360 DM	Data	Batch data synch - Asynch	Customer data will be loaded from the legacy CRMs to C360 data manager using Informatica ETL. C360 DM will identify duplicate records and assign a Global party ID to the uniquely identified records. C360 will use fuzzy logic and complex matching algorithms. At a later stage, data will be exported from C360 DM and loaded into Salesforce.	HTTPS (one way SSL/ TLS)	oAuth 2.0 web-server flow
Mig-002	ERPs -> C360 DM -> ERPs	Data	Batch data synch - Asynch	Customer records will be extracted from the ERPs (knowing that we have duplicates) and loaded into C360 DM. We have already loaded the customer records in Mig-001. C360 will identify duplicate records and assign a Global party ID to the uniquely identified records. C360 will use fuzzy logic and complex matching algorithms. We will tag all input data with the Global party ID generated. This data will then be used to update back the records in the ERPs. This activity will ensure that we have the customer's Global IDs attached to all relevant records in the ERPs.	HTTPS (one way SSL/ TLS)	oAuth 2.0 web-server flow
Mig-003	C360 DM -> Informatica -> Salesforce	Data	Batch data synch - Asynch	The unique customers identified by C360 DM after loading data into it via Mig-001 will now have a Global IDs (also known as Global party IDs) associated each record. This data will be loaded into Salesforce using Informatica ETL.	HTTPS (one way SSL/ TLS)	oAuth 2.0 web-server flow
Mig-004	Legacy CRM apps -> Informatica -> Salesforce	Data	Batch data synch - Asynch	Meter records will be migrated from the legacy CRMs to Informatica MDM where they get deduplicated based on simple logic (relying on the meter ID). Once that is accomplished, deduplicated meter records will be loaded into Salesforce.	HTTPS (one way SSL/ TLS)	oAuth 2.0 web-server flow

Figure 15.4 – Data migration interfaces – final

We learned in *Chapter 13, Present and Defend – First Mock*, that we need to address the following questions:

- How are you planning to get the data from their data sources?

- How would you eventually load them into Salesforce? What are the considerations that the client needs to be aware of and how do we mitigate the potential risks?

- What is the proposed migration plan?

- What is your migrated approach (big bang versus ongoing accumulative approach)? Why?

Let's cover these later in this chapter, when we formulate our data migration presentation. For the time being, we need to review our LDV mitigation strategy. We have penciled several objects as potential LDVs in our data model, but we still need to do the math to confirm it. Once we do, we need to craft a mitigation strategy. Let's tackle this challenge next.

Reviewing identified LDVs and developing a mitigation strategy

Going through the scenario, we can identify several objects that could potentially be LDVs. Let's list them all and do the math to determine whether they are LDVs or not. You can use a table like the following:

Object	Expected number of records	Is LDV?	Mitigation strategy
Account	6,700,000 customer records (B2B and B2C) plus properties (specific account record type), which is assumed to be equal to 25% more than the number of customers (some customers are related to more than one property). That is nearly 8.5 million records. In total, we can assume nearly 15,200,000 records.	Yes	We need to keep this object as slim as possible by archiving inactive customers whenever possible. Accounts will be archived using big objects.
Contact	Every person account consumes an account and a contact record. This means we have nearly 6 million B2C customer contacts. We can also have up to five contacts per B2B account, which is almost 1.4 million records. In total, we have nearly 7.4 million records.	Yes. Although the number of records is not massive, this object will be directly impacted by the Account archiving strategy	We need to keep this object as slim as possible by archiving inactive contacts whenever possible. Contacts will be archived using big objects.
Asset	6 million B2C customers. On average, 1.5 of them have subscriptions to both electricity and gas. 80% of B2B customers are signed up for both electricity and gas. Key customers will have an average of 10 properties. We roughly have 12,150,000 total assets.	Yes	We need to keep this object as slim as possible by archiving inactive assets whenever possible. Assets will be archived using big objects.
Contract_Line_item__c	Similar to Assets. 12,150,000 total assets.	Yes	Similar to assets. This object will be archived using big objects

Object	Expected number of records	Is LDV?	Mitigation strategy
Contract	We can assume one active contract per customer (which covers one or more products). This means we have around 6,700,000 potential records.	Yes. Although the number of records is not massive.	This object is tightly related to Assets and `Contract_Line_item__c`. It should be archived in a similar way to them. Contracts will be archived using big objects.
`Meter__c`	10 million	No	This object doesn't grow much in size; therefore, it is not considered an LDV.
`Meter_Reading__c`	24.5 million (per year)	Yes	All meter readings more than 2 years old should be archived using big objects.
`Quote`	A quote is generated for each new online signup process. This is assumed to be less than 1 million per year.	No	
`Opportunity`	Opportunity is only used for B2B deals. This is assumed to be less than 500,000 per year.	No	
`Case`	PLU has an average of three cases per customer per year. This is nearly 20 million records. Not including other types of cases (reporting a failure).	Yes	All cases of more than 1 year old should be archived using big objects.
`AccountContact Relation`	This object will be heavily utilized to control record visibility. We can assume more than 10 million records (based on 8.5 million properties and 6.7 million customers, some are related to more than one property).	Yes	This object is tightly related to accounts (person account, property) and contact. It should be archived in a similar way to them. The AccountContactRelation object will be archived using big objects (for the sake of data integrity only, as it won't be driving any record visibility anymore).

Table 15.1 – Main objects and identified LDVs

We have several LDV objects, many that we can't shift to an off-platform solution because we need the data to exist in Salesforce to execute business logic (such as auto-renewals, lead generation, and more).

We can mitigate these objects' LDV impact by ensuring they stay as slim as possible and archive records whenever possible. Some business rules have been shared in the scenario, while we have to assume others.

PLU doesn't currently have a data warehouse to archive the records to. We can either propose one, archive to **Heroku**, or archive to **Salesforce big objects**.

We don't have Heroku in our landscape but don't let that stop you from proposing it. Data archiving is a fair enough reason to justify that. However, keep in mind that big objects are also great for such use cases. We compared the two products in *Chapter 7, Designing a Scalable Salesforce Data Architecture*. For this scenario, let's use **big objects**.

We can populate the big objects using APEX, but there is a more scalable and easier-to-manage way. We already have an ETL in our landscape; let's utilize it. Informatica will be handling all the archiving jobs from **sObjects** to **big objects**.

Objects mastered in the ERPs such as `Invoice_Header__x`, `Invoice_Line_Item__x`, and `Payment__x` are not a concern for us considering that their data is stored outside the Salesforce platform.

Let's update our landscape architecture, list of interfaces, and data model. Your data model could look like the following:

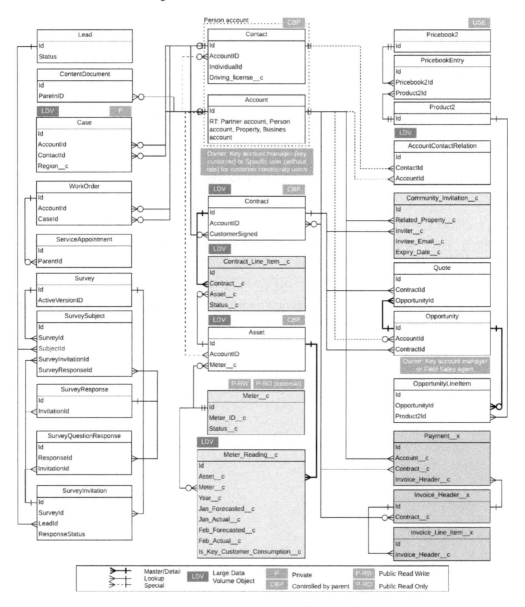

Figure 15.5 – Data model – fourth draft

Let's now move forward and start analyzing the accessibility and security requirements, which is usually the second most tricky part of an exam scenario.

Analyzing the accessibility and security requirements

The accessibility and security section requirements are usually the second most difficult to tackle after the business processes requirements. In contrast to the business process requirements, they don't tend to be lengthy, but rather more technically challenging.

You might need to adjust your data model, role hierarchy, and possibly your actors and licenses diagram. The good news is that there is a limited number of possible sharing functionalities available. You have a small pool of tools to choose from. However, you have to know each of these tools well in order to select the correct combination.

Let's start with the first shared requirement, as follows.

Key customers and their meter readings are only visible to the key customer manager

In our proposed solution for the key customer management process in *Chapter 14, Practice the Review Board – Second Mock*, we mentioned that a **key customer manager** would eventually own the **key customer's business account**. We also noted that other relevant **key customer managers** would be added to the **account team**. This will ensure these users and their managers have access to the required **account** record.

The OWD of the Account object is private, which means other users can't access these records. We can grant the support agents visibility using **criteria-based sharing rules**. The support agents require access to all accounts actually, including key customers. We can create a sharing rule that shares all Account records with the support agent role and anyone on top in the hierarchy.

The Meter_Reading__c object is linked via a master/detail relationship with the relevant **asset**, which, in turn, is related to a **property** (a special Account record type). To fulfill the requirement, we need to ensure that the property record is visible to the right users only.

The **parent account** relationship is not enough to grant record visibility. A possible approach would be to copy the **account team** members to all relevant **properties**. We can rely on a **Lightning flow** to do the job, but we need a *condition* to control it. The condition could simply rely on an Is_Key_Customer__c flag on the business account.

Once that flag is checked, the **flow** will copy all account team members to the relevant properties. The flow will also execute every time we add a new account team member to the business account.

We will also need another flow that fires upon linking a new property to a business account to automatically copy the account team members to the newly connected property record.

Update your data model diagram, and let's move on to the next requirement, as follows.

The key customer manager should be able to delegate the visibility of a customer account to another manager for a specific period

Once the specified period of visibility is passed, the record should not be visible anymore to the delegated manager.

Salesforce provides a way to delegate approvals to other users, but it doesn't offer the requested functionality out of the box. If you are unaware of a third-party product (for example, from AppExchange) that offers such capability, then you need to design it yourself.

You can propose doing this in multiple ways, including the following:

- Define a new **account team role** with a name that indicates a pre-defined duration (for example, `Temp Admin - 7 days`). The **key account manager** can add a new **account team member** using that role. This will grant the user access to the `Account` record. We can then have a scheduled job that queries records based on their creation date and names (for example, query all `AccountTeamMember` records created more than 7 days ago and has the role `Temp Admin - 7 days`) and deletes them. This will ensure that the delegated users do not get access beyond the allowed period.

- Create a similar logic using a new custom object. You can define the exact start and end dates on that custom object. The batch job would either create or delete **account team member** entries based on the settings in the custom object. You can even extend this solution beyond the `Account` object and include other standard or custom objects. In that case, you won't be utilizing the **account teams**. Instead, you would create **share** records via APEX.

  This solution offers more customization capabilities and enables more advanced use cases, such as defining time-based delegated sharing for all records of a particular object.

Let's pick the second option as it is more flexible and future-embracing. Don't be shy about explaining both options during the presentation as long as you have enough time.

Now, let's introduce a new custom object, `Delegated_Record_Access__c`, add it to our data model, and move on to the next requirement.

A complaint is only visible to the agent who is managing it and their manager

Complaints are modeled as cases in our solution. This means the `Case` object's OWD will be **private**. The agent managing a complaint will also own it, making the record visible to the agent and the agent's manager by default.

Finally, we can simply grant the set of superusers the **View All** permission on the `Case` object. But this will grant them visibility to all types of cases, not just complaints. Alternatively, we can create a public group, add the designated users to it, and then create a **criteria-based sharing rule** to share all complaints.

Be very careful when proposing a solution that relies on the **View All** or **Modify All** object permissions. The advantage of using these permissions is that they allow users to access records without evaluating the record-sharing settings. This enhances performance. However, they might be granting the users more access than they should. It is recommended to avoid them unless there is a valid reason to justify using them. We covered that earlier in *Chapter 6, Formulating a Secure Architecture in Salesforce*.

Let's now move on to the next shared requirement.

Inquiries should be visible to all support agents

Inquiries are modeled as cases in our solution. We can create a criteria-based sharing rule to share all inquiries with the support agents role. Let's move on to the next requirement, as follows.

The maintenance partners records should be visible to the support agents only

Maintenance partner account records should be visible, but not editable, to all support agents. We can achieve that by creating a criteria-based sharing rule to share the relevant accounts with the support agents role. The access level on the sharing rule can be set to **Read Only**.

Support agents who manage the direct relationship with that partner will also own the partner's `Account` record. Therefore, they have edit permission by default.

Let's now move on to the next requirement.

B2B customers should be able to manage all properties and meters related to their account

We already solved this requirement in *Chapter 14, Practice the Review Board – Second Mock*, while designing the data model. We utilized a combination of **sharing sets** and `AccountContactRelation` records to achieve the desired behavior.

It is worth mentioning that sharing sets were available for **Customer Community** licenses only, but Salesforce extended that feature to both the **Partner** and **Customer Community Plus** licenses in summer 2018 (at that time, it was public beta). More details can be found at the following link: `https://trailblazer.salesforce.com/ideaView?id=0873000000l4NcAAI`.

Let's move on to the next and final requirement.

B2C customers should be able to manage all their related properties. It is common to have a B2C customer associated with more than one property

We solved this requirement in *Chapter 14, Practice the Review Board – Second Mock*, as part of our proposed data model. We used person accounts to represent B2C customers. We utilized a combination of sharing sets and `AccountContactRelation` records to allow Community users to access multiple properties (an `Account` record type).

This concludes the accessibility and security section requirements. By now, you have covered nearly 80–85% of the scenario (complexity wise). We still have a few more requirements to solve, but we have passed most of the tricky topics. Let's continue pushing forward. Our next target is reporting requirements.

Analyzing the reporting requirements

In *Chapter 13, Present and Defend – First Mock*, we came to know that reporting requirements could occasionally impact your data model, particularly when deciding to adopt a denormalized data model to reduce the number of generated records.

Reporting could also impact your landscape architecture, list of integrations, or the licenses associated with the actors. Let's go through the requirements shared by PLU and solve them one at a time.

The global SVP of service would like a report showing service requests handled by the maintenance partners for a given year compared to data from four other years

Maintenance requests are modeled as cases in our solution. We are planning to archive all cases more than 1 year old. Although the data still technically exists on the platform (in big objects), we still can't use standard reports and dashboards with it.

There are two potential ways to fulfill this requirement:

- Using **Async SOQL** to extract aggregated data. You can use Async SOQL to extract and aggregate your archived data and load it into a custom object. You can then use standard reports and dashboards with this object.

- Use an analytics tool such as **Tableau CRM**. This option will allow further flexibility and the ability to drill into the data behind dashboards. Tableau CRM (formerly **Einstein Analytics**) has a connector that can retrieve data from big objects.

Let's use the second approach. It doesn't require custom development and provides more flexibility to embrace future requirements.

Update your landscape architecture and list of integration interfaces, then let's move on to the next requirement, as follows.

The global SVP of the service would like a dashboard showing the number of inquiries and complaints received and resolved broken down by country and region

This requirement can be fulfilled using standard reports and dashboards, assuming that the past year's data is enough. The SVP already has access to the mentioned data. The question didn't specify a timeframe for the data. Let's not overcomplicate things for ourselves and simply assume that data from the past year is good enough to meet the expectations.

Let's move on to the next requirement.

Key customer managers would like a set of business intelligence reports showing business improvements gained by switching the key customers from the previous tariffs to new tariffs

Reporting requirements that indicate *business intelligence* are generally beyond the grasp of the standard platform capabilities. Standard **reports and dashboards** will fall short of such requirements, except if you invest in developing a custom solution that creates aggregated data that you can report on.

For such requirements, you should consider an analytics and business intelligence tool such as Tableau CRM. Luckily, we already have it in our landscape architecture. Let's use it for this requirement too. Ensure you call that out during your presentation.

Let's now move on to the next requirement.

PLU would like to offer their customers a dashboard showing the change in their consumption across the past 2 years

We maintain meter readings on the platform for 2 years using the custom `Meter_Reading__c` object. We can easily develop a report that shows the change in consumption using that object.

Are we missing anything here? Yes, Customer Community users don't have access to standard reports and dashboards, but Customer Community Plus users do. Shall we adjust our proposed solution and use Customer Community Plus licenses with both B2C and B2B customers?

The answer is *no*. We selected the B2C licenses based on solid logic. We had millions of customers, and we needed a license suitable for that number of users. Don't lose faith in your logic because of such requirements. Hold your ground and think of a potential solution.

You can easily develop a custom Lightning component with a nice graph showing user consumption. This will indeed require custom development (which we usually try to avoid) but it is well justified.

Switching to the Customer Community Plus license will have far more impact on the solution, not only from a cost perspective but, more importantly, from a technical perspective. Customer Community Plus users consume portal roles, which are limited. We covered that in detail in *Chapter 6, Formulating a Secure Architecture in Salesforce*.

Let's stick with our proposed customer licenses and use a custom-developed Lightning component to fulfill this requirement. Our rationale is clear and our design decision is justified.

That concludes the requirements of the reporting section. We are getting closer now. The last part of the scenario normally lists requirements related to the governance and development life cycle. Keep that momentum, and let's tackle the next set of requirements.

Analyzing the project development requirements

This part of the scenario would generally focus on the tools and techniques used to govern the development and release process in a Salesforce project. As mentioned before in *Chapter 13, Present and Defend – First Mock*, the artifacts we created earlier in *Chapter 10, Development Life Cycle and Deployment Planning*, such as *Figure 10.3 – Proposed CoE structure, Figure 10.4 – Proposed DA structure*, and *Figure 10.7 – Development life cycle diagram – final*, are handy to pass this part of the scenario.

You need to fully understand and *believe in* the values that organizational structures such as the **CoE** or the **Design Authority** (**DA**) bring. You need to know *why* customers should consider *CI/CD*; not just the market hype, but the actual *value* brought up by these techniques to the development and release strategy.

We will now go through the different PLU requirements and see how we can put these artifacts into action to resolve some of the raised challenges. Let's start with the first requirement.

PLU would like to start realizing value quickly and get Salesforce functionalities as soon as possible

This requirement represents a common trend in today's enterprise world. Enterprises are all eager to switch to a more agile fashion of product adoption. It is simply not acceptable for enterprises to wait for years to start realizing their investment's value. They are willing to embark on an understandably long journey to roll out a new system across the enterprise fully, but they want to start reaping some of the value as soon as possible.

This is why the concept of **Minimum Viable Product** (**MVP**) has gained so much traction in the past few years. The MVP concept promises a quick reap of value with minimal efforts and, therefore, financial risk. An MVP contains core functionalities that the full product would eventually include. These core functionalities allow additional features to be developed around and extended with time.

Think about it this way. You can theoretically start reaping out the benefits of your newly built house as long as you have it in a habitable form. You can later on make it homelier by adding decorations, tidying up the garden, adding a nice garage, and so on.

The MVP allows enterprises to start gaining benefits without waiting until the end of the program. This effectively reduces the overall risk as the users will start using the new system in a matter of weeks/a few months rather than years.

The art of determining what belongs to an MVP scope and what does not is out of scope for this book and is at the heart of modern **product management**. You can read more about this from other books such as *Lean Product Management* by Mangalam Nandakumar.

Note

Solid product management alone won't be enough to develop a scalable MVP solution. In real life, you need to combine that with the right technical guidance (offered by the design authority), overall governance (provided by the CoE), and the right delivery methodology. Otherwise, you could risk developing an MVP that doesn't extend or scale well.

This is particularly relevant to Salesforce projects mainly because the platform is flexible, dynamic, and full of ready-to-use functionalities, which could be tempting to quickly put together an MVP solution, which, without proper planning and governance, could easily miss its future potential.

Coming back to PLU's requirement, this can be met by adopting an MVP style of product design and development. In your presentation, you need to briefly explain what an MVP solution is, the value it brings, and how you can ensure it meets its future potential. Let's now move on to the next requirement.

The team maintaining the ERPs work in a 6-month release cycle, and they are unable to modify their timeline to suit this project

This could potentially be a risk. You need to bring up any foreseen risks during your presentation. Considering the ERPs' release cycle, we might encounter situations where a Salesforce release is held back until the next ERP release. This means there will be a need to carefully manage and select the released Salesforce features in any version.

Moreover, you should have the right environment structure to control feature developments and the right integration strategy to enable loose coupling.

Our proposed environment structure and development life cycle strategy should cater to these requirements and clearly explain how they would address this risk. We will cover this in our presentation pitch later on in this chapter.

Let's move on to the next requirement, as follows.

Historically, the customer support team is used to high-productivity systems, and they have a regulatory requirement to handle calls in no more than 10 minutes

We can improve the productivity of the customer support team using the **Service Cloud** console. The console allows configuring some shortcuts as well to meet PLU's expectations. Also, **Service Cloud Voice** allows automatic contact lookup based on the caller's phone number. **Salesforce** macros can also be used to speed up some repetitive tasks (such as sending an email to the customer and updating the case record with a single click).

All these features will further improve the productivity and response time of the customer support team.

Let's now move on to the next requirement.

PLU would like to get support in identifying potential project risks

We have already come across three potential risks:

- The design and governance of the MVP solution

- Aligning the relatively slow release cycle of the ERPs with the quick release cycle adopted by Salesforce

- Managing the user expectations and performance while switching to a cloud- / browser-based solution compared to a high-productivity desktop application

We need to call each of these out during the presentation and clearly explain how we plan to mitigate each of them. We will do that later on in this chapter.

Let's now move on to the next requirement.

PLU would like to have a clear, traceable way to track features developed throughout the project life cycle

In *Chapter 10*, *Development Life Cycle and Deployment Planning*, we came across several techniques to govern a release cycle, including tracking developed features.

We have also learned that the best mechanism to handle such situations in Salesforce is by implementing **source code-driven development** using a **multi-layered development environment**.

Source code-driven development will allow you to maintain a trackable audit trail that shows the developed features at any given time of your project life cycle.

This requirement is also related to the next. Let's go through that to help us formulate a comprehensive response for both. The next requirement is as follows.

PLU is looking for recommendations for the right environment management strategy to ensure the proper tests are executed at each stage

This requirement could be asked in several different ways. The answer will always lead you to what we described in *Chapter 10*, *Development Life Cycle and Deployment Planning*. The multi-layered development environment and automated release management and test automation tools and techniques should be used to fulfill this requirement.

We saw a sample development life cycle diagram, *Figure 10.7 – Development life cycle diagram – final*, which we used as the base for our proposed environment management and development life cycle diagram in *Chapter 13, Present and Defend – First Mock*. We will use the same diagram as the base for this scenario too. We can assume one development stream in this case. Your diagram could look like the following:

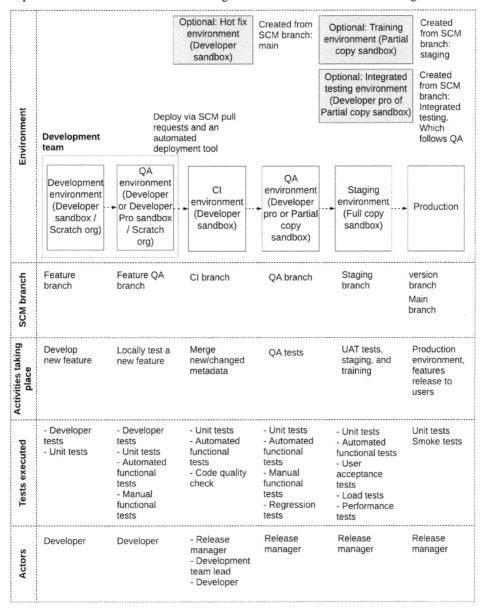

Figure 15.6 – Development life cycle diagram – final

You'll notice that we still have a CI sandbox (also known as the *build* sandbox) and QA sandboxes before and after the CI environment. Why do we need them? After all, we only have one development stream, and things will be more straightforward with fewer environments, right? Not exactly.

Your release strategy should be *future-embracing*. It should never be short-sighted to cover near-future requirements only. Your strategy should be able to extend and accommodate multiple project streams developing new/updated features concurrently, even if this is not currently an urgent requirement.

In most Salesforce projects, there will be at least two concurrent streams at any given time: a stream building and developing new features, and a stream maintaining production, fixing, and patching any encountered bugs. All code changes should ideally be merged into the CI environment to follow the designed pipeline (apart from some exceptional cases). Your environment strategy should be able to cater to that and more.

Local QA environments help the development team test their functionalities before they can progress any further. Shared QA environments are typically managed by dedicated testing teams who ensure that everything fits together and works as expected.

Things will indeed get more complicated with additional environments, except if you have the right tools in place to support you. This is why **source control management (SCM)** and **automated build and release management** tools are crucial for any enterprise-scale Salesforce project's success.

For PLU's scenario, we need to suggest an automated build and release tool. Let's propose a tool such as **Copado**. We also need to add an automated testing tool such as **Provar**. Keep in mind that you still need to explain how your unit tests would work side by side with **Provar** to provide a comprehensive testing experience. We will cover that later on in this chapter while crafting our presentation pitch.

Add **Copado** and **Provar** to your landscape diagram, and let's move on to the next and final requirement.

PLU is looking for an appropriate methodology to manage the project delivery and ensure proper technical governance

This is a combined requirement that you can address using the knowledge you gained regarding the various developing methodologies and the different governance bodies we came to know about in *Chapter 10, Development Life Cycle and Deployment Planning*.

You need a delivery methodology capable of supporting the MVP solution. A methodology that caters for a *blueprinting phase* to *plan* the *program's outcome* and define how that would be achieved, preferably with some **proofs of concept**. However, the methodology should also be flexible enough to *accommodate* and *embrace* other requirements beyond the MVP phase. This all should point you to the **hybrid methodology**.

To ensure technical governance, you need a governing body capable of bringing together the right people at the right time to make decisions, empowered by executive sponsorship, and supported by expertise from around the enterprise. This is precisely what the CoE is.

Besides, you need to have an ongoing activity to validate, challenge, and ratify each design decision required during the project delivery, which is exactly what the **DA** is meant to do. MVP solutions accumulate additional functionalities with time and become more complex. With the DA structure in place, we ensure that every user story's solution is challenged and technically validated by the right people before we start delivering it.

That concludes the requirements of the project development section. The next section is usually limited and contains other general topics and challenges. Let's maintain our momentum and continue on to the next set of requirements.

Analyzing the other requirements

The *other requirements* section in a full mock scenario could contain further requirements about anything else that has not yet been covered by the other sections. There are usually a limited number of requirements in this section.

Your experience and broad knowledge about the Salesforce platform and its ecosystem would play a vital role at this stage. Let's explore the shared requirements.

PLU has recently acquired a company working in renewable energy

They manufacture and install solar panels as well as electric batteries. The acquired company is also utilizing Salesforce as their central CRM. PLU would like to know whether they should plan to merge this Salesforce instance with theirs or keep it separate and are looking for your support with this decision.

The org strategy is something you need to consider for every review board scenario you come across. You should come up with a clear recommendation and a valid rationale behind whether you decide to propose a single org or multi-orgs. We listed some pros and cons for each in *Chapter 5, Developing a Scalable System Architecture*.

In this scenario, we come across a use case where there is already a second org inherited via company acquisition. The efforts to merge this Salesforce instance with PLU's should be considered and never underestimated.

Moreover, the newly acquired company works in a slightly different business. Manufacturing, distributing, and installing solar panels and electric batteries will understandably have a completely different set of sales and service processes and activities. In such cases, you will typically find limited interaction between the two businesses.

The acquired company will likely have its own set of supporting systems, such as ERPs and HR solutions. It is also common to keep the two companies' financials separate or embark on a 3–5-year transition period.

For all of these reasons, it is safer to assume a multi-org strategy. Global reporting requirements—if any—can be accommodated using business intelligence tools such as Tableau CRM.

As we don't know much about this new org, we will not include it in our landscape architecture diagram. You can simply explain the proposed org strategy and the rationale behind it during the presentation.

Your landscape architecture diagram could now look like the following:

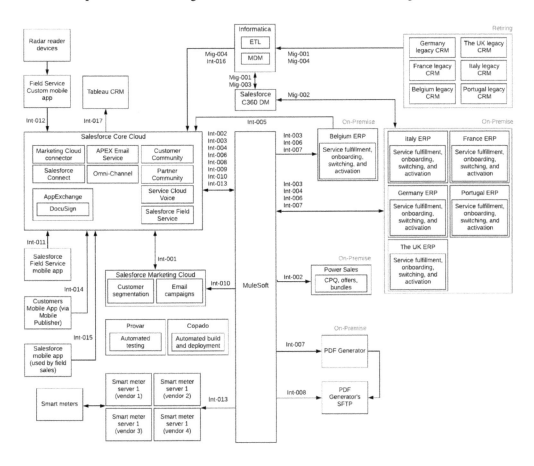

Figure 15.7 – Landscape architecture – final

We split the list of integration interfaces into two diagrams to improve readability. The first part of the list of integration interfaces could look like the following:

Interface Code	Source / Destination	Integration Layer	Integration Pattern	Description	Security	Authentication
Int-001	Salesforce <-> Marketing cloud	Data	Batch Data Synchronizatio n - Asynch	Synch data such as contacts and leads from Salesforce to Marketing cloud and vice versa using the marketing cloud connector	HTTPS (one way SSL/TLS)	oAuth 2.0 Client Credentials flow (to authenticate to Marketing cloud) oAuth 2.0 web-server flow (to authenticate to Salesforce)
Int-002	Salesforce -> MuleSoft -> Power Sales	Business logic	Remote process invocation - request and reply - Blocking	Invoke multiple methods and get back quote details from Power Cloud. The APIs can be invoked using buttons within a custom UI in Salesforce. Once the button is clicked, an APEX controller would invoke the MuleSoft API. Once invoked, MuleSoft will determine if it is going to call one of Power Sales APIs or connect directly to its database to execute the logic (such as creating a quote). Once the result is returned, the APEX controller creates a Salesforce Quote record and link it to the relevant Opportunity	HTTPS (two way SSL/TLS) between Salesforce and MuleSoft. HTTPS (one way SSL/TLS) Between MuleSoft and Power Sales	oAuth 2.0 web-server flow (then refresh token flow) with mutual authentication between Salesforce and MuleSoft. Simple authentication between MuleSoft and Power Sales
Int-003	Salesforce -> MuleSoft -> The right ERP	Data	Remote Process Invocation— Fire and Forget	Fire a platform event from Salesforce. This will be subscribed to by MuleSoft. MuleSoft will use the data in the Platform Event to determine the right ERP to send the data to.	HTTPS (one way SSL/TLS)	oAuth 2.0 JWT bearer token flow

Interface Code	Source / Destination	Integration Layer	Integration Pattern	Description	Security	Authentication
Int-004	ERPs (except Belgium's) -> MuleSoft -> Salesforce	Data	Remote Call-In	The ERPs will send a message to MuleSoft to indicate the completion of the Switching process. MuleSoft would then invoke the standard Salesforce REST API to update the relevant record.	HTTPS (two way SSL/TLS) between Salesforce and MuleSoft. HTTPS (one way SSL/TLS) Between MuleSoft and the ERPs	oAuth 2.0 web-server flow (then refresh token flow) with mutual authentication between Salesforce and MuleSoft. Simple authentication between MuleSoft and the ERPs
Int-005	Belgium ERP -> Salesforce	Data	Remote Call-In (Email)	An email sent by the Belgium ERP using an SMTP server and received by a Salesforce custom APEX Email Service	HTTPS (one way SSL/TLS)	None (to Salesforce). Simple authentication with the SMTP server.
Int-006	MuleSoft -> Salesforce	UI	Data Virtualization / Mashup / oData	Invoices, invoice line items, and Payments are displayed in Salesforce using Salesforce Connect. MuleSoft fetches the data from the relevant ERPs and aggregate them using an oData interface.	HTTPS (one way SSL/TLS)	oAuth 2.0 web-server flow (then refresh token flow)
Int-007	MuleSoft -> ERPs MuleSoft -> PDF generator	Business logic	Remote process invocation - request and reply - Blocking	A scheduled MuleSoft job retrieves new invoice data and pass them to the PDF Generator to generate PDF invoices.	HTTPS (one way SSL/TLS)	Simple authentication
Int-008	MuleSoft -> SFTP MuleSoft -> Salesforce	Data	Batch Data Synchronization - Asynch	A scheduled MuleSoft job retrieves PDF invoices from the SFTP and transfers them to Salesforce	HTTPS (two way SSL/TLS) between Salesforce and MuleSoft. HTTPS (one way SSL/TLS) Between MuleSoft and SFTP	oAuth 2.0 web-server flow (then refresh token flow) with mutual authentication between Salesforce and MuleSoft. Simple authentication between MuleSoft and the SFTP

Figure 15.8 Integration interfaces (part one) – final

The second part of the list of the integration interfaces could look like the following:

Interface Code	Source / Destination	Integration Layer	Integration Pattern	Description	Security	Authentication
Int-009	Salesforce -> MuleSoft	Data	Remote Process Invocation— Fire and Forget	Fire a platform event from Salesforce for any newly created Critical Incident (Case). This will be subscribed to by MuleSoft. MuleSoft will use the data in the Platform Event to query back Salesforce for additional details	HTTPS (one way SSL/TLS)	oAuth 2.0 JWT bearer token flow
Int-010	MuleSoft -> Salesforce MuleSoft -> Marketing Cloud	Business logic	Remote process invocation - request and reply - Blocking	MuleSoft queries Salesforce for Customer records that are impacted by a critical Incident (Case). Then invokes the Marketing Cloud Transactional Messaging API to send SMS notifications to these customers	HTTPS (two way SSL/TLS) between Salesforce and MuleSoft. HTTPS (one way SSL/TLS) Between MuleSoft and Marketing Cloud	oAuth 2.0 web-server flow (then refresh token flow)
Int-012	Custom mobile app <-> Salesforce	Data	Remote Call-In	The mobile application communicate with the Radar reader via Bluetooth, read values, cache them locally, then transfer them to Salesforce using the REST API	HTTPS (one way SSL/TLS)	OpenID connect flow (then refresh token flow)
Int-013	MuleSoft -> Smart meter platforms MuleSoft -> Salesforce	Data	Remote Call-In	A scheduled MuleSoft job that retrieves meter readings from the different platforms. The data is then transformed to a unified structure and combined together. The combined data set is then used to update Salesforce.	HTTPS (two way SSL/TLS) between Salesforce and MuleSoft. HTTPS (one way SSL/TLS) Between MuleSoft and the Platforms	oAuth 2.0 web-server flow (then refresh token flow) with mutual authentication between Salesforce and MuleSoft. Simple authentication between MuleSoft and the Platforms

Interface Code	Source / Destination	Integration Layer	Integration Pattern	Description	Security	Authentication
Int-014	Salesforce Mobile app (via Mobile publisher) -> Salesforce	Data	Remote Call-In	The mobile application will invoke the REST API to query, create, or update records	HTTPS (one way SSL/TLS)	OpenID connect flow (then refresh token flow)
Int-015	Salesforce Mobile app -> Salesforce	Data	Remote Call-In	The mobile application will invoke the REST API to query, create, or update records	HTTPS (one way SSL/TLS)	OpenID connect flow (then refresh token flow)
Int-016	Informatica -> Salesforce	Data	Remote Call-In	Informatica will handle archiving all identified LDV objects into Big Objects. Informatica will also hard- delete all archived records from sObjects	HTTPS (one way SSL/TLS)	oAuth 2.0 web-server flow (then refresh token flow)
Int-017	Salesforce -> Tableau CRM	Data	Batch Data Synchronizatio n - Asynch	A selected set of Salesforce data in standard, custom, and big objects are copied to Tableau CRM to enable historical and trending reports. The data is pulled/retrieved from Salesforce using Tableau CRM's connector.	HTTPS (one way SSL/TLS)	oAuth 2.0 web-server flow (then refresh token flow)

Figure 15.9 – Integration interfaces (part two) – final

Your actors and licenses diagram could look like the following:

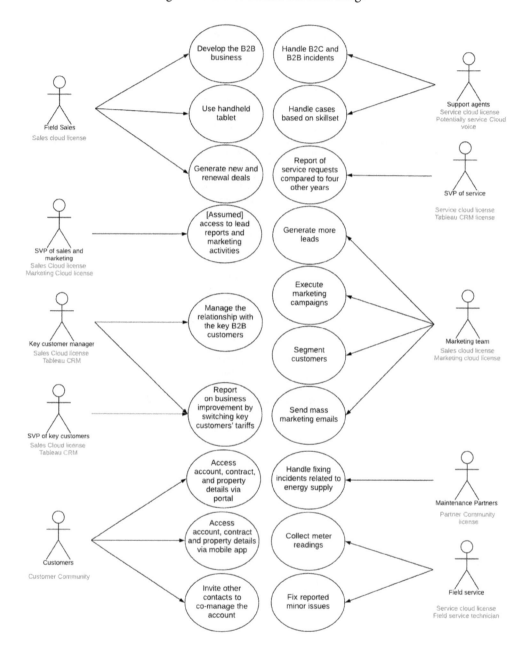

Figure 15.10 – Actors and licenses – final

Your data model diagram could look like the following:

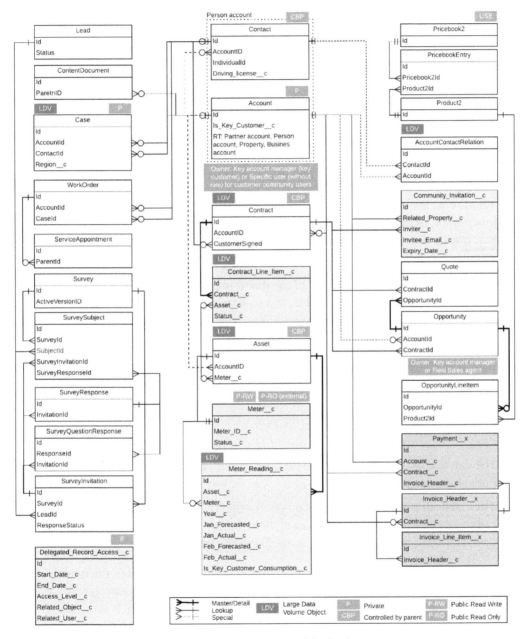

Figure 15.11 – Data model – final

No changes occurred in the role hierarchy diagram.

Congratulations! You managed to complete your second full scenario. You have created a scalable and secure end-to-end solution. We need to pair that now with a strong, engaging, and attractive presentation to nail down as many marks as possible and leave the Q&A stage to close down a few gaps only.

Ready for the next stage? Let's do it.

Presenting and justifying your solution

It is now time to create your presentation. This is something you would have to do on the go during the review board as you would likely consume all 3 hours creating the solution and supporting artifacts.

As we mentioned before in *Chapter 13, Present and Defend – First Mock*, you need to plan your presentation upfront and use your time management skills to ensure you describe the solution with enough details in the given time. We will discuss some time-keeping techniques in *Appendix, Tips and Tricks, and the Way Forward*.

You are now familiar with the structure of the board presentation. We start with the structured part of our presentation, and then we switch to the catch-all mode. As a reminder, these two different presentation phases include the following:

- **The structured part**: In this part, you describe specific pre-planned elements of your solution, starting with an overall solution introduction, including a brief walk through the created artifacts. Then, you start tackling the business processes one by one and—using the diagrams and artifacts—explain how your solution will fulfill them. After that, you need to describe your LDV mitigation and data migration strategies.

  You can add more topics as you see appropriate, assuming you have planned and budgeted enough time for that.

- **The catch-all part**: This is where you go through the requirements one by one and call out those that you haven't covered in the first part. You do this to ensure you haven't missed any requirements, particularly the straightforward ones.

In this chapter, we will create presentation pitches for the following topics: the overall solution and artifact introduction, one of the business processes, and the project development requirements. We will pick the *Customer service* process as it is the most complex and lengthy.

We will then hold our ground and defend and justify our solution, knowing that we might need to adjust our solution based on newly introduced challenges.

Let's begin creating the presentation pitches for the structured part. We will start with an overall introduction of the solution and artifacts.

Introducing the overall solution and artifacts

Similar to what we did in *Chapter 13, Present and Defend – First Mock*, start by introducing yourself; this shouldn't be more than a single paragraph. It should be as simple as the following:

> *My name is [your name], and I am here today to present the proposed solution for [the company's name in the scenario].*

Then, proceed with another short paragraph that briefly describes the company's business. This will help *you* to get into presentation mode and break the ice. You can simply utilize a shortened version of the first paragraph in the scenario, such as the following:

> *Packt Lightning Utilities (PLU) is a European electric utility company that serves several cities across Germany, Italy, France, Portugal, Belgium, and the UK. PLU operates in 40 cities. PLU offers services to both B2C customers (residential) and small and medium B2B customers*

Remember that you shouldn't use more than a minute to present yourself and set the scene. Now you can start explaining the key need of PLU using a brief paragraph, such as the following:

> *PLU has been struggling with its existing CRM solutions for many years, and as a new strategic movement, decided to switch to Salesforce. PLU is looking to use its new CRM to launch a global, unified new set of Sales and Service processes.*

It is now time to explain the current and to-be landscape architecture. Use and show your **landscape architecture diagram** to guide the audience through it; never just stand next to it and speak in a *monotone*. You should be able to look at your diagram and describe the as-is and to-be landscape. Your pitch could be as follows:

> *PLU uses six different ERP systems. They are used for service fulfillment, customer onboarding, switching, and activation. The plan is to retain all of them and integrate the new solution with them using their APIs. It is worth mentioning that the Belgium ERP doesn't offer an API.*

Data will be traveling from Salesforce to these systems and vice versa. To develop a scalable and flexible architecture, we should aim to have a unified communication interface between Salesforce and the ERP systems. Middleware such as MuleSoft would provide that capability. It will also offer the ability to orchestrate the data flow between these systems and handle any encountered exceptions.

MuleSoft will also be able to communicate directly with the flat-file database that the Belgium ERP is based on using its built-in connectors. MuleSoft won't be transferring a massive amount of data. This is what pointed me to the need for an ESB rather than an ETL. However, I am also proposing an ETL to handle data migration.

PLU uses a heavily customized CPQ solution that they are planning to retain. We will integrate with that solution using fine-grained APIs exposed by MuleSoft as the solution itself offers a poor API. Power Sales will be invoked at the right stage to calculate the price for a customer quote.

PLU also relies on electricity and gas smart meters and regular radar-based meters that need to be supported. MuleSoft will again play a key role here as a unified integration middleware.

The proposed solution is replacing a set of legacy CRM solutions across the target countries. We will explain the data migration strategy later on, but we propose an ETL tool such as Informatica to facilitate that.

The proposed solution is based on a single Salesforce org. We understand that PLU has recently acquired a new company that is also using Salesforce as their core CRM solution. But we believe that the two businesses are different and would likely need a different set of business processes. Furthermore, I assumed that the acquired company would continue to operate independently for a few years.

Based on that, I believe that we can start with a single org to accommodate PLU's requirements. This org will host all of the functionalities described in this scenario. The acquired Salesforce org will continue to operate independently, and MuleSoft will be used to link that org with other systems.

The proposed solution will also utilize Marketing Cloud for customer segmentation, email, and mobile communications. We will also use some third-party applications from AppExchange, such as DocuSign.

I have created a full list of required integration interfaces and the authentication mechanism for each. I have also created a data model diagram, which I will explain further during this presentation.

You have set the scene and briefly explained your solution. Remember to mention your org strategy (and the rationale behind it) during your presentation. You can now proceed by explaining the licenses they need to invest in. Switch to the actors and licenses diagram and continue with your pitch. Remember to use your body language to assert your authority on the stage by moving across it (if you are doing the presentation in person). Your presentation could be as follows:

I have identified the following actors. They will need different types of licenses based on their expected roles. For example, the Field Sales agents [point at them on the diagram] will need a Sales Cloud license because they need to manage the new and renewal opportunities for customers.

The Service agents will utilize a Service Cloud license as they need to work with the Case object (which represents incidents and queries). Cases will be assigned to the right agent based on the required skills. Salesforce Omni-Channel will be used for that, which also explains the need for the Service Cloud license. The Service agents will also use the Service console and Salesforce Service Cloud Voice to answer support calls.

SVPs will be using licenses that grant them access to all objects their teams have access to. They would also need a Tableau CRM license to access some trending reports that rely on data that doesn't exist in Salesforce standard or custom objects.

The key customer managers will use a Sales Cloud license as they need to use the Opportunity object to manage deals with key customers.

The marketing team will require both Sales Cloud and Marketing Cloud licenses to create and nurture leads across both systems. Moreover, they will be executing marketing campaigns and sending mass emails using Marketing Cloud.

The Field Service team will use Service Cloud and Salesforce Field Service licenses. They need access to the Salesforce Field Service capabilities, such as the mobile application, the Field Service data model, and the optimized scheduling capability.

Maintenance partners will be using the Partner Community license. We don't have many details on the tasks they do apart from handling energy supply incidents. I assumed they would need some advanced sharing capabilities and visibility to some opportunities.

Finally, customers will be using a Salesforce Customer Community Login license. It will be a good fit considering that PLU has nearly 6 million customers. This license is tailored for a vast number of users. We can manage their accessibility requirements using functionalities such as sharing sets.

That concludes the overall high-level solution presentation. This part should take no more than 5–6 minutes to cover end to end. You can use your own words, of course, but you need to adjust your speed to ensure that you cover all the required information in the given time. Keep practicing until you manage to do that. Time management is *crucial* for this exam.

Now, let's move on to the most significant part of your presentation, where you will explain how your solution will solve the shared business processes.

Presenting the business processes' end-to-end solution

We are still in the *structured* part of your presentation. If you have created a business process diagram for a business process, then this is the time to use it. Besides, you will typically use the landscape architecture diagram, the data model, and the list of interfaces to explain your end-to-end solution. You can start this part with a short intro, such as the following:

PLU shared six business processes. I will go through each and explain how the solution fulfils it.

We will create a sample presentation for the customer service business process.

Customer service

Similar to what we did in *Chapter 13, Present and Defend – First Mock*, we will try to *tell a story* that explains how their process will be realized using the new system. Your pitch could be as follows:

I will now explain how the proposed solution will fulfill the customer service process requirements.

The customer can raise inquires and complaints using an online portal or by calling the call center number. The inquires and complaints will be modeled using the standard Case object. I propose using Salesforce Omni-Channel to assign the Case record to the right agent based on the required skills, such as language. There will be a need to evaluate multiple skills. Therefore, I decided to use Omni-Channel instead of queues.

Salesforce communities will be used to create an online portal. As mentioned before, customers will be utilizing the Customer Community login license.

Salesforce Service Cloud Voice can be used to set up a phone number for the call center. Service Cloud Voice will also integrate with the Service Cloud console and provide a softphone that the agents can use to pick up calls and create cases.

I will use the case escalation rules to escalate complaints that are not resolved in 7 days. The SVP of the service will receive an email once a complaint is escalated.

One of the shared requirements indicates that the system should automatically generate a forecasted meter reading for the next month based on the previous month's reading. Considering the number of customers and meters we have in the system, and considering that we have two figures to capture each month per meter (which are the forecasted and actual consumption), I estimated a need for around 146 million records to hold this data.

This number is enormous and will directly impact the performance of the target object's CRUD operations. It will also consume a considerable amount of data storage and could have other performance impacts based on lookup skew.

I will explain all identified LDVs and how I am planning to mitigate them later on. The meter readings will be stored in a custom denormalized object. This will significantly reduce the number of needed records to capture the monthly forecasted and actual consumption [point at the Meter_Reading__c object on your data model diagram].

I will use a before-save flow to populate the next month's forecasted consumption once the actual consumption for the previous month is captured. For example, the flow will automatically populate the Feb_Forecasted__c field's value once the Jan_Actual__c field is updated.

The Meter_Reading__c object will be linked to the Asset object using a master-detail relationship. This way, any user who has access to the Asset record will be able to view its related Meter_Reading__c. Customer Community users will get access to the assets related to the Account records they have access to; therefore, they will be able to view their relevant Meter_Reading__c records.

I have assumed that invoices and payments are stored in the ERPs. I propose exposing them to customers in Salesforce using Salesforce Connect. MuleSoft connects to all the ERPs, retrieves the invoices, aggregates, and exposes them as an OData interface that Salesforce can subscribe to. I have added the following external objects to my data model [point to the Payment__x, Invoice_Header__x, and Invoice_Line_Item__x objects on your data model diagram].

Invoice PDFs will be generated via a batch MuleSoft job that runs every month, retrieves the invoice details from the ERPs, and passes them to the PDF generator system to generate PDFs [point to Int-007 on your landscape diagram and your list of interfaces]. MuleSoft would then retrieve all files stored on the SFTP and transfer them to Salesforce [point to Int-008 on your landscape diagram and your list of interfaces]. We can use a specific file naming convention that includes the account ID. This will allow MuleSoft to attach the files to the correct Account record. The PDFs will be stored using Salesforce Files [point at the Content Document object on your data model diagram].

Next, we have a requirement to create a critical incident in case of energy failure and assign it to the right maintenance partner based on the property's address. The critical incident will be another Case record type. We will use case assignment rules to assign the critical incident case to the right partner user or queue, assuming we have a field that indicates the relevant case region.

Once that is done, we need to identify all customers relevant to that particular region and send them all an SMS notification. This is a mass SMS send, a capability not available out of the box on the Salesforce platform. Therefore, we will use Marketing Cloud to fulfill this requirement.

We will send transaction emails and SMS using the Marketing Cloud Transactional Messaging API.

Once a critical incident case is created, we will fire a platform event from Salesforce to MuleSoft with the necessary case details [point at Int-009 on your landscape diagram and your list of interfaces]. MuleSoft will then query Salesforce to find out the relevant/impacted customers, then invoke Marketing Cloud's Transactional Messaging API [point at Int-010 on your landscape diagram and your list of interfaces]. MuleSoft can orchestrate the entire process in a scalable and performant way.

All communications between Salesforce and MuleSoft will be protected using two-way TLS and authenticated using OAuth 2.0 web server flow (initially, then the refresh token flow going forward).

This is a lengthy business process, but presenting its solution should not take more than 5–6 minutes. The other business processes should take less time. Practice the presentation using your own words and keep practicing until you are comfortable with delivering a similar pitch in no more than 6 minutes.

We have also seeded some questions, such as the full description of the OAuth 2.0 web server flow. If the judges feel a need to get more details, they will come back to this point during the Q&A.

Communicating Your Assumptions

We have included our assumptions in the context of the presentation. You can use this approach or simply list all your assumptions upfront. I prefer the former approach as I find it more natural and engaging.

We are not going to create a pitch for the LDV mitigation strategy. However, you can utilize the table we created earlier in this chapter. It contains a list of all identified LDV objects, the expected number of records, and the mitigation strategy.

Let's now move on to the next element of our structured presentation.

Presenting the project development and release strategy

At this stage, you have probably consumed most of the time allocated for your *structured presentation*. Let's prepare our concise project development and release strategy pitch:

PLU would like to start realizing value quickly. To achieve that, I propose following an MVP's concept in defining the functionalities included in each release. The MVP allows enterprises to start gaining benefits without waiting until the end of the program. This effectively reduces the overall risk as the users will start using the new system quickly and get additional capabilities with incremental releases.

I have identified at least three potential risks in this project; they are, firstly, the design and governance of the MVP solution. To mitigate this, we will use a governance body consisting of two parts: a CoE (Center of Excellence) to ensure the strategic decisions are taken with the involvement of all stakeholders and a DA (Design Authority) responsible for tackling the daily project challenges and coming up with a justified and audible solution based on best practices.

Next is aligning the relatively slow release cycle of the ERPs with the quick release cycle adopted by Salesforce. We will use a multi-layered development environment and integrate it with the right ERP environment to mitigate this. We will establish a loosely coupled integration between the systems using MuleSoft, which will allow us to utilize a two-speed architecture concept. The two-speed architecture will allow the integrated systems to develop at their own pace with minimal dependencies in between. A transparent backlog across the project will ensure everyone is aware of the features being developed. The CoE will ensure the right features are selected for the correct release.

The final risk is managing the user expectations and performance while switching to a cloud-/browser-based solution compared to a high-productivity desktop application. To mitigate this, we need to ensure we have the right change management process in place, including any communication campaigns, training, the definition of trailblazers/superusers, and continuous support from the executive team. We will use tools that closely match the desktop application's performance.

We will use source code-driven development using a multi-layered development environment. Source code-driven development will allow you to maintain a trackable audit trail that shows the developed features at any given time of your project life cycle.

In this diagram [point at the development life cycle diagram], you can see that we will initially have one development stream.

The team in this stream will be using a development sandbox to develop new features. They will use another developer sandbox to test the developed features without disruption from any development activities. There will be a sandbox used for the continuous merging of newly developed features from all streams.

On top of that, there will be a QA environment sandbox managed by the testing team, a staging environment, and a production environment.

Hotfixes can take place on a separate sandbox then get deployed into CI, staging, and production.

This setup will allow future streams to work in parallel and ensure that all teams are always using the latest codebase and avoiding conflicts.

I propose using an automated deployment and release management tool such as Copado and an automated test management suite such as Provar. An APEX unit test will still be used to test all critical functionalities, in addition to functionalities that cannot be tested using a UI-based automated test.

Each time a functionality is deployed from one environment to another, all APEX unit tests will be invoked. Automated test scripts will also be automatically invoked. Together, they will ensure that all regression tests are executed and newly developed features meet all the acceptance criteria. There will still be manual tests, of course, but we should aim at automating the most critical use cases.

The judges will most probably ask questions related to this domain in the Q&A stage, such as the structure of a CoE, the proposed development methodology, the rationale behind the CI environment, the use of branches in the SCM, how to keep all development environments up to date, and how to ensure the tests are consistently being invoked.

We have seeded some questions here as well. For example, we have briefly mentioned that the CI setup will allow teams to avoid conflict, but we didn't explain precisely how. We will tackle that question later on in this chapter.

Let's now move on to the catch-all phase of our presentation.

Going through the scenario and catching all the remaining requirements

At this part of the presentation, we will go through the requirements one by one and ensure we have covered each one.

We saw this approach's benefits in *Chapter 13, Present and Defend – First Mock*, where it helped us spot and solve a missed requirement. Even if you've created a perfectly structured presentation, it is recommended to leave some room to go through the requirements again and ensure you haven't missed any.

If you are doing an in-person review board, you will receive a printed version of the scenario. You will also have access to a set of pens and markers. When you read and solve the scenario, highlight or underline the requirements. If you have a solution in mind, write it next to it. This will help you during the *catch-all* part of the scenario.

If you are doing a virtual review board, you will get access to a digital version of the scenario. You have access to MS PowerPoint and Excel, and you can copy requirements to your slides/sheets and then use that during the presentation.

That concludes our presentation. The next part is the Q&A, the stage where the judges will ask questions to fill in any gaps that you have missed or not clearly explained during the presentation.

Justifying and defending your solution

We'll now move on to the Q&A, the stage that should be your friend. Relax and be proud of what you have achieved so far. You are very close to achieving your dream.

During the Q&A, you should also expect that the judges will change some requirements to test your ability to solve *on the fly*. This is all part of the exam. Let's see some example questions and answers.

The judges might decide to challenge one of your proposed solutions. This doesn't necessarily mean that it is wrong. Even if the tone suggests so, trust in yourself and your solution. Defend, but don't over-defend. If you figure out that you have made a mistake, accept it humbly and rectify your solution. The judges will appreciate that.

For example, a judge might ask the following question:

> *You proposed introducing an integration interface to pull the smart meter readings from the devices in your solution. This means that we are unable to get a real-time reading of the meters where possible. Why have you proposed this solution, and is there any alternate way that can give us real-time data?*

While answering such a question, make sure your answer is sharp and to the point. Don't try to muddy the water and hope they won't notice. Your answer could be as follows:

> *The question indicated that only two systems could push the meter readings to the server (via pub/sub). Moreover, the requirement was to read these meters once a month. PDU was keen on developing a unified mechanism to retrieve the smart meter data from all its vendors.*
>
> *This is why I thought of developing a scheduled monthly MuleSoft job in MuleSoft that pulls the meter readings from all these platforms, then update Salesforce with the readings.*
>
> *Alternatively, we could investigate whether we can introduce a pub/sub layer on top of the two systems that don't support it. This could be achieved by connecting MuleSoft to their database and periodically checking for changes, assuming that these systems can provide a mechanism to retrieve the delta of changed data, something similar to the CDC concept.*
>
> *If these systems didn't support this capability, we could consider integrating with these systems in two different ways. The first would be the unified pull interface, while the second could use MuleSoft to subscribe to the pub/sub channels provided by two systems. This way, we get the updates from two out of four systems in real time. This will be against PLU's original requirements, though.*
>
> *I favor the pulling mechanism because it ensures we don't update Salesforce records unnecessarily. This will ensure we adhere to the governance limits and avoid any performance challenges.*

Your answer should not take more than 2–3 minutes. Remember that you have a limited Q&A time, and you better leave room for the judges to ask as many questions as possible. *The Q&A phase is your friend.*

Let's explore another question raised by the judges:

> *You mentioned that MuleSoft would be using an OAuth 2.0 web server flow followed by the refresh token flow to authenticate to Salesforce. Is there an alternative authentication flow that you could have used, and when would you use each one?*

MuleSoft is authenticating to and communicating with Salesforce. This is a server-to-server or machine-to-machine kind of authentication. This could have been accomplished using the JWT flow, which is commonly used for similar scenarios and supported by both platforms. Your answer could be as follows:

> *I could have used the OAuth 2.0 JWT flow. It is a flow that supports machine-to-machine authentication. Both flows can fulfill this requirement. However, the JWT flow is more useful when authenticating using a context user rather than a named principal/integration user/service user. We can enable more advanced auditing capabilities and support different access privileges using the combination of context user authentication and JWT tokens.*

> *The web server flow (followed by the refresh token flow) is not the best fit for deep machine-to-machine context user-based authentication as it involves a manual authentication step per user. This is not a problem when authenticating using a single named principal. The web server flow could be easier to set up for a named principal considering that we don't need to exchange and host multiple TLS certificates on both ends. This is why I opted for this solution for PLU.*

Be ready to draw the sequence diagram for all these authentication flows. You are likely to be asked to explain one or more of them. There is no better and more comprehensive way to describe them than using sequence diagrams. You can find these diagrams in *Chapter 4, Core Architectural Concepts – Identity and Access Management*.

Diagrams are the unified language for architects

I have mentored many candidates, some of who knew about the sequence diagrams but felt that it is overkill to use them. Remember that you are expected to explain the flow in detail in front of three seasoned CTAs. The sequence diagram is the best tool to achieve that.

Let's explore another question raised by the judges:

> *In your environment and release strategy, can you explain further who would be moving the metadata between the environments and how? Can you also explain how the conflicts will be detected and resolved, and by whom?*

This is a question we have seeded during our presentation. You should be ready to answer it:

> *The developers would be working on a new feature branch for every developed feature. Once they are done, they can initiate a pull request to merge this branch with the CI/build branch.*

> *The pull request will notify the release manager (who is sometimes known as the DevOps admin). The release manager will validate the pull request and detect any conflicts. SCMs provide mechanisms and tools for that. The release manager will attempt to resolve minor conflicts (such as changes in page layouts) and revert the pull request for more complicated conflicts. The developer will have to fix it and initiate another pull request.*

> *Once the pull request is accepted, the automated build tool will attempt to deploy the codebase in the SCM to the build environment. The release manager will deploy these functionalities to upper environments in due time based on pre-defined criteria (such as being accepted by the QA team).*

Remember not to get carried away with too many details. Keep an eye on the remaining time.

That concludes the Q&A stage. We tried to cover different questions than what you came across in *Chapter 11, Communicating and Socializing Your Solution*, and *Chapter 13, Present and Defend – First Mock*. But, as you would expect, there is a vast number of possible questions. However, you have learned how to handle them.

Understand the questions, accept being challenged, defend and adjust your solution if needed, and answer with enough details without losing valuable time.

Enjoy being challenged by such senior and talented architects. This is not an experience that you'll come across many times in your career.

Summary

In this chapter, we continued developing the solution for our second full mock scenario. We explored more challenging data modeling, accessibility, and security requirements. We also created comprehensive LDV mitigation and data migration strategies. We tackled challenges with reporting and had a good look at the development and release management process and its supporting governance model.

We then picked up specific topics and created an engagement presentation pitch that describes the proposed solution end to end. We used our diagrams to help us explain the architecture more thoroughly and practiced the Q&A stage using various potential questions.

Congratulations! You have now completed two full mock scenarios. You can practice solving these scenarios as many times as possible. You can also try to add or remove requirements to them to make things more challenging. The mini scenarios we used in this book are also handy to practice a shorter version from time to time.

In the *Appendix*, we will go through some tips and tricks that can help you pass the review board. We will learn of some best practices and lessons learned. Finally, we will discuss your next steps.

Appendix
Tips and Tricks, and the Way Forward

You have covered many topics throughout this book and learned how to deal with different challenges you may encounter during the review board. In this chapter, we will learn about an additional set of tips and tricks that can help you pass your review board exam.

It is true that this exam puts a lot of mental pressure on the candidate. However, the reward is equally worthy. Passing the exam grants access to an exclusive elite club and provides a significant career boost.

You have to prepare mentally for the exam. You need to go into your review board (or join it online) relaxed, fresh, and focused.

Have a good night's sleep. Put on your war helmet on the exam day. Find out what makes you energized and do it. For some, it is the feeling of being challenged. For others, it is the desire to prove themselves.

Your motives should be positive. The fear of failing is not a good one. You have to find something positive to push you forward. Something that makes you aggressive and ready to fight until the last minute of that exam.

We will discuss various tips and tricks you can follow to prepare for the review board exam. In this chapter, we're going to cover the following main topics:

- The anatomy of a review board scenario
- General solving tips
- Managing the board
- Time management
- Your presentation – make or break
- Your exam, your way
- Next steps
- The community and available training

By the end of this chapter, you will have learned a set of tips, tricks, and techniques that you can use to increase your chances of passing. This will cover activities that you can do before and during the exam.

You will also learn where to go from here onward – what to do next and where to find additional useful information.

The anatomy of a review board scenario

As you have seen in *Chapter 12, Practice the Review Board – First Mock*, and in *Chapter 14, Practice the Review Board – Second Mock*, the review board scenarios are usually structured in a specific way. They typically contain the following sections:

- **Project overview**: This section provides general information about the company (which is what the scenario all about), its services, pain points, geographic locations covered by the company, growth plans, and so on. This section is generally helpful for you to understand the bigger picture. It can also help you develop your initial understanding of potential actors (the group of users who would eventually interact with the solution).

    This section might include some important figures (however, this is not necessarily the only place where such figures might exist). We have learned from many previous scenarios that these figures could significantly impact the target data volume.

- **Current landscape**: The scenario typically has a section that explains the existing system landscape for the customer. This section is very helpful for you to start drafting your landscape architecture. As you have learned in past chapters, including retiring systems in your landscape will help you explain the full picture. Moreover, this section will give you a good early understanding of the task accomplished by each system.

  This section might also include brief information about supported business functionalities, the company's strategy in retaining or replacing some of its existing systems, and overall general pain points and risks.

- **Business use cases/business process requirements**: We mentioned before that this section is the meatiest and, most likely, the longest in the scenario. The business processes are usually described using a series of bullet points. Each could include one or more requirements. The business process will consist of functional, data, and integration requirements.

  In previous chapters, we learned that the best way to handle this section is by creating a business process diagram (per process). This will help you not only present the business process in a structured and attractive way but also organize your thoughts and spot potential gaps.

- **Data migration requirements**: This might exist as a standalone section or as a part of another section. This section will normally describe the expected data volumes in source systems. The figures should help you craft your data migration strategy and plan. This section might also impact your definition of LDVs as well as your mitigation strategy.

- **Accessibility requirements**: This section usually contains IAM requirements, mobile accessibility specifications, and internal and external expected user experience. You can expect information such as where the user's credentials are stored and whether there is a need to support social sign-in for external users. This section might add more requirements to those shared in the business processes section, particularly when it comes to system and data accessibility. This section could be combined with the security requirements section.

- **Security requirements**: This is one of the most critical sections, and I like to think of it as the second most complex (after the business requirements section). This section normally contains application and network security requirements. It may also include requirements to challenge your knowledge of several platform security features (such as sharing rules, profiles, permission sets, platform encryption, MFA, sharing sets, and so on).

- **Reporting requirements**: This section includes a description of key required reports. It might also indicate the necessary data for these reports (for example, records from multiple systems). The availability of these reports and the impacted actors are also likely to be included.

- **Project development requirements**: This section will include a description of the current release process. It may also list some pain points that would help you define the right development and release strategy and the appropriate governance model to control it.

- **Other requirements**: This section may or may not exist. It could contain other requirements that haven't been covered by any of the previous sections. Sometimes, it contains information and risks that impact your proposed governance model. In some cases, it might simply be combined with the project development requirements section.

The naming of these sections could vary from one scenario to another. This can be considered a general structure but expect the real scenario to include more or fewer sections.

Salesforce has the right to define and change the structure of its exams. What is listed here should not be considered an official document as it is based on the author's knowledge and experience only.

Let's now go through a set of general solving tips, things that you should keep in mind while crafting your end-to-end solution.

General solving tips

Let's start with a set of general tips on tackling, organizing, and structuring your solution. We have come across many examples in the previous chapters. Let's go through a few more.

Go through the scenario and annotate first

This is something we've repeated many times in previous chapters. Before you start with your incremental solving, go through the whole scenario, take notes, and add annotations next to each requirement.

You won't get a printed version of the scenario on a virtual review board. You will get an editable Word document instead. You can highlight sections and add annotations on the Word document directly. You can also use different colors to annotate various topics, for example, potential LDVs.

567 General solving tips

This activity should help you during both the incremental solving and the catch-all presentation stages. The review board scenarios are complex and lengthy (as you have experienced yourself in the previous four chapters). You can easily miss or forget some requirements if you don't highlight/annotate them clearly.

Provide a solution, not a set of options

As a CTA, you are expected to come up with a clear and justified solution for a particular requirement. Providing a salad of solutions won't be acceptable. For example, when dealing with LDVs, you can't simply list the possible solutions, such as custom indexes, archiving, skinny tables, and so on. You have to be specific and select a solution based on the shared requirements and justify it.

It is okay to mention the other solution options that you have considered (if you have enough time for that), but you have to be crisp and clear about your recommended solution and the rationale behind it.

Avoid the extensive use of buzzwords. For example, you won't get marks for knowing the buzzword *CI/CD* but will if you explain what exactly it is, its benefits, and how it would fit into your solution to address a shared requirement.

You have a limited set of tools to solve a problem

There is actually a finite number of possible solutions for most, if not all, the requirements. You might feel a bit overwhelmed while creating your solution and get the feeling that you have an unlimited toolset to choose from. This is not actually true.

Take LDVs as an example. There is a limited number of options to choose from. Sharing is another example; you have a limited number of features that you can use in Salesforce, such as sharing sets, sharing rules, manual sharing, groups, APEX, and so on.

One of these options will be the ideal solution based on a set of considerations extracted from the scenario or assumptions you can make.

Act like an architect, use the common architects' language

You need to use the common language of architects. Diagrams are crucial to visualize a solution and communicate with your audience. They can also help you organize your thoughts and ensure you cover all that needs to be covered.

Use standard diagrams wherever applicable. For example, use standard sequence diagrams to explain a sequence of activities rather than coming up with an unusual diagram. This is like speaking a common language understood by everyone.

Sometimes, you might need to come up with a non-standard diagram to explain a particular topic. Don't feel shy about doing so. Just make sure that you use standard diagrams wherever possible and easy-to-follow custom diagrams otherwise.

Let's now move on to a set of tips and tricks that you can follow to help you manage the board.

Managing the board

The judges in the review board are seasoned CTAs who are trained to act as judges. They are trained to not show emotion. They will maintain a poker face during your presentation and Q&A. This way, they avoid disturbing or misleading the candidate by showing positive or adverse reactions.

However, you can use the following simple tips to help you manage the board.

Help them to keep up with you

When you present your solution, help the judges follow you by highlighting the relevant requirement's location in the scenario. They can't read your mind, and they might miss one of your statements. Help them by pointing them to the requirement you are solving whenever you feel a need for that.

Tie your solution back to the requirement

Avoid presenting a dry solution that is untied to a requirement (also known as a solution without a requirement). Make sure you articulate the relationship between your proposed solution and a shared requirement.

This shows that you understand the requirement. You can then explain the assumptions, rationale, and trade-offs you followed in choosing a particular solution among the possible others.

Watch and observe their reaction if possible

The judges are trained not to show any emotion. However, they will be taking notes during your presentation and Q&A. They usually do that using their laptops. Sometimes, you might be able to observe whether they are typing something or not.

This is particularly helpful during the Q&A. If you are explaining something and they are not typing, then perhaps you are not adding anything to what you have previously described.

Seed some questions

We came across this technique in *Chapter 9*, *Forging an Integrated Solution*, and experienced it again in *Chapter 13*, *Present and Defend – First Mock*, and *Chapter 15*, *Present and Defend – Second Mock*.

You can use this technique during the presentation to draw the judges' attention to a particular topic that you haven't covered in full detail. If that point is interesting to them, they will come back to it during the Q&A to ask for further information.

You usually seed questions that you are comfortable with answering. For example, you could describe an integration interface with just enough details and mention the authentication flow that it will be using. If the judges are interested in knowing more about that flow or want to test your knowledge, they will come back to this point during the Q&A. You can then use a sequence diagram to explain the flow with all the required details.

Be careful not to abuse this technique. You still need to explain the solution end to end with all the required details. We did that many times throughout this book. You can seed a question where the level of detail is *not impacting* the *clarity* or *completeness* of your proposed solution.

Show your professional attitude

During the presentation and Q&A phases, show your professional attitude. Don't attempt to bluff your way through a challenging question. That will simply backfire. The judges will know that, trust me, and you will show unprofessional behavior in addition to failing to answer the question.

Show that you can listen and understand well during the Q&A. Be confident, defend your solution, and hold your ground, but also be humble and accept that your answer might be incorrect. If that happens, admit the mistake professionally and adjust if needed. After all, communicating and socializing your solution is one of the domains you need to demonstrate that you've mastered.

Time management

Time management is absolutely crucial in this exam. I can't stress that enough, no matter how many times I've repeated it throughout this book. If Salesforce decided to introduce a new domain to this certificate, I would confidently propose time management.

Here are some tips and tricks to help you manage your time during the review board exam.

Plan ahead and stick to your plan

You have to have a time plan for every stage of the exam: a time plan for the solving, the presentation, and the Q&A stages. Your solving stage's time plan could look like the following:

Activity	Sub activity	Minimum time (mins)	Maximum time (mins)	Recommended time (mins)
Scenario full read through and annotation	Read, understand, and highlight or annotate potential solutions	20	40	30
	Creation of draft artifact scribbles			
Detailed solving	Read, understand, and solve creation	90	130	110
	Draft artifacts' creation			
Solution review	Review your solution and adjust it if needed	10	25	15
Artifact finalization	Create the final version of the artifacts	10	30	20
Buffer	Buffer	5	10	5

Table Appendix.1 – Proposed time plan – solving stage

You can develop your own time plan based on your own skills and abilities. For example, you could be a slow reader but a speedy diagram creator. In that case, you can increase the time allocated for the initial scenario reading and annotation and reduce the time allocated for the artifacts' finalization.

It is recommended not to go above or below the maximum and minimum suggested boundaries.

Your presentation stage's time plan could look like the following:

Activity	Sub activity	Minimum time (mins)	Maximum time (mins)	Recommended time (mins)
Intro	Self-introduction	1	3	1.5
	High-level scenario and client overview			
The structured presentation	High-level solution intro	5	10	5
	Introduce the actors and licenses and the rationale behind the license selection			
	Introduce the landscape architecture and the rationale behind product selection			
	Business processes – proposed solution	10	25	15
	Accessibility and security – proposed solution	5	10	5
	LDV mitigation strategy	3	5	3
	Data migration strategy	3	5	3
	Governance, including the development and release strategy	3	5	3
The catch-all presentation	Go through the scenario and call out any missing points	3	10	9.5
	Buffer			

Table Appendix.2 – Proposed time plan – presentation stage

Time management is a little bit trickier during the presentation. The catch-all stage could act as a buffer if you run over slightly in one of the previous sections. A lot of that depends on the nature of the scenario.

The scenario might include more challenging business processes or security requirements, and you might need to extend their respective presentation slots accordingly.

Remember that these are suggested figures only, and you need to come up with *your own time plan* based on *your own skills, abilities, and comfort zones*. For example, you might know the governance pitch so well that you can cover it in less than 3 minutes.

You can start practicing with a specific plan in your head and adjust if needed until you find your *zen zone*.

Rehearse and perfect your timing

You have to practice and perfect your time plan before attempting the review board. It might feel tough at the beginning, but everything is possible with practice and perseverance.

Ask a colleague or friend to help you with timekeeping during your mock presentations. This activity will be very rewarding during the review board.

During the review board, you will be given a timer or have access to a clock, depending on the facility and the exam's nature (in person/virtual). You should always keep an eye on it. Ensure you include that in your practices as well.

Practice the 2-minute pitch

You have probably come across the term **2-minute pitch** or heard of Einstein's famous quote: *If you can't explain it simply, you don't understand it well enough.*

Stick to that principle, and practice it during your mocks and rehearsals. Try to explain a topic to a colleague or a friend in 2 minutes. Focus on the key arguments and the rationale behind proposing one approach over the others.

In addition to time management, this skill is essential to having a fair chance of passing the review board.

Balance where you spend your time

In past years, I noticed a common pitfall that many of my mentees struggled with initially. Candidates tend to spend too much time in areas that fall within their comfort zones. For example, some candidates could spend 10 minutes merely explaining the release management strategy.

Similarly, I noticed that some candidates tend to avoid topics that they are not necessarily comfortable with and hope it will pass unnoticed.

Try to avoid this. Don't leave any point unanswered; they all count. Stick to your time plan and give every requirement section the deserved amount of attention.

The presentation stage is crucial, and probably the most difficult to master. Let's explore more tips and tricks that can help you overcome that challenge.

Your presentation – make or break

You are now aware of the importance of the review board presentation phase. We discussed time management techniques and different ways to manage the board. Let's now go through a set of tips that are mainly related to your soft presentation skills.

Show confidence

It is a challenging exam and a difficult presentation. You might feel nervous and under a lot of pressure. But you have to control these feelings and radiate confidence throughout the presentation and Q&A.

You need to practice the way you stand in front of the board. This involves nothing special, but try not to look stressed or afraid. Look at them and make some eye contact. They won't show any emotion (as they are trained not to), but you still have to demonstrate your ability to communicate with the audience.

Try holding an object in your hand – a cup, a pen, or paper. Some people feel more confident when they do so.

Cut down the *ah* and *ehm* sounds. Be direct and clear. If you have to speed up during the presentation, make sure that is caused by the limited time and not because you are nervous.

Control the tempo

Don't worry if you usually feel uncomfortable in front of an audience. Everything is possible with practice and perseverance. You need to be honest with yourself and know your strengths and weaknesses. Overconfidence can also be a weakness.

Learn some tricks to control your emotions during presentations. You can try to take 10 seconds to break from time to time during the presentation. Take a sip of water. And take your time in doing so. You have budgeted 10 seconds to take that sip of water, so use it. Those seconds are not wasted. They are very helpful to organize your thoughts and control your emotions.

Some people are natural public speakers. Others are not. Don't feel less than anyone and remember the quote: *Everyone is a genius. But if you judge a fish by its ability to climb a tree, it will live its whole life believing that it is stupid.*

Understand your strengths and weaknesses, and develop, practice, and perfect your attack strategy accordingly.

Own the stage

Move around the stage, point at the board (or at a specific part of the slide), and use your body language to show the audience that you own the stage.

During the Q&A, relax and move closer toward the person asking you a question. Give the judges the feeling that they are dealing with a peer.

Use your artifacts

I've mentioned this point a dozen times before, but I've decided to include it here once more to emphasize its importance.

We create artifacts such as the landscape architecture diagram, the data model diagram, the role hierarchy, and others for a reason. The main reason is to *use them* to convey your end-to-end solution. In real life, you also use them to *document* your solution. Besides, the creation of these artifacts would also help you organize your thoughts and spot anything that you're missing.

Make sure you use your diagrams well. Point clearly at the relevant section. The judges (and any audience) can't read your mind. A successful presenter delivers their complete message easily and smoothly to the audience.

You have invested a lot of time to develop a great set of tools to help you during your presentation. Make sure you use them well.

Enjoy it

You don't get many chances to present to such a brilliant audience. Enjoy the experience. This will be reflected in all your actions during the presentation and Q&A and will leave a good impression.

Enjoy the Q&A. Being able to stand in front of these technical rockstars, answer their questions, challenge them, and defend your opinion is a joyful experience.

Show them what you are capable of. You wanted the certificate to prove that you belong to this prestigious club. There is no better chance to do so than this.

Go to the review board with the right mindset and you will enjoy the experience.

Your exam, your way

You have read this book and gone through several suggestions and recommendations. You will also read and hear a lot more from other CTAs, coaches, candidates, and experts while you prepare for your review board.

Some would recommend approaches different than others. If you speak to 10 different CTAs, you would probably hear 10 various bits of feedback on how they prepared and attended the review board. There will be significant overlap, but there will also be different points of view.

For example, some would recommend using PowerPoint presentations instead of flip charts. Others would recommend a different structure and time plan. Some might be entirely against the *catch-all* presentation stage, while others might support it. This feedback could be coming from actual CTAs, which means that what they have recommended actually worked. Yet, it might not work for you.

What you need to keep in mind that *there is no right approach*. You need to figure out the approach that works best for you. Use this book and the other resources available to prepare. While preparing, try to figure out what approach fits you best.

You need to ensure that you are still covering what needs to be covered. We saw several examples throughout this book. How you do that is up to you to figure out based on your own style, skills, experience, strengths, and weaknesses.

Determine your own strategy to identify requirements, your own presentation structure and time plan, and your own technique to put together an end-to-end solution. Fine-tune them with practice, and stick to it during the exam day. Whatever your plan is, don't change it during the exam. That is a guaranteed recipe for failure.

Next steps

You have come a long way now. You have practiced solving several scenarios and successfully handled different functional and technical challenges. Let's plan your next steps together.

Practice and practice more

Practice makes it perfect. This is applicable for pretty much everything in life, including preparing for the CTA review board.

To put it simply, the more mocks you do, the better chance you will have of passing. Put yourself under conditions as close as possible to the real thing. Practice using a timer and presenting to someone.

I expect my mentees to do between five and nine full mocks before they are considered ready for the review board. If you get a chance to do more, grab it. The more mocks you do (especially using different scenarios), the more you will know about your preferred style and strategy to tackle this exam.

You can even do mocks using the same scenario several times. There is value in using a new scenario. The surprise factor will put you under pressure, similar to what you will experience during the real review board. However, there is still a lot of value gained from doing the same scenario multiple times.

You can also try to create your own variation of a scenario. Some CTAs have already shared some tips about that. Other CTAs have published some free mock scenarios as well. We will list a set of resources at the end of this chapter.

Plan some time off before the exam

You are likely busy with a thousand different things at work. Add social and family responsibilities, and your day is nearly full.

You might be able to squeeze in some study activities from time to time. That can help you prepare for the review board, assuming you are utilizing your work time to practice some of the activities listed throughout this book.

Plan some time off before the review board date for intense preparation activities, that is, a boot camp: 2 or 3 weeks of intense study, mock, and practice. This is very important to help you close any remaining gaps and put you in the right mindset.

Get in touch with the community and study groups

There are several study groups available nowadays. This is a luxury that didn't exist a few years back. Make use of it. You can get in touch with peers to exchange ideas and experiences.

These study groups also host CTAs from time to time and do live mocks. Time zones could be difficult for many candidates but seek local/nearby study groups that you can join. If none exist, create your own. Others will join.

We will list some of these study groups at the end of this chapter.

Stay connected and share your experience

There are several blogs written by CTAs and candidates who were unsuccessful at the review board. Have a look at them and try to make use of their feedback.

Also, don't be shy about sharing your own experience. You don't know who might benefit from it. It is an excellent gesture to give back to the community. As a CTA, you have a responsibility to develop future architects and help them reach their potential.

The community and available training

The market demand for architects is higher than ever. It is beneficial for everyone to develop highly skilled architects: Salesforce, Salesforce partners, clients, and the architects themselves. There are several valuable resources that can help you prepare for your review board. Here are some.

Salesforce training and study groups

Salesforce has developed two valuable trainings to prepare candidates for the CTA review board: the **CTA-601** and the **CTA-602**. In addition, they have launched a regular office hours webinar to get in touch with candidates and share practical knowledge. There are also several other study groups with valuable information. Make yourself familiar with the following:

- **Certified Technical Architect Preparation Workshop (CTA-601)**: This is a workshop-style training. It will help you understand the exam objectives and develop your skills to create an end-to-end solution. More info can be found at the following links: `https://help.salesforce.com/HTTrainingCourseDetail?id=a230M0000001C0U` and `https://help.salesforce.com/HTTrainingCourseDetail?id=a230M000000A5UJ`.

- **Architect Review Board Readiness Diagnostic (CTA-602)**: This is a full mock review board exam. It allows you to practice solving, presenting, and defending a full review board mock scenario. You will also receive feedback with a clear summary and recommendations based on your performance. I personally highly recommend this training. More info can be found at the following links: `https://trailhead.salesforce.com/en/academy/classes/cta602-architect-review-board-readiness-diagnostic/`

  and

  `https://help.salesforce.com/HTTrainingCourseDetail?id=a230M000000cqk5QAA`.

- **CTA office hours**: A Chatter group with regular online meetups and activities: `https://success.salesforce.com/_ui/core/chatter/groups/GroupProfilePage?g=0F93A000000Lm2P`.

- **Ladies Be Architects**: This is a study group that was initially created to inspire female architects. However, it soon developed to become one of the key success groups that provide valuable information to all Salesforce professionals: `https://success.salesforce.com/_ui/core/chatter/groups/GroupProfilePage?g=0F93A0000001zan`

  and

  `https://architechclub.com/`.

- **APAC Architects**: A study group for architects in the **Asia Pacific (APAC)** region: `https://success.salesforce.com/_ui/core/chatter/groups/GroupProfilePage?g=0F93A0000009Vpd`.

- **Trailhead Architect Enablement**: A Chatter group with valuable knowledge and materials for architects: `https://partners.salesforce.com/_ui/core/chatter/groups/GroupProfilePage?g=0F9300000009PD5`.

- **Architect Trailblazer Community**: A Chatter group with valuable knowledge and materials for architects: `https://success.salesforce.com/_ui/core/chatter/groups/GroupProfilePage?g=0F930000000blKv`.

- **Customer Architect Community**: A Chatter group with valuable knowledge and materials for architects: `https://success.salesforce.com/_ui/core/chatter/groups/GroupProfilePage?g=0F9300000009Q1X`.

- **Salesforce CTA Study Group Benelux**: A study group initially created to cover the **Belgium, Netherlands, Luxembourg (Benelux)** region but grew quickly to become international: `https://www.meetup.com/Benelux-Salesforce-CTA-to-Be/`.

Several other resources can be found on official Salesforce channels. There are also additional ones created regularly. Keep Googling and looking.

Stories and lessons learned

Many architects have shared their experiences with the review board. Here is a selected list:

- `http://bobbuzzard.blogspot.com/2012/02/certified-salesforce-technical.html`
- `https://bob-buzzard.medium.com/salesforce-certified-technical-architect-154a2cf76cd8`
- `https://www.linkedin.com/pulse/how-i-became-certified-technical-architect-jannis-bott-/`
- `https://www.linkedin.com/pulse/becoming-salesforce-certified-technical-architect-sam-jenkins/`
- `https://www.linkedin.com/pulse/my-journeytocta-admin-cta-lead-program-architect-sebastian-wagner/`
- `https://enterpriseforcearchitect.com/2014/03/12/my-journey-to-salesforce-com-certified-technical-architect/`
- `https://ericsantiago.com/2012/05/16/salesforce-technical-architect-certification-part-2-review-board/`
- `http://salesforcediaries.blogspot.com/2019/06/the-role-of-technical-architect.html`

Many other architects have shared their experiences. Some have done that via recorded videos, while others chose blogs. More materials are added regularly. Keep Googling and looking.

Blogs and training providers

In additon to the training launched by Salesforce to prepare for the CTA review board, they launched the following:

- **Bob Buzzard**: One of the most famous blogs for Salesforce-related knowledge: `http://bobbuzzard.blogspot.com/`
- **Salesforce Ben**: One of the most famous blogs for Salesforce-related knowledge: `https://www.salesforceben.com/`

- **Gemma Blezard**: A blog containing many valuable resources for Salesforce professionals: `http://gemmablezard.com/`

- **Flow Republic**: A coaching and mentoring academy run by multiple talented CTAs: `https://flowrepublic.com/`

- **Cloud Johan**: A blog containing many valuable resources and tips for Salesforce architects: `https://cloudjohann.com/`

- **CTA 202**: A blog containing many valuable resources and tips for Salesforce architects, including sample CTA mock scenarios: `http://cta202.com/`

Again, this is a limited list from a vast pool of valuable knowledge available on the net. We are all lucky to have Google around.

Finally, I would like to add one last tip to close this chapter. Reward yourself after attending the review board exam. You will feel tired and exhausted, and in many cases, you will feel unsure of the result. Just relax and wait for your result and try to do something cheerful and fun for the rest of that day (and probably one or two more days to come).

You are now closer than ever to becoming a Salesforce Certified Technical Architect. Keep up the good spirit and carry on with the next step toward your dream!

Journey Towards Becoming a Salesforce CTA – Book Club

We have created an exclusive book club for you on our Packt Community page, to share knowledge and have insightful discussions around the topics covered in this book. This book club is for all the readers, existing architects, and anyone who aims to achieve the Salesforce CTA certification.

You are welcome to discuss the book, share your own experiences, views, and best practices on designing modern, practical, and robust architectures on the Salesforce platform, and help us grow the number of Salesforce CTAs globally.

Scan the code to join the book club

Packt.com

Subscribe to our online digital library for full access to over 7,000 books and videos, as well as industry leading tools to help you plan your personal development and advance your career. For more information, please visit our website.

Why subscribe?

- Spend less time learning and more time coding with practical eBooks and Videos from over 4,000 industry professionals

- Improve your learning with Skill Plans built especially for you

- Get a free eBook or video every month

- Fully searchable for easy access to vital information

- Copy and paste, print, and bookmark content

Did you know that Packt offers eBook versions of every book published, with PDF and ePub files available? You can upgrade to the eBook version at packt.com and as a print book customer, you are entitled to a discount on the eBook copy. Get in touch with us at customercare@packtpub.com for more details.

At www.packt.com, you can also read a collection of free technical articles, sign up for a range of free newsletters, and receive exclusive discounts and offers on Packt books and eBooks.

Other Books You May Enjoy

If you enjoyed this book, you may be interested in these other books by Packt:

Salesforce Lightning Platform Enterprise Architecture - Third Edition

Andrew Fawcett

ISBN: 978-1-78995-671-9

- Create and deploy AppExchange packages and manage upgrades
- Understand Enterprise Application Architecture patterns
- Customize mobile and desktop user experience with Lightning Web Components
- Manage large data volumes with asynchronous processing and big data strategies
- Implement Source Control and Continuous Integration
- Add AI to your application with Einstein
- Use Lightning External Services to integrate external code and data with your Lightning Application

Hands-On Low-Code Application Development with Salesforce

Enrico Murru

ISBN: 978-1-80020-977-0

- Get to grips with the fundamentals of data modeling to enhance data quality
- Deliver dynamic configuration capabilities using custom settings and metadata types
- Secure your data by implementing the Salesforce security model
- Customize Salesforce applications with Lightning App Builder
- Create impressive pages for your community using Experience Builder
- Use Data Loader to import and export data without writing any code
- Embrace the Salesforce Ohana culture to share knowledge and learn from the global Salesforce community

Packt is searching for authors like you

If you're interested in becoming an author for Packt, please visit `authors.packtpub.com` and apply today. We have worked with thousands of developers and tech professionals, just like you, to help them share their insight with the global tech community. You can make a general application, apply for a specific hot topic that we are recruiting an author for, or submit your own idea.

Leave a review - let other readers know what you think

Please share your thoughts on this book with others by leaving a review on the site that you bought it from. If you purchased the book from Amazon, please leave us an honest review on this book's Amazon page. This is vital so that other potential readers can see and use your unbiased opinion to make purchasing decisions, we can understand what our customers think about our products, and our authors can see your feedback on the title that they have worked with Packt to create. It will only take a few minutes of your time, but is valuable to other potential customers, our authors, and Packt. Thank you!

Index

Symbols

2-minute pitch 572

A

access grants
  explicit grants 185
  group membership grants 185
  implicit grants 185
  inherited grants 185
accessibility and security requirements
  analyzing 420-430, 527-530
  examples 455-457
accessibility and security requirements,
    Packt Pioneer Auto (PPA) 374
access token 115
AccountContactRelation 476
account data skew 222
ACID 27
Act on the Protection of Personal
    Information (APPI) 35
actors diagram 13, 14
administrator 99
Adobe Sign 266
Advanced Encryption System (AES) 85

agile
  versus waterfall 318
APAC Architects
  reference link 578
APEX trigger 388
API gateways 76
API-led architecture 80
API monetization 96
APIs
  experience APIs 80
  process APIs 80
  system APIs 80
AppExchange solutions 150
application programmable
    interfaces (APIs) 66
Apttus Contract Management 265
Architect Review Board Readiness
    Diagnostic (CTA-602)
  reference link 578
Architect Trailblazer Community
  reference link 578
Architectural Description Language 11
architecture diagram 11
artifacts 447-449
asset token flow 142, 143, 401

asymmetric cryptography
    algorithms 83, 89
asymmetric cryptography
    algorithms, use cases
  digital signature 90
  message confidentiality 90
Async SOQL 531
authentication 98
authentication flows
  about 110, 120
  OAuth 2.0/OpenID Connect flows 126
  SAML 2.0 flows 121
authenticity 85
authorization 99
authorization code 119
authorization code flow 127
authorization server 126
automated build and release
    management 538
AWS 163

B

backup and restore solutions 33
BASE 28
Batch Apex
  about 221
  reference link 221
batch data synchronization
  about 285
  description 285
  key use cases 285
  operational layer 285
  patterns 285
  reference link 285
  relevant Salesforce features 285
  timing 285
big data 42

biometric authentication 106
block cipher 85, 86
Bluefin 388
bridge table 57
bring your own encryption (BYOE) 84
bring your own key (BYOK) 84
build environment 325
built-in sharing 185
Bulk API
  about 220
  reference link 221
Business Intelligence (BI) 239
business processes end-to-end solution
  customer registration 450-452
  presenting 450
business process flow diagram 21, 22
business process, presentation
  about 552
  customer service 553-555
  project development and release
      strategy 556-558
business process requirements, Packt
    Lightning Utilities (PLU)
  about 464, 480
  customer registration 467, 468, 503
  customer services 492-497
  field sales 468, 504, 508
  Key Customer Management
      465, 481-490
  scheduled automatic meter
      reading 467, 499, 500
  scheduled manual meter
      reading 466, 498, 499
business process requirements,
    Packt Pioneer Auto (PPA)
  car check-in 372, 392-394
  car check-out 372, 395-400
  car reservation 371, 386-392

car status update 373, 401-411
customer registration 370, 381-385
penalty settlement 373, 401-411

C

California Consumer Privacy
    Act (CCPA) 35
canonical data format 74
Case Escalation Rule 490
CA-signed certificate 85
Center of Excellent (CoE) 321
certificate 85
certificate authority (CA) 85
Certified Technical Architect Preparation
    Workshop (CTA-601)
  reference link 577
change data capture (CDC) 285
Chargent 388
CI concept 328
ciphertext 82
claims 115
classic RDBMS
  versus Salesforce 26-30
client app 126
client ID 127
client secret 127
clinical research organizations
    (CROs) 257
closed-lost stage 258
cloud information model (CIM) 74
Cloudingo 262
CoE structure 322
coexistence style 40
communication 342
conceptual-level data
    architecture design 46
Configure, Price, Quote (CPQ) 484

Conga Contracts 265
consolidation style
  about 40
  versus registry MDM style 518
consumer ID 127
consumer secret 127
contextual SSO flow diagram 23, 24
context user 101
context user authentication 109
continuous delivery (CD) 328
Continuous Integration and Continuous
    Deployment (CI/CD) 23
continuous integration (CI) tools
  need for 327-329
contract life cycle management
    (CLM) solutions 265
create, read, update, and
    delete (CRUD) 49
cryptography
  concepts 82-85
  use cases 90
cryptography algorithms
  asymmetric cryptography algorithms 89
  symmetric cryptography algorithms 86
CTA office hours
  reference link 578
CTA review board
  exam structure 9-11
  format 6, 7
  structure 6, 7
Customer Architect Community
  reference link 578
customer community plus license 183
customer experience (CX) 96
Customer identity and access
    management (CIAM) 96
customer relationship
    management (CRM) 60

custom indexes
  about 217
  reference link 217

D

DA structure 324
data access-control levels
  field-level 181
  object-level 181
  org-level 181
  record-level 181
data access control tools 182
data architecture concepts
  about 45
  conceptual-level data
    architecture design 46
  logical-level data architecture design 46
  physical-level data architecture
    design 47, 48
data architecture domain mini
    hypothetical scenario 225
data archiving 218-220
database administrators 31
database management system (DBMS) 26
database relationships
  many-to-many relationship 57
  one-to-many relationship 56
  one-to-one relationship 56
  using 55, 58
data categories
  big data 42
  exploring 38
  master data 38, 39
  master data management 38
  metadata 41
  reference data 38, 41
  reporting data 41

transactional data 38
unstructured data 42
data clearing 34
data consumption analysis
  about 221
  reference link 221
data custodian 31
data destruction 34
data encryption 32
data encryption, solutions
  encryption at rest 32
  encryption in transit 32
  Salesforce Shield 32
data encryption standard (DES) 86
data erasure 34
data extraction 72
data flow diagrams 345
data governance 30
data governance, artefacts
  about 31
  business glossary 31
  data catalogue 31
  data mapping and classification 31
data lakes 43
data loading 72
Data manipulation language (DML) 500
data masking 33
data obfuscation 33
data migration approach
  determining 224
data migration requirements
  analyzing 414-516
  duplicate customers, in legacy
    CRMs 516-519
  number of meters, in legacy
    CRMs 519-522
data migration requirements, Packt
    Lightning Utilities (PLU) 468

data migration requirements, Packt
    Pioneer Auto (PPA) 373
data migration strategy
  data backup and restore 225
  determining 224
  key topics 224
  presenting 454, 455
data migration tools
  determining 224
data model
  designing 48
  documenting 48
data model diagram 15
data modeling 46
data modeling concepts
  about 222
  account data skew 222
  impact, on database's design 222
  lookup skew 222, 223
  ownership skew 223
data obfuscation 33
data regulatory compliance 35-38
data restoration, solutions
  backup and restore solutions 33
data security 32
data steward 31
data transformation 72
data virtualization
  about 287
  description 287
  key use cases 287
  operational layer 287
  reference link 287
  relevant Salesforce features 287
  timing 287
data warehouse (DW) 43
data wiping 34

declarative and/or programmatic features
    used, for controlling record-
    level security 184
declarative and programmatic
    functionalities
  selecting 253, 254
deferred sharing calculation
  about 220
  reference link 220
delegated authentication 187-190
demilitarized zones (DMZs) 73
denial of service (DOS) attacks 76
denormalization
  about 49
  versus normalization 49-52
de-provisioning 103
Design Authority (DA) 322, 533
design decisions
  communicating 342-344
Development and Operations
    (DevOps) 78
device flow 140, 141, 401
diagrams, review board exam
    considerations 12
digital enterprise landscape 60
divisions 218
document management
    solutions (DMSes)
  determining 156
document management system (DMS)
  selecting 44, 45
documents 45
DocuSign 266, 486
DocuSign CLM 265
duplicate rules 352, 415

E

email notifications 285
encryption 82
encryption at rest 32
encryption in transit 32
encryption key 83
end-to-end identity management solution
  designing 187
end-to-end solution
  creating 414, 516
enterprise content management (ECM)
  about 44
  key capabilities 44
enterprise data warehouse (EDW) 43
enterprise integration
  needs 61
enterprise integration
    architecture technology
  determining 281, 282
enterprise integration interfaces
  designing, to build connected
    solution 293
enterprise resource planning (ERP) 60
Enterprise Resource Platform (ERP) 291
Enterprise Service Bus (ESB) 67, 74
Enterprise Territory Management
  reference link 472
environment diagram 22, 23
environment management strategy
  crafting, while considering platform
    capabilities 325-327
  crafting, while considering platform
    limitations 325-327
event 81
event-driven architecture 81
exact matching 40
executive vice president (EVP) 191

explicit grants 185
eXtensible Markup Language (XML) 41
extract, transform, and load
  (ETL) 43, 72, 73

F

Fair and Accurate Credit Transactions
  Act of 2003 (FACTA) 35
federated identifier 101
file-based systems 26
files 44
Files Connect 45, 166
file transfer 65
File Transfer Protocol (FTP) 73
first normal form
  database conditions 52
flowcharts 344
functionality spillover 61
future methods 285
fuzzy matching 40

G

General Data Protection Regulation
  (GDPR) 35, 97
Gliffy 347
Globally Unique Identifier (GUID) 388
golden record 40, 517
group membership grants 185
group memberships 99, 104

H

hashing algorithms
  about 87
  mechanism 88
  properties 87

Health Insurance Portability and
    Accountability Act (HIPAA) 35
HelloSign 266
Heroku 163, 525
Heroku Connect 163, 218, 403
HTML5 apps 357
hub-and-spoke approach 68
hybrid apps 357
hybrid methodology 319, 539

I

IAM solution, components
  identity repository 97
  management toolbox 97
  monitoring platform 97
  policy enforcer 97
IAM standards
  about 110, 111
  Kerberos 114
  Open authorization (OAuth) 112, 113
  OpenID Connect (OIDC) 113, 114
  Security Assertion Markup
    Language (SAML) 111
IAM, terms and definitions
  authentication 98
  authorization 99
  de-provisioning 103
  identity 98
  identity provider (IDP) 99, 100
  identity store 99
  Multi-Factor Authentication (MFA) 103
  provisioning 103
  Role-Based Access (RBA) 104
  service provider (SP) 100
  Single Sign On (SSO) 100, 101
identified LDVs
  reviewing 418, 419, 522, 525, 526

identity 98
identity and access management (IAM)
  about 82
  concepts 96, 97
Identity as a service (IDaaS) 107
identity provider (IDP) 99, 100
identity store 99
ID token 113, 116
impact development methodologies
  agile 317
  hybrid 318
  waterfall 317
impact development methodologies,
  on workstreams 317
implicit flow 134
implicit grants 185
Informatica 416
Informatica MDM 352, 517
inherited grants 185
initialization vector 84
integrated testing 315
Integrated Windows Authentication
    (IWA) 114
integration architecture
  design principles 62-64
integration interface
  designing, with integration pattern 283
integration landscape
  recommending 280, 281
integration pattern
  used, for designing integration
    interface 283
integration styles
  about 64
  file transfer 65
  messaging 67
  remote procedure invocation (RPI) 66
  unified datastore 65, 66

integration tools
  about 67
  API gateways 76
  Enterprise Service Bus (ESB) 74
  extract, transform, and load (ETL) 72
  point-to-point integration (P2P) 67
  reverse proxy 75
  stream-processing platforms 76
Intermediate Document (IDoc) 74
internal level 47
Internet of Things (IoT) 401
issuer 85

J

Java Database Connectivity (JDBC) 73
JSON Web Tokens (JWTs) 115
junction table 57
JWT
  URL 115
JWT bearer flow 137-139
JWT flow 384
JWT token 117, 118

K

Kerberos 114
key 83
keyed-hash message authentication
    code (HMAC) 88
key management 83

L

Ladies Be Architects
  reference link 578
Large Data Volume (LDV) 51

Large Data Volume (LDV) Objects
  impact 214, 215
  optimization methods 214
  platform considerations 214
lazy loading 287
LDV mitigation strategy
  presenting 453
LDV mitigation, techniques
  data archiving 218-220
  divisions 218
  off-platform data storage 218
  skinny tables 216
  standard and custom indexes 217
LDV mitigation, tools
  about 220
  Batch Apex 221
  Bulk API 220
  data consumption analysis 221
  deferred sharing calculations 220
  query optimizer 220
LDV objects' impact
  mitigating 216
licenses
  for solutions 155
licenses diagram 13
lightning web component (LWC) 253
Lightweight Directory Access
    Protocol (LDAP) 108
logical-level data architecture design
  about 46
  stages 46, 47
lookup data 41
lookup skew 222
Lucidchart 347

M

MAC algorithms
  about 88
  mechanism 89
machine-to-machine (M2M)
     processes 403
managed APIs 80
man-in-the-middle attacks 32
many-to-many relationship 57
Marketing Cloud 171, 254
Marketing Cloud Transactional
     Messaging API 497
master data 38, 39
master data management (MDM) 38, 39
MDM implementation styles
  coexistence style 40, 517
  consolidation style 40, 517
  registry style 39, 517
MDM matching mechanisms
  exact matching 40
  fuzzy matching 40
merge fields 388
message authentication code (MAC) 86
message-digest algorithm (MD5) 87
messaging 67
metadata 41
microservices
  about 78
  versus service-oriented
     architecture (SOA) 78, 79
Microsoft Active Directory (AD) 99, 108
Microsoft Active Directory Federation
     Services (ADFS) 108
Minimum Viable Product (MVP) 533
mitigation strategy
  developing 418-526
mixed diagrams 345

mix of systems
  determining 150, 160
mobile applications
  in solutions 154
mobile strategy 155
modern integration approaches
  API-led architecture 80
  event-driven architecture 81
  exploring 77
  microservices 78
  service-oriented architecture (SOA) 77
Mulesoft CloudHub 94
Multi-Factor Authentication (MFA) 103
multi-layered development
     environment 536
mutual authentication 82, 90

N

native apps 357
non-relational databases (NoSQL) 27
  use cases 28
normal forms 49, 52
normalization
  about 49
  versus denormalization 49-52
not only SQL 27
NT Lan Manager (NTLM) 114
NYDFS 97

O

OAuth 2.0 187, 384
OAuth2.0 client credentials flow 171
OAuth 2.0/OpenID Connect flows
  asset token flow 142, 143
  device flow 140, 141
  JWT bearer flow 137-139

refresh token flow 132-134
user agent flow 134-137
username password flow 144, 145
web server flow 127
OAuth2.0 standards 183
objection
    handling 348
    managing 351
object relations
    impact, on sharing architecture 186
off-platform data storage 218
one-time-password token (OTP) 103
one-to-many relationship 56
one-to-one relationship 56
one-way TLS 384
online analytical processing (OLAP) 51
online payments, payment
        gateway integration ways
    hosted checkout approach 36
    onsite checkout approach 37
online transaction processing (OLTP) 51
Open authorization (OAuth) 112, 113
Open Database Connectivity (ODBC) 73
OpenID Connect
        (OIDC) 113, 114, 183, 187
OpenID Connect User-Agent Flow 393
order management system (OMS) 60
org strategy
    about 152
    multi-org 153, 154
    single org 152, 153
org wide defaults (OWD) 183, 201
outbound messages 285
oversimplified diagrams 346
ownership skew 223

P

Packt Digital (PD)
    about 348
    current situation 350, 351
    requirements 350
    scenario 349
    shared requirements 352-363
Packt Innovative Retailers (PIR)
    current situation 191-200
    requirements 192-210
    scenario 191
Packt Lightning Utilities (PLU)
    about 462
    accessibility and security
        requirements 469
    actors, determining 473-476
    business process requirements 464
    current landscape 464
    current situation 471, 472
    data migration requirements 468
    draft data model, creating 476-479
    draft end-to-end solution, creating 471
    landscape architecture, compiling 480
    licenses, determining 473-476
    project overview 462, 463
    reporting requirements 469
    requirements, analyzing 471
Packt Medical Equipment (PME)
    about 290
    current situation 291-294
    requirements 292
    scenario 291
    shared requirements 294-310
Packt Modern Furniture (PMF)
    about 329, 330
    current situation 330-333

requirements 334-339
scenario 330
Packt Online Wizz (POZ)
about 225
current situation 226-232
requirements 226-234, 239-249
scenario 225
Packt Pioneer Auto (PPA)
about 368
accessibility and security
requirements 374
business process requirements 370, 381
current landscape 369, 370
current situation 377-380
data migration requirements 373
draft end-to-end solution, creating 376
project development requirements 375
project overview 368, 369
reporting requirements 375
requirements 376
requirements, analyzing 376
Packt United Builder (PUB)
about 157
current situation 160, 162
external stakeholders 158
internal stakeholders 157
requirements 158-160
shared requirements 162-177
Packt visiting angels (PVA)
about 256
current situation 257-261
requirements 257-276
scenario 257
Pardot 254
parties 38
Payment Card Industry Data Security
Standard (PCI DSS) 35

personally identifiable
information (PII) 33
physical-level data architecture
design 47, 48
plaintext 82
platform events 285, 487
platform security features
using, to control object and field
access permissions 186
platform security mechanisms
utilizing 180-183
platform-specific integration capabilities
justifying 288
selecting 288-290
point-to-point integration (P2P)
about 67
high dependencies 71
IT, turning into blocker 71
limited capabilities 71
overall reliability 70, 71
process orchestration 70
scalability 71
unique channel establishment 68, 69
Power BI 151
pre-game/blueprinting phase 318
presentation
creating 548
scenario and requirements 558
solution and artifacts 549-552
solution, justifying 558-561
structure 446, 447
presentation, phases
catch-all part 548
structured part 548
primary key 27
principals 99
private key 89
process orchestration 70

project development requirements
    analyzing 433-437, 533
    customer support team,
        productivity improving 535
    developed features, tracking 536
    developing methodologies 539
    environment management
        strategy 536, 538
    ERPs release cycle 534
    governance bodies 539
    potential project risks, identifying 535
    Salesforce functionalities,
        obtaining 533, 534
project development requirements, Packt
    Lightning Utilities (PLU) 470
project development requirements,
    Packt Pioneer Auto (PPA) 375
project governance
    recommending, to support technical
        decision-making 321-324
project risks and developing
        mitigation strategies
    conflicting processes 316
    conflicting release cycles 315, 316
    high resistance 316, 317
    identifying 315
    low adoption 316, 317
proofs of concept 539
provisioning 103
public key 85, 89
public-key cryptography algorithms 89
push notifications 285

Q

query optimizer 220
question seeding 295
queueable classes 285

R

reciprocal ciphers 86
record access data
    calculating 184
    creating 184
record-level security
    controlling, with declarative and/
        or programmatic features 184
reference data 38, 41
refresh token 116
refresh token flow 132-134, 384
registry MDM style
    versus consolidation style 518
registry style 39, 517
relational databases 27
relational databases transactions,
        characteristics
    atomic 27
    consistent 27
    durable 27
    isolated 27
release management
    source control, need 327-329
remote call-in
    about 286, 393
    description 286
    key use cases 286
    operational layers 286
    patterns 286
    reference link 286
    relevant Salesforce features 286
    timing 286
Remote Process Invocation (RPI)
    about 66, 283
    fire and forget 284
    reference link 284
    request and reply 283, 284

reporting and analytics
  design considerations 151
reporting data 41
reporting requirements
  analyzing 430-433, 530
  business intelligence reports 532
  meter readings, maintaining 532
  number of inquiries and complaints 531
  service requests, displaying 531
reporting requirements, Packt
    Lightning Utilities (PLU) 469
reporting requirements, Packt
    Pioneer Auto (PPA) 375
requirements
  analyzing 414, 438-445, 516, 539
  renewable energy, working with 540-548
resource server 126
reverse proxy 75
review board
  managing 568, 569
  presentation phase 573-575
review board exam
  approaches 575
  blogs and training providers 579, 580
  community and available
    training 577-579
  experiences 579
  Salesforce training and study
    groups 577-579
  solving tips 566, 567
  steps 576, 577
  time management 570-573
review board scenario, anatomy
  accessibility requirements 565
  business use cases/business
    process requirements 565
  current landscape 565
  data migration requirements 565

project development requirements 566
project overview 564
reporting requirements 566
requirements 566
security requirements 565
RingLead 262
risk-based authentication (RBA) 108
Role-based access control (RBAC) 104
Role-Based Access (RBA) 104
Role Hierarchy
  reference link 472
role hierarchy diagram 20

S

Salesforce
  about 29
  versus classic RDBMS 26-30
Salesforce Big Objects 219, 525
Salesforce Canvas 484
Salesforce Certified Technical Architect
  becoming 7, 8
  profile 4-6
Salesforce community 183
Salesforce Connect 218, 491
Salesforce Core Cloud (Force.
    com platform) 480
Salesforce CRM Content 44
Salesforce CTA Study Group Benelux
  reference link 578
Salesforce data architect
  objectives 214
Salesforce development life cycle and
    deployment architect 314
Salesforce external objects
  reference link 218
Salesforce External Services 384
Salesforce Field Service 499

Salesforce Flow 384
Salesforce Heroku 401
Salesforce integration architect
    objectives 280
Salesforce Knowledge 45, 234
Salesforce licenses 156
Salesforce Lightning Design
    System (SLDS) 501
Salesforce macros 535
Salesforce mobile app 357
Salesforce Mobile publisher 357
Salesforce Object Query
    Language (SOQL) 29
Salesforce security token 120
Salesforce Shield 32
Salesforce solution architect 253
Salesforce streaming API 285
Salesforce system architect 150
Salesforce Technical Solution Architecture
    artefacts 11
salt 84
SAML 2.0 187
SAML 2.0 flows 121
SAML assertion 119
SAML IDP-initiated flow 111, 121, 122
SAML SP-initiated flow 111, 122-126
SAML V1.1 111
SAML V2.0 111
sandbox cloning 328
scratch orgs 328
second normal form
    database conditions 53
secure hash algorithm (SHA) 87
secure portal architecture
    designing 183
Secure Sockets Layer (SSL) 91
security architect 180
security architecture domain 190

Security Assertion Markup
    Language (SAML) 111
self-reciprocal ciphers 86
Senior Vice President (SVP) 462
Service Cloud console 535
service implementers (SIs) 375
service-oriented architecture (SOA)
    about 77, 78
    versus microservices 78, 79
service provider (SP) 100
service user 108
session key 92
session token 119
shared secret 92
Simple Mail Transfer Protocol
    (SMTP) 490
Single Sign On (SSO) 100, 101
skinny table
    about 216
    reference link 217
solution
    about 447-449
    augmenting, with external
        applications 255, 256
    articulating 351
    building 160
    communicating 342
    defending 457-460
    justifying 446, 457-460
    presenting 446
solution architecture domain mini
        hypothetical scenario 256
source code-driven development 536
source control
    need, in release management 327-329
source control management
        (SCM) 329, 538
sprints 317

SSH File Transfer Protocol (SFTP) 73
standard indexes 217
stream ciphers 86
stream-processing platforms 76
super user 99
symmetric cryptography algorithms
  about 83, 86
  hashing algorithms 87
  MAC algorithms 88
system architecture domain mini
    hypothetical scenario 156
System for Cross-domain Identity
    Management (SCIM) 105
system landscape diagram 16, 17
System of record (SOR) 352

T

Tableau 151, 172
Tableau CRM 151, 172, 240, 531
test strategies recommendation
  for migrating project risks 319-321
third normal form
  database conditions 54, 55
TLS 82
tokens
  about 115
  access token 115
  authorization code 119
  ID token 116
  JWT token 117, 118
  refresh tokens 116
  Salesforce security token 120
  SAML assertion 119
  session token 119
Trailhead Architect Enablement
  reference link 578
transactional data 38

Transport Layer Security (TLS)
  working 91, 92
Two-Factor Authentication (2FA) 103
two-way-SSL 90
two-way TLS
  about 82, 90
  working 93

U

UI update, based on changes in data
  about 286
  description 286
  key use cases 287
  operational layer 287
  reference link 287
  relevant Salesforce features 287
  timing 287
unified datastore 65, 66
unique channel 68
United Kingdom version of
    GDPR (UK-GDPR) 35
unstructured data 42
user agent flow 134-137
username password flow 144

V

version control 329
Visio 347
visualization skills
  demonstrating, to articulate
    solution 344
Visual Studio Code (VSC) 330

W

waterfall
  versus agile 318
web server authentication flow 384
web server flow 127-132
wireframes 345

X

XML Signature Wrapping 111, 119

Lightning Source UK Ltd.
Milton Keynes UK
UKHW050916240223
417581UK00008B/892

9 781800 568754